国家社会科学基金项目"我国体育赛事监管体系研究"(19BTY018)

体育赛事英语(一)

温 阳 陶宏军 编著

东南大学出版社
SOUTHEAST UNIVERSITY PRESS
·南京·

内容提要

本书由国家社会科学基金项目资助,课题组成员在美国佐治亚大学学习期间,收集了大量的体育赛事专业英文资料。在此基础上,课题组成员历经4年整理,归类出了各个运动项目发展历史、体育赛事管理机构、重要赛事、比赛规则以及术语词汇等专业英语,并翻译成中文供对照。

本书为体育赛事英语系列书籍的第一册,采用中英对照形式。本书分为10章,内容是同场对抗球类赛事专业英语,包括足球、篮球、草地曲棍球、手球、美式橄榄球、马球、棒球、门球、冰球和水球。

本书是国内第一本系统研究体育赛事英语理论和实践问题的著作,可作为体育专业院校的教材,也可作为对体育赛事和体育英语感兴趣的读者的学习和参考用书。

图书在版编目(CIP)数据

体育赛事英语. 一 / 温阳,陶宏军编著. -- 南京:东南大学出版社,2024.12. -- ISBN 978-7-5766-1727-6

Ⅰ.G808.2

中国国家版本馆 CIP 数据核字第 2024LG5333 号

责任编辑:张绍来　　责任校对:张万莹　　封面设计:王玥　　责任印制:周荣虎

体育赛事英语(一)
Tiyu Saishi Yingyu(Yi)

编　　著:温　阳　陶宏军
出版发行:东南大学出版社
社　　址:南京四牌楼2号　邮编:210096　电话:025-83793330
出 版 人:白云飞
网　　址:http://www.seupress.com
电子邮件:press@seupress.com
经　　销:全国各地新华书店
印　　刷:苏州市古得堡数码印刷有限公司
开　　本:787 mm×1092 mm　1/16
印　　张:23
字　　数:580千字
版　　次:2024年12月第1版
印　　次:2024年12月第1次印刷
书　　号:ISBN 978-7-5766-1727-6
定　　价:59.00元

本社图书若有印装质量问题,请直接与营销部联系。电话(传真):025-83791830。

前言 PREFACE

自20世纪以来，在国际奥林匹克运动的推动下，国际体育赛事规模日益扩大，体育赛事数量日益增多。当前，世界各国都十分重视体育赛事活动的开展，把举办体育赛事作为一项重要的工作来开展。体育赛事已成国际化产业，吸引着全球数百万人的关注。随着2008年北京夏季奥运会、2022年北京冬季奥运会、2022年杭州亚运会、2023年成都世界大学生夏季运动会等国际大赛的顺利举办，体育赛事已经成为我国政府、社会和企业关注的热点，越来越多城市积极申办、承办各类国际体育赛事，以实现经济、文化和社会的多重收益。

随着全球体育产业的不断发展和国际交流的加深，我国在组织国际大赛时体育专业英语人才不足所带来的问题也逐渐凸显，比如当地组委会与体育单项国际组织沟通不畅、国外运动员与赛事志愿者信息不对称等等。在大型国际体育赛事中，英语通常作为官方语言，掌握专业的体育赛事英语词汇是体育赛事管理人才的必备条件，专业英语翻译在体育赛事的沟通中也起着决定性作用。然而，目前国内体育赛事中从事语言服务的人员大部分为英语专业出身，但缺乏相应的体育专业知识，导致沟通的准确性下降，影响大赛的举办质量。在体育赛事专业英语翻译人才匮乏的现状下，培养高水平的复合型体育赛事管理人才已成为我国体育院校和高校体育专业的重要任务。因此，在体育赛事英语的专业性书籍缺乏的背景下，本著作填补了该领域的空白，顺应了当前国家大力发展体育赛事的政策导向和趋势。

在国家社会科学基金项目"我国体育赛事监管体系研究"（19BTY018）和国家一流本科专业建设的资助下，本书课题组成员在美国佐治亚大学学习期间，收集了大量的体育赛事专业英文资料。团队成员在此基础上，历经4年研究和分析相关文献，整理和归类出了各个运动项目的发展历史、体育赛事主要管理机构、重要赛事、比赛规则以及术语词汇等专业英语，并翻译成相应中文供对照。本书为系列书籍第一本，分为10章，为同场对抗球类项目体育赛事专业英语，包括足球、篮球、草地曲棍球、手球、美式橄榄球、马球、棒球、门球、冰球和水球等。从研究现状来看，本书是国内第一本系统研究体育赛事英语理论和实践问题的著作。

本书有三个特色：第一，内容采用中英双语对照形式，便于读者了解和掌握各个运动项目的英语表达方式以及提高英语阅读能力；第二，在术语部分，提供了比较详尽的中英文对照的专业术语词汇，为读者理解专业术语提供了帮助;第三,在内容安排方面,从体育赛事的角度全面反映了各个运动项目的全景,包括各个运动项目的产生和发展,以及规则的不断演化,有助于加深读者对于各个运动项目的理解。

　　本书由温阳教授和陶宏军副教授主编,温阳教授负责本书的统筹管理和中文部分,陶宏军副教授负责英文部分。编者带领袁家乐、罗靖凯、兰天一、刘雨欣、姜雨嫣等南京体育学院体育经济与管理专业学生整理资料,南京体育学院研究生杨欣怡和陈文茜、南京师范大学研究生徐诺渲、武汉大学信息管理学院骆雪菲、江苏科技大学外国语学院骆雨菲等负责书籍中文翻译工作,南京市第二十九中学高中部语文老师章翼和谢正华对书稿中文的校对和英语老师渠立爽和茆静芳对书稿英文的校对投入了大量的精力。在此,对以上师生的辛勤付出一并表示感谢。

　　在编写过程中,我们参考了大量的中文和英文资料,英文部分主要参考了维基百科,并尽最大努力进行了参考文献的标注。在此,我们向参考文献的作者表达诚挚的敬意。东南大学出版社在本书出版过程中提供的指导和帮助,使本书得以顺利出版,在此深表感谢!

　　由于本书内容采用双语对照形式,编写的工作量巨大,加之我们的水平有限,还存在许多不足之处,还有很多问题需要进一步探讨,敬请专家和读者批评指正并提出宝贵意见。

温　阳

2024 年 12 月于南京体育学院

目录 | CONTENTS

Chapter 1　Association Football (Soccer) ·········· 001
　　Section 1　Introduction ·········· 001
　　Section 2　Major Governing Body ·········· 003
　　Section 3　Major Events ·········· 004
　　Section 4　Rules ·········· 009
　　Section 5　Basic Strategies ·········· 018

Chapter 2　Basketball ·········· 023
　　Section 1　Introduction ·········· 023
　　Section 2　Major Governing Body ·········· 025
　　Section 3　Major Events ·········· 026
　　Section 4　Rules ·········· 029
　　Section 5　Common Techniques ·········· 035
　　Section 6　Basic Strategies ·········· 040

Chapter 3　Field Hockey ·········· 044
　　Section 1　Introduction ·········· 044
　　Section 2　Major Governing Body ·········· 045
　　Section 3　Major Events ·········· 045
　　Section 4　Rules ·········· 047
　　Section 5　Basic Tactics ·········· 062

Chapter 4　Handball ·········· 066
　　Section 1　Introduction ·········· 066
　　Section 2　Major Governing Body ·········· 067
　　Section 3　Major Events ·········· 068
　　Section 4　Rules ·········· 070
　　Section 5　Basic Tactics ·········· 080

Chapter 5　American Football ·········· 086
　　Section 1　Introduction ·········· 086
　　Section 2　Major Governing Body ·········· 087

Section 3	Major Events	088
Section 4	Rules	091
Section 5	Basic Tactics	105

Chapter 6   Polo · 109
Section 1	Introduction	109
Section 2	Major Governing Body	110
Section 3	Major Events	110
Section 4	Rules	112
Section 5	Basic Tactics	120

Chapter 7   Baseball · 123
Section 1	Introduction	123
Section 2	Major Governing Body	124
Section 3	Major Events	125
Section 4	Rules	127
Section 5	Basic Tactics	132

Chapter 8   Gateball · 137
Section 1	Introduction	137
Section 2	Major Governing Body	138
Section 3	Major Events	138
Section 4	Rules	138
Section 5	Basic Tactics	143

Chapter 9   Ice Hockey · 145
Section 1	Introduction	145
Section 2	Major Governing Body	146
Section 3	Major Events	147
Section 4	Rules	149
Section 5	Basic Tactics	166

Chapter 10   Water Polo · 172
Section 1	Introduction	172
Section 2	Major Governing Body	173
Section 3	Major Events	174
Section 4	Rules	176
Section 5	Basic Strategies	190

第一章　足球 196
第一节　概述 196
第二节　主要管理机构 198
第三节　重要赛事 198
第四节　比赛规则 202
第五节　基本战术 209

第二章　篮球 213
第一节　概述 213
第二节　主要管理机构 214
第三节　重要赛事 215
第四节　比赛规则 218
第五节　常用技术 223
第六节　基本战术 226

第三章　草地曲棍球 230
第一节　概述 230
第二节　主要管理机构 231
第三节　重要赛事 231
第四节　比赛规则 233
第五节　基本战术 244

第四章　手球 247
第一节　概述 247
第二节　主要管理机构 248
第三节　重要赛事 248
第四节　比赛规则 250
第五节　基本战术 258

第五章　美式橄榄球 264
第一节　概述 264
第二节　主要管理机构 265
第三节　重要赛事 266
第四节　比赛规则 268
第五节　基本战术 280

第六章　马球 283
第一节　概述 283

第二节　主要管理机构 ·· 284
　　第三节　重要赛事 ·· 284
　　第四节　比赛规则 ·· 285
　　第五节　基本战术 ·· 292

第七章　棒球 ·· 295
　　第一节　概述 ··· 295
　　第二节　主要管理机构 ·· 296
　　第三节　重要赛事 ·· 297
　　第四节　比赛规则 ·· 298
　　第五节　基本战术 ·· 302

第八章　门球 ·· 307
　　第一节　概述 ··· 307
　　第二节　主要管理机构 ·· 308
　　第三节　重要赛事 ·· 308
　　第四节　比赛规则 ·· 308
　　第五节　基本策略 ·· 312

第九章　冰球 ·· 314
　　第一节　概述 ··· 314
　　第二节　主要管理机构 ·· 315
　　第三节　重要赛事 ·· 315
　　第四节　比赛规则 ·· 317
　　第五节　基本战术 ·· 331

第十章　水球 ·· 337
　　第一节　概述 ··· 337
　　第二节　主要管理机构 ·· 338
　　第三节　重要赛事 ·· 338
　　第四节　比赛规则 ·· 340
　　第五节　基本战术 ·· 352

参考文献 ·· 357

Chapter 1

Association Football (Soccer)

Goals

1. Understand the development history of football
2. Master the major governing body and major events of football matches
3. Be familiar with football game rules and professional terminology

Section 1   Introduction

Figure 1.1   Inside Soccer City in Johannesburg, South Africa, during a match at the 2010 FIFA World Cup. By Steve Evans

Association football, more commonly known as football or soccer, is a team sport played between two teams of 11 players each, who primarily use their feet to propel a ball around a rectangular field called a pitch. The objective of the game is to score more goals than the opposing team by moving the ball beyond the goal line into a rectangular-framed goal defended by the opposing team. Traditionally, the game has been played over two 45-minute halves, for a total match time of 90 minutes. With an estimated 250 million players active in over 200 countries and territories, it is the world's most popular sport.

The game of association football is played in accordance with the Laws of the Game, a set of rules that has been in effect since 1863 and maintained by the IFAB since 1886. The game is played with a football that is 68–70 cm (27–28 in) in circumference. The two teams compete to get the ball into the other team's goal (between the posts, under the bar, and across the goal line), thereby scoring a goal. When the ball is in play, the players mainly use their feet, but may use any other part of the body, except for their hands or arms, to control, strike, or pass the ball. Only the goalkeepers may use their hands and arms within the penalty area. The team that has scored more goals at the end of the game is the winner. There are situations where a goal can be disallowed, such as an offside call or a foul in the build-up to the goal. Depending on the format of the competition, an equal number of goals scored may result in a draw being declared, or the game goes into extra time or a penalty shoot-out.

Internationally, association football is governed by FIFA. Under FIFA, there are six continental confederations: AFC, CAF, CONCACAF, CONMEBOL, OFC, and UEFA. Of these confederations, CONMEBOL is the oldest one, being founded in 1916. National associations (e.g. The FA or CFA) are responsible for managing both the professionally and amateur games in their own countries, and coordinating competitions in accordance with the Laws of the Game. The most senior and prestigious international competitions are the FIFA World Cup, also referred to as the FIFA Men's World Cup, and the FIFA Women's World Cup. The Men's World Cup is the most-viewed sporting event in the world, surpassing the Olympic Games. The two most prestigious competitions in European club football are the UEFA Champions League, also referred to as the UEFA Men's Champion League, and the UEFA Women's Champions League, which attract an extensive television audience throughout the world. Since 2009, the final of the UEFA Men's Champions League has been the most-watched annual sporting event in the world.

The Chinese competitive game *cuju* (蹴鞠, literally "kick ball"; also known as tsu chu) resembles modern association football. *Cuju* players could use any part of the body apart from hands and the intent was to kick a ball through an opening into a net. During the Han dynasty (206 BCE–220 CE), *cuju* games were standardised and rules were established. Other East Asian games, including *kemari* in Japan and chuk-guk in Korea were both influenced by *cuju*. *Kemari*

Figure 1.2 On the left, an episkyros player on an ancient stone carving, c. 375-400 BCE, exhibited at the National Archaeological Museum, By Wikimedia Commons; on the right, children playing cuju in Song dynasty China, 12th century. The right one By Su Hanchen

originated after the year 600 during the Asuka period. It was a ceremonial rather than a competitive game, and involved the kicking of a mari, a ball made of animal skin. In North America, *pasuckuakohowog* was a ball game played by the Algonquians; it was described as "almost identical to the kind of folk football being played in Europe at the same time, in which the ball was kicked through goals".

Association football itself does not have a classical history. Notwithstanding any similarities to other ball games played around the world, FIFA has described that no historical connection exists with any game played in antiquity outside Europe. The history of football in England dates back to at least the eighth century. The modern rules of association football are based on the mid-19th century efforts to standardize the widely varying forms of football played in the public schools of England.

Section 2 Major Governing Body

The Fédération Internationale de Football Association (French for "International Association Football Federation"; abbreviated as FIFA and pronounced in English as /ˈfiːfə/) is the international governing body of association football, beach soccer, and futsal. It was founded in 1904 to oversee international competitions among the national associations of Belgium, Denmark, France, Germany, the Netherlands, Spain (represented by the Madrid Football Club), Sweden, and Switzerland. Headquartered in Zürich, Switzerland, its membership now comprises 211 national associations. These national associations must also be members of one of the six regional confederations into which the world is divided: CAF, AFC, UEFA, CONCACAF, OFC, and CONMEBOL.

FIFA outlines several objectives in its organizational statutes, including developing association football internationally, providing efforts to ensure it is accessible to everyone, and advocating for integrity and fair play. It is responsible for the organization and promotion of association football's major international tournaments, notably the World Cup which commenced in 1930, and the Women's World Cup which began in 1991. FIFA does not independently set the Laws of the Game, which is the responsibility of the International Football Association Board (IFAB). As a member of IFAB, FIFA applies and enforces the rules across all FIFA competitions. All FIFA tournaments generate revenue from sponsorships; in 2022, FIFA had revenues of over $5.8 billion, ending the 2019-2022 cycle with a net positive of $1.2 billion, and cash reserves of over $3.9 billion.

Section 3　Major Events

3.1　FIFA World Cup

The **FIFA World Cup**, often simply called the World Cup, is an international association football competition between the senior men's national teams of the members of FIFA, the sport's global governing body. The tournament has been held every four years since the inaugural tournament in 1930, with the exception of 1942 and 1946 due to the Second World War. The reigning champions are Argentina, who won their third title at the 2022 tournament.

The contest starts with the qualification phase, which takes place over the preceding three years to determine which teams qualify for the tournament phase. In the tournament phase, 32 teams compete for the title at venues within the host nation(s) over the course of about a month. The host nation(s) automatically qualify for the group stage of the tournament. The next FIFA World Cup is scheduled to expand to 48 teams for the 2026 tournament.

Figure 1.3　*French footballer Ousmane Dembélé holding the FIFA World Cup Trophy after the tournament's final match on* **15 July 2018**. *By Антон Зайцев*

As of the 2022 FIFA World Cup, 22 final tournaments have been held since the event's inception in 1930, and a total of 80 national teams have competed. The trophy has been won by eight national teams. Brazil, with five wins, is the only team to have played in every tournament. The other World Cup winners are: Germany and Italy, with four titles each; Argentina, with three titles; France and inaugural winner Uruguay, each with two titles; and England and Spain, with one title each.

The World Cup is the most prestigious association football tournament in the world, as well as the most widely viewed and followed single sporting event in the world. The viewership of the 2018 World Cup was estimated to be 3.57 billion, close to half of the global population, while the engagement with the 2022 World Cup was estimated to be 5 billion, with about 1.5 billion people watching the final match.

Seventeen countries have hosted the World Cup, most recently Qatar, which hosted the 2022 event. The 2026 tournament will be jointly hosted by Canada, the United States, and Mexico, which will give Mexico the distinction of being the first country to host games in three World Cups.

3.2 FIFA Women's World Cup

Figure 1.4   *FIFA Women's World* 2019 *Final Alex Morgan vs. Stefanie van der Gragt. By Holly Cheng*

The **FIFA Women's World Cup** is an international association football competition contested by the senior women's national teams of the members of Fédération Internationale de Football Association (FIFA), the sport's international governing body. The competition has been held every four years and one year after the Men's FIFA World Cup since 1991, when the inaugural tournament, then called the FIFA Women's World Championship, was held in China. Under the tournament's current format, national teams vie for the remaining 31 slots in a three-year qualification phase. The host nation's team is automatically entered as the first slot. The final of the tournament, called the World Cup Finals, is contested at venues within the host nation(s) over about one month.

The nine FIFA Women's World Cup tournaments have been won by five national teams. The United States has won four times. The other winners are Germany, with two titles, and Japan, Norway, and Spain with one title each.

Eight countries have hosted the Women's World Cup. China and the United States have each hosted the tournament twice, while Australia, Canada, France, Germany, New Zealand, and Sweden have each hosted it once.

The 2023 competition was hosted by Australia and New Zealand, making it the first Women's World Cup to be held in the Southern Hemisphere, and the first edition to be hosted by two countries.

3.3 Football at the Summer Olympics

Football at the Summer Olympics, also referred to as the Olympic Football Tournament, has been included in every Summer Olympic Games as a men's competition sport, except 1896 (the inaugural Games) and 1932 (in an attempt to promote the new FIFA World Cup tournament). Women's football was added to the official program at the Atlanta 1996 Games.

In order to avoid competition with the World Cup, FIFA has restricted the participation of elite players in the men's tournament in various ways: currently, squads for the men's tournament are required to be composed of players under 23 years of age, with three permitted exceptions.

By comparison, the women's football tournament is a full senior-level international tournament, second in prestige only to the FIFA Women's World Cup.

3.4 UEFA European Football Championship

The **UEFA European Football Championship**, less formally the **European Championship** and informally the **Euro**, is the primary association football tournament organized by the Union of European Football Associations (UEFA). The competition is contested by senior men's national teams of the UEFA members, determining the continental champion of Europe. It is the second most-watched football tournament in the world after the FIFA World Cup. The Euro 2012 final was watched by a global audience of around 300 million. The competition has been held every four years since 1960, except for 2020, when it was postponed until 2021 due to the COVID-19 pandemic in Europe, but kept the name Euro 2020. Scheduled to be in the even-numbered year between FIFA World Cup tournaments, it was originally called the European Nations' Cup before changing to its current name in 1968. Since 1996, the individual events have been branded as "UEFA Euro [year]".

Figure 1.5 *Spanish footballers Fernando Torres, Juan Mata, and Sergio Ramos celebrating winning the UEFA European Championship in 2012. By Football. ua*

Before entering the tournament, all teams other than the host nations (which qualify automatically) compete in a qualifying process. Until 2016, the championship winners could compete in the following year's FIFA Confederations Cup, but were not obliged to do so. From the 2020 edition onwards, the winner competes in the CONMEBOL-UEFA Cup of Champions.

The sixteen European Championship tournaments have been won by ten national teams: Germany and Spain have each won three titles, Italy and France have won two titles, and the Soviet Union, Czechoslovakia, the Netherlands, Denmark, Greece, and Portugal have won one title each. To date, Spain is the only team to have won consecutive titles, doing so in 2008 and 2012.

3.5 FIFA Confederations Cup

The **FIFA Confederations Cup** was an international association football tournament for men's national teams, held every four years by FIFA. It was contested by the winners of each of the six continental championships (AFC, CAF, CONCACAF, CONMEBOL, OFC, and UEFA), along with the current FIFA World Cup winner and the host nation, to bring the number of teams up to eight.

Between 2001 and 2017 (with the exception of 2003), the tournament was held in the country that would host the World Cup next year, acting as a test event for the larger tournament.

In March 2019, FIFA confirmed that the tournament would no longer be staged, with its slot replaced by an expansion of the FIFA Club World Cup.

3.6　UEFA Champions League

The **UEFA Champions League** (historically known as the **European Cup** and mostly abbreviated worldwide as the UCL) is an annual club association football competition organized by the Union of European Football Associations (UEFA). It is contested by top-division European clubs, with the winners determined through a round-robin group stage to qualify for a double-legged knockout format, and a single-leg final. It is the most-watched club competition in the world and the third most-watched football competition overall, behind only the FIFA World Cup and the UEFA European Championship. It is one of the most prestigious football tournaments in the world and the most prestigious club competition in European football, played by the national league champions (and, for some nations, one or more runners-up) of their national associations.

Introduced in 1955 as the Coupe des Clubs Champions Européens (French for European Champion Clubs' Cup), and commonly known as the European Cup, it was initially a straight knockout tournament open only to the champions of Europe's domestic leagues, with its winner reckoned as the European club champion. The competition took on its current name and format in 1992, adding a round-robin group stage in 1991 and allowing multiple entrants from certain countries since the 1997-98 season. It has since been expanded, and while most of Europe's national leagues can still only enter their champion, the strongest leagues now provide up to four teams. Clubs that finish next-in-line in their national league, having not qualified for the Champions League, are eligible for the second-tier UEFA Europa League competition, and since 2021, for the third-tier UEFA Europa Conference League.

In its present format, the Champions League begins in late June with a preliminary round, three qualifying rounds, and a play-off round, all played over two legs. The six surviving teams enter the group stage, joining 26 teams qualified in advance. The 32 teams are drawn into 8 groups of four teams each for a double round-robin stage. The eight group winners and eight runners-up proceed to the knockout phase, with the final match taking place in late May or early June. The winner of the Champions League automatically qualifies for the following year's Champions League, entering at the group stage, the UEFA Super Cup, the FIFA Club World Cup, and as of 2024 the new FIFA Intercontinental Cup which serves as a replacement for the previous annual format of the Club World Cup.

Spanish clubs have the highest number of victories (19 wins), followed by England (15 wins) and Italy (12 wins). England has the largest number of winning teams, with 6 clubs having won the title. The competition has been won by 23 clubs, 13 of which have won it more than once, and 8 successfully defended their title. Real Madrid is the most successful club in the tournament's history, having won it 14 times. Manchester City are the current European champions, having beaten Inter Milan 1-0 in the 2023 final for their first title.

Section 4　Rules

4.1　Gameplay

Association football is played in accordance with a set of rules known as the Laws of the Game. Two teams of eleven players each compete to get the ball into the other team's goal (between the posts and under the bar), thereby scoring a goal. The team that has scored more goals at the end of the game is the winner; if both teams have scored an equal number of goals, then the game is a draw. Each team is led by a captain who has only one official responsibility as mandated by the Laws of the Game: to represent their team in the coin toss prior to kick-off or penalty kicks.

Figure 1.6　A kick-off. Players other than the kicker are required to be in their team's own half of the pitch and opposing players may not be in the 10-yard diameter centre circle. By Michael Barera

The primary law is that players other than goalkeepers may not deliberately handle the ball with their hands or arms during play, though they must use both their hands during a throw-in restart. Although players usually use their feet to move the ball around they may use any part of their body (notably, "heading" with the forehead) other than their hands or arms. Within normal play, all players are free to play the ball in any direction and move throughout the pitch, though players may not pass to teammates who are in an offside position.

During the game, players attempt to create goal-scoring opportunities through individual control of the ball, such as by dribbling, passing the ball to a teammate, and by taking shots at the goal, which is guarded by the opposing goalkeeper. Opposing players may try to regain control of the ball by intercepting a pass or through tackling the opponent in possession of the ball; however, physical contact between opponents is restricted. Football is generally a free-flowing game, with play stopping only when the ball has left the field of play or when play is stopped by the referee for an infringement of the rules. After a stoppage, play recommences with a specified restart.

Figure 1.7 *A player executing a slide tackle to dispossess an opponent.*
By D League

At a professional level, most matches produce only a few goals. For example, the 2005-06 season of the English Premier League produced an average of 2.48 goals per match. The Laws of the Game do not specify any player positions other than goalkeeper, but a number of specialized have evolved. Broadly, these include three main categories: strikers, or forwards, whose main task is to score goals; defenders, who specialize in preventing their opponents from scoring; and midfielders, who dispossess the opposition and keep possession of the ball to pass it to the forwards on their team. Players in these positions are referred to as outfield players, to be distinguished from the goalkeeper.

These positions are further subdivided according to the area of the field in which the player spends most of the time. For example, there are central defenders and left and right midfielders. The ten outfield players may be arranged in any combination. The number of players in each position determines the style of the team's play; more forwards and fewer defenders create a more aggressive and offensive-minded game, while the reverse creates a slower, more defensive style of play. While players typically spend most of the game in a specific position, there are few restrictions on their movement, and players can switch positions at any time. The layout of a team's players is known as a formation. Defining the team's formation and tactics is usually the prerogative of the team's manager.

4.2 Players, equipment and officials

Each team consists of a maximum of eleven players (excluding substitutes), one of whom must be the goalkeeper. Competition rules may state a minimum number of players required to constitute a team, which is usually seven. Goalkeepers are the only players allowed to play the ball with their hands or arms, provided they do so within the penalty area in front of their own goal. Though there are a variety of positions in which the outfield (non-goalkeeper) players are strategically placed by a coach, these positions are not defined or required by the Laws.

The basic equipment or kit players are required to wear includes a shirt, shorts, socks, footwear, and adequate shin guards. An athletic supporter and protective cup are highly recommended for male players by

Figure 1.8 The referee officiates in a football match. By thetelf

medical experts and professionals. Headgear is not a required piece of basic equipment, but players today may choose to wear it to protect themselves from head injury. Players are forbidden to wear or use anything dangerous to themselves or another player, such as jewels or watches. The goalkeeper must wear clothing that is easily distinguishable from that worn by the other players and the match officials.

A number of players may be replaced by substitutes during the course of the game. The maximum number of substitutions permitted in most competitive international and domestic league games is 3 in 90 minutes with each team being allowed one more if the game should go into extra-time, though the permitted number may vary in other competitions or in friendly matches. Common reasons for a substitution include injury, tiredness, ineffectiveness, a tactical switch, or timewasting at the end of a finely poised game. In standard adult matches, a player who has been substituted may not take further part in a match. IFAB recommends "that a match should not continue if there are fewer than 7 players in either team". Any decision regarding points awarded for abandoned games is left to the individual football associations.

A game is officiated by a referee, who has "full authority to enforce the Laws of the Game in connection with the match to which he has been appointed" (Law 5), and whose decisions are final. The referee is assisted by two assistant referees. In many high-level games, there is also a fourth official who assists the referee and may replace other officials when necessary.

Goal-line technology is used to measure if the whole ball has crossed the goal line, thereby determining whether a goal has been scored or not; this was brought in to prevent there being controversy. Video assistant referees (VAR) have also been increasingly introduced in high-level matches to assist officials through video replays to correct clear and obvious mistakes. There are four types of calls that can be reviewed: mistaken identity in awarding a red or yellow card, the awarding of a goal, decisions concerning whether there was a violation during the buildup, direct red card decisions, and penalty decisions.

4.3 Ball

The ball is spherical with a circumference of between 68 and 70 cm (27 and 28 in), a weight in the range of 410 to 450 g (14 to 16 oz), and a pressure between 0.6 and 1.1 standard atmospheric pressure (8.5 and 15.6 pounds per square inch) at sea level. In the past, the ball was made up of leather panels sewn together, with a latex bladder for pressurization but modern balls at all levels of the game are now synthetic.

Figure 1.9 A typical ball. By Steffen Prößdorf

4.4 Pitch

As the Laws were formulated in England, and were initially administered solely by the four British football associations within IFAB, the standard dimensions of a football pitch were

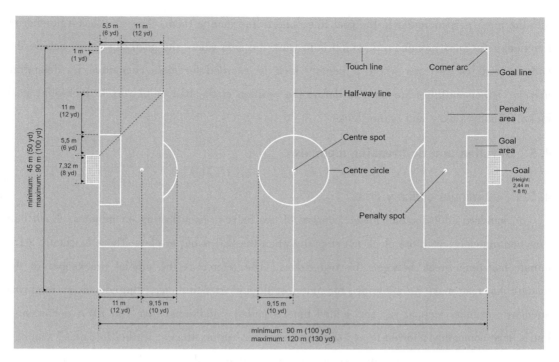

Figure 1.10 Standard pitch measurements. By Bildersindtoll

originally expressed in imperial units. The Laws now stipulate that the dimensions of a football field should be expressed in approximate metric units (followed by imperial units in brackets). In spite of this, the use of imperial units remains popular in English-speaking countries with a relatively short history of metrication (or those only partially using the metric system), such as Britain.

The length of the pitch, or field, for international adult matches is in the range of 100–110 m (110–120 yd) and the width is in the range of 64–75 m (70–80 yd). Fields for non-international matches may be 90–120 m (100–130 yd) in length and 45–90 m (50–100 yd) in width, provided that the pitch does not become square. In 2008, the IFAB initially approved a fixed size of 105 m (115 yd) long and 68 m (74 yd) wide as a standard pitch dimension for international matches; however, this decision was later put on hold and was never actually implemented.

The longer boundary lines are touchlines, while the shorter boundary lines (on which the goals are placed) are goal lines. A rectangular goal is positioned on each goal line, midway between the two touchlines. The inner edges of the vertical goalposts must be 7.32 m (24 ft) apart, and the lower edge of the horizontal crossbar supported by the goalposts must be 2.44 m (8 ft) above the ground. Nets are usually placed behind the goal, but are not required by the Laws.

In front of the goal is the penalty area. This area is enclosed by four lines: the goal line, two lines starting on the goal line 16.5 m (18 yd) from the goalposts and extending 16.5 m (18 yd) into the pitch perpendicular to the goal line, and a line joining them. This area has a number of functions, the most prominent of which is to mark the area where the goalkeeper may handle the ball, as well as the area where a penalty kick is awarded for fouls committed by defending players. Other markings are used to define the position of the ball or players at kick-offs, goal kicks, penalty kicks, and corner kicks.

4.5 Duration and tie-breaking methods

4.5.1 90-minute ordinary time

A standard adult football match consists of two halves, each lasting 45 minutes. Each half runs continuously, with the clock not stopping when the ball is out of play. There is usually a 15-minute half-time break between the two halves. The referee is the official timekeeper of the match, and may make an allowance for time lost through substitutions, injured players requiring attention, or other stoppages. This added time is called "additional time" in FIFA documents, but is most commonly referred to as "stoppage time" or "injury time", while "lost time" can also be used as a synonym. The duration of stoppage time is at the sole discretion of the referee. Stoppage time does not fully compensate for the time in which the ball is out of play. A 90-minute game typically involves about an hour of "effective playing time". Only the referee can signal the end of the match. In matches where a fourth official is appointed, towards the end of each half, the referee signals how many minutes of stoppage time they intend to add. The fourth official then informs the players and spectators by holding up a board showing this number. The signaled stoppage time may be further extended by the referee. Added time was introduced because of an incident which happened in 1891 during a match between Stoke City F.C. and Aston Villa F.C.. Trailing 0 – 1 and with just two minutes remaining, Stoke City were awarded a penalty. However, Villa's goalkeeper kicked the ball out of the ground, and by the time the ball was recovered, 90 minutes had elapsed and the game was over. As a result, the law states that the duration of either half is extended until the penalty kick or retaken penalty kick is completed, thus no game shall end with a penalty to be taken.

4.5.2 Tie-breaking

In league competitions, games may end in a draw. In knockout competitions where a winner is required, various methods may be employed to break the deadlock, such as some competitions may invoke replays. A game tied at the end of regulation time may go into extra time, which consists of two additional 15-minute halves. If the score is still tied after extra time, some competitions allow the use of penalty shootouts (known officially in the Laws of the Game as "kicks from the penalty mark") to determine which team will progress to the next stage of the

Figure 1.11 *Most knockout competitions use a penalty shootout to decide the winner if a match ends as a draw. By rayand*

tournament. Goals scored during extra-time periods count towards the final score of the game, but penalty shootouts are only used to decide which team progresses to the next round (with goals scored in a penalty shootout not making up part of the final score).

In competitions using two-legged matches, each team plays one match at home, and the aggregate score from the two matches determines which team progresses. Where aggregates are equal, the away goals rule may be used to determine the winners, in which case the winner is the team that scored more goals in the leg they played away from home. If the result is still equal, extra time and potentially a penalty shootout are required.

4.6 Ball in and out of play

Under the Laws, the two basic states of play during a game are ball in play and ball out of play. From the kick-off of each half until the end of the half, the ball is in play at all times, unless it leaves the field of play, or play is stopped by the referee. When the ball becomes out of play, play is restarted by one of the 8 restart methods, depending on how it went out of play:

① Kick-off: The kick-off is used to start each period in soccer and to restart the game after a goal.

② Throw-in: When the ball has crossed the touchline, a throw-in is awarded to the opposing team which last touched the ball.

③ Goal kick: When the ball has wholly crossed the goal line without a goal having been scored and having last been touched by a player of the attacking team, a goal kick is awarded to

Figure 1.12 *A player takes a free kick while the opposition form a wall to try to block the ball.*
By Neier

the defending team.

④ Corner kick: When the ball has wholly crossed the goal line without a goal having been scored and having last been touched by a player of the defending team, a corner kick is awarded to the attacking team.

⑤ Indirect free kick: An indirect free kick is awarded to the opposing team following "non-penal" fouls, certain technical infringements, or when play is stopped to caution or dismiss an opponent without a specific foul having occurred. A goal may not be scored directly (without the ball first touching another player) from an indirect free kick.

⑥ Direct free kick: A direct free kick is awarded to fouled team following certain listed "penal" fouls. A goal may be scored directly from a direct free kick.

⑦ Penalty kick: A penalty kick is awarded to the fouled team following a foul usually punishable by a direct free kick but that has occurred within their opponent's penalty area.

⑧ Dropped ball: A dropped ball occurs when the referee has stopped play for any other reason, such as a serious injury to a player, interference by an external party, or a ball becoming defective.

4.7 Violations

4.7.1 On-field

A foul occurs when a player commits an offence listed in the Laws of the Game while the ball is in play. The offences that constitute a foul are listed in Law 12. Handling the ball deliberately, tripping an opponent, or pushing an opponent, are examples of "penal fouls", punishable by a direct free kick or penalty kick depending on where the offence occurred. Other fouls are punishable by an indirect free kick.

The referee may punish a player's or substitute's misconduct by a caution (yellow card) or dismissal (red card). A second yellow card in the same game leads to a red card, which results in a dismissal. A player given a yellow card is said to have been "booked", the referee writing the player's name in their official notebook. If a player has been dismissed, no substitute can be brought on in their place and the player may not participate in

Figure 1.13 *Players are cautioned with a yellow card, and dismissed from the game with a red card. These colours were first introduced at the* 1970 *FIFA World Cup and used consistently since.*

further play. Misconduct may occur at any time, and while the offences that constitute misconduct are listed, the definitions are broad. In particular, the offence of "unsporting behavior" may be used to deal with most events that violate the spirit of the game, even if they are not listed as specific offences. A referee can show a yellow or red card to a player, substitute or substituted player. Non-players such as managers and support staff cannot be shown the yellow or red card but may be expelled from the technical area if they fail to conduct themselves in a responsible manner.

Rather than stopping play, the referee may allow play to continue if doing so will benefit the team against which an offence has been committed. This is known as "playing an advantage". The referee may "call back" play and penalize the original offence if the anticipated advantage does not ensue within "a few seconds". Even if an offence is not penalized due to the advantage being played, the offender may still be sanctioned for misconduct at the next stoppage of play.

The referee's decision in all on-pitch matters is considered final. The score of a match cannot be altered after the game, even if later evidence shows that decisions (including awards/non-awards of goals) were incorrect.

4.7.2 Off-field

Along with the general administration of the sport, football associations and competition organizers also enforce good conduct in wider aspects of the game, dealing with issues such as comments to the press, clubs' financial management, doping, age fraud, and match-fixing. Most competitions enforce mandatory suspensions for players who are sent off in a game. Some on-field incidents, if considered very serious (such as allegations of racial abuse), may result in competitions deciding to impose heavier sanctions than those normally associated with a red card. Some associations allow for appeals against player suspensions incurred on-field if clubs feel a referee was incorrect or unduly harsh.

Sanctions for such infractions may be levied on individuals or on clubs as a whole. Penalties may include fines, points deductions (in league competitions) or even expulsion from competitions. For example, the English Football League deducts 12 points from any team that enters financial administration. Among other administrative sanctions are penalties against game forfeiture. Teams that had forfeited a game or had been forfeited against would be awarded a technical loss or win.

Section 5 Basic Strategies

Although soccer may seem like a relatively simple sport, it is only simple in the rules and the basic gameplay. The strategy of the game can be quite complex especially at high levels of play like professional and World Cup.

5.1 Basic strategy for the offense

The team that has possession of the soccer ball is on the offense. When on offense, a soccer team may take a number of different tactics or strategies depending on which players are in the game at the time and on the skill level and type of the players.

One general strategy of offensive play that all soccer players should employ is **passing and moving**. This means that you should never just stand still on offense. Whenever a player has the ball, he/she needs to either pass the ball or dribble. Just standing still is a sure way to lose possession. This also applies to any offensive player near the player with the ball. They should always be moving and looking for an opening and providing passing lanes for their teammates.

Another good strategy is to pass the ball and then move quickly to another open space closer to the goal. By continuing to move and create passing lanes, the offense can put the defense at a disadvantage.

Another good offensive soccer strategy is to **switch the attack**. This is a long pass to another area of the field that has fewer defenders. It may be backwards towards one's own goal or all the way across the field. This gives the offense a chance to re-group and form a new attack on goal.

Some offensive soccer teams will play **possession ball**. This is when the team tries to keep possession of the ball for a long period. Players may pass the ball backwards side-to-side with no real apparent attack. This can be a good strategy for periods over a long soccer game. Passing the ball takes much less effort than dribbling or chasing the ball. The defensive soccer team will use much more energy to try and chase the ball down than the offensive team do to pass the ball around. This can also be a good soccer strategy when the offensive team has a good lead and wants to take some time off the clock.

5.2 Basic strategy for the defense

The team that does not have possession of the ball is the defense. Good team defense is essential to winning any soccer game. Defense is not just the goalie's job, but the job of all 11 players.

A good defensive soccer team will learn to communicate and form walls of defense against the offense. A player or two should always remain between the ball and the goal. Other players should be covering the other offensive players to make sure that they can't get open for a short goal shot. This is often called "marking".

It is a good idea for defenders to force the player with the ball towards the sidelines. By playing the right angle and turning the body, the defensive player can guide or channel the offensive player to the sidelines. This makes it hard for the offense to get off a good shot or get a good angle for a pass. It can also cause them to lose the soccer ball over the sideline, and therefore, get the possession back.

Some teams have a player who is often called the sweeper. This is a defensive player that positions in the center of the soccer field usually a bit deeper than the rest of the defense. The sweeper roams the backfield looking to steal or "sweep" any ball that gets through the defense.

Defenses can also trap the offensive player with the ball with two players preventing them from getting off a pass and stealing the ball. This can be a risky but rewarding play.

Defenses should take advantage of the soccer offside rule. By coordinating the last line of defense and keeping track of the offensive player's locations, a defense can trap a player offsides and cause a turnover of the ball.

Football Terminology

FIFA /ˈfiːfə/: The acronym used for the Federation Internationale de Football Association, the world governing body for the game of association football, which is based in Switzerland.

Confederation: Organization responsible for football in specific regions.

Pitch /pɪtʃ/: The soccer field of play.

Center Spot: The spot marked at the center of the field from which the kickoff is made.

Corner Flag: The flag marking each of the four corners of the field.

Touch Line: The line that defines the outer edge of the longer sides of the field of play.

Goal Line: The two boundary lines located at each end of the field.

Goal Area: The rectangular area in front of the goal. It is also knows as the 6-yard box because of its dimensions.

Penalty Area: The rectangular area in front of the goal in which the goalkeeper may handle the ball. It is also known as the 18-yard box because of its dimensions.

Penalty Spot: The marked spot 12 yards from the goal line from which a penalty kick is taken.

Far Post: The goalpost farthest from the ball.

Near Post: The goalpost closest to the ball.

Referee /ˌrefəˈriː/: The official who is in charge of the game.

Striker /ˈstraɪkə(r)/: An attacking player whose job is to finish attacking plays by scoring a goal.

Wingers /ˈwɪŋəz/: Attackers who play on the wings/flanks of the field.

Midfielder: The playing position for players that are responsible for linking play between attackers and defenders.

Defender /dɪˈfendə(r)/: A player whose job is to stop the opposition attacking players from goal scoring.

Goalkeeper: The specialized player who is the last line of defense and is allowed to control the ball with his hands when in the goal area.

Sweeper /ˈswiːpə(r)/: A defensive player whose job is to roam behind the other defenders. A sweeper has no specific marking duties and is the last line of defense before the goalkeeper.

Kickoff: The kickoff is taken from the centre spot at the start of play at the beginning of each half and after a goal has been scored.

Penalty /ˈpenəlti/: A penalty kick is awarded when a foul has been committed inside the penalty area in front of the goal. A penalty is taken by one player opposed only by the goalkeeper.

Corner Kick: A corner kick is a free kick taken from the corner of the field by an attacker. It is awarded when the ball has passed over the goal line after last touching a defensive player. The shot is taken from the corner closest to where the ball went out.

Free Kick: A free kick is awarded to an opposition player when a player has committed a foul, which falls under the category of place kicks. Free kicks can be either direct or indirect.

Direct Free Kick: A free kick from which a goal may be scored by the player taking the free kick.

Indirect Free Kick: A free kick awarded to a player from which a goal may not be scored directly by the player taking the free kick.

Goal Kick: A goal kick is awarded to the defending team when the ball is played over the goal line by the attacking team. It can be taken by any player though it is normally taken by the goalkeeper.

Dribble /ˈdrɪbl/: Keeping control of the ball while running.

Shot /ʃɒt/: A kick, header, or any intended deflection of the ball toward a goal by a player attempting to score a goal.

Header /ˈhedə(r)/: Using the head to pass or control the ball.

Throw-in /ˈθrəʊ ɪn/: The ball is thrown in after the ball has crossed the touch line. A player taking a throw-in must have both feet on or behind the touch line, must maintain contact with the ground, and must use a two-handed throw made from behind the head. A goal cannot be scored directly from a throw-in.

Toe Poke: Using the toe to strike the ball.

Backheel: A type of pass or shot in which a player uses his heel to propel the ball backward to another player or to the goal.

Volley /ˈvɒli/: Striking the ball in mid-air with either foot.

Bicycle Kick: A spectacular move in which a player jumps in the air in a backflip motion, kicking the ball backward over their head. The name comes from action which mimics their legs moving as if pedaling a bicycle.

Bend /bend/: A skill attribute in which players strike the ball in a manner that applies spin, resulting in the flight of the ball curving, or bending, in mid-air.

Back Pass: A pass that a player makes back toward their own goal, and that is usually made back to the goalkeeper. This is often a defensive move to restart a new phase of play.

Through Pass: A pass played past defenders into free space to allow a teammate to run onto the ball.

Sliding Tackle: A tackle in which the defender slides along the surface of the field of play before making one-footed contact with the ball.

Tackle /ˈtæk(ə)l/: To take the ball away from the opponent using the feet.

Offside /ˌɒfˈsaɪd/: A player is in an offside position if he is closer to his opponent's goal line than both the ball and the second-to-last opponent. This does not apply if the player is on his half of the field. An indirect free kick is awarded to the opposing team at the place where the offside occurred.

Offside Trap: A technique used by defenders to put attacking players in an offside position, by moving quickly away from their own goal to leave attackers offside.

One-Touch Pass: A pass in which the ball is played with a player's first touch.

Give and Go: (also known as a 1-2) When a player passes the ball to a teammate, who immediately one-touch passes the ball back to the first player.

Man to Man Marking: A defensive system where defenders are designated one attacking player to track continuously.

Zonal marking: System of marking, in which each player is responsible for an area of the pitch, rather than an opposing player.

Foul /faʊl/: Any illegal play.

Obstruction /əbˈstrʌkʃn/: Causing obstruction, which is blocking an opponent with the body, is penalized by awarding an indirect free kick to the opposition.

Yellow Card: A yellow card is held up by a referee to signal a caution for a minor infringement.

Red Card: A red card is issued to a player when that player has committed a serious infraction or has been issued with two yellow cards within the same game. The red card is held up by the referee to signal that a player is being sent off. The player sent off cannot be replaced.

Review Questions

1. What is the world governing body of soccer?
2. Please name three major international soccer events.
3. What are the length and width of a standard soccer field?
4. Which country did the ancient game of soccer originate in? What was it called then?

Chapter 2

Basketball

Goals

1. Understand the development history of basketball
2. Master the major governing body and major events of basketball matches
3. Be familiar with basketball game rules and professional terminology

Project Overview

Section 1　Introduction

Figure 2.1　The inside of the arena.　By Max12Max

Basketball is a team sport in which two teams, most commonly of five players each, opposing one another on a rectangular court. The two teams compete with the primary objective of shooting a basketball through the defender's hoop while preventing the opposing team from shooting through their own hoop. A field goal is worth two points unless it's behind the three-point line, when it is worth three. After a foul, timed play stops and the player fault or designated to shoot a technical foul is given one, two, or three free throws with each worth one point. The team with more points at the end of the game wins, but if the regulation game expires with the score tied, an extra play period(overtime) is mandatory.

Players advance the ball by bouncing it while walking or running (dribbling) or by passing it to a teammate, both of which require considerable skill. On offense, players may use a variety of shots—the lay-up, the jump shot, or a dunk; on defense, they may steal the ball from a dribbler, intercept passes, or block shots; either offense or defense may collect a rebound, that is, a missed shot that bounces off the rim or backboard. It is a violation to lift or drag one's pivot foot without dribbling the ball, to carry it, or to hold the ball with both hands and then resume dribbling.

The five players on each side fall into five playing positions. The tallest player is usually the center, the second-tallest and strongest is the power forward, a slightly shorter but more agile player is the small forward, and the shortest players or the best ball handlers are the shooting guard and the point guard. The point guard implements the coach's game plan by managing the execution of offensive and defensive plays (player positioning). Informally, players may play three-on-three, two-on-two, and one-on-one.

Invented in 1891 by Canadian-American gym teacher James Naismith in Springfield, Massachusetts, in the United States, basketball has evolved to become one of the world's most popular and widely viewed sports. The National Basketball Association (NBA) is the most significant professional basketball league in the world in terms of popularity, salaries, talent, and level of competition (drawing most of its talent from U.S. college basketball teams). Outside North America, the top clubs from national leagues qualify for continental championships such as the EuroLeague and the Basketball Champions League Americas. The FIBA Basketball World Cup and Men's Olympic Basketball Tournament are the major international events of the sport and attract top national teams from around the world. Each continent hosts regional competitions for national teams, like EuroBasket and FIBA AmeriCup.

The FIBA Women's Basketball World Cup and Women's Olympic Basketball Tournament feature top national teams from continental championships. The main North American league is the Women's National Basketball Association (WNBA) (NCAA Women's Division I Basketball Championship is also popular), whereas the strongest European clubs participate in the EuroLeague Women.

Section 2　Major Governing Body

Figure 2.2　FIBA headquarters in Mies, Switzerland.
By Richard Ruilliart

The **International Basketball Federation** (**FIBA**) is an association of national organizations which governs the sport of basketball worldwide. Originally known as the Fédération Internationale de Basketball Amateur (hence FIBA), in 1989 it dropped the word amateur from its name but retained the acronym; the "BA" now represents the first two letters of basketball.

FIBA defines the rules of basketball, specifies the equipment and facilities required, organizes international competitions, regulates the transfer of athletes between countries, and controls the appointment of international referees. A total of 213 national federations has been members since its inception in 1932, and organized since 1989 in five zones: Africa, America, Asia, Europe, and Oceania.

FIBA organizes both the men's and women's FIBA World Olympic Qualifying Tournament and the Summer Olympics Basketball Tournament, which are sanctioned by the International Olympic Committee (IOC). The FIBA Basketball World Cup is a world tournament for men's national teams held every four years. Teams compete for the Naismith Trophy, named in honor of basketball's Canadian-American creator James Naismith. The tournament structure is similar but not identical to that of the FIFA World Cup in association football; these tournaments occurred in the same year from 1970 through 2014, but starting in 2019, the Basketball World Cup will move to the year following the FIFA World Cup. A parallel event for women's teams, the FIBA Women's Basketball World Cup, is also held quadrennial; from 1986 through 2014, it was held in the same year as the men's event but in a different country.

Section 3 Major Events

3.1 Olympic Basketball Tournament

The Olympic Basketball Tournament has been a sport for men consistently since 1936. Prior to its inclusion as a medal sport, basketball was held as a demonstration event in 1904. Women's basketball made its debut at the 1976 Summer Olympics. FIBA organizes both the male and female FIBA World Olympic Qualifying Tournaments and the Summer Olympics basketball tournaments, which are sanctioned by the IOC.

The United States is by far the most successful country in Olympic basketball, with United States men's teams having won 16 of 19 tournaments in which they participated, including 7 consecutive titles from 1936 to 1968. United States women's teams have won 8 titles out of the 10 tournaments in which they competed, including seven in a row from 1996 to 2020. Besides the United States, Argentina is the only existing nation that has won both the men's and women's tournament. The Soviet Union, Yugoslavia, and the Unified Team are the countries no longer in existence who have won the tournament.

On June 9, 2017, the Executive Board of the International Olympic Committee announced that 3×3 basketball would become an official Olympic sport as of the 2020 Summer Olympics in Tokyo, Japan, for both men and women.

3.2 FIBA Basketball World Cup

The **FIBA Basketball World Cup**, also known as the **FIBA World Cup of Basketball** or simply the **FIBA World Cup**, between 1950 and 2010 known as the FIBA World Championship, is an international basketball competition contested by the senior men's national teams of the members of the International Basketball Federation (FIBA), the sport's global governing body. It is considered the flagship event of FIBA.

The tournament structure is similar, but not identical, to that of the FIFA World Cup; both of these international competitions were played in the same year from 1970 to 2014. A parallel event for women's teams, now known as the FIBA Women's Basketball World Cup, is also held quadrennially. Between 1986 and 2014, the men's and women's championships were held in the same year, but in different countries. The current format of the tournament involves 32 teams competing for the title at venues within the host nation. The winning team receives the Naismith Trophy, first awarded in 1967.

Following the 2014 FIBA championships for men and women, the men's World Cup was scheduled on a new four-year cycle to avoid conflict with the FIFA World Cup. The men's World Cup was held in 2019, in the year following the FIFA World Cup. The women's championship, which was renamed from "FIBA World Championship for Women" to "FIBA Women's Basketball World Cup", after its 2014 edition, will remain on the previous four-year cycle, with championships in the same year as the FIFA World Cup.

The 1994 FIBA World Championship, which was held in Canada, was the first FIBA World Cup tournament in which currently active US NBA players, who had also already played in an official NBA regular season game, were allowed to participate. All FIBA World Championship/World Cup tournaments since then, are thus considered fully professional level tournaments.

3.3 FIBA Women's Basketball World Cup

The **FIBA Women's Basketball World Cup**, also known as the **Basketball World Cup for Women** or simply the **FIBA Women's World Cup**, is an international basketball tournament for women's national teams which is held quadrennially. It was created by the International Basketball Federation (FIBA). Its inaugural game was in 1953 in Chile, three years after the first Men's World Championship. For most of its early history, it was not held in the same year as the men's championship, and was not granted a consistent quadrennial cycle until 1967. After the 1983 event, FIBA changed the scheduling so that the women's tournament would be held in even-numbered non-Olympic years, a change that had come to the men's tournament in 1970.

Formerly known as the FIBA World Championship for Women, the name changed shortly after its 2014 edition. From 1986 through 2014, the tournament was held in the same year as the FIBA Men's Basketball World Cup, though in different countries. After the 2014 editions of both championships, the men's event was rescheduled on a new four-year cycle (the latest in 2019) to avoid conflict with the Men's FIFA World Cup, but the Women's World Cup remains on the same four-year cycle, with editions held in the same years as the Men's FIFA World Cup and the finals tournament played a few months after it.

3.4 National Basketball Association

The **National Basketball Association** (**NBA**) is a professional basketball league in North America. The league is composed of 30 teams (29 in the United States and 1 in Canada) and is one of the four major professional sports leagues in the United States and Canada. It is the premier

*Figure 2.3 Chicago Bulls and New Jersey Nets, March 28, 1991.
By The Eloquent Peasant*

men's professional basketball league in the world.

The league was founded in New York City on June 6, 1946, as the Basketball Association of America (BAA). It changed its name to the National Basketball Association on August 3, 1949, after merging with the competing National Basketball League (NBL). The league's several international as well as individual team offices are directed out of its head offices in Midtown Manhattan.

In North America, the NBA is the third wealthiest professional sports league after the National Football League (NFL) and Major League Baseball (MLB) by revenue and is among the top four in the world. As of 2020, NBA players are the world's best-paid athletes by average annual salary per player.

The current league organization divides 30 teams into two conferences of three divisions with five teams each. The current divisional alignment was introduced in the 2004-05 season. Most teams are in the eastern half of the country: 13 teams are in the Eastern Time Zone, nine in the Central, three in the Mountain, and five in the Pacific. The league's regular season runs from October to April and the playoff tournament extends into June.

During the regular season, each team plays 82 games, 41 each home and away. A team faces opponents in its own division four times a year (16 games). Each team plays six of the teams from the other two divisions in its conference four times (24 games), and the remaining four teams three times (12 games). Finally, each team plays all the teams in the other conference twice apiece (30 games).

Starting with the 2023–24 season, the regular season will include an in-season tournament, in which all games in the tournament (except for the final) will count towards the regular season.

The NBA playoffs begin in April after the conclusion of the regular season with the top eight teams in each conference, regardless of divisional alignment, competing for the league's championship title.

The playoffs follow a tournament format. Each team plays an opponent in a best-of-seven series, with the first team to win four games advancing into the next round, while the other team is eliminated from the playoffs. In the next round, the successful team plays against another advancing team of the same conference. All but one team in each conference is eliminated from the playoffs.

The final playoff round, a best-of-seven series between the victors of both conferences, is known as the NBA Finals and is held annually in June (sometimes, the series will start in late May). The winner of the NBA Finals receives the Larry O'Brien Championship Trophy. Each player and major contributor—including coaches and the general manager—on the winning team receive a championship ring.

Section 4 Rules

The object of the game is to outscore one's opponents by throwing the ball through the opponents' basket from above while preventing the opponents from doing so on their own. An attempt to score in this way is called a shot. A successful shot is worth two points, or three points if it is taken from beyond the three-point arc 6.75 m (22 ft 2 in) from the basket in international games and 7.24 m (23 ft 9 in) in NBA games. A one-point shot can be earned when shooting from the foul line after a foul is made. After a team has scored from a field goal or free throw, play is resumed with a throw-in awarded to the non-scoring team taken from a point beyond the end line of the court where the points(s) were scored.

4.1 Playing regulations

Games are played in four quarters of 10 (FIBA) or 12 minutes (NBA). College men's games use two 20-minute halves, college women's games use 10-minute quarters, and most United States high school varsity games use 8-minute quarters; however, this varies from state to state. 15 minutes are allowed for a half-time break under FIBA, NBA, and NCAA rules and 10 minutes in

United States high schools. Overtime periods are five minutes in length except for high school, which is four minutes in length. Teams exchange baskets for the second half. The time allowed is actual playing time; the clock is stopped while the play is not active. Therefore, games generally take much longer to complete than the allotted game time, typically about two hours.

Five players from each team may be on the court at one time. Substitutions are unlimited but can only be done when play is stopped. Teams also have a coach, who oversees the development and strategies of the team, and other team personnel such as assistant coaches, managers, statisticians, doctors and trainers.

For both men's and women's teams, a standard uniform consists of a pair of shorts and a jersey with a clearly visible number, unique within the team, printed on both the front and back. Players wear high-top sneakers that provide extra ankle support. Typically, team names, players' names and, outside of North America, sponsors are printed on the uniforms.

A limited number of time-outs and clock stoppages requested by a coach (or sometimes mandated in the NBA) for a short meeting with the players, are allowed. They generally last no longer than one minute (100 seconds in the NBA) unless, for televised games, a commercial break is needed.

The game is controlled by the officials consisting of the referee (referred to as crew chief in the NBA), one or two umpires (referred to as referees in the NBA) and the table officials. For college, the NBA, and many high schools, there are a total of three referees on the court. The table officials are responsible for keeping track of each team's scoring, timekeeping, individual and team fouls, player substitutions, team possession arrow, and the shot clock.

4.2 Violations

The ball may be advanced toward the basket by being shot, passed between players, thrown, tapped, rolled or dribbled (bouncing the ball while running).

The ball must stay on the court; the last team to touch the ball before it travels out of bounds forfeits possession. The ball is out of bounds if it touches a boundary line, or touches any player or object that is out of bounds.

There are limits placed on the steps a player may take without dribbling, which commonly results in an infraction known as traveling. Nor may a player stop his dribble and then resume dribbling. A dribble that touches both hands is considered stopping the dribbling, giving this infraction the name double dribble. Within a dribble, the player cannot carry the ball by placing his hand on the bottom of the ball; doing so is known as carrying the ball. A team, once having established ball control in the front half of their court, may not return the ball to the backcourt and be the first to touch it. A violation of these rules results in loss of possession.

The ball may not be kicked, nor be struck with a fist. For the offense, a violation of these rules results in loss of possession; for the defense, most leagues reset the shot clock and the offensive team is given possession of the ball out of bounds.

There are limits imposed on the time taken before progressing the ball past halfway (8 seconds in FIBA and the NBA), before attempting a shot (24 seconds in FIBA and the NBA), holding the ball while closely guarded (5 seconds), and remaining in the restricted area known as the free-throw lane (or the "key") (3 seconds). These rules are designed to promote more offense.

There are also limits on how players may block an opponent's field goal attempt or help a teammate's field goal attempt. Goaltending is a defender's touching of a ball that is on a downward flight toward the basket, while the related violation of basket interference is the touching of a ball that is on the rim or above the basket, or by a player reaching through the basket from below.

4.3 Fouls

Figure 2.4 Zoran Dragić(right) contacts Carl English and commits a foul. By Carlos Delgado

An attempt to unfairly disadvantage an opponent through certain types of physical contact is illegal and is called a personal foul. These are most commonly committed by defensive players;

however, they can be committed by offensive players as well. Players who are fouled either receive the ball to pass inbounds again, or receive one or more free throws if they are fouled in the act of shooting, depending on whether the shot was successful. One point is awarded for making a free throw, which is attempted from a line 15 ft (4.6 m) from the basket.

The referee is responsible for judging whether contact is illegal, sometimes resulting in controversy. The calling of fouls can vary between games, leagues and referees.

There is a second category of fouls called technical fouls, which may be charged for various rule violations including failure to

Figure 2.5 The referee signals that a foul has been committed. By Wikipedia

Figure 2.6 When shooting a free throw for a technical foul, only the free throw shooter, in this case of Andrei Ivanov, is allowed to be within the area below the free throw line extended. By Artem Korzhimanov

properly record a player in the scorebook, or for unsportsmanlike conduct. These infractions result in one or two free throws, which may be taken by any of the five players on the court at the time. Repeated incidents can result in disqualification. A blatant foul involving physical contact that is either excessive or unnecessary is called an intentional foul (flagrant foul in the NBA). In FIBA and NCAA women's basketball, a foul resulting in ejection is called a disqualifying foul.

If a team exceeds a certain limit of team fouls in a given period (quarter or half) — four for NBA, NCAA women, and international games — the opposing team is awarded one or two free throws on all subsequent non-shooting fouls for that period, the number depending on the league. In the US college men's games and high school games for both sexes, if a team reaches 7 fouls in a half, the opposing team is awarded one free throw, along with a second shot if the first is made. This is called shooting "one-and-one". If a team exceeds 10 fouls in the half, the opposing team is awarded two free throws on all subsequent fouls for the half.

When a team shoots foul shots, the opponents may not interfere with the shooter, nor may they try to regain possession until the last or potentially last free throw is in the air.

After a team has committed a specified number of fouls, the other team is said to be "in the bonus". On scoreboards, this is usually signified with an indicator light reading "Bonus" or "Penalty" with an illuminated directional arrow or dot indicating that the team is to receive free throws when fouled by the opposing team. (Some scoreboards also indicate the number of fouls committed.)

If a team misses the first shot of a two-shot situation, the opposing team must wait for the completion of the second shot before attempting to reclaim possession of the ball and continuing play.

If a player is fouled while attempting a shot and the shot is unsuccessful, the player is awarded a number of free throws equal to the value of the attempted shot. A player fouled while attempting a regular two-point shot thus receives two shots, and a player fouled while attempting a three-point shot receives three shots.

If a player is fouled while attempting a shot and the shot is successful, typically the player will be awarded one additional free throw for one point. In combination with a regular shot, this is called a "three-point play" or "four-point play" (or more colloquially, an "and one") because of the basket made at the time of the foul (2 or 3 points) and the additional free throw (1 point).

4.4 Equipment

The only essential equipment in a basketball game is the ball and the court: a flat, rectangular surface with baskets at opposite ends. Competitive levels require the use of more equipment such as clocks, score sheets, scoreboard(s), alternating possession arrows, and whistle-operated stop-clock systems.

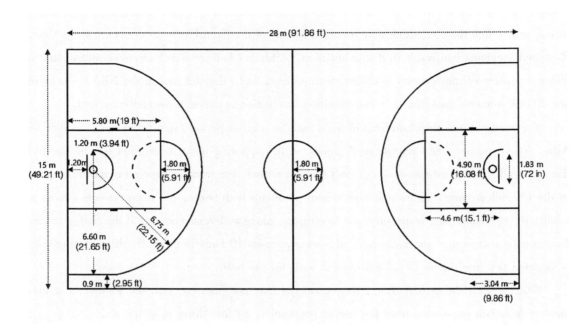

Figure 2.7 Basketball court. By Lencer

4.4.1 Basketball court

A standard basketball court in international games is 28 m (92 ft) long and 15 m (49 ft) wide. In the NBA and NCAA, the court is 29 by 15 m (94 by 50 ft). Most courts have wood flooring, usually constructed from maple planks running in the same direction as the longer court dimension. The name and logo of the home team are usually painted on or around the center circle.

4.4.2 Basket

The basket is a steel rim 46 cm (18 in) in diameter with an attached net affixed to a backboard that measures 1.8 by 1.1 m (6 by 3.5 ft) and one basket is at each end of the court. The white outlined box on the backboard is 46 cm (18 in) high and 61 cm (2 ft) wide.

At almost all levels of competition, the top of the rim is exactly 3.05 m (10 ft) above the court and 1.22 m (4 ft) inside the baseline. While variation is possible in the dimensions of the court and backboard, it is considered important for the basket to be of the correct

Figure 2.8 Basketball falling through the hoop. By Class Kerelin Molina

height — a rim that is off by just a few inches can have an adverse effect on shooting. The net must "check the ball momentarily as it passes through the basket" to aid the visual confirmation that the ball went through. The act of checking the ball has the further advantage of slowing down the ball so the rebound doesn't go as far.

4.4.3 Basketball

The size of the basketball is also regulated. For men, the official ball is 75 cm (29.5 in) in circumference (size 7, or a "295 ball") and weighs 22 oz (623.69 grams). If women are playing, the official basketball size is 72 cm (28.5 in) in circumference (size 6, or a "285 ball") with a weight of 20 oz (567 grams). In 3×3, a formalized version of the halfcourt 3-on-3 game, a dedicated ball with the circumference of a size 6 ball but the weight of a size 7 ball is used in all competitions (men's, women's, and mixed teams).

Figure 2.9 Traditional eight-panel basketball. By Reisio

Section 5　Common Techniques

5.1 Position

Although the rules do not specify any positions whatsoever, they have evolved as part of basketball. During the early years of basketball's evolution, two guards, two forwards, and one center were used. In more recent times specific positions have evolved, but the current trend, advocated by many top coaches including Mike Krzyzewski, is towards positionless basketball, where big players are free to shoot from outside and dribble if their skills allow it. Popular descriptions of positions include:

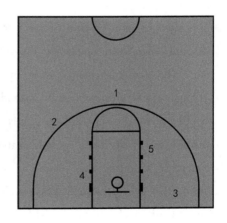

1—Point guard;　2—Shooting guard;
3—Small forward;　4—Power forward;
5—Center.

Figure 2.10 Basketball positions in the offensive zone. By Wikipedia

Point guard (often called the "1"): usually the fastest player on the team, organizes the team's offense by controlling the ball and ensuring that it gets to the right player at the right time.

Shooting guard (often called the "2"): creates a high volume of shots on offense, mainly long-ranged; and guards the opponent's best perimeter player on defense.

Small forward (often called the "3"): often primarily responsible for scoring points via cuts to the basket and dribble penetration; on defense seeks rebounds and steals, but sometimes plays more actively.

Power forward (often called the "4"): plays offensively often with their back to the basket; on defense, plays under the basket (in a zone defense) or against the opposing power forward (in man-to-man defense).

Center (often called the "5"): uses height and size to score (on offense), to protect the basket closely (on defense), or to rebound.

The above descriptions are flexible. For most teams today, the shooting guard and small forward have very similar responsibilities and are often called the wings, as do the power forward and center, who are often called post players. While most teams describe two players as guards, two as forwards, and one as a center, on some occasions teams choose to call them by different designations.

5.2　Shooting

Shooting is the act of attempting to score points by throwing the ball through the basket, methods varying with players and situations.

Typically, a player faces the basket with both feet facing the basket. A player will rest the ball on the fingertips of the dominant hand (the shooting arm) slightly above the head, with the other hand supporting the side of the ball. The ball is usually shot by jumping (though not always) and extending the shooting arm. The shooting arm, fully extended with the wrist fully bent, is held stationary for a moment following the release of the ball, known as a follow-through. Players often try to put a steady backspin on the ball to absorb its impact with the rim. The ideal trajectory of the shot is somewhat controversial, but generally, a proper arc is recommended. Players may shoot directly into the basket or may use the backboard to redirect the ball into the basket.

The two most common shots that use the above-described setup are the set shot and the

Figure 2.11　A short jump shot. By Wikimedia

jump shot. Both are preceded by a crouching action which preloads the muscles and increases the power of the shot. In a set shot, the shooter straightens up and throws from a standing position with neither foot leaving the floor; this is typically used for free throws. For a jump shot, the throw is taken in mid-air with the ball being released near the top of the jump. This provides much greater power and range, and it also allows the player to elevate over the defender. Failure to release the ball before the feet return to the floor is considered a traveling violation.

Another common shot is called the layup. This shot requires the player to be in motion toward the basket, and to "lay" the ball "up" into the basket, typically off the backboard (the backboard-free, underhand version is called a finger roll). The shot with the greatest poplanty and the highest rate of accuracy is the slam dunk, in which the player jumps very high and throws the ball downward through the basket, with his hands touching the ball.

Another shot that is less common than the lay-up, is the "circus shot". The circus shot is a low-percentage shot that is flipped, heaved, scooped, or flung toward the hoop while the shooter is off-balance, airborne, falling down, or facing away from the basket. A back-shot is a shot taken when the player is facing away from the basket, and may be shot with the dominant hand, or both; but there is a very low chance that the shot will be successful.

A shot that misses both the rim and the backboard completely is referred to as an air ball. A particularly bad shot, or one that only hits the backboard, is jocularly called a brick. The hang time is the length of time a player stays in the air after jumping, either to make a slam dunk, lay-up, or jump shot.

5.3 Rebounding

The objective of rebounding is to successfully gain possession of the basketball as it rebounds from the hoop or backboard after a missed field goal or free throw. This plays a major role in the game, as most possessions end when a team misses a shot. There are two categories of rebounds: offensive rebounds, in which the ball is recovered by the offensive side and does not change possession, and defensive rebounds, in which the defending team gains possession

Figure 2.12 A player making an offensive rebound. By Tony The Tiger

of the loose ball. The majority of rebounds are defensive, as the team on defense tends to be in a better position to recover missed shots.

5.4　Passing

A pass is a method of moving the ball between players. Most passes are accompanied by a step forward to increase power and are followed through with the hands to ensure accuracy.

The staple pass is the chest pass. The ball is passed directly from the passer's chest to the receiver's chest. A proper chest pass involves an outward snap of the thumbs to add velocity and leaves the defense little time to react.

Another type of pass is the bounce pass. Here, the passer bounces the ball crisply about two-thirds of the way from his own chest to the receiver. The ball strikes the court and bounces up toward the receiver. The bounce pass takes longer to complete than the chest pass, but it is also harder for the opposing team to intercept (kicking the ball deliberately is a violation). Thus, players often use the bounce pass in crowded moments, or to pass around a defender.

The overhead pass is used to pass the ball over a defender. The ball is released while over the passer's head.

The outlet pass occurs after a team gets a defensive rebound. The next pass after the rebound is the outlet pass.

The crucial aspect of any good pass is that it is difficult to intercept. Good passers can pass the ball with great accuracy and they know exactly where each of their other teammates prefers to receive the ball. A special way of doing this is passing the ball without looking at the receiving teammate. This is called a no-look pass.

Another advanced style of passing is the behind-the-back pass, which, as the description implies, involves throwing the ball behind the passer's back to a teammate. Although some players can perform such a pass effectively, many coaches discourage no-look or behind-the-back passes, believing them to be difficult to control and more likely to result in turnovers or violations.

5.5　Dribbling

Dribbling is the act of bouncing the ball continuously with one hand and is a requirement for a player taking steps with the ball. To dribble, a player pushes the ball down towards the ground with the fingertips rather than patting it; this ensures greater control.

When dribbling past an opponent, the dribbler should dribble with the hand farthest from the opponent and making it more difficult for the defensive player to get to the ball. It is therefore important for a player to be able to dribble competently with both hands.

Good dribblers (or "ball handlers") tend to bounce the ball low to the ground, reducing the travelling distance of the ball from the floor to the hand, making it more difficult for the defender to "steal" the ball. Good ball handlers frequently dribble behind their backs, between their legs, and switch directions suddenly, making a less predictable dribbling pattern that is more difficult to defend against. This is called a crossover, which is the most effective way to move past defenders while dribbling.

A skilled player can dribble without watching the ball, using the dribbling motion or peripheral vision to keep track of the ball's location. By not having to focus on the ball, a player can look for teammates or scoring opportunities, as well as avoid the danger of having someone steal the ball away from him/her.

Figure 2.13 *A player (left) posts up a defender. By Damon J. Moritz*

5.6 Blocking

Figure 2.14 *Blocking. By Wikimedia*

A block is performed when, after a shot is attempted, a defender succeeds in altering the shot by touching the ball. In almost all variants of play, it is illegal to touch the ball after it is in the downward path of its arc, which is known as goaltending. It is also illegal under NBA and Men's NCAA basketball to block a shot after it has touched the backboard, or when any part of the ball is directly above the rim. Under international rules, it is illegal to block a shot that is in the downward path of its arc or one that has touched the backboard until the ball has hit the rim. After the ball hits the rim, it is again legal to touch it even though it is no longer considered as a block performed.

To block a shot, a player has to be able to reach a point higher than where the shot is released. Thus, height can be an advantage in blocking. Players who are taller and playing the power forward or center positions generally record more blocks than players who are shorter and playing the guard positions. However, with good timing and a sufficiently high vertical leap, even shorter players can be effective shot blockers.

Section 6　Basic Strategies

There are two main defensive strategies: zone defense and man-to-man defense. In a zone defense, each player is assigned to guard a specific area of the court. Zone defenses often allow the defense to double-team the ball, a maneuver known as a trap. In a man-to-man defense, each defensive player guards a specific opponent.

Offensive plays are more varied, normally involving planned passes and movement by players without the ball. A quick movement by an offensive player without the ball to gain an advantageous position is known as a cut. A legal attempt by an offensive player to stop an opponent from guarding a teammate, by standing in the defender's way such that the teammate cuts next to him, is a screen or pick. The two plays are combined in the pick and roll, in which a player sets a pick and then "rolls" away from the pick towards the basket. Screens and cuts are very important in offensive plays; these allow quick passes and teamwork, which can lead to a successful basket. Teams almost always have several offensive plays planned to ensure their movement is not predictable. On the court, the point guard is usually responsible for indicating which play will occur.

Basketball Terminology

Center(C): One of five total positions in the game of basketball. Centers are generally the tallest players on the floor, mainly responsible for scoring, rebounding, and defense near the basket.

Small Forward (SF): One of the five positions in basketball. Small forwards are generally the most versatile players and typically the third-tallest on the floor.

Power Forward (PF): Usually the second-tallest player on the court. The power forward plays a similar role to the center.

Point Guard (PG): The shortest player and best ball-handler on the court. The point guard is responsible for directing the team's offense.

Shooting Guard (SG): One of the five positions in basketball. The shooting guard is generally the team's best scorer and the second-shortest player.

Elbow Zone: The position where both ends of the free-throw line meet the three-second zone.

Low Post: The area of the court around the basket on either side of the bottom of the key.

High Post: The area of the court at the top of the key on either end of the free-throw line.

Restricted Area: Referred to as the three-second zone, an area within the free-throw lane, designated by a semicircle in front of the basket.

Free-Throw Line: A line 15 feet from the perpendicular of the rebound, parallel to the baseline, from which the free-throw player shoots.

Backboard /ˈbækbɔːd/: A square board of wood or fiberglass connected to the basket.

Shot Clock: A timer designed to increase the pace (and, consequently, the frequency of scoring) by requiring a shot to be released before the timer expires; if the ball does not touch the rim or enter the basket, a shot-clock violation is called, which results in a loss of possession for the shooting team. The time limit is 24 seconds in the NBA, WNBA, and FIBA play.

Jump Ball: Two opposing athletes jump up and compete for a basketball thrown by the referee over their center.

Lay-up: The offensive action of a player sending the ball into the basket while running.

Long Pass: The first pass made by the attacking team after grabbing the backcourt rebound, to complete the attack as quickly as possible.

Rebound /rɪˈbaʊnd, ˈriːbaʊnd/: A player grabs a ball that falls from the basket or rebounds after a shot.

Bank shot: A shot that hits the backboard before hitting the rim or going through the net.

Hollow Basket: The basketball hit by shooting only touches the net, but does not touch the basket, and makes a "swish" sound (swish is an Onomatopoeia).

Air Ball: In basketball, an air ball is an unblocked shot that misses the basket, rim, and backboard entirely.

Alley-oop /æliˈuːp/: An alley-oop in basketball is an offensive play in which one player passes the ball near the basket to a teammate who jumps, catches the ball in mid-air and dunks or lays it in before touching the ground.

Cut: A basketball cut is an offensive skill that occurs when a player without possession of the ball uses a specific action to move from one location on the court to another with the primary purpose of creating space and getting open from a defender.

Block out: Also box out, to maintain a better rebounding position than an opposing player by widening your stance and arms and using your body as a barrier.

Shielding /ˈʃiːldɪŋ/: Offensive players stand between teammates and defensive players, creating opportunities for teammates to shoot in open spaces.

Pick and Roll: The attacking player without the ball uses his own body to block the forward direction of the defender. The player without the ball can only stand still to pick and roll, otherwise it will be deemed an offensive or mobile pick and roll foul.

Blocking /ˈblɒkɪŋ/: The defensive player tips or deflects a shooter's shot to alter its flight so that the shot misses.

Assist /əˈsɪst/: If a player passes the basketball to a teammate and the teammate directly scores after receiving the ball, then one assist will be recorded for the player on the technical statistics table.

Turnover /ˈtɜːnəʊvə(r)/: A loss of possession, either during ordinary play or as the result of a penalty for an infraction of the rules.

Three-Second Violation: The attacking player stands in the paint area for more than three seconds.

Double Dribble /ˈdʌbl ˈdrɪbl/: The player uses two hands to dribble the ball at the same time, or starts to dribble again after the dribble stopped, which is a violation.

Travel /ˈtræv(ə)l/: To move one's pivot foot illegally, to fall to the floor without maintaining a pivot foot, or to take three or more steps without dribbling the ball.

Offensive Foul: A foul committed by an offensive player.

Charge: An offensive foul which occurs when a player with the ball rushes into a non-moving defender.

Flop /flɒp/: A deliberate or exaggerated fall by a player after little or no physical contact from an opponent, with the goal of drawing a personal foul call against the opponent.

Free Throw: An unhindered shot in basketball made from behind a set line and awarded because of a foul by an opponent.

And-One: A free throw awarded to a shooter who is fouled while scoring, especially when the shot is successfuly done despite the disturbance of the opponent.

Post up: An offensive strategy in which a player gets the ball in the post area with his or her back to the basket.

Fast Break: An offensive tactic in which a team attempts to advance the ball and score as quickly as possible, giving the other team no time to defend effectively. It is often the result of a steal or blocked shot.

Man-to-Man Defense: A defense in which each player guards a single opposing player.

Zone Defense: A type of defense where each defender is responsible for an area of the court and must defend any opponent who enters that area.

Full-Court Press: A full-court press is a basketball term for a defensive style in which the defense applies pressure to the offensive team the entire length of the court before and after the inbound pass. Pressure may be applied man-to-man, or via a zone press using a zone defense. Some presses attempt to deny the initial inbounds pass and trap ball handlers either in the backcourt or at midcourt.

Review Questions

1. What is the international governing body of basketball?
2. Which country and year did basketball originate in?
3. What are the main positions of the players on the court in a basketball game?

Chapter 3

Field Hockey

Goals

1. Understand the development history of field hockey
2. Master the major governing body and major events of field hockey matches
3. Be familiar with field hockey game rules and professional terminology

Project Overview

Section 1 Introduction

Figure 3.1 Field hockey at the 2018 Summer Youth Olympics. By BugWarp

Field hockey (or simply **hockey**) is a team sport structured in standard hockey format, in which each team plays with 11 players in total, made up of 10 field players and a goalkeeper. Teams must move a hockey ball around a pitch by hitting it with a hockey stick towards the rival team's shooting circle and then into the goal. The match is won by the team that scores the most goals. Matches are played on grass, watered turf, artificial turf, or indoor boarded surface.

The modern game was developed at public schools in 19th-century England and it is now played globally. Its major governing bodly is FIH. Men and women are represented internationally in competitions including the Olympic Games, World Cup, FIH Pro League, Junior World Cup and in the past also World League, Champions Trophy. Many countries run extensive junior, senior, and masters club competitions. The FIH is also responsible for organizing the Hockey Rules Board and developing the sport's rules.

The sport is known simply as "hockey" in countries where it is the more common form of hockey. The term "field hockey" is used primarily in Canada and the United States, where "hockey" more often refers to ice hockey. In Sweden, the term "landhockey" is used. A popular variant of field hockey is the indoor field hockey, which differs in a number of respects while embodying the primary principles of hockey.

Section 2　Major Governing Body

The Fédération Internationale de Hockey (English: International Hockey Federation), commonly known by the acronym FIH, is the international governing body of field hockey and indoor field hockey. Its headquarters are in Lausanne, Switzerland. FIH is responsible for field hockey's major international tournaments, notably the Hockey World Cup.

FIH was founded on 7 January 1924 in Paris by Paul Léautey, who became the first president, in response to field hockey's omission from the programme of the 1924 Summer Olympics. Prior to this, the Paris Olympic Cimmittee had refused to include hockey as there was no international body governing the sport. First members complete to join the seven founding members were Austria, Belgium, Czechoslovakia, France, Hungary, Spain, and Switzerland.

In 1982, the FIH merged with the International Federation of Women's Hockey Associations (IFWHA), which had been founded in 1927 by Australia, Denmark, England, Ireland, Scotland, South Africa, the United States, and Wales.

Section 3　Major Events

3.1　Olympic Hockey Competition

Field hockey was introduced at the Olympic Games as a men's competition at the 1908 Games in London, with six teams, including four from the United Kingdom of Great Britain and Ireland.

Figure 3.2　The field hockey stadium at the 2008 Summer Olympics (Germany v. China female teams playing) By Andre Kiwitz

Field hockey was removed from the Summer Olympic Games at the 1924 Paris Games because of the lack of an international sporting structure. The International Hockey Federation (FIH, International Hockey League) was founded in Paris that year as a response to field hockey's omission. Men's field hockey became a permanent feature at the next Olympic Games, the 1928 Games in Amsterdam.

The first women's Olympic field hockey competition was introduced by the IOC at the 1980 Summer Olympics. Olympic field hockey games were first played on artificial turf at the 1976 Montreal Olympic Games.

Until the 1988 Olympics, the tournament was invitational but FIH introduced a qualification system at the 1992 Games. The Netherlands is the leading team in the overall medal tally with 18 medals (6 gold, 6 silver, and 6 bronze). India leads in the greatest number of gold medals.

3.2　FIH Hockey World Cup

The **Men's FIH Hockey World Cup** is an international field hockey competition organized by the International Hockey Federation (FIH). The tournament was started in 1971. It is held every four years, bridging the four years between the Summer Olympics. Pakistan is the most successful team, having won the tournament four times. The Netherlands, Australia, and Germany have each won three titles. Belgium and India have both won the tournament once. The World Cup expanded to 16 teams in 2018.

The **Women's FIH Hockey World Cup** is an international field hockey competition for women, whose format for qualification and the final tournament is similar to the men's. It has been held since 1974. The tournament has been organized by the International Hockey Federation (FIH) since it merged with the International Federation of Women's Hockey Associations (IFWHA) in 1982. Since 1986, it has been held regularly once every four years, in the same year as the men's competition.

The Hockey World Cup consists of a qualification stage and a final tournament stage. The format for each stage is the same.

The qualification stage has been a part of the Hockey World Cup since 1977. All participating teams play in the qualification round. The teams are divided into two or more pools and compete for a berth in the final tournament. The top two teams are automatically qualified and the rest of the berths are decided in playoffs.

The final tournament features the continental champions and other qualified teams. Sometimes it also features the winners of the Summer Olympics' hockey competition or the continental runners-up. The teams are divided into pools once more and play a round-robin tournament. The composition of the pools is determined using the current FIH World Rankings.

3.3 FIH Pro League

The **Men's FIH Pro League** is an international men's field hockey competition organized by the International Hockey Federation (FIH), which replaces the Men's FIH Hockey World League. The competition also serves as a qualifier for the Hockey World Cup and the Olympic Games. The first edition started in 2019. Nine teams secured their places for four years.

The **Women's FIH Pro League** is an international women's field hockey competition organized by the International Hockey Federation (FIH), which replaces the Women's FIH Hockey World League. The competition also serves as a qualifier for the Hockey World Cup and the Olympic Games. The first edition started in 2019. Nine teams secured their places for four years.

Nine men's and women's teams compete in a round-robin tournament with home and away matches, played from October to June, with the top team at the end of the season winning the league. From 2022−23 onwards, the bottom team at the end of the season will be relegated and will be replaced by the winner of a new competition called the Men's FIH Nations Cup/Women's FIH Nations Cup.

Section 4   Rules

4.1 Overview

Hockey's outdoor competition surface is a smooth, flat surface that is 91.4 m long by 55 m wide. Two teams of 11 athletes each compete for 70 minutes. One of each team's 11 players is typically a goalkeeper. Each athlete carries a stick and uses it to move the hockey ball. The hockey stick is about 1 yard long and weighs about one and a half (1.5) pounds. At one end is a narrow, round handle (like a broom handle). The stick expands to a blade-like playing end that is flat on one side and is usually round on the other. Athletes dribble and pass a hard, plastic ball to teammates while their opponents try to gain possession. The hockey ball is similar in size to a baseball but is bigger, heavier, and harder. While hockey's tactics and strategies are very similar to football, hockey is unique because the player in possession of the ball may not use their body, equipment, or a teammate to screen, pick, or otherwise obstruct their opponent from reaching the ball. This requires the development of expert dribbling, passing, and receiving skills. Both teams are trying to dribble or pass the ball into the scoring zone, called the circle, and shoot it across the goal line into a goal cage. The circle is actually shaped more like the letter D. Goals can only be scored when an attacker has legally played (pushed, flicked, scooped, hit, or deflected) the ball from within the circle. The team with more goals at the end of the game is the winner.

4.2 The game

The match is officiated by two field umpires. Traditionally each umpire generally controls half of the field, divided roughly diagonally. These umpires are often assisted by a technical bench including a timekeeper and record keeper.

Prior to the start of the game, a coin is tossed and the winning captain can choose a starting end or whether to start with the ball. Since 2017 the game consists of four periods of 15 minutes with a 2-minute break after every period, and a 15-minute intermission at halftime before changing ends. At the start of each period, as well as after goals are scored, play is started with a pass from the center of the field. All players must start in their defensive half (apart from the player making the pass), but the ball may be played in any direction along the floor. Each team starts with the ball in one half, and the team that conceded the goal has possession for the restart. Teams trade sides at halftime.

Field players may only play the ball with the face of the stick. If the back side of the

Figure 3.3 A Virginia Cavaliers field player passing the ball. By Jack Marion

stick is used, it is a penalty and the other team will get the ball back. Tackling is permitted as long as the tackler does not make contact with the attacker or the other person's stick before playing the ball (contact after the tackle may also be penalized when the tackle was made from a position where contact was inevitable). Further, the player with the ball may not deliberately use his body to push a defender out of the way.

Field players may not play the ball with their feet, but if the ball accidentally hits the feet, and the player gains no benefit from the contact, then the contact is not penalized.

Obstruction typically occurs in three circumstances — when a defender comes between the player with possession and the ball in order to prevent him from tackling; when a defender's stick comes between the attacker's stick and the ball or makes contact with the attacker's stick or body; and also when blocking the opposition's attempt to tackle a teammate with the ball (called third-party obstruction).

When the ball passes completely over the sidelines (on the sideline is still in), it is returned to play with a sideline hit, taken by a member of the team whose players were not the last to touch the ball before crossing the sideline. The ball must be placed on the sideline, with the hit taken from as near the place the ball went out of play as possible. If it crosses the back line after last touched by an attacker, a 16 yd (15 m) hit is awarded to the defensive side. A 16 yd hit is also awarded for offenses committed by the attacking side within 16 yd of the end of the pitch they are attacking.

4.3 Positions

When hockey positions are discussed, notions of fluidity are very common. Each team can be fielded with a maximum of 11 players and will typically arrange themselves into forwards, midfielders, and defensive players (fullbacks) with players who frequently move between these lines with the flow of play. Each team may also play with:
- a goalkeeper who wears a shirt with a different color and full protective equipment comprising at least headgear, leg guards and kickers;
- only field players; no player has goalkeeping privileges or wears a different color shirt; no player may wear protective headgear except a face mask when defending a penalty corner or stroke.

4.3.1 Formations

As hockey has a very dynamic style of play, it is difficult to simplify positions to the static formations which are common in association football. Although positions will typically be categorized as either fullback, halfback, midfield/inner or striker, it is important for players to have an understanding of every position on the field. For example, it is not uncommon to see a halfback overlap and end up in either attacking position, with the midfield and strikers being responsible for re-adjusting to fill the space they left. Movement between lines like this is particularly common across all positions.

4.3.2 Goalkeepers

When the ball is inside the circle, goalkeepers wearing full protective equipment are permitted to use their stick, feet, kickers or leg guards to propel the ball and to use their stick, feet, kickers, leg guards or any other part of their body to stop the ball or deflect it in any direction including over the back line. Similarly, field players are permitted to use their sticks. They are not allowed to use their feet and legs to propel the ball, stop the ball, or deflect it in any

Figure 3.4 Goalkeeper Filip Neusser in full gear. By Neusserf

direction including over the back line. However, neither goalkeepers, nor players with goalkeeping privileges are permitted to conduct themselves in a manner which is dangerous to other players by taking advantage of the protective equipment they wear.

Neither goalkeepers or players with goalkeeping privileges may lie on the ball; however, they are permitted to use arms, hands, and any other part of their body to push the ball away. Lying on the ball deliberately will result in a penalty stroke, whereas if an umpire deems a goalkeeper has lain on the ball accidentally (e.g. it gets stuck in their protective equipment), a penalty corner is awarded.

When the ball is outside the circle they are defending, goalkeepers or players with goalkeeping privileges are only permitted to play the ball with their stick. Further, a goalkeeper, or player with goalkeeping privileges who is wearing a helmet, must not take part in the match outside the 23 m area they are defending, except when taking a penalty stroke. A goalkeeper must wear protective headgear at all times, except when taking a penalty stroke.

4.4 Set plays

4.4.1 Free hits

Free hits are awarded when offenses are committed outside the scoring circles. The ball may be hit, pushed, or lifted in any direction by the team offended against. The ball can be lifted from a free hit but not by hitting, you must flick or scoop to lift it from a free hit. Opponents must move 5 m (5.5 yd) from the ball when a free hit is awarded. A free hit must be taken from within playing distance of the place of the offense for which it was awarded and the ball must be stationary when the free hit is taken.

As mentioned above, a 15 m hit is awarded if an attacking player commits a foul forward of that line, or if the ball passes over the back line by an attacker. When an attacking free hit is awarded within 5 m of the circle everyone including the person taking the penalty must be 5 m from the circle and everyone apart from the person taking the free hit must be 5 m away from the ball. When taking an attacking free hit, the ball may not be hit straight into the circle if you are within your attacking 23-meter area (25-yard area). It has to travel 5 m before going in.

Figure 3.5 Sideline hit. By Dimitri Aguero

4.4.2 Long corner

A free hit from the 23-meter line — called a long corner — is awarded to the attacking team if the ball goes over the back line after last being touched by a defender, provided they do not play it over the back line deliberately, in which case a penalty corner is awarded. This free hit is played by the attacking team from a spot on the 23-meter line, in line with where the ball went out of play.

4.4.3 Penalty corner

Figure 3.6 Penalty corner for China against South Korea during the London Olympics 2012. By The Hammer

The short or penalty corner is awarded:

1. for an offense by a defender in the circle which does not prevent the probable scoring of a goal;

2. for an intentional offense in the circle by a defender against an opponent who does not have possession of the ball or an opportunity to play the ball;

3. for an intentional offense by a defender outside the circle but within the 23-meter area they are defending;

4. for intentionally playing the ball over the back line by a defender;

5. when the ball becomes lodged in a player's clothing or equipment while in the circle they are defending.

Short corners begin with five defenders (usually including the goal keeper) positioned behind the back line and the ball placed at least 10 yards from the nearest goal post. All other players in the defending team must be beyond the center line, that is not in their "own" half of the pitch, until the ball is in play. Attacking players begin the play standing outside the scoring circle, except for one attacker who starts the corner by playing the ball from a mark 10 m on either side of the goal (the circle has a 14.63 m radius). This player puts the ball into play by pushing or hitting the ball to the other attackers outside the circle; the ball must be passed outside the circle and then be put back into the circle before the attackers may make a shot at the goal from which a goal can be scored.

Figure 3.7 A player is to take a penalty corner from the 10 m mark. The 5 m line above demarcates the closest position a defender may stand. By Rega Photography

For safety reasons, the first shot of a penalty corner must not exceed 460 mm high (the height of the "backboard" of the goal) at the point it crosses the goal line if it is hit. However, if the ball is deemed to be below backboard height, the ball can be subsequently deflected above this height by another player (defender or attacker), providing that this deflection does not lead to danger. The "slap" stroke (a sweeping motion towards the ball, where the stick is kept on or close to the ground when striking the ball) is classed as a hit, and so the first shot at goal must be below backboard height for this type of shot also.

If the first shot at goal in a short corner situation is a push, flick or scoop, in particular the drag flick, the shot is permitted to rise above the height of the backboard, as long as the shot is not deemed dangerous to any opponent. This form of shooting was developed because it is not height-restricted in the same way as the first hit shot at the goal and players with good technique are able to drag-flick with as much power as many others can hit a ball.

4.4.4 Penalty stroke

Figure 3.8 A penalty stroke consisting of a single stroke by an attacker against the goalkeeper from the penalty spot. By Dimitri Aguero

A penalty stroke is awarded when a defender commits a foul in the circle (accidental or otherwise) that prevents a probable goal or commits a deliberate foul in the circle or if defenders repeatedly run from the back line too early at a penalty corner. The penalty stroke is taken by a single attacker in the circle, against the goalkeeper, from a spot 6.4 m from the goal. The ball is played only once at goal by the attacker using a push, flick, or scoop stroke. If the shot is saved, play is restarted with a 15 m hit to the defenders. When a goal is scored, play is restarted in the normal way.

4.5 Dangerous play and raised balls

According to the Rules of Hockey 2015 issued by the FIH there are only two criteria for a dangerously played ball. The first is legitimate evasive action by an opponent (what constitutes legitimate evasive action is an umpiring judgment). The second is specific to the rule concerning a shot at goal at a penalty corner but is generally, if somewhat inconsistently, applied throughout the game and in all parts of the pitch: it is that a ball lifted above knee height and at an opponent who is within 5 m of the ball is certainly dangerous.

The velocity of the ball is not mentioned in the rules concerning a dangerously played ball. A ball that hits a player above the knee may on some occasions not be penalized, this is at the umpire's discretion. A jab tackle, for example, might accidentally lift the ball above knee height into an opponent from close range but at such low velocity as not to be, in the opinion of the umpire, dangerous play. In contrast, a high-velocity hit at very close range into an opponent, but below knee height, could be considered to be dangerous or reckless play in the view of the umpire, especially when safer alternatives are open to the striker of the ball.

A ball that has been lifted high so that it will fall among close opponents may be deemed to be potentially dangerous and play may be stopped for that reason. A lifted ball that is falling to a player in clear space may be made potentially dangerous by the actions of an opponent closing to within 5 m of the receiver before the ball has been controlled to ground — a rule which is often only loosely applied; the distance allowed is often only what might be described as playing distance, 2-3 m, and opponents tend to be permitted to close to the ball as soon as the receiver plays it. These unofficial variations are often based on the umpire's perception of the skill of the players, in other words, on the level of the game. According to FIH Rules of Hockey 2015 and FIH Umpire's Briefings 2015, in order to maintain game flow, umpires are in general instructed not to penalize when it is unnecessary to do so; this is also a matter at the umpire's discretion.

The term "falling ball" is important in what may be termed encroaching offenses. It is generally only considered an offense to encroach on an opponent receiving a lifted ball that has been lifted to above head height (although the height is not specified in the rule) and is falling.

In general, even potentially dangerous play is not penalized if an opponent is not disadvantaged by it or, obviously, not injured by it so that he cannot continue. A personal penalty, that is a caution or a suspension, rather than a team penalty, such as a free ball or a penalty corner, may be issued to the guilty party after an advantage allowed by the umpire has been played out in any situation where an offense has occurred, including dangerous play (but once advantage has been allowed the umpire cannot then call play back and award a team penalty).

It is not an offense to lift the ball over an opponent's stick (or body on the ground), provided that it is done with consideration for the safety of the opponent and not dangerously. For example, a skillful attacker may lift the ball over a defender's stick or prone body and run past them; however, if the attacker lifts the ball into or at the defender's body, this would almost certainly be regarded as dangerous.

It is not against the rules to bounce the ball on the stick and even to run with it while doing so, as long as that does not lead to a potentially dangerous conflict with an opponent who is attempting to make a tackle. For example, two players trying to play at the ball in the air at the same time would probably be considered a dangerous situation, and it is likely that the player who first put the ball up or who was so "carrying" it would be penalized.

Dangerous play rules also apply to the usage of the stick when approaching the ball, making a stroke at it (replacing what was at one time referred to as the "sticks" rule, which once forbade the raising of any part of the stick above the shoulder during any play. This last restriction has been removed but the stick should still not be used in a way that endangers an opponent) or attempting to tackle (fouls relating to tripping, impeding, and obstruction). The use of the stick to strike an opponent will usually be much more severely dealt with by the umpires than offenses such as barging, impeding, and obstruction with the body, although these are also dealt with firmly, especially when these fouls are intentional.

4.6 Warnings and suspensions

Hockey uses a three-tier penalty card system of warnings and suspensions:

- When shown a green card, the player may have to leave the field for two minutes, depending on national regulations, though at international standards the player has to leave the field for two minutes, any further infractions will result in a yellow or red card.

Figure 3.9 Green card (warning with 2-minute suspension); yellow card (suspension of 5/10 minutes depending on the intensity of foul); red card (permanent suspension). By Wikipedia

- A yellow card is an official suspension similar to the penalty box in ice hockey. The duration is decided by the umpire issuing the card and the player must go to a pre-defined area of the pitch as chosen by the umpires, or by the local/state/national association of that country. Most umpires will opt for a minimum of 5-minute duration without substitution; the maximum time is at the discretion of the umpire, depending on the seriousness of the offense, for example the second yellow card to the same player or the first for danger might be given 10 minutes (In some modes, including indoor ones, shorter periods of suspension are applied, dependent on local rules.). However, it is possible to send a player off for the remainder of the match if the penalty time is longer than the time remaining in the match.
- A red card, just like in association football, is a permanent exclusion from the rest of the game, without substitution, and usually results in the player being banned for a certain period of time or a number of matches (this is governed by local playing conditions, rather than the rules of field hockey). The player must also leave the pitch and surrounding areas.

If a coach is sent off, depending on local rules, a player may have to leave the field for the remaining length of the match.

*Figure 3.10   A Penn State field hockey player receives a green card.
By Cathi Alloway*

In addition to their colors, field hockey penalty cards are often shaped differently, so they can be recognized easily. Green cards are normally triangular, yellow cards rectangular, and red cards circular.

Unlike football, a player may receive more than one green or yellow card. However, they cannot receive the same card for the same offense (for example, two yellows for dangerous play), and the second must always be a more serious card. In the case of a second yellow card for a different breach of the rules (for example, a yellow for deliberate foot, and a second later in the game for dangerous play), the temporary suspension would be expected to be of considerably longer duration than the first.

Umpires, if the free hit would have been in the attacking 23 m area, may upgrade the free hit to a penalty corner for dissent or other misconduct after the free hit has been awarded.

4.7   Scoring

The teams' object is to play the ball into their attacking circle and, from there, hit, push, or flick the ball into the goal to score a goal. The team with more goals after 60 minutes wins the game. The playing time may be shortened, particularly when younger players are involved, or for some tournament play. If the game is played in a countdown clock, like ice hockey, a goal can only count if the ball completely crosses the goal line and into the goal before time expires, not when the ball leaves the stick in the act of shooting.

If the score is tied at the end of the game, either a draw is declared or the game goes into extra time, or there is a penalty shoot-out, depending on the format of the competition. In many competitions (such as regular club competitions, or pool games in FIH international tournaments such as the Olympics or the World Cup), a tied result stands and the overall competition standings are adjusted accordingly. Since March 2013, when a tie-breaker is required, the official FIH Tournament Regulations mandate to no longer have extra time and go directly into a penalty shoot-out when a classification match ends in a tie. However, many associations follow the previous procedure consisting of two periods of 7.5 minutes of "golden goal" extra time during which the game ends as soon as one team scores.

There are many variations to overtime play that depend on the league or tournament rules. In American college play, a seven-a-side overtime period consists of a 10-minute golden goal period with 7 players for each team. If the scores remain equal, the game enters a one-on-one competition where each team chooses 5 players to dribble from the 23-meter (25 yd) line down to the circle against the opposing goalkeeper. The player has eight seconds to score against the goalkeeper while keeping the ball in bounds. The game ends after a goal is scored, the ball goes out of bounds, a foul is committed (ending in either a penalty stroke or flick or the end of the one-on-one) or time expires. If the tie still persists, more rounds are played until one team has scored.

4.8 Field of play

4.8.1 Hockey field

The pitch is a 91.4 m×55 m (100.0 yd×60.1 yd) rectangular field. At each end is a goal 2.14 m (7 ft) high and 3.66 m (12 ft) wide, as well as lines across the field 22.90 m (25 yd) from each end-line (generally referred to as the 23-meter lines or the 25-yard lines) and a line in the center of the field. A spot 0.15 m (6 in) in diameter, called the penalty spot or stroke mark, is placed with its center 6.40 m (7 yd) from the center of each goal. The shooting circle is 15 m (16 yd) from the base line.

4.8.2 Field hockey goals

Field hockey goals are made of two upright posts, joined at the top by a horizontal crossbar,

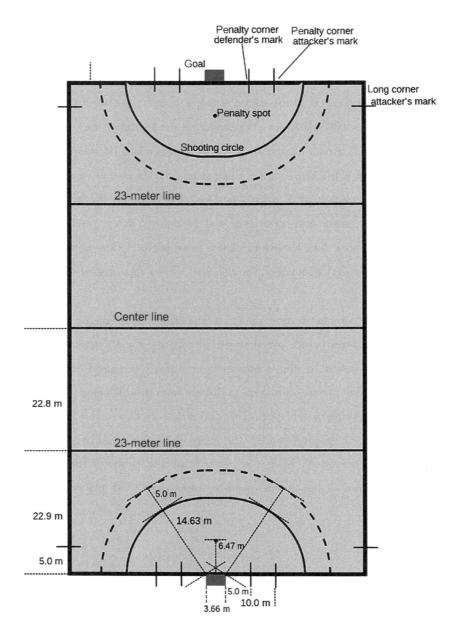

Figure **3. 11** *Diagram of a hockey field. By Hockey field. svg*

with a net positioned to catch the ball when it passes through the goalposts. The goalposts and crossbar must be white and rectangular and should be 51 mm (2 in) wide and 51-76 mm (2-3 in) deep. Field hockey goals also include sideboards and a backboard, which stand 50 cm (20 in) from the ground. The backboard runs the full 3. 66 m (12. 0 ft) width of the goal, while the sideboards are 1. 2 m (3 ft 11 in) deep.

Chapter 3 Field Hockey

Figure 3.12 Field hockey goals. By sportsequip. co. uk

4.8.3 Playing surface

Figure 3.13 Sydney Olympic Park Hockey Center during the 2000 Summer Olympics. By Jimmy Harris

Historically the game developed on natural grass turf. In the early 1970s, synthetic grass fields began to be used for hockey, with the first Olympic Games on this surface being held in

Montreal in 1976. Synthetic pitches are now mandatory for all international tournaments and for most national competitions.

4.9 Equipment

4.9.1 Field hockey ball

Standard field hockey balls are hard spherical balls, made of solid plastic (sometimes over a cork core), and are usually white, although they can be any color as long as they contrast with the playing surface. The balls have a diameter of 71.3−74.8 mm (2.81−2.94 in) and a mass of 156−163 g (5.5−5.7 oz). The ball is often covered with indentations to reduce aquaplaning that can cause an inconsistent ball speed on wet surfaces.

Figure 3.14 A field hockey ball with a 5 franc coin. By Clément Bucco

4.9.2 Field hockey stick

Each player carries a hockey stick that normally measures between 80−95 cm (31−37 in); shorter or longer sticks are available. The length of the stick is based on the player's individual height: the top of the stick usually comes to the player's hip, and taller players typically have longer sticks. Goalkeepers can use either a specialized stick, or an ordinary field hockey stick. The specific goal-keeping sticks have another curve at the end of the stick, to give it more surface area to block the ball.

Sticks were traditionally made of wood, but are now often made also with fiberglass, kevlar, or carbon fiber composites. Metal is forbidden from use in field hockey sticks, due to the risk of injury from sharp edges if the stick were to break. The stick has a round handle, has a J-shaped hook at the bottom, and is flattened on the left side (when looking down the handle with the hook facing upwards). All sticks must be right-handed; left-handed ones are prohibited.

There was traditionally a slight curve (called the bow, or rake) from the top to bottom of the face side of the stick and another on the "heel" edge to the top of the handle (usually made according to the angle at which the handle part was inserted into the splice of the head part of the stick), which assisted in the positioning of the stick head in relation to the ball and made striking the ball easier and more accurate.

4.9.3 Goalkeeper equipment

The Rules of Hockey 2007 saw major changes regarding goalkeepers. A fully equipped goalkeeper must wear a helmet, leg guards and kickers, and like all players, he must carry a

Figure 3.15 A hockey stick. By Martin Conlon

Figure 3.16 A goalkeeper makes a glove save. Equipment worn here is typical gear for a field hockey goalkeeper. By Wikimedia

stick. Goalkeepers may use either a field player's stick or a specialized goalkeeping stick provided always the stick is of legal dimensions. Usually, field hockey goalkeepers also wear extensive additional protective equipment including chest guards, padded shorts, heavily padded hand protectors, groin protectors, neck protectors, and arm guards. A goalie may not cross the 23 m line, the sole exception to this being if the goalkeeper is to take a penalty stroke at the other end of the field when the clock is stopped. The goalkeeper can also remove his helmet for this action. While goalkeepers are allowed to use their feet and hands to clear the ball, like field players they may only use one side of their stick. Slide tackling is permitted as long as it is with the intention of clearing the ball, not aimed at a player.

It is now also even possible for teams to have a full eleven outfield players and no goalkeeper at all. In such circumstance, no player may wear a helmet or other goalkeeping equipment, neither will any player be able to play the ball with any other part of the body than with their stick. This may be used to offer a tactical advantage. For example, if a team is trailing with only a short time to play, increase in the number of on-field players will promote its rate of winning;

this new rule will also allow for play to commence if no goalkeeper or kit is available.

Section 5　Basic Tactics

The basic tactic in field hockey, as in association football and many other team games, is to outnumber the opponent in a particular area of the field at a moment in time. When in possession of the ball, this temporary numerical superiority can be used to pass the ball around opponents so that they cannot effect a tackle because they cannot get within playing reach of the ball and to further use this numerical advantage to gain time and create clear space for making scoring shots on the opponent's goal. When not in possession of the ball, numerical superiority is used to isolate and channel an opponent in possession and "mark out" any passing options so that an interception or a tackle may be made to gain possession. Highly skillful players can sometimes get the better of more than one opponent and retain the ball and successfully pass or shoot, but this tends to use more energy than quick early passing.

Every player has a role depending on their relationship to the ball if the team communicates throughout the play of the game. There will be players on the ball (offensively — ball carriers; defensively — pressure, support players, and movement players).

The main methods by which the ball is moved around the field by players are (a) passing (b) pushing the ball and running with it controlled to the front or right of the body and (c) "dribbling"; where the player controls the ball with the stick and moves in various directions with it to elude opponents. To make a pass the ball may be propelled with a pushing stroke, where the player uses their wrists to push the stick head through the ball while the stick head is in contact with it; the "flick" or "scoop", similar to the push but with an additional arm and leg and rotational actions to lift the ball off the ground; and the "hit", where a swing at the ball is taken and contact with it is often made very forcefully, causing the ball to be propelled at velocities in excess of 70 mph (110 km/h). In order to produce a powerful hit, usually for travel over long distances or shooting at the goal, the stick is raised higher and swung with maximum power at the ball, a stroke sometimes known as a "drive".

Tackles are made by placing the stick into the path of the ball or playing the stick head or shaft directly at the ball. To increase the effectiveness of the tackle, players will often place the entire stick close to the ground horizontally, thus representing a wider barrier. To avoid the tackle, the ball carrier will either pass the ball to a teammate using any of the push, flick, or hit strokes, or attempt to maneuver or "drag" the ball around the tackle, trying to deceive the tackler.

In recent years, the penalty corner has gained importance as a goal-scoring opportunity, particularly with the technical development of the drag flick. Tactics at penalty corners to set up time for a shot with a drag flick or a hit shot at the goal involve various complex plays, including multiple passes before deflections towards the goal but the most common method of shooting is the direct flick or hit at the goal.

At the highest level, field hockey is a fast-moving, highly skilled game, with players using fast moves with the stick, quick accurate passing, and hard hits, in attempts to keep possession and move the ball towards the goal. Tackling with physical contact and otherwise physically obstructing players is not permitted. Some of the tactics used resemble football (soccer), but with greater ball speed.

With the 2009 changes to the rules regarding free hits in the attacking 23 m area, the common tactic of hitting the ball hard into the circle was forbidden. Although at higher levels this was considered tactically risky and low-percentage at creating scoring opportunities, it was used with some effect to "win" penalty corners by forcing the ball onto a defender's foot or to deflect high (and dangerously) off a defender's stick. The FIH felt it was a dangerous practice that could easily lead to raised deflections and injuries in the circle, which is often crowded in a free-hit situation, and outlawed it.

Field Hockey Terms

Field Player: A participant in the game who is not a goalkeeper.

Striker /ˈstraɪkə(r)/: The players who play as forwards and mainly score the goals for a team.

Wings: A position at which the players play near the sidelines.

Centre Forward: An offensive position that covers the middle of the offensive area and takes shots on goal, which is often referred to as the "striker".

Midfielder: A position that covers the middle of the field. Players at this position have both offensive and defensive responsibilities. Their job is to get the ball from their team's defense and move it up the field to the offense.

Inner /ˈɪnə(r)/: A forward or midfield position that has the player(s) positioned at or near the centre of the field when there are more than three players on one line.

Fullback: A position on the defensive side of the field that focuses on keeping the opposing team's forwards from scoring.

Bully: Used to restart the play when possession is unclear. The ball is placed between two opposing players, and they must tap their sticks above the ball three times before playing.

Center Pass: This is the pass taken at the start of each half to start the game; it is also taken by one team after they have been scored against.

Penalty Corner/Short Corner: When the defending team fouls in the shooting circle, or if the defenders send the ball over the end line intentionally, a penalty corner will be awarded to the attacking team. The ball is placed on the backline 10 m (11 yd) from the nearest goalpost and ejected by an offensive player to his/her team waiting on the outside of the shooting circle to take a shot on goal.

Long Corner: A free hit for the offense on the sideline five yards from the backline. This is awarded to the offense when the defense hits the ball back over the backline.

Penalty Strok: In field hockey, a penalty stroke, sometimes known as a penalty flick, is the most severe penalty given. It is predominantly awarded when a foul has prevented a certain goal from being scored or for a deliberate infringement by a defender in the penalty circle.

16-Yard Hit/15-Meter Hit: This is a hit taken by the team in defense 16 yd from the goal line after the attacking team hits the ball over the baseline.

Push-in: Free hit awarded to a team after the opponent hits the ball out of bounds over the sideline.

Drag Flick: It is used as an attacking technique, mainly within penalty corners involving two main components known as the scoop and flick. The technique involves a running-up, and then forceful "slinging" technique of the ball around your body, towards the goals.

Flick /flɪk/: To raise the ball from the ground into the air with a quick movement of the stick. The ball must not rise more than 18 in above the playing surface.

Scoop /skuːp/: It means that a player raises the ball off the ground by getting the head of the stick under the ball and using a lifting motion.

Push /pʊʃ/: It means that a player moves the field hockey ball along the ground using a pushing motion.

Sweep Hit: The method by which a player uses the motion of swinging the stick low to the turf in a sweeping motion.

Crosshit: The method by which a player uses his arm and waist strength to swing the bat from behind to forward to hit the ball. It is characterized by high power, fast ball speed and long running distance.

Indian Dribble: A type of dribble that became popular after the addition of synthetic turf. The dribble includes moving the ball left and right by turning the stick over the ball.

Obstruction /əbˈstrʌkʃn/: A foul called by the referee if a player uses either the stick or the body to block or keep another player from hitting the ball.

Stick Interference: A foul called for using the stick to hit an opponent's stick, whether intentionally or unintentionally.

Tackle /ˈtækl/: An action taken by one player to stop another player from keeping possession of the ball.

Dangerous Play: A foul called for anything that could likely result in injury, such as pushing, tripping, hacking, or raising the ball toward an opponent who is less than five yards away.

Shooting Circle: An area in the shape of a capital "D" and made up of two quarter-circles. It measures 16 yards out from each goal post and is joined by a short straight line. An attacking player must be within this area to score. It is also known as the "D".

Review Questions

1. What is the international governing body of hockey?
2. What are hockey balls usually made of?

Chapter 4

Handball

Goals

1. Understand the development history of handball
2. Master the major governing body and major events of handball matches
3. Be familiar with handball game rules and professional terminology

Project Overview

Section 1 Introduction

Figure **4.1** *A handball game in progress at SAP Arena in Mannheim, Germany. By D. roller. saparena*

Handball (*also known as* **team handball**, **European handball**, or **Olympic handball**) is a team sport in which two teams of 7 players each (6 outcourt players and 1 goalkeeper) pass a ball using their hands with the aim of throwing it into the goal of the other team. A standard match consists of two periods of 30 minutes, and the team that scores more goals wins.

Modern handball is played on a court of 40 by 20 m (131 by 66 ft), with a goal in the middle of each endline. The goals are surrounded by a 6 m (20 ft) zone where only the defending goalkeeper is allowed; goals must be scored by throwing the ball from outside the zone or while "diving" into it. The sport is usually played indoors, while outdoor variants exist in the forms of field handball, Czech handball (which was more common in the past), and beach handball. The game is fast and high-scoring: professional teams now typically score between 20 and 35 goals each, though lower scores were not uncommon until a few decades ago. Players may score hat tricks. Body contact is permitted for the defenders trying to stop the attackers from approaching the goal. No protective equipment is mandated, but players may wear soft protective bands, pads, and mouth guards.

The game was codified in Denmark at the end of the 19th century. The modern set of rules was published on 29 October 1917 in Berlin, which is seen as the date of birth of the sport, and has several revisions since. The first official handball match was played in the same year in Germany. The first international games were played under these rules for men in 1925 and for women in 1930. Men's handball was first played as outdoors at the 1936 Summer Olympics in Berlin, the next time as indoors at the 1972 Summer Olympics in Munich, and has been an Olympic sport since. Women's team handball was added at the 1976 Summer Olympics.

The sport is most popular in Europe, and European countries have won all medals but one in the men's world championships since 1938. In the women's world championships, only two non-European countries have won the title: South Korea and Brazil. The game also enjoys popularity in East Asia, North Africa, and parts of South America.

Section 2 Major Governing Body

The **International Handball Federation** (**IHF**) is the administrative and controlling body for handball and beach handball. IHF is responsible for the organization of handball's major international tournaments, notably the IHF World Men's Handball Championship, which commenced in 1938, and the IHF World Women's Handball Championship, which commenced in 1957.

IHF was founded in 1946 to oversee international competitions. Headquartered in Basel, its membership now comprises 210 national federations. Each member country must also be a member of one of the six regional confederations: Africa, Asia, Europe, North America and the Caribbean, Oceania, and South and Central America.

Section 3 Major Events

3.1 Handball at the Summer Olympics

Figure **4.2** *Handball at the Summer Olympics. By Wikimedia*

Handball at the Summer Olympics refers to two different sports. Field handball was introduced for men at the 1936 Summer Olympics in Berlin, but dropped after that. At the 1952 Olympics, field handball was a demonstration sport. (Indoor) handball was introduced for men at the 1972 Summer Olympics, also on German territory. Women's handball competition was introduced at the 1976 Summer Olympics in Montreal.

3.2 Handball World Championships

The **IHF Men's Handball World Championship** has been organized indoors by the International Handball Federation since 1938.

The first indoor championship took place in Germany in 1938, involving four teams from Europe made up of 7 players who competed in a round-robin stage to find a winner. It wouldn't be until sixteen years later when the second World Championship was held in the country of Sweden. Throughout their history, the World Championships have been dominated by European teams, with no medals being won by non-European countries until 2015, by Qatar. Over the years, the organization of the World Championships has changed. Initially, there were group games in both the preliminary and main rounds, but since the 1995 edition, a knockout system has been applied after the preliminary round.

The **IHF Women's Handball World Championship** has been organized by the International Handball Federation since 1957. European teams have won every time except the 1995 edition where South Korea won as the first team outside Europe and 2013 where Brazil won as the first American team. The biggest winners are Russia and Norway with four titles each.

Nine teams participated in the first championship, which number has grown in steps to 32 (from 2021). In 1977 a B-tournament was introduced and later in 1986 a C-tournament which served as qualification for the real championship or A-tournament. The B-and-C-tournament qualifications were replaced by the present qualification system based on continental confederations in 1993.

Between 1978 and 1990 it was held every fourth alternating with the Olympic tournament (introduced women's handball in 1976). Since 1993 it has been held every other year. The first five tournaments were held in the summer or early fall whereas the rest were held in November or December.

3.3 European Handball Championship

The **European Men's Handball Championship** is the official competition for senior men's national handball teams of Europe and has taken place every two years since 1994, in the even-numbered year between the World Championships. In addition to crowning the European champions, the tournament also serves as a qualifying tournament for the Olympic Games and World Championship. The most successful team is Sweden which has won five titles. Spain, however, has won the most medals.

The **European Women's Handball Championship** is the official competition for senior women's national handball teams of Europe, and takes place every two years. In addition to crowning the European champions, the tournament also serves as a qualifying tournament for the Olympic Games and World Championship. As of December 2022, the only teams that have ever won the championship are Norway (nine times), Denmark (three times), Hungary, Montenegro and France (each once).

In 1946, the International Handball Federation was founded by eight European nations, and though non-European nations competed at the World Championships, the medals had always been taken by European nations. European Handball Federation was founded in 1991. In 1995, the World Championship was changed from a quadrennial to a biannual event, and the European Handball Federation now began its own championship — which also acted as a regional qualifier for the World Championship.

3.4　North American and the Caribbean Handball Championship

The **North American and the Caribbean Men's Handball Championship** is the official competition for Men's national handball teams of North America and the Caribbean. In addition to crowning the North American and the Caribbean champions, the tournament also served as a qualifying tournament for the Pan American Handball Championship. Starting from the 2020 edition the tournament is a qualifying event for the IHF World Men's Handball Championship.

The **North American and the Caribbean Women's Handball Championship** is the official competition for Women's national handball teams in North America and Caribbean. In addition to crowning the North American and the Caribbean champions, the tournament also served as a qualifying tournament for the Pan American Handball Championship. Starting from the 2019 edition the tournament is a qualifying event for the IHF World Women's Handball Championship.

Section 4　Rules

4.1　Summary

2 teams of 7 players (6 court players plus 1 goalkeeper) take the court and attempt to score points by putting the game ball into the opposing team's goal. In handling the ball, players are subject to the following restrictions:

- After receiving the ball, players can pass, keep possession, or shoot the ball.
- Players are not allowed to touch the ball with their feet, and the goalkeeper is the only one allowed to use their feet but only within the goal area.
- If possessing the ball, players must dribble (not similar to a basketball dribble), or can take up to three steps for up to three seconds at a time without dribbling.
- No attacking or defending players other than the defending goalkeeper are allowed to touch the floor of the goal area (within 6 m of the goal). A shot or pass in the goal area is valid if completed before touching the floor. Goalkeepers are allowed outside the goal area, but are not allowed to cross the goal area boundary with the ball in their hands.
- The ball may not be passed back to the goalkeeper when he is positioned in the goal area.

Notable scoring opportunities can occur when attacking players jump into the goal area. For example, an attacking player may catch a pass while launching inside the goal area, and then shoot or pass before touching the floor. The chance of scoring will double when a diving attacking player passes to another diving teammate.

4.2 Duration

A standard match has two 30-minute halves with a 10-minute or 15-minute (mainly in Championships/Olympics) halftime intermission. At halftime, teams switch sides of the court as well as benches. For youths, the length of the halves is reduced—25 minutes at ages 12 to 15, and 20 minutes at ages 8 to 11; though national federations of some countries may differ in their implementation from the official guidelines.

If a decision must be reached in a particular match (e.g., in a tournament) and it ends in a draw after regular time, there are at maximum two overtimes, each consisting of two straight 5-minute periods with a 1-minute break in between. If these do not decide the game either, the winning team is determined in a penalty shootout (best-of-five rounds; if still tied, extra rounds are added until one team wins).

The referees may call timeout according to their sole discretion; typical reasons are injuries, suspensions, or court cleaning, such as a change of the goalkeeper.

Since 2012, teams can call 3 team timeouts per game (up to 2 per half), which last 1 minute each. This right may only be invoked by the team in possession of the ball. Team representatives must show a green card marked with a black T on the timekeeper's desk. The timekeeper then immediately interrupts the game by sounding an acoustic signal to stop the clock. Before 2012, teams were allowed only one timeout per half. For the purpose of calling timeouts, overtime and shootouts are extensions of the second half.

4.3 Referees

A handball match is adjudicated by two referees with equal rights. Some national bodies allow games with only a single referee in special cases like illness on short notice. Should the referees disagree on any occasion, a decision is made on mutual agreement during a short timeout; or, in case of punishments, the more severe of the two comes into effect. The referees are obliged to make their decisions "on the basis of their observations of facts". Their judgments are final and can be appealed against only if not in compliance with the rules.

The referees position themselves in such a way that the team players are confined between them. They stand diagonally aligned so that each can observe one side line. Depending on their positions, one is called field referee and the other goal referee. These positions automatically switch on ball turnover. They physically exchange their positions approximately every 10 minutes (long exchange), and change sides every 5 minutes (short exchange).

The IHF defines 18 hand signals for quick visual communication with players and officials.

Figure 4.3   The referees (in blue shirts) keep both teams between them.   By Wikipedia

The signal for warning is accompanied by a yellow card. A disqualification for the game is indicated by a red card, followed by a blue card if the disqualification will be accompanied by a report. The referees also use whistle blows to indicate infractions or to restart the play.

The referees are supported by a scorekeeper and a timekeeper who attend to formal things such as keeping track of goals and suspensions, or starting and stopping the clock, respectively. They also keep an eye on the benches and notify the referees of substitution errors. Their desk is located between the two substitution areas.

4.4   Team players, goalkeeper, and team officials

Each team consists of 7 players on the court and 7 substitute players on the bench. One player on the court must be the designated goalkeeper, differing in his clothing from the rest of the field players. Substitution of players can be done in any number and at any time during gameplay. An exchange takes place over the substitution line. Prior notification of the referees is not necessary.

Some national bodies, such as the Deutsche Handball Bund (DHB, "German Handball Federation"), allow substitution in junior teams only when in ball possession or during timeouts. This restriction is intended to prevent the early specialization of players to offense or defense.

4.4.1   Court players

Court players are allowed to touch the ball with any part of their bodies above and including the knee. As in several other team sports, a distinction is made between catching and dribbling. A player who is in possession of the ball may stand stationary for only 3 seconds, and may take only 3 steps. They must then either shoot, pass, or dribble the ball. Taking more than three steps at any time is considered traveling, and results in a turnover. A player may dribble as many times as they want (though, since passing is faster, it is the preferred method of attack), as long as during each dribble the hand contacts only the top of the ball. Therefore, carrying is completely prohibited, and results in a turnover. After the dribble is picked up, the player has the right to another 3 seconds or 3 steps. The ball must then be passed or shot, as further holding or dribbling will result in a double dribble turnover and a free throw for the other team. Other offensive infractions that result in a turnover include charging and setting an illegal screen.

4.4.2 Goalkeeper

Figure 4.4 A woman goalkeeper during a seven-meter throw.
By Armin Kuebelbeck

Only the goalkeepers are allowed to move freely within the goal perimeter, although they may not cross the goal perimeter line while carrying or dribbling the ball. Within the zone, they are allowed to touch the ball with all parts of their bodies, including their feet, with a defensive aim (for other actions, they are subject to the same restrictions as the court players). The goalkeepers may participate in the normal play of their teammates, if a team elects to use this scheme in order to outnumber the defending players. A regular court player may also substitute for the goalkeeper. Prior to 2015, this court player became the designated goalkeeper on the court and had to wear a vest or bib of the same color as the goalkeeper's shirt to be identified as such. A rule change meant to make the game more offensive now allows any player to substitute for the goalkeeper without becoming a designated goalkeeper. The new rule resembles the one used in ice hockey. This rule was first used in the IHF Women's Handball World Championship in December 2015. It has since been used by the European Men's Handball Championship in January 2016 and by both genders in the Olympic tournament in 2016. This rule change has led to a drastic increase in empty net goals.

If either goalkeeper deflects the ball over the outer goal line, their team stays in possession of the ball, in contrast to other sports like football. The goalkeeper resumes the play with a throw from within the zone ("goalkeeper throw"). In a penalty shot, throwing the ball against the head of a goalkeeper who is not moving will lead to a direct disqualification ("red card"). Hitting a non-moving goalkeeper's head out of regular play will lead to a two-minute suspension as long as the player throws without obstruction.

Outside the D-zone, the goalkeeper is treated as an ordinary court player, and has to follow court players' rules; holding or tackling an opponent player outside the area risks a direct disqualification. The goalkeeper may not return to the area with the ball. Passing to one's own goalkeeper results in a turnover.

4.4.3 Team officials

Each team is allowed to have a maximum of 4 team officials seated on the benches. An official is anybody who is neither a player nor a substitute. One official must be the designated representative who is usually the team manager. Since 2012, representatives can call up to 3 team timeouts (up to twice per half), and may address the scorekeeper, timekeeper, and referees (before that, it was once per half); overtime and shootouts are considered extensions of the second half. Other officials typically include physicians or managers. Neither official is allowed to enter the playing court without the permission of the referees.

4.5 Ball

The ball is spherical and must be made either of leather or a synthetic material. It is not allowed to have a shiny or slippery surface. As the ball is intended to be operated by a single hand, its official sizes vary depending on the age and gender of the participating teams.

Figure 4.5 A size III handball.
By Armin Kuebelbeck

Table 4.1 Official Sizes of Handball

Size	Class	Circumference/cm	Weight/g
I	Junior over 8	50–52	290–330
II	Women over 14, men over 12	54–56	325–375
III	Men over 16	58–60	425–475

4.6 Awarded throw

The referees may award a special throw to a team. This usually happens after certain events such as scored goals, off-court balls, turnovers, and timeouts. All of these special throws require the thrower to obtain a certain position and pose restrictions on the positions of all other players. Sometimes the execution must wait for a whistle blow by the referee.

4.6.1 Throw-off

A throw-off takes place from the center of the court. The thrower must touch the middle line with one foot, and all the other offensive players must stay in their half until the referee restarts the game. The defending players must keep a distance of at least three meters from the thrower until the ball leaves his hand. A throw-off occurs at the beginning of each period and after the opposing team scores a goal. It must be cleared by the referees.

Modern handball introduced the "fast throw-off" concept, i.e. the play will be immediately restarted by the referees as soon as the executing team fulfills its requirements. Many teams leverage this rule to score easy goals before the opposition has time to form a stable defense line.

4.6.2 Throw-in

The team which did not touch the ball last is awarded a throw-in when the ball fully crosses the side line or touches the ceiling. If the ball crosses the outer goal line, a throw-in is awarded only if the defending field players touched the ball last. Execution requires the thrower to place one foot on the nearest outer line to the cause. All defending players must keep three meters (9.8 ft). However, they are allowed to stand immediately outside their own goal area even when the distance is less than three meters.

4.6.3 Goalkeeper throw

If the ball crosses the outer goal line without interference from the defending team or is deflected by the defending team's goalkeeper, or when the attacking team violates the D-zone as described above, a goalkeeper throw is awarded to the defending team. This is the most common turnover. The goalkeeper resumes the play with a throw from anywhere within the goal area.

4.6.4 Free throw

A free throw restarts the play after an interruption by the referees. It takes place from the spot where the interruption was caused if this spot is outside of the free-throw line of the opposing team. In the latter case, the throw is deferred to the nearest spot on the free-throw line. Free throws are the equivalent to free kicks in association football; however, conceding them is typically not seen as poor sportsmanship for the defending side, and in itself, they carry no major disadvantages (In particular, being awarded a free throw while being on warning for passive play will not reset the warning, whereas a shot on goal will.). The thrower may take a direct attempt for a goal which, however, is rarely feasible if the defending team has organized a defense. However, if a free throw is awarded and the half or game ends, a direct throw at the goal is typically attempted, which occasionally goes in.

4.6.5 Seven-meter throw

Figure **4.6** *A seven-meter throw. By Frank*

A seven-meter throw is awarded when a clear chance of scoring is illegally prevented anywhere on the court by an opposing team player, official, or spectator. It is also awarded when the referees have interrupted a legitimate scoring chance for any reason. The thrower steps with one foot behind the seven-meter (23 ft) line with only the defending goalkeeper between him and the goal. The goalkeeper must keep three meters (9.8 ft), which is marked by a short tick on the floor. All other players must remain behind the free-throw line until execution and the defending field players must keep three meters. The thrower must await the whistle blow of the referee. A 7 m throw is the equivalent of a penalty kick in association football; however, it is far more common and typically occurs several times in a single game.

4.7 Penalties

Penalties are given to players, in a progressive format, for fouls that require more punishment than just a free throw. Actions directed mainly at the opponent and not the ball (such

*Figure 4.7 A yellow card shown in a handball match.
By Armin Kuebelbeck*

as reaching around, holding, pushing, tripping, and jumping into the opponent) as well as contact from the side, from behind a player or impeding the opponent's counterattack are all considered illegal and are subject to penalty. Any infraction that prevents a clear scoring opportunity will result in a seven-meter penalty shot.

Typically, the referee will give a warning yellow card for an illegal action; but, if the contact is particularly dangerous, like striking the opponent in the head, neck, or throat, the referee can forego the warning for an immediate two-minute suspension. Players are warned once before being given a yellow card; they risk being red-carded if they draw three yellows.

A red card results in an ejection from the game and a two-minute penalty for the team. A player may receive a red card directly for particularly rough penalties. For instance, any contact from behind during a fast break is now treated with a red card as does any deliberate intent to injure opponents. A red-carded player must leave the playing area completely. A player who is disqualified may be substituted with another player after the 2-minute penalty is served. A coach or official can also be penalized progressively. Any coach or official who receives a 2-minute suspension will have to pull out one of their players for two minutes; however, the player is not the one punished and can be substituted again, as the penalty consists of the team playing with one fewer player than the opposing team.

After referees award the ball to the opponents for whatever reason, the player currently in possession of the ball must lay it down quickly or risk a two-minute suspension. Also, gesticulating or verbally questioning the referee's order, as well as arguing with the officials' decisions, will normally risk a yellow card. If the suspended player protests further, does not walk straight off the field to the bench, or if the referee deems the tempo deliberately slow, that player risks a double yellow card. Illegal substitution (outside of the dedicated area, or if the replacement player enters too early) is prohibited; if they do, they risk a yellow card.

4.8 Playing court

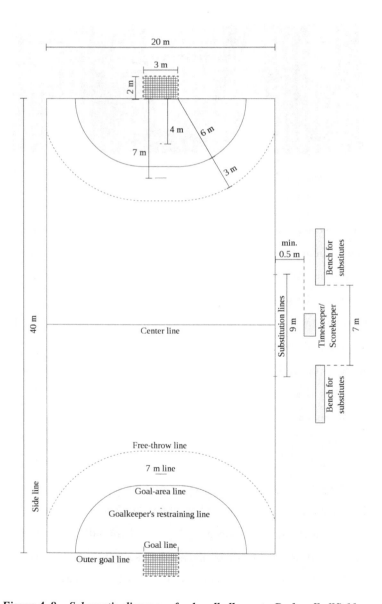

Figure 4.8 Schematic diagram of a handball court. By handballfield.svg

Handball is played on a court 40 by 20 m (131 ft 2.80 in × 65 ft 7.40 in), with a goal in the center of each end. The goals are surrounded by a near-semicircular area, called the zone or the crease, defined by a line 6 m from the goal. A dashed near-semicircular line nine meters from the goal marks the free-throw line. A line of each line on the court is part of the area it encompasses. A part of this implies that the middle line belongs to both halves at the same time.

4.8.1 Goals

The goals are 2 m high and 3 m wide. They must be securely bolted either to the floor or the wall behind.

The goal posts and the crossbar must be made out of the same material (e.g., wood or aluminum) and feature a quadratic cross section with sides of 8 cm (3 in). The three sides of the beams visible from the playing field must be painted alternatingly in two contrasting colors which both have to contrast against the background. The colors on both goals must be the same.

Each goal must feature a net. This must be fastened in such a way that a ball thrown into the goal does not leave or pass the goal under normal circumstances.

4.8.2 Crease

The goals are surrounded by the crease, also called the zone. This area is delineated by 2-quarter circles with a radius of 6 m around the far corners of each goal post and a connecting line parallel to the goal line. Only the defending goalkeeper is allowed inside this zone. However, court players may catch and touch the ball in the air within it as long as the player starts their jump outside the zone and releases the ball before they land (landing inside the perimeter is allowed in this case as long as the ball has been released).

If a player without the ball contacts the ground inside the goal perimeter, or the line surrounding the perimeter, they must take the most direct path out of it. Should a player cross the zone to gain an advantage (e.g., better position) their team cedes the ball. Similarly, violation of the zone by a defending player is penalized only if they do so in order to gain an advantage in defending.

4.8.3 Substitution area

Outside of one long edge of the court to both sides of the middle line are the substitution areas for each team. Team officials, substitutes, and suspended players must wait within this area. A team's area is the same side as the goal the team is defending; during halftime, substitution areas are swapped. Any player entering or leaving the play must cross the substitution line which is part of the sideline and extends 4.5 m (15 ft) from the middle line to the team's side.

Section 5 Basic Tactics

5.1 Formations

Players are typically referred to by the positions they are playing. The positions are always denoted from the view of the respective goalkeeper, so that a defender on the right opposes an attacker on the left.

5.1.1 Offense

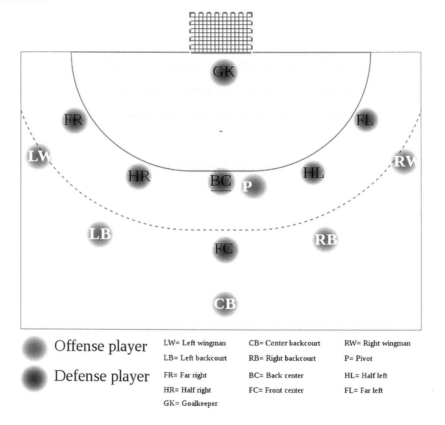

Figure 4.9 Positions of attacking (red) and defending players (blue), in a 5-1 defense formation. By Kuebi

① Left and right wingman. These typically are fast players who excel at ball control and wide jumps from the outside of the goal perimeter in order to get into a better shooting angle at the goal. Teams usually try to occupy the left position with a right-handed player and vice versa.

② Left and right backcourt. Goal attempts by these players are typically made by jumping high and shooting over the defenders. Thus, it is usually advantageous to have tall players with a powerful shot for these positions.

③ Center backcourt. A player with experience is preferred in this position who acts as a playmaker and the handball equivalent of a basketball point guard.

④ Pivot. This player tends to intermingle with the defense, setting picks and attempting to disrupt the defense's formation. This position requires the least jumping skills, but ball control and physical strength are advantages.

Sometimes, the offense uses formations with two pivot players.

5.1.2 Defense

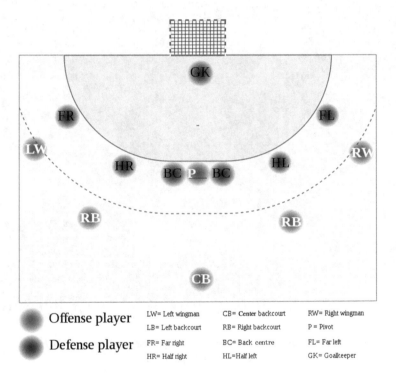

Figure 4.10 Positions of attacking (red) and defending players (blue), in a 6-0 defense formation. By Kuebi

There are many variations in defensive formations. Usually, they are described as $n:m$ formations, where n is the number of players defending at the goal line and m the number of players defending more offensive. Exceptions are the 3 : 2 : 1 defense and $n+m$ formation (e.g. 5+1), where m players defend in man coverage (instead of the usual zone coverage).

① Far left and far right. The opponents of the wingmen.

② Half left and half right. The opponents of the left and right backcourts.

③ Back center. The opponent of the pivot.

④ Front center. The opponent of the center backcourt, who may also be set against another specific backcourt player.

5.2 Offensive play

Attacks are played with all court players on the side of the defenders. Depending on the speed of the attack, one distinguishes between three attack *waves* with a decreasing chance of success:

5.2.1 First-wave attack

Figure **4.11** *Women's handball — a jump shot completes a fast break.*
By Armin Kuebelbeck

First-wave attacks are characterized by the absence of defending players around their goal perimeter. The chance of success is very high, as the throwing player is unhindered in his scoring attempt. Such attacks typically occur after an intercepted pass or a steal, and if the defending team can switch fast to offense. The far left or far right will usually try to run the attack, as they are not as tightly bound in the defense. On a turnover, they immediately sprint forward and receive the ball halfway to the other goal. Thus, these positions are commonly held by quick players.

5.2.2 Second-wave attack

If the first wave is not successful and some defending players have gained their positions around the zone, the second wave comes into play: the remaining offensive players advance with quick passes to locally outnumber the retreating defenders. If one player manages to step up to the perimeter or catches the ball at this spot, he becomes unstoppable by legal defensive means. From this position, the chance of success is naturally very high. Second-wave attacks became much more important with the "fast throw-off" rule.

5.2.3 Third-wave attack

Figure 4.12 Men's handball — a jump shot. By Kuebi

The time during which the second wave may be successful is very short, as then the defenders close the gaps around the zone. In the third wave, the attackers use standardized attack patterns usually involving crossing and passing between the backcourt players who either try to pass the ball through a gap to their pivot, take a jumping shot from the backcourt at the goal, or lure the defense away from a wingman.

The third wave evolves into the normal offensive play when all defenders not only reach the zone, but gain their accustomed positions. Some teams then substitute specialized offense players. However, this implies that these players must play in the defense should the opposing team be able to switch quickly to offense. Teams with a fast attacking rhythmn are good at launching fast breaks when switching from defense to attack.

If the attacking team does not make sufficient progress (eventually releasing a shot on goal), the referees can call passive play (since 1995, the referee gives an advance warning by holding one hand high, signaling that the attacking team should release a shot soon), turning control over to the other team. A shot on goal or an infringement leading to a yellow card or two-minute penalty will mark the start of a new attack, causing the hand to be taken down; but a shot blocked by the defense or a normal free throw will not. This rule prevents an attacking team from stalling the game indefinitely。

5.3 Defensive play

The usual formations of the defense include the 6-0, when all the defense players line up between the 6 m (20 ft) and 9 m (30 ft) lines to form a wall; the 5-1, when one of the players cruises outside the 9 m (30 ft) perimeter, usually targeting the center forwards while the other 5 line up on the 6 m (20 ft) line; and the less common 4-2 when there are two such defenders out front. Very fast teams will also try a 3-3 formation which is close to a switching man-to-man style. The formations vary greatly from country to country and reflect each country's style of play. 6-0 is sometimes known as "flat defense", and all other formations are usually called "offensive defense"!

Handball Terms

Court Player: The players playing on the court except goalkeepers are known as court players.

Goalie /ˈɡəʊli/: A player who defends the goal while the opposition attempts to score goals. A goalie or goalkeeper is permitted to play inside the goal area.

Throw-off: A throw-off takes place from the center of the court. The thrower must touch the middle line with one foot, and all the other offensive players must stay in their half until the referee restarts the game. The defending players must keep a distance of at least 3 m from the thrower until the ball leaves his hand. A throw-off occurs at the beginning of each period and after the opposing team scores a goal. It must be cleared by the referees.

Goal Throw: A goal throw is awarded to the defending team when the ball goes over the end line and is last touched by the offensive team or by the defending goalkeeper.

Throw-in: A throw-in is awarded to the defending team when the ball goes out of bounds on the sideline; a throw-in is taken from the spot where the ball crosses the sideline. The thrower must place one foot on the sideline to execute the one-handed throw. All opposing players must stay 3 m from the ball.

Corner Throw: This is thrown by an attacking player from the corner of the court. It is done by throwing the ball by using either hand. A corner throw is given to an attacking player while the ball is played over the goal line by a defending player or either side of the goal.

Free Throw: It is awarded to the opposition team while the other team does a foul during the game. The ball is thrown from a line 9 m away from the goal.

Seven-meter Throw: The penalty shot is thrown from a mark at a distance of 7 m from the goal. In a penalty throw a player is allotted to score a goal through a direct throw into the goal center.

Referees Throw: This throw is done by referees to resume the game after an interruption of play caused by some reasons, during a handball match.

Dive Shot: It is a way of putting the shot, in order to score a goal, by jumping above the floor towards the goal. It is done without touching the D-line.

Warning (yellow card): A warning occurs when the referee, as in soccer, warns a player. The next time, he or she will have to sit out two minutes and his or her team must play short-handed. A second such penalty on the same player results in another two-minute penalty whereas a third warrants a red card and the player is disqualified from the game. The disqualified player's team must play the next two minutes short-handed before being able to return to even strength.

Disqualification (red card): A disqualified player must leave the court and bench, but the team can replace the player after the two-minute suspension expires.

Exclusion: An exclusion is given for a severe infraction, similar to a red card in soccer. The excluded player's team continues minus one player for the rest of the game.

Review Questions

1. How many 30-minute halves are there in handball matches in international championships and Olympic Games?
2. What is the international governing body of handball?
3. Which continent did modern handball first originate in?

Chapter 5

American Football

Goals

1. Understand the development history of American football
2. Master the major governing body and major events of American football matches
3. Be familiar with American football game rules and professional terminology

Project Overview

Section 1 Introduction

American football (referred to simply as football in the United States and Canada), also known as **gridiron football**, is a team sport played by two teams of eleven players on a rectangular field with goalposts at each end. The offense, the team with possession of the oval-shaped football, attempts to advance down the field by running with the ball or throwing it, while the defense, the team without possession of the ball, aims to stop the offense's advance and to take control of the ball for themselves. The offense must advance at least 10 yd in 4 downs or plays; if they fail, they turn over the football to the defense,

Figure 5.1 Estadio Emilio Royo in Panama City. By Pedro Arenas

but if they succeed, they are given a new set of 4 downs to continue the drive. A game is won by the team with the higher number of points, which are scored primarily by advancing the ball into the opposing team's end zone for a touchdown or kicking the ball through the opponent's goalposts for a field goal.

American football evolved in the United States, and originated in the sports of soccer and rugby. The first American football match was played on November 6th, 1869, between two college teams, Rutgers and Princeton, using rules based on the rules of soccer at the time. A set of rule changes drawn up from 1880 onward by Walter Camp, the "Father of American Football", "established the snap, the line of scrimmage, 11-player teams, and the concept of downs. Later rule changes legalized the forward pass, created the neutral zone, and specified the size and shape of the football. The sport is closely related to Canadian football, which evolved in parallel with and at the same time as the American game (although their rules were developed independently from those of Camp). Most of the features that distinguish American football from rugby and soccer are also present in Canadian football. The two sports are considered the primary variants of gridiron football.

American football is the most popular sport in the United States in terms of broadcast viewership audience. The most popular forms of the game are professional and college football, with the other major levels being high-school and youth football. As of 2022, nearly 1.04 million high-school athletes play the sport in the U.S., with another 81,000 college athletes in the National Collegiate Athletic Association (NCAA) and the NAIA. The National Football League (NFL) has the highest average attendance of any professional sports league in the world. Its championship game, the Super Bowl, ranks among the most-watched club sporting events globally. In 2022, the league had an annual revenue of around $18.6 billion, making it the most valuable sports league in the world. Other professional and amateur leagues exist worldwide, but the sport does not have the international popularity of other American sports like baseball or basketball; the sport maintains a growing following in the rest of North America, Europe, Brazil, and Japan.

Section 2　Major Governing Body

2.1　International Federation of American Football

The International Federation of American Football (IFAF) is the international governing body for the sport of American Football. The IFAF oversees the organization and promotion of all amateur international competitions across both contact and non-contact versions of the game, including the IFAF World Championship of American Football, which is held every four years. The IFAF became a provisionary member of Global Association of International Sports Federations (GAISF) in 2003 and became a full GAISF member in 2005. The organization's head office is located in the French commune of La Courneuve, in the Île-de-France region.

The IFAF recognizes in their respective areas the following branches and has 75 members as of May 2024: IFAF Africa: 12; IFAF America: 16; IFAF Asia: 13; IFAF Europe: 29 (European Championship of American football); IFAF Oceania: 5.

2.2　USA Football

USA Football is the governing body of American football in the United States. It is the United States' member of the International Federation of American Football (IFAF), and a recognized sports organization of the U.S. Olympic & Paralympic Committee. It selects and organizes the U.S. men's national team and the U.S. women's national team to take part in federation-sanctioned international competitions.

USA Football is an independent non-profit organization headgquartered in Indianapolis, Indiana, whose mission includes designing and delivering premier educational, development, and competitive programs for American football, including tackle and flag football. It partners with leaders in medicine, child advocacy, and athletics to support positive football experience for youth, high school, and other amateur players.

USA Football was endowed by the National Football League (NFL) and the National Football League Players Association (NFLPA) in 2002.

Section 3　Major Events

3.1　IFAF World Championship of Football

The IFAF World Championship of Football (also known as the IFAF World Cup) is an international gridiron competition held every four years and contested by teams representing member nations. The competition is run by the International Federation of American Football (IFAF), the international governing body for the sport. 71 nations have a national American football team.

At the 2011 championship, the championship tournament consisted of 8 teams divided into 2 groups of 4 (there were 6 teams in 1999 and 2007, 4 in 2003, and 7 in 2015). The opening round featured a round-robin tournament within the groups, with each team playing each other once. However, as opposed to a tournament bracket after the games were completed, the teams with the best record from each group met in the gold medal game, with the second-place teams in each group playing for the bronze medal, the 3rd-place teams playing in the 5th-place game, and the 4th-place teams playing in the 7th-place game, thus guaranteeing each team 4 games.

Automatic berths included the host nation and the defending champions. Both finalists from the European Championship of American Football received berths. Two teams from the Pan American Federation of American Football received berths, as did one member each from the Asian Federation of American Football and from the Oceania Federation of American Football.

For the 2019 championship (postponed to 2023, then 2025), the tournament will expand to 12 teams. Teams will be divided into four groups, each consisting of three teams. Teams will play the other two teams in their group once each, for a total of two group-stage games. Teams will then advance to the second round, and from there to the placement and medal games.

Because American football is far more dominant in the United States than anywhere else in the world, the United States did not field a team in the tournament for its first two editions. The United States has fielded a squad for the last three iterations, but with extremely restrictive criteria that make most American football players ineligible for the team. Despite the restrictions, the United States has won all three world championships in which they have competed. Similarly, Canada did not participate until the 2011 competition, when the Canadian team finished second to the United States.

3.2 National Football League (NFL)

The National Football League (NFL) is a professional American football league that consists of 32 teams, divided equally between the American Football Conference (AFC) and the National Football Conference (NFC). In addition, each Conference is divided into four divisions (east, south, west, north), each of which is composed of four teams. The NFL is one of the major professional sports leagues in the United States and Canada and the highest professional level of American football in the world.

Each NFL season begins annually with a three-week preseason in August, followed by the 18-week regular season which runs from early September to early January, with each team playing 17 games and having one bye week. Following the conclusion of the regular season, seven teams from each conference (four division winners and three wild card teams) advance to the playoffs, a single-elimination tournament that culminates in the Super Bowl, which is contested in February and is played between the winners of the AFC and NFC championship games.

The NFL was formed in 1920 as the American Professional Football Association (APFA) before renaming itself the National Football League for the 1922 season. After initially determining champions through end-of-season standings, a playoff system was implemented in 1933 that culminated with the NFL Championship Game until 1966. Following an agreement to merge the NFL with the rival American Football League (AFL), the Super Bowl was first held in 1967 to determine a champion between the best teams from the two leagues and has remained the final game of each NFL season since the merger was completed in 1970.

The NFL is the wealthiest professional sports league in the world by revenue and the sports league with the most valuable teams. The NFL also has the highest average attendance (69,582, 2023) of any professional sports league in the world and is the most popular sports league in the United States. The Super Bowl is also among the biggest club sporting events in the world, with the individual games accounting for many of the most watched television programs in American history and all occupying Nielsen's top 5 tally of the all-time most watched U.S. television broadcasts by 2015. The NFL is headquartered in Midtown Manhattan.

The Green Bay Packers hold the most combined NFL championships with 13, winning 9 titles before the Super Bowl era and 4 Super Bowls afterwards. Since the creation of the Super Bowl, the New England Patriots and Pittsburgh Steelers are tied for the most Super Bowl victories at 6 each.

3.3 NCAA Division I Football Bowl Subdivision

The NCAA Division I Football Bowl Subdivision (FBS), formerly known as Division I-A, is the highest level of college football in the United States. The FBS consists of the largest schools in the National Collegiate Athletic Association (NCAA). As of the 2024 season, there are 10 conferences and 134 schools in FBS.

College football is one of the most popular spectator sports throughout much of the United States. The top schools generate tens of millions of dollars in yearly revenue. Top FBS teams draw tens of thousands of fans to games, and the fifteen largest American stadiums by capacity all host FBS teams or games. Since July 1, 2021, college athletes have been able to receive payments for the use of their name, image, and likeness. Prior to this date, colleges were only allowed to provide players with non-monetary compensation such as athletic scholarships that provide for tuition, housing, and books.

The FBS season begins in late August or early September and ends in January with the College Football Playoff National Championship game. Most FBS teams play 12 regular season games per year, with 8 or 9 of those games coming against conference opponents. All 10 FBS conferences hold a conference championship game to determine the winner of the conference. Between conference games, non-conference games, a conference championship game, and up to two bowl games if ranked among the top four college teams in the country by the College Football Playoff Committee. Only the four playoff teams are eligible to participate in two bowl games in one postseason instead of a single one for the rest, and only the winners of the two playoff semifinal bowl games will play a 15th game when they meet in the College Football Playoff National Championship.

Section 4 Rules

4.1 Team and positions

A football game is played between two teams of 11 players each. Playing with more on the field is punishable by a penalty. Teams may substitute any number of their players between downs; this "platoon" system replaces the original system, which featured limited substitution rules, and has resulted in teams utilizing specialized offensive unit, defensive unit, and special teams unit. The number of players allowed on an active roster varies by league: the NFL has a 53-man roster, while NCAA Division I allows teams to have 63 scholarship players in the FCS (Football Championship Subdivision) and 85 scholarship players in the FBS, respectively.

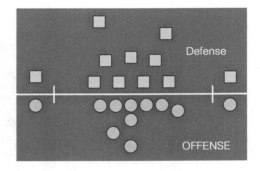

Figure 5.2 A diagram of a typical pre-snap formation. The Offense (red) is lined up in a variation of the I formation, while the defense (blue) is lined up in the 4-3 defense. Both formations are legal. By Killervogel5

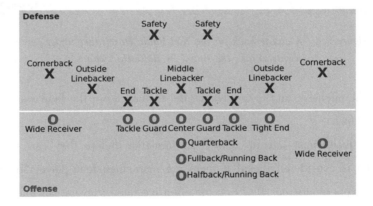

Figure 5.3 A diagram showing an I formation on offense and a 4-3 formation on defense. By Kainaw

Individual players in a football game must be designated with a uniform number between 1 and 99, though some teams may "retire" certain numbers, making them unavailable to players. NFL teams are required to number their players by a league-approved numbering system, and any exceptions must be approved by the commissioner.

Although the sport is played almost exclusively by men, women are eligible to play in high school, college, and professional football. No woman has ever played in the NFL, but women have played in high school and college football games. In 2018, 1,100 of the 225,000 players in Pop Warner Little Scholars youth football were girls, and around 11% of the 5.5 million Americans who report playing tackle football are female according to the Sports and Fitness Industry Association.

4.1.1 Offensive unit

Figure 5.4 A quarterback for the Kiel Baltic Hurricanes under center, ready to take the snap. By BalticHurricanes

The role of the offensive unit is to advance the football down the field with the ultimate goal of scoring a touchdown.

The offensive team must line up in a legal formation before they can snap the ball. An offensive formation is considered illegal if there are more than four players in the backfield or fewer than five players numbered 50-79 on the offensive line. Players can line up temporarily in a position whose eligibility is different from what their number permits as long as they report the change immediately to the referee, who then informs the defensive team of the change. Neither team's players, except the center (C), are allowed to line up in or cross the neutral zone until the ball is snapped. Interior offensive linemen are not allowed to move until the snap of the ball.

The main backfield positions are the quarterback (QB), halfback/tailback (HB/TB), and fullback (FB). The quarterback is the leader of the offense. Either the quarterback or a coach calls the plays. Quarterbacks typically inform the rest of the offense of the play in the huddle before the team lines up. The quarterback lines up behind the center to take the snap and then hands the ball off, throws it, or runs with it.

The primary role of the halfback, also known as the running back or tailback, is to carry the ball on running plays. Halfbacks may also serve as receivers. Fullbacks tend to be larger than halfbacks and function primarily as blockers, but they are sometimes used as runners in short-yardage or goal-line situations. They are seldom used as receivers.

The offensive line (OL) consists of several players whose primary function is to block members of the defensive line from tackling the ball carrier on running plays or sacking the quarterback on passing plays. The leader of the offensive line is the center, who is responsible for snapping the ball to the quarterback, blocking, and for making sure that the other linemen do their jobs during the play. On either side of the center are the guards (G), while tackles (T) line up outside the guards.

The principal receivers are the wide receivers (WR) and the tight ends (TE). Wide receivers line up on or near the line of scrimmage, split outside the line. The main goal of the wide receiver is to catch passes thrown by the quarterback, but they may also function as decoys or as blockers during running plays. Tight ends line up outside the tackles and function both as receivers and as blockers.

4.1.2 Defensive unit

Figure **5.5** *Dallas Cowboys defensive players force Houston Texans running back Arian Foster to fumble the ball. By AJ Guel*

The role of the defense is to prevent the offense from scoring by tackling the ball carrier or by forcing turnovers (interceptions or fumbles).

The defensive line (DL) consists of defensive ends (DE) and defensive tackles (DT). Defensive ends line up on the ends of the line, while defensive tackles line up inside, between the defensive ends. The primary responsibilities of defensive ends and defensive tackles are to stop running plays on the outside and inside, respectively, to pressure the quarterback on passing plays, and to occupy the line so that the linebackers can break through.

Figure 5.6 Cornerback Brent Grimes of the Hamburg Sea Devils intercepts a pass. By Torsten Bolten

Linebackers line up behind the defensive line but in front of the defensive backfield. They are divided into two types: middle linebackers (MLB) and outside linebackers (OLB). Linebackers tend to serve as the defensive leaders and call the defensive plays, given their vantage point of the offensive backfield. Their roles include defending the run, pressuring the quarterback, and tackling backs, wide receivers, and tight ends in the passing game.

The defensive backfield, often called the secondary, consists of cornerbacks (CB) and safeties (S). Safeties are themselves divided into free safeties (FS) and strong safeties (SS). Cornerbacks line up outside the defensive formation, typically opposite a receiver to be able to cover them. Safeties line up between the cornerbacks but farther back in the secondary. Safeties tend to be viewed as "the last line of defense" and are responsible for stopping deep passing plays as well as breakout running plays.

4.1.3 Special teams unit

The special teams unit is responsible for all kicking plays. The special teams unit of the team

*Figure 5.7　Kicker Jeff Reed of the Pittsburgh Steelers executes a kickoff.
By Joey Gannon*

in control of the ball tries to execute field-goal-attempts, punts, and kickoffs, while the opposing team's unit will aim to block or return them.

Three positions are specific to the field goal (FG) and PAT (point-after-touchdown) unit: the placekicker (K or PK), holder (H), and long snapper (LS). The long snapper's job is to snap the football to the holder, who will catch and position it for the placekicker. There is not usually a holder on kickoffs, because the ball is kicked off a tee; however, a holder may be used in certain situations, such as if wind is preventing the ball from remaining upright on the tee. The player on the receiving team who catches the ball is known as the kickoff returner (KR).

The positions specific to punt plays are the punter (P), long snapper, upback, and gunner (G). The long snapper snaps the football directly to the punter, who then drops and kicks it before it hits the ground. Gunners line up split outside the line and race down the field, aiming to tackle the punt returner (PR)—the player who catches the punt. Upbacks line up a short distance behind the line of scrimmage, providing additional protection to the punter.

4.2　Scoring

In football, the winner is the team that has scored more points at the end of the game. There are multiple ways to score in a football game. The touchdown (TD), worth six points, is the most valuable scoring play in American football. A touchdown is scored when a live ball is advanced into, caught, or recovered in the opposing team's end zone. The scoring team then attempts a try,

Figure 5.8 *A player for the Navy Midshipmen (in dark jersey) scores a touchdown while a defender from the Tulsa Golden Hurricane (in white) looks on. The goal line is marked by the small orange pylon. By Christop*

more commonly known as the point(s)-after-touchdown (PAT) or conversion, which is a single scoring opportunity. This is generally attempted from the two- or three-yard line, depending on the level of play. If the PAT is scored by a place kick or drop kick through the goalposts, it is worth one point, typically called the extra point. If the PAT is scored by what would normally be a touchdown, it is worth two points; this is known as a two-point conversion. In general, the extra point is almost always successful, while the two-point conversion is a much riskier play with a higher probability of failure; accordingly, extra-point attempts are far more common than two-point conversion attempts.

A field goal (FG), worth three points, is scored when the ball is place-kicked or drop-kicked through the uprights and over the crossbars of the defense's goalposts. In practice, almost all field goal attempts are done via a place kicks. While drop kicks were common in the early days of the sport, the shape of modern footballs makes it difficult to drop-kick the ball reliably. The last successful scoring play by a drop kick in the NFL was accomplished in 2006; prior to that, the last successful drop kick had been made in 1941. After a PAT attempt or successful field goal, the scoring team must kick the ball off to the other team.

A safety is scored when the ball carrier is tackled in his own end zone. Safeties are worth two points, which are awarded to the defense. In addition, the team that conceded the safety must kick the ball to the scoring team via a free kick.

4.3 Field and equipment

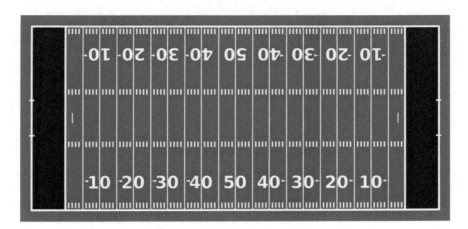

Figure 5.9 Diagram of a modern American football field. By Xyzzy n

Football games are played on a rectangular field that measures 120 yd (109.7 m) long and 53.33 yd (48.76 m) wide. Lines marked along the ends and sides of the field are known as the end lines and sidelines. The marked line in front of the end line is called the goal line, and the distance between the two goal lines is 100 yd (91.44 m). Goal lines are marked 10 yd (9.144 m) inward from each end line.

Weighted pylons are placed at the inside corner of the intersections of the sidelines with the goal lines and end lines. White markings on the field identify the distance from the end zone. Inbound lines, or hash marks, are short parallel lines that mark off 1-yard (0.9144 m) increments. Yard lines, which can run the width of the field, are marked every 5 yd (4.57 m). A 1-yard line is placed at each end of the field; this line is marked at the center of the 2-yard line in professional play and the 3-yard line in college play. Numerals that display the distance from the closest goal line in yards are placed on both sides of the field every 10 yd.

Goalposts are located at the center of the plane of the two end lines. The crossbar of these posts is 10 ft (3.0 m) above the ground, with vertical uprights at the end of the crossbar 18 ft 6 in (5.64 m) apart for professional and collegiate play, and 23 ft 4 in (7.11 m) apart for high school play. The uprights extend vertically 35 ft (11 m) on professional fields, a minimum of 10 yd (9.144 m) on college fields, and a minimum of 10 ft (3.0 m) on high school fields. Goalposts are padded at the base, and orange ribbons are normally placed at the tip of each upright as indicators of wind strength and direction.

The football itself is a prolate spheroid leather ball, similar to the balls used in rugby or Australian rules football. To contain the compressed air within it, a pig's bladder was commonly

Figure 5.10   *A football field as seen from behind one end zone. The tall, yellow goalposts mark where the ball must pass for a successful field goal or extra point. By Clstds*

used before the advent of artificial rubber inside the leather outer shell to sustain crushing forces. At all levels of play, the football is inflated to 12.5 to 13.5 pounds per square inch (86 to 93 kPa), or just under one atmosphere, and weighs 14 to 15 ounces (396.9 to 425.3 g); beyond that, the exact dimensions vary slightly. In professional play, the ball has a long axis of 11 to 11.25 in (28 to 29 cm), a long circumference of 28 to 28.5 in (71 to 72 cm), and a short circumference of 21 to 21.25 in (53.4 to 54 cm). In college and high school play the ball has a long axis of 10.875 to 11.4375 in (27.6 to 29.1 cm), a long circumference of 27.75 to 28.5 in (70 to 72 cm), and a short circumference of 20.75 to 21.25 in (52.7 to 54 cm).

4.4   Duration and time stoppages

Football games last for a total of 60 minutes in professional and college play and are divided into two halves of 30 minutes and four quarters of 15 minutes. High school football games last 48 minutes with two halves of 24 minutes and four quarters of 12 minutes. The two halves are separated by a halftime period, and the first and third quarters are followed by a short break. Before the game starts, the referee and each team's captain meet at midfield for a coin toss. The visiting team can call either "heads" or "tails"; the winner of the toss chooses whether to receive or kick off the ball or which goal they wish to defend. They can defer their choice until the second half. Unless the winning team decides to defer, the losing team chooses the option the winning team did not select—to receive, kick, or select a goal to defend to begin the second half. Most teams choose to receive or defer because choosing to kick the ball to start the game allows the other team to choose which goal to defend. Teams switch goals following the first and third quarters. If a down is in progress when a quarter ends, play continues until the down is completed. If certain fouls are committed during play while time has expired, the quarter may be extended through an untimed down.

Games last longer than their defined length due to play stoppages—the average NFL game lasts slightly over three hours. Time in a football game is measured by the game clock. An operator is responsible for starting, stopping, and operating the game clock based on the direction of the appropriate official. A separate play clock is used to show the amount of time within which the offense must initiate a play. The play clock is set to 25 seconds after certain administrative stoppages in play and to 40 seconds when play is proceeding without such stoppages. If the offense fails to start a play before the play clock reads "00", a delay of game foul is called on the offense.

4.5 Advancing the ball and downs

Figure **5.11** *Carolina Panthers quarterback Jake Delhomme (number* **17**) *in the motion of throwing a forward pass. By Tomasland*

There are two main ways the offense can advance the ball: running and passing. In typical play, the center passes the ball backward and between their legs to the quarterback in a process known as the snap. The quarterback then either hands the ball off to a running back, throws the ball, or runs with it. The play ends when the player with the ball is tackled or goes out-of-bounds or a pass hits the ground without a player having caught it. A forward pass can be legally attempted only if the passer is behind the line of scrimmage; only one forward pass can be attempted per down. As in rugby, players can also pass the ball backward at any point during a play. In the NFL, a down also ends immediately if the runner's helmet comes off.

The offense is given a series of four plays, known as downs. If the offense advances 10 or more yards in the 4 downs, they are awarded a new set of 4 downs. If they fail to advance ten yards, possession of the football is turned over to the defense. In most situations, if the offense reaches their 4th down they will punt the ball to the other team, which forces them to begin their drive from farther down the field; if they are in field goal range, they might attempt to score a field goal instead. A group of officials, the chain crew, keeps track of both the downs and the distance measurements. On television, a yellow line is electronically superimposed on the field to show the first down line to the viewing audience.

4.6 Kicking

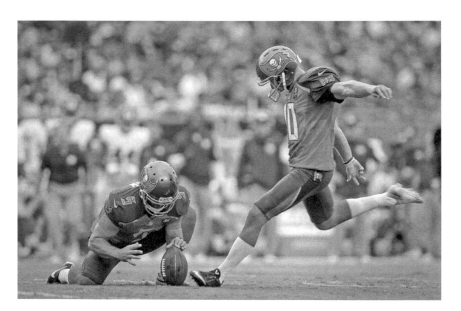

Figure 5.12 *Tampa Bay Buccaneers, placekicker Connor Barth attempts a field goal by kicking the ball from the hands of a holder. This is the standard method to score field goals or extra points. By Ned T. Johns*

There are two categories of kicks in football: scrimmage kicks, which can be executed by the offensive team on any down from behind or on the line of scrimmage, and free kicks. The free kicks are the kickoff, which starts the first and third quarters and overtime and follows a try attempt or a successful field goal; the safety kick follows a safety.

On a kickoff, the ball is placed at the 35-yard line of the kicking team in professional and college play and at the 40-yard line in high school play. The ball may be drop-kicked or place-kicked. If a place kick is chosen, the ball can be placed on the ground or a tee; a holder may be used in either case. On a safety kick, the kicking team kicks the ball from their own 20-yard line. They can punt, drop-kick or place-kick the ball, but a tee may not be used in professional play. Any member of the receiving team may catch or advance the ball. The ball may be recovered by the kicking team once it has gone at least 10 yd and has touched the ground or has been touched by any member of the receiving team.

The three types of scrimmage kicks are place kicks, drop kicks, and punts. Only place kicks and drop kicks can score points. The place kick is the standard method used to score points, because the pointy shape of the football makes it difficult to drop-kick reliably. Once the ball has been kicked from a scrimmage kick, it can be advanced by the kicking team only if it is caught or recovered behind the line of scrimmage. If it is touched or recovered by the kicking team beyond this line, it becomes dead at the spot where it was touched. The kicking team is prohibited from interfering with the receiver's opportunity to catch the ball. The receiving team has the option of signaling for a fair catch, which prohibits the defense from blocking into or tackling the receiver. The play ends as soon as the ball is caught, and the ball may not be advanced.

4.7 Officials and fouls

Officials are responsible for enforcing game rules and monitoring the clock. All officials carry a whistle and wear black-and-white striped shirts and black hats except for the referee, whose hat is white. Each carries a weighted yellow flag that is thrown to the ground to signal that a foul has been called. An official who spots multiple fouls will throw their hat as a secondary signal. Women can serve as officials; Sarah Thomas became the NFL's first female official in 2015. The 7 officials (of a standard 7-man crew; lower levels of play up to the college level use fewer officials) on the field are each tasked with a different set of responsibilities:

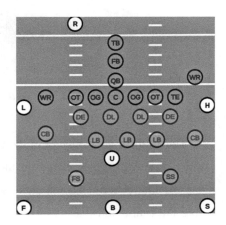

Figure 5. 13 Diagram showing the relative positions of the traditional 7-official system (in white) in relation to the typical offensive (in blue) and defensive (in red) formations. By Zzyzx11

The **referee** is positioned behind and to the side of the offensive backs. The referee is charged with oversight and control of the game and is the authority on the score, the down number, and any rule interpretations in discussions among the other officials. The referee announces all penalties and discusses the infraction with the offending team's captain, monitors illegal hits against the quarterback, makes requests for first-down measurements, and notifies the head coach whenever a player is ejected. The referee positions themselves to the passing arm side of the quarterback. In most games, the referee is responsible for spotting the football prior to a play from scrimmage.

Figure 5.14   Officials meeting at midfield.   By Belinda Hankins Miller

The **umpire** is positioned in the defensive backfield, except in the NFL, where the umpire is positioned lateral to the referee on the opposite side of the formation. The umpire watches play along the line of scrimmage to make sure that no more than 11 offensive players are on the field before the snap, and that no offensive linemen are illegally downfield on pass plays. The umpire monitors contact between offensive and defensive linemen and calls most of the holding penalties. The umpire records the number of timeouts taken and the winner of the coin toss and game score. They also assist the referee in situations involving possession of the ball close to the line of scrimmage, determine whether player equipment is legal, and dry wet balls prior to the snap if a game is played in rain.

The **back judge** is positioned deep in the defensive backfield, behind the umpire. The back judge ensures that the defensive team has no more than 11 players on the field and determines whether catches are legal, whether field goal or extra point attempts are good, and whether a pass interference violation occurs. The back judge is also responsible for the play clock, the time between each play, when a visible play clock is not used.

Figure 5.15   Officials use the chains to measure a first down. Here, the ball is just short of the pole and therefore short of a first down. By BrokenSphere

Figure 5.16   Back judge Lee Dyer picks up a penalty flag during a game on November 16, 2008, between the San Francisco 49ers and St. Louis Rams. By BrokenSphere

The **head linesman/down judge** is positioned at one end of the line of scrimmage. The head linesman/down judge watches for any line-of-scrimmage and illegal use-of-hands violations and assists the line judge with illegal shift or illegal motion calls. The head linesman/down judge also rules on out-of-bounds calls that happen on their side of the field, oversees the chain crew, and marks the forward progress of a runner when a play has been whistled dead.

The **side judge** is positioned 20 yd downfield from the head linesman. The side judge mainly duplicates the functions of the field judge. On field goal and extra point attempts, the side judge is positioned lateral to the umpire.

The **line judge** is positioned at the end of the line of scrimmage, opposite the head linesman. They supervise player substitutions, the line of scrimmage during punts, and game timing. The line judge notifies the referee when time has expired at the end of a quarter and notifies the head coach of the home team when 5 minutes remain for halftime. In the NFL, the line judge also alerts the referee when 2 minutes remain in the half. If the clock malfunctions or becomes inoperable, the line judge becomes the official timekeeper.

The **field judge** is positioned twenty yards downfield from the line judge. The field judge monitors and controls the play clock, counts the number of defensive players on the field, and watches for offensive pass interference and illegal use-of-hands violations by offensive players. The field judge also makes decisions regarding catches, recoveries, the ball spot when a player goes out of bounds, and illegal touching of fumbled balls that have crossed the line of scrimmage. On field goal and extra point attempts, the field judge is stationed under the upright opposite the back judge.

The **center judge** is an 8th official used only in the top level of college football. The center judge stands lateral to the referee, the same way the umpire does in the NFL. The center judge is responsible for spotting the football after each play and has many of the same responsibilities as the referee, except announcing penalties.

Another set of officials, the **chain crew**, is responsible for moving the chains. The chains, consisting of two large sticks with a 10-yard-long chain between them, are used to measure a first down. The chain crew stays on the sidelines during the game, but if requested by the officials they will briefly bring the chains onto the field to measure. A typical chain crew will have at least three people—two members of the chain crew will hold either of the two sticks, while a third will hold the down marker. The down marker, a large stick with a dial on it, is flipped after each play to indicate the current down and is typically moved to the approximate spot of the ball. The chain crew system has been used for over 100 years and is considered an accurate measure of distance, rarely subject to criticism from either side.

Figure 5.17　*Chain crew. By Rickyrab*

Figure 5.18　*First down marker. By DoubleBlue*

Section 5　Basic Tactics

Tactics play a crucial role in American football. Both teams carefully plan various aspects of their gameplay in an effort to win. This includes deciding formations, selecting players for specific positions, and assigning roles and instructions to each player on offense and defense.

Throughout the game, each team constantly adjusts their tactics, responding to the other's strengths and weaknesses. They experiment with different approaches to outmaneuver or overpower their opponent. On offense, a team's objective is to score through touchdowns and field goals, all while remaining vigilant of the opposing team's defensive tactics. On defense, the goal is to prevent the offense from scoring, as well as attempting to intercept the ball and shift momentum in their favor.

Tactics include: play-action pass, delayed hand-off, draw play, screen pass, quarterback short pass to running back tactics. There are two types: line move forward, usually a running play; line move backward, usually a passing play.

Generally speaking, running play is safer than passing play. However, there are also some more conservative passing plays and more adventurous running plays. In order to deceive the opponent, some passing plays will be set up to look like running plays, and vice versa. American football has many strategies, such as sometimes forming a kicking formation, but then suddenly trying to pass or rush. A successful high-stakes ploy is exciting to watch. Of course, if the opponent has figured out the strategy, it will also bring unfortunate results to the team.

American Football Terms

Offensive Unit: The role of the offensive unit is to advance the football down the field with the ultimate goal of scoring a touchdown.

Offensive Line: The human wall of 5 men who block for and protect the quarterback and ball carriers. Every line has a center (who snaps the ball), two guards, and two tackles.

Defensive Unit: The role of the defense is to prevent the offense from scoring by tackling the ball carrier or by forcing turnovers (interceptions or fumbles).

Defensive Line: The defensive line consists of one or two defensive tackles and two defensive ends who play outside the defensive tackles. The defensive line works with the linebackers to try to control the line of scrimmage.

Backfield /ˈbækfiːld/: The area of an American football field behind the line of scrimmage. The backfield or offensive backfield can also refer to members of the offense who begin plays behind the line, typically including any backs on the field, such as the quarterback, running back, and fullback.

Special Teams: The units that handle kickoffs, punts, free kicks, and field goal attempts. They're often made up of second- and third-team players.

Huddle /ˈhʌdl/: When the 11 players on the field come together to discuss strategy between plays.

Down /daʊn/: A period of action that starts when the ball is put into play and ends when the ball is ruled dead (meaning the play is completed). The offense gets four downs to advance the ball 10 yards. If it fails to do so, it must surrender the ball to the opponent, usually by punting on the fourth down.

End Zone: A 10-yard-long area at each end of the field. You score a touchdown when you enter the end zone in control of the football. If you're tackled in your own end zone while in possession of the football, the other team gets a safety.

Touchdown /ˈtʌtʃdaʊn/: A score, worth six points, that occurs when a player in possession of the ball crosses the plane of the opponent's goal line, when a player catches the ball while in the opponent's end zone, or when a defensive player recovers a loose ball in the opponent's end zone.

Extra Point: A kick, worth one point, that's typically attempted after every touchdown (it's also known as the point after touchdown or PAT). The ball is placed on either the 2-yard line (in the NFL) or the 3-yard line (in college and high school) and is generally kicked from inside the 10-yard line after being snapped to the holder. It must sail between the uprights and above the crossbar of the goalpost to be considered good.

Safety /ˈseɪfti/: A score, worth two points, that the defense earns by tackling an offensive player in possession of the ball in his own end zone.

Line of Scrimmage: An imaginary line that extends from where the football is placed at the end of a play to both sides of the field. Neither the offense nor the defense can cross the line until the football is put in play again.

Secondary /ˈsekəndəri/: The four defensive players who defend against the pass and line up behind the linebackers and wide on the corners of the field opposite the receivers.

Snap /snæp/: The action in which the ball is hiked (tossed between the legs) by the center to the quarterback, to the holder on a kick attempt, or to the punter. When the snap occurs, the ball is officially in play and action begins.

Kickoff /ˈkɪkˈɒf/: A free kick (meaning the receiving team can't make an attempt to block it) that puts the ball into play. A kickoff is used at the start of the first and third quarters and after every touchdown and successful field goal.

Field Goal: A kick, worth three points, that can be attempted from anywhere on the field but is usually attempted within 40 yd of the goalpost. Like an extra point, a kick must sail above the crossbar and between the uprights of the goalpost to be ruled good.

Punt /pʌnt, pʊnt/: A kick made when a player drops the ball and kicks it while it falls toward his foot. A punt is usually made on a fourth down when the offense must surrender possession of the ball to the defense because it couldn't advance 10 yd.

Handoff /ˈhændɒf/: The act of giving the ball to another player. Handoff usually occurs between the quarterback and a running back.

Rushing /ˈrʌʃɪŋ/: To advance the ball by running, not passing. A running back is sometimes called a rusher.

Sack /sæk/: When a defensive player tackles the quarterback behind the line of scrimmage for a loss of yardage.

Interception /ˌɪntə(ː)ˈsɛpʃən/: A pass that is caught by a defensive player, ending the offense's possession of the ball.

Fair Catch: When the player returning a punt waves his extended arm from side to side over his head. After signaling for a fair catch, a player can't run with the ball, and those attempting to tackle him can't touch him.

Incompletion: A forward pass that falls to the ground because no receiver could catch it, or a pass that a receiver dropped or caught out of bounds.

Fumble /ˈfʌmbl/: The act of losing possession of the ball while running with it or being tackled. Members of the offense and defense can recover a fumble. If the defense recovers the fumble, the fumble is called a turnover.

Return /rɪˈtɜːn/: The act of progressing the ball down the field after a change of possession, such as a kick or interception.

Review Questions

1. How many players does each team have in an American football game?
2. Name three American football terms.
3. Which American football event is one of the most watched sporting events in the world?

Chapter 6

Polo

Goals

1. Understand the development history of polo
2. Master the major governing body and major events of polo matches
3. Be familiar with polo game rules and professional terminology

Project Overview

Section 1 Introduction

Polo is a horseback ball game, a traditional field sport, and one of the world's oldest known team sports. The idea of the game is to score by using a long-handled wooden mallet to strike a small, hard ball through the goal of the other team. The game often lasts one to two hours and is broken into intervals known as "chukkas" or "chukkers." Each team has four mounted riders.

Polo has been called "the sport of kings", and has become a spectator sport for equestrians and high society, often supported by sponsorship. The concept of the game and its variants date back from the 6th century BC to the 1st century AD, originating from equestrian games played by nomadic Iranian peoples. The sport was at first a training game for Persian cavalry

Figure 6.1 *Tang dynasty Chinese courtiers on horseback playing a game of polo*, **706 AD**. *By Wikimedia*

units, usually the royal guard or other elite troops. A notable example is Saladin, who was known for being a skilled polo player, and this sport contributed to his military training. It is now popular around the world, with well over 100 member countries in the Federation of International Polo, played professionally in 16 countries, and was an Olympic sport from 1900 to 1936.

Arena polo is an indoor/semi-outdoor variant with similar rules and is played with three riders per team. The playing field is smaller, enclosed, and usually of compacted sand or fine aggregate, and often indoors. Arena polo has more maneuvering due to space limitations and uses an air-inflated ball slightly larger than the hard solid ball used in field polo. Standard mallets are used, though slightly larger-head arena mallets are an option.

Section 2 Major Governing Body

The **Federation of International Polo** is the international federation representing the sport of polo, officially recognized by the International Olympic Committee. It was founded in 1982 by representatives of 11 national polo associations, and currently represents the national polo associations of more than 90 countries. FIP's principal aim is to enhance the image and status of the great game of polo internationally.

FIP's mission is to promote the practice of the sport of polo worldwide in order to defend and ensure the spirit of fair play and moral fortitude, with the objective of forming the sporting attitude of gentlemanly behavior during and after the game, on the playing fields and wherever polo players should meet, to form one great world polo family.

Section 3 Major Events

3.1 World Polo Championship

The **World Polo Championship** is a polo competition between countries. The event is organized by the sport's governing body, the Federation of International Polo (FIP), and is contested by the national teams. There is no restriction on the gender of the players. The inaugural tournament was held in 1987, hosted by Argentina, and is now contested every three or four years.

The participating teams must have a handicap of up to 14 goals. It's for this reason that, unlike other sports, the best players can't play the World Polo Championship.

Figure 6.2 World Polo Championship — Argentina 2011. By Emanuel Agustin Lorenzoni Macchi

3.2 FIP Arena Polo European Championship

The **FIP Arena Polo European Championship** is a tournament contested by 4 international teams. The teams are national teams, nominated by their respective national federations which are all FIP members. The handicap of the tournament is 10-12 goals per team (arena handicap). The games will have 4 Chukkers.

3.3 FIP Snow Polo World Cup Invitational

The FIP Snow Polo World Cup Invitational is an invitational snow polo tournament that was started in 2012 and is held annually at the Metropolitan Polo Club in Tianjin, China.

The FIP Snow Polo World Cup Invitational Tournament marks a milestone in FIP's mission to promote the sport worldwide and enhance the image and stature of this great game.

Played on a flat area of compacted snow or a frozen lake, snow polo provides the same speed and physicality as traditional field polo, but is considered much quicker due to the smaller playing field. Snow Polo audiences also get to see the game at much closer quarters thanks to the high sideboards right at the edge of the pitch.

3.4 FIP Super Nations Cup

Gathering four professional teams from the world's leading polo nations, this 24-goal tournament, one of the highest-goal international tournaments in the world, is held at Tianjin Goldin Metropolitan Polo Club, in Tianjin, China.

3.5　The Ambassador's Cup

Within a few years of FIP's foundation, 19 countries had signed up, with 10 more provisional members. The main vehicle for recruiting new member countries was a series of tournaments that became known as Ambassador's Cups. These tournaments originated as a competition for FIP members and collaborators to engage them in the sport of polo beyond organizational issues. At the beginning the proposal was to play polo in different parts of the world, getting to know all the FIP friends and collaborators and inviting new people to start playing, to expand polo across the world.

One of the first Ambassador's Cups was held in Moscow with the idea of reviving the sport, which had been abolished by the Russian Revolution in 1918. The tournament was played as indoor polo in a circus tent since there were no fields. It took a lot of hard work to organize, but since then polo has begun to be played in Russia again and it is still growing.

Section 4　Rules

The rules of polo are written to include the safety of both players and horses. Games are monitored by umpires. A whistle is blown when an infraction occurs, and penalties are awarded. Strategic plays in polo are based on the "line of the ball", an imaginary line that extends through the ball in the line of travel. This line traces the ball's path and extends past the ball along that trajectory. The line of the ball defines rules for players to approach the ball safely. The "line of the ball" changes each time the ball changes direction. The player who hits the ball generally has the right of way, and other players cannot cross the line of the ball in front of that player. As players approach the ball, they ride on either side of the line of the ball giving players on each side access to the ball. A player can cross the line of the ball when it does not create a dangerous situation. Most infractions and penalties are related to players improperly crossing the line of the ball or the right of way. When players have the line of the ball on their right, they have the right of way. A "ride-off" is when a player moves another player off the line of the ball by making shoulder-to-shoulder contact of his own horse with the other players' horses.

The defending player has a variety of opportunities for their team to gain possession of the ball. They can push the opponent off the line or steal the ball from the opponent. Another common defensive play is called "hooking." While a player is taking a swing at the ball, their opponent can block the swing by using their mallet to hook the mallet of the player swinging at the ball. A player may hook only if they are on the side where the swing is being made or directly behind an opponent. A player may not purposely touch another player, another player's tack, or a pony with their mallet. Unsafe hooking is a foul that will result in a penalty shot being awarded to the other team. For example, it is a foul for a player to reach over an opponent's mount in an attempt to hook.

The other basic defensive play is called the bump or ride-off. It's similar to a body check in ice hockey. In a ride-off, a player rides their pony alongside an opponent's mount to move an opponent away from the ball or to take them out of a play. It must be executed properly so that it does not endanger the horses or the players. The angle of contact must be safe and can not knock the horses off balance, or harm the horses in any way. Two players following the line of the ball and riding one another off have the right of way over a single man coming from any direction.

Like in hockey, ice hockey, or basketball, fouls are potentially dangerous plays that infringe on the rules of the game. To the novice spectator, fouls may be difficult to discern. There are degrees of dangerous and unfair play and penalty shots are awarded depending on the severity of the foul and where the foul was committed on the polo field. White lines on the polo field indicate where the mid-field is and where the 60-, 40-, and 30-yard penalties are taken.

The official set of rules and rules interpretations are reviewed and published annually by each country's polo association. Most of the smaller associations follow the rules of the Hurlingham Polo Association (the national governing body of the sport of polo in the United Kingdom) and the United States Polo Association.

4.1 Outdoor polo

Figure 6.3 Indonesia plays against Thailand in SEA Games Polo 2007. By Dirgayuza Setiawan

Outdoor or field polo lasts about 1.5 - 2 hours and consists of 4 to 8 7-minute chukkas, between or during which players change mounts. At the end of each 7-minute chukka, play continues for an additional 30 seconds or until a stoppage in play, whichever comes first. There is a three-minute interval between chukkas and a five-minute halftime. Play is continuous and is only stopped for rule infractions, broken tack (equipment), or injury to a horse or player. The object is to score goals by hitting the ball between the goalposts, no matter how high in the air. If the ball goes wide of the goal, the defending team is allowed a free "knock-in" from the place where the ball crossed the goal line, thus getting the ball back into play.

4.2 Indoor and arena polo

Arena polo has rules like the field version and is less strenuous for the player. It is played in a 300 × 150 ft (91 × 46 m) enclosed arena, much like those used for other equestrian sports; the minimum size is 150 × 75 ft (46 × 23 m). There are many arena clubs in the United States, and most major polo clubs, including the Santa Barbara Polo & Racquet Club, have active arena programmers. The major differences between the outdoor and indoor games are: speed (outdoor being faster), physicality/roughness (indoor/arena is more physical), ball size (indoor is larger), goal size (because the arena is smaller the goal is smaller), and some penalties. In the United States and Canada, collegiate polo is arena polo; in the UK, collegiate polo is both.

Forms of arena polo include beach polo, played in many countries between teams of three riders on a sand surface, and cowboy polo, played almost exclusively in the western United States by teams of five riders on a dirt surface.

Another modern variant is snow polo, which is played on a flat area of compacted snow or a frozen lake. The format of snow polo varies depending on the space available. Each team generally consists of three players and a brightly colored plastic ball is preferred.

4.3 Field

The playing field is 300 × 160 yd (270 × 150 m), the area of approximately 6 soccer fields or 9 American football fields (10 acres), while the field of arena polo is 96 × 46 m. The playing field is equipped with carefully maintained and closely mowed turf, providing a safe and reliable playing surface. Goals are posts which are set 8 yd apart, centered at each end of the field. The surface of a polo field requires careful and constant ground maintenance to keep the surface in good playing condition. During half-time of a match, spectators are invited to go onto the field to participate in a polo tradition called "divot stamping", which was developed not only to help replace the mounds of earth (divots) that are torn up by the horses' hooves, but also to afford spectators the opportunity to walk about and socialize.

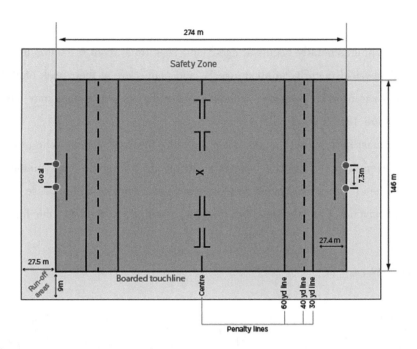

Figure 6.4 Polo field dimensions. By Wikipedia

4.4 Polo ponies

The mounts used are called "polo ponies", although the term pony is purely traditional, and the mount is a full-sized horse. They range from 14.2–16 hands (58–64 in, 147–163 cm) high at the withers, and weigh 900 – 1,100 lb (410 – 500 kg). The polo pony is selected carefully for quick bursts of speed, stamina, agility, and maneuverability. Temperament is critical: the horse must remain responsive under pressure and not become excited or difficult to control. Not to mention that it requires intelligence to know what is happening in the field, follow the game, and have a notion of

Figure 6.5 A polo pony. By Wikimedia

the other players, the other horses, and the changes that may occur. Many are Thoroughbreds or Thoroughbred crosses. They are trained to be handled with one hand on the reins, and to respond to the rider's leg and weight cues for moving forward, turning, and stopping. A well-trained horse will carry its rider smoothly and swiftly to the ball and can account for 60%–75% of the player's skill and net worth to his team.

Polo pony training generally begins at age 3 and lasts from about 6 months to 2 years. Most horses reach full physical maturity at about age 5, and ponies are at their peak of athleticism and training at around age 6 or 7. However, without any accidents, polo ponies may have the ability to play until they are 18-20 years old.

Each player must have more than one horse, to allow for tired mounts to be replaced by fresh ones between or even during chukkas. A player's "string" of polo ponies may number two or three in Low Goal matches (with ponies being rested for at least a chukka before reuse), four or more for Medium Goal matches (at least one per chukka), and even more for the highest levels of competition.

4.5 Players

Figure 6.6 Argentine Polo Open Championship. By Roger Schultz

Each team consists of four mounted players, which can be mixed teams of both men and women.

Each position assigned to a player has certain responsibilities:

① Number One is the most offense-oriented position on the field. The Number One position generally covers the opposing team's Number Four and is usually the rookie of the team;

② Number Two has an important role in offense, either running through and scoring themselves, or passing to Number One and getting in behind them. Defensively, they will cover the opposing team's Number Three, generally the other team's best player. Given the difficulty of this position, it is not uncommon for the best player on the team to play Number Two so long as another strong player is available to play Number Three;

③ Number Three is the tactical leader and must be a long powerful hitter to feed balls to Number Two and Number One as well as maintain a solid defense. The best player on the team is usually the Number Three player, usually wielding the highest handicap;

④ Number Four is the primary defense player. They can move anywhere on the field, but they usually try to prevent scoring. The emphasis on defense by the Number Four allows the Number Three to attempt more offensive plays, since they know that they will be covered if they lose the ball;

⑤ Polo must be played right-handed in order to prevent head-on collisions.

4.6 Equipment

4.6.1 Safety equipment of the players and mounts

The rules for equipment vary in detail between the hosting authorities but are always for the safety of the players and mounts.

Mandatory equipment includes a protective helmet with chinstrap always worn by all players and mounted grooms. They must be to the locally accepted safety standards — PAS015 (UK) and NOCSAE (USA). A face guard is commonly integral to a helmet.

Figure 6.7 Polo helmet with face guard. By Montanabw

Figure 6.8 Polo player wearing kneepads, riding off an opponent. By Trebaxus

Polo boots and knee guards are mandatory in the UK during official play, and boots are recommended for all play everywhere. The UK also recommends goggles, elbow pads, and gum shields. A shirt or jersey is required that distinguishes the player's team and is not black and white stripes like an umpire shirt.

White polo pants or trousers are worn during official play. Polo gloves are commonly worn to protect from working the reins and mallet.

Not permitted is any equipment that may harm horses, such as certain spurs or whips.

4.6.2 Ball

The modern outdoor polo ball is made of high-impact plastic. Historically they have been made of bamboo, leather-covered cork, hard rubber, and years of willow root. Originally the British used a white-painted leather-covered cricket ball.

The regulation outdoor polo ball is 3–3.5 in (7.6–8.9 cm) in diameter and weighs 99–130 g (3.5–4.5 oz).

Plastic balls were introduced in the 1970s. They are less prone to breakage and much cheaper.

Figure 6.9 Polo mallets and ball. By Montanabw

The indoor and arena polo ball is leather-covered and inflated and is about 4.25 in (11 cm) in diameter.

It must be not less than 12.5 in (32 cm) or more than 15 in (38 cm) in circumference. The weight must be not less than 170 g (6.0 oz) or more than 182 g (6.4 oz). In a bounce test from 9 ft (2.7 m) on concrete at 70 °F (21 °C), the rebound should be a minimum of 54 in (140 cm) and a maximum of 64 in (160 cm) at the inflation rate specified by the manufacturer. This provides for a hard and lively ball.

4.6.3 Mallet

Figure 6.10 Polo mallets. By Wikimedia

The polo mallet comprises a cane shaft with a rubber-wrapped grip, a webbed thong, called a sling, for wrapping around the thumb, and a wooden cigar-shaped head. The shaft is made of manau-cane (not bamboo, which is hollow) although a small number of mallets today are made from composite materials. Composite materials are usually not preferred by top players because the shaft of composite mallets can't absorb vibrations as well as traditional cane mallets. The mallet head is generally made from a hardwood called tepa, approximately 9.25 in long. The mallet head weighs from 160–240 g (5.6–8.5 oz), depending on player preference and the type of wood used, and the shaft can vary in weight and flexibility depending on the player's preference. The weight of the mallet head is of important consideration for the more seasoned players. Female players often use lighter mallets than male players. For some polo players, the length of the mallet depends on the size of the horse: the taller the horse, the longer the mallet. However, some players prefer to use a single length of mallet regardless of the height of the horse. Either way, playing with horses of differing heights requires some adjustment by the rider. Variable lengths of the mallet typically range from 127 cm (50 in) to 134 cm (53 in). The term mallet is used exclusively in US English; British English prefers the term polo stick. The ball is struck with the broad sides of the mallet head rather than its round and flat tips.

4.6.4 Saddle

Figure 6.11 Polo saddle. By Wikimedia

Polo saddles are English-style, close contact, similar to jumping saddles; although most polo saddles lack a flap under the billets. Some players will not use a saddle blanket. The saddle has a flat seat and no knee support; the rider adopts a forward-leaning seat and closed knees dissimilar to a classical dressage seat. A breastplate is added, usually attached to the front billet.

A standing martingale must be used, so a breastplate is a necessity for safety. The tie-down is usually supported by a neck strap. Many saddles also have a girth. The stirrup irons are heavier than most, and the stirrup leathers are wider and thicker, for added safety when the player stands in the stirrups. The legs of the pony are wrapped with polo wraps from below the knee to the fetlock to minimize pain. Jumping (open front) or gallop boots are sometimes used along with the polo wraps for added protection. Often, these wraps match the team colors. The pony's mane is most often roached (hogged), and its tail is docked or braided so that it will not snag the rider's mallet.

Polo is ridden with double reins for greater accuracy of signals. The bit is frequently a gag bit or Pelham bit. In both cases, the gag or shank rein will be the bottom rein in the rider's hands, while the snaffle rein will be the top rein. If a gag bit is used, there will be a drop noseband in addition to the cavesson, supporting the tie-down. One of the rein sets may alternately be draw reins.

Section 5 Basic Tactics

5.1 Coordination between rider and horse

The coordination between the rider and the horse is the most crucial element in polo. The rider must be able to direct the horse precisely, especially when changing directions quickly or accelerating to compete for the ball. It takes a long period of training to develop understanding, trust and coordination between the rider and horse.

5.2 Strategic positioning

In polo, positioning is everything. Players need to know how to move to secure the right space for themselves and their team. Good players master the art of quickly reading the game and determining where they should be to assist in either attack or defense.

5.3 Team play and communication

The team with the highest level of communication and coordination has a greater chance of winning. Using hand signals and verbal communication between players can help break through the opponent's defenses and organize effective attacks.

5.4 Defensive positioning

Players must be aware of their defensive roles, whether it's protecting teammates or chasing down opposing players. Knowing when to pressure the player with the ball and when to stay back to guard the goal is crucial.

5.5 Fast attacks

The speed of transitioning from defense to attack is one of the key traits of successful teams. It is preferable for the team to quickly move the ball and rush towards the goal before the opponent can reorganize their defense.

Polo Terms

Draw Reins: These reins go from the rider's hand through the bit to the side of the saddle. They give increased leverage and control over a strong horse and help keep its head down.

Gag Bit: This is a circle bit on the side that pulls the horse's head up when stopping.

Pelham Bit: This is a lever and chain that pulls the horse's head down when stopping.

Martingale: This is the strap that goes from the bridle to the girth. It keeps the horse from throwing its head up into the rider. It is very important to check this strap is not too tight nor too loose. It should just follow the contour under the horse's neck when at rest.

Girth /gɜːrθ/: This is the strap under the horse that holds the saddle on the horse. This strap should be tight, so you can slide only two fingers inside. Always check that the girth is tight before mounting the horse.

Bowl-in: When the umpire starts or resumes play by rolling the ball down the center of a lineup of players.

Out of Bounds: When a ball crosses the sidelines or goes over the sideboards, it is considered out of bounds and the umpire throws in another ball between the two teams at that point. No time-out is allowed for an out-of-bounds ball.

Knock-in: Should a team, in an offensive drive, hit the ball across the opponent's backline, the defending team resumes the game with a free hit from their backline.

Safety /'seɪftɪ/: Also known as a Penalty, a safety is awarded when a defending player hits the ball over his own backline, the shot is taken 60 yd out from the backline, opposite the point at which the ball went over. It is equivalent to a corner in soccer and no defender can be nearer than 30 yards from the ball when it is played.

Chukka /'tʃʌkə/: Also called a period. There are six chukkas in a polo game (four in arena polo and low-goal polo) each lasting seven minutes plus up to 30 seconds in overtime. If, during the 30 seconds, the ball hits the sideboards or goes out of bounds, or if the umpire blows his whistle, the chukka is over. There is no overtime at the end of the sixth chukka unless the score is tied, at which time a seventh chukka will be played until the first goal is scored. A player returns to each chukka on a different horse, though they may rest them for a chukka or two and play the horse again.

Boards /bɔːdz/: Games can be "boarded" or "unboarded", though those with spectators typically have sideboards to keep the ball in play and avoid any accidents. The sideboards must not exceed 28cm in height and are positioned along the sidelines only.

Line of the Ball: When you hit the ball, there is a line from the point where you hit to ball to where it goes. This is the line of the ball and it is very important because you cannot cross this line. If you cross this line, you can cause a dangerous foul.

Near Side: The left hand of the horse.

Off Side: The right-hand side of the horse.

Neck Shot: A ball that is hit under the horse's neck from either side.

Playing Diagonals: Polo is all about judging the angles. Running straight down the field should be avoided. Instead, move across to the field's right side so your teammate can pass the ball to you. In some cases, if the left is opening then the ball can also be passed to the left. From one end towards, the board the ball moves in a diagonal pattern.

Ride off: Two riders may make contact and push each other off the line to prevent the other from striking the ball. It is primarily intended for the ponies to do the pushing, but a player is allowed to use his body, but not his elbows.

Bump /bʌmp/: A player is permitted to ride into another player so as to spoil their shot. The angle of the collision must be slight causing no more than a jar, and the faster the horse travels, the smaller the angle must be.

Hook /hʊk/: A player spoils another's shot by putting his mallet in the way of a striking player. A cross hook occurs when the player reaches over his opponent's mount to hook; this is considered a foul.

Review Questions

1. What is polo?
2. How many chukkas does the polo match consist of?

Chapter 7

Baseball

Goals

1. Understand the development history of baseball
2. Master the major governing body and major events of baseball matches
3. Be familiar with baseball rules and professional terminology

Section 1 Introduction

Figure 7.1 Fenway Park, home of the Boston Red Sox. By Kevin Read

Baseball is a bat-and-ball game played between two opposing teams who take turns batting and fielding. The game proceeds when a player on the fielding team, called the pitcher, throws a ball which a player on the batting team tries to hit with a bat. The objective of the offensive team (batting team) is to hit the ball into the field of play, allowing its players to run the bases, having them advance counter-clockwise around four bases to score what are called "runs". The objective of the defensive team (fielding team) is to prevent batters from becoming runners, and to prevent runners' advance around the bases. A run is scored when a runner legally advances around the bases in order and touches home plate (the place where the player started as a batter). The team that scores the most runs by the end of the game is the winner.

The first objective of the batting team is to have a player reach first base safely. A player on the batting team who reaches first base without being called "out" can attempt to advance to subsequent bases as a runner, either immediately or during teammates' turns batting. The fielding team tries to prevent runs by getting batters or runners "out", which forces them out of the field of play. Both the pitcher and fielders have methods of getting the batting team's players out. The opposing teams switch back and forth between batting and fielding; the batting team's turn to bat is over once the fielding team records three outs. One turn batting for each team constitutes an inning. A game is usually composed of 9 innings, and the team with the greater number of runs at the end of the game wins. If scores are tied at the end of 9 innings, extra innings are usually played. Baseball has no game clock, although most games end in the 9th inning.

Baseball evolved from older bat-and-ball games already being played in England by the mid-18th century. This game was brought by immigrants to North America, where the modern version developed. By the late 19th century, baseball was widely recognized as the national sport of the United States. Baseball is popular in North America, parts of Central and South America, the Caribbean, and East Asia, particularly in Japan, South Korea, and Taiwan, China.

In the United States and Canada, professional Major League Baseball (MLB) teams are divided into the National League (NL) and American League (AL), each with three divisions: East, West, and Central. The MLB champion is determined by playoffs that culminate in the World Series (WS). The top level of play is similarly split in Japan between the Central and Pacific Leagues and in Cuba between the West League and East League. The World Baseball Classic (WBC), organized by the World Baseball Softball Confederation (WBSC), is the major international competition of the sport and attracts the top national teams from around the world.

Section 2　Major Governing Body

2.1　World Baseball Softball Confederation

World Baseball Softball Confederation (**WBSC**) is the world governing body for the sports of baseball and softball. It was established in 2013 by the merger of the International

Baseball Federation (IBAF) and the International Softball Federation (ISF), the former world governing bodies for baseball and softball, respectively. Under WBSC's organizational structure, IBAF and ISF now serve as the Baseball Division and Softball Division of WBSC. Each division is governed by an executive committee, while the WBSC is governed by an executive board.

Headquartered in Pully, Switzerland, the WBSC was granted recognition as the sole competent global authority for both the sports of baseball and softball by the International Olympic Committee at the 125th IOC Session on 8 September 2013.

The WBSC has 190 National Federation Members in 136 countries and territories across Asia, Africa, the Americas, Europe, and Oceania. Professional baseball organizations as well as youth organizations are also included and form an arm of the WBSC as associate members.

As the recognized governing body in baseball/softball, the WBSC is charged with overseeing all international competitions and holds the exclusive rights to all competitions, tournaments, and world championships featuring National Teams. These rights extend to the Olympic Games. Baseball was played at the Olympic Games from 1992 to 2008 and was reinstated in 2020. WBSC's members hold the right to organize and select National Teams. This exclusive authority of the WBSC and its members in each constituent country to sanction and regulate the sport of baseball applies in the 136 territories in which the WBSC has an associated National Federation.

2.2 Major League Baseball

Major League Baseball (**MLB**) is a professional baseball organization. As one of the major professional sports leagues in the United States and Canada, MLB comprises 30 teams, divided equally between the National League (NL) and the American League (AL), with 29 in the United States and 1 in Canada. Formed in 1876 and 1901, respectively, the NL and AL cemented their cooperation with the National Agreement in 1903, making MLB the oldest major professional sports league in the world. They remained legally separate entities until 2000, when they merged into a single organization led by the Commissioner of Baseball. MLB is headquartered in Midtown Manhattan.

Section 3 Major Events

3.1 Baseball at the Summer Olympics

Baseball at the Summer Olympics unofficially debuted at the 1904 Summer Olympics and became an official Olympic sport at the 1992 Summer Olympics. Baseball was played at the Olympic Games from 1992 to 2008, then was dropped from the Summer Olympic program and was reinstated in 2020. Olympic baseball is governed by the World Baseball Softball Confederation (WBSC).

3.2 World Baseball Classic

The **World Baseball Classic (WBC)** is an international baseball tournament sanctioned from 2006 to 2013 by the the International Baseball Federation (IBAF) and after 2013 by the World Baseball Softball Confederation (WBSC) in partnership with the Major League Baseball (MLB). It was proposed to the IBAF by the Major League Baseball (MLB), the Major League Baseball Players Association (MLBPA), and other professional baseball leagues and their players associations around the world. It is one of the two main senior baseball tournaments sanctioned by the WBSC, alongside the Premier12, but the Classic is the only one which grants the winner the title of "World Champion".

The tournament is the first of its kind to have national teams featuring professional players from the major leagues around the world, including the Major League Baseball. In addition to providing a format for the best baseball players in the world to compete against one another while representing their home countries, the World Baseball Classic was created to further promote the game around the globe.

3.3 The WBSC Premier12

The **WBSC Premier12** is the international baseball tournament organized by the World Baseball Softball Confederation (WBSC), featuring the 12 highest-ranked national baseball teams in the world. The first tournament was held in November 2015. The second tournament, the 2019 WBSC Premier12, was held in November 2019, and served as a qualifier for two teams for baseball at the 2020 Summer Olympics.

3.4 Women's Baseball World Cup

The **Women's Baseball World Cup** is an international tournament in which national women's baseball teams from around the world compete. Through its 2012 edition, it was sanctioned by the International Baseball Federation; following the 2013 merger of the IBAF with the International Softball Federation (ISF), subsequent tournaments are sanctioned by the World Baseball Softball Confederation (WBSC). In the eight that have been held, the tournament has been won twice by the United States and six consecutive times by Japan in 2008, 2010, 2012, 2014, 2016, and 2018.

Section 4 Rules

4.1 Game

Figure 7.2 The batter, awaiting a pitch, with the catcher and umpire. By Wikimedia

A baseball game is played between two teams, each composed of 9 players, that take turns playing offense (batting and baserunning) and defense (pitching and fielding). A pair of turns, one at bat and one in the field, by each team constitutes an inning. A game consists of nine innings (7 innings at the high school level and in doubleheaders in the College, Minor League Baseball, and since the 2020 season, the Major League Baseball; and 6 innings at the Little League level). One team—customarily the visiting team—bats in the top, or first half, of every inning. The other team—customarily the home team—bats in the bottom, or second half, of every inning. The goal of the game is to score more points (runs) than the other team. The players on the team at bat attempt to score runs by touching all four bases, in order, set at the corners of the square-shaped baseball diamond. A player bats at home plate and must attempt to safely reach a base before proceeding, counterclockwise, from first base to second base, third base, and back home to score a run. The team in the field attempts to prevent runs from scoring by recording outs, which removes opposing players from offensive action, until their next turn at bat comes up again. When three outs are recorded, the teams switch roles for the next half-inning. If the score of the game is tied after 9 innings, extra innings are played to resolve the contest. Many amateur games, particularly unorganized ones, involve different numbers of players and innings.

4.2　Personnel

4.2.1　Players

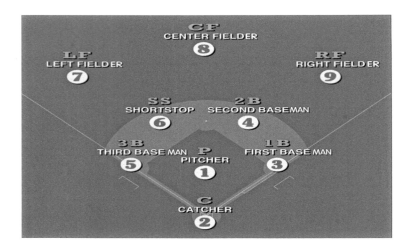

Figure 7.3　Defensive positions on a baseball field, with abbreviations and scorekeeper's position numbers (not uniform numbers). By Michael J

The number of players on a baseball roster, or squad, varies by league and by the level of organized play. A Major League Baseball (MLB) team has a roster of 26 players with specific roles. A typical roster features the following players:

① 8 position players: 1 catcher, 4 infielders, and 3 outfielders—all of whom play on a regular basis.

② 5 starting pitchers who constitute the team's pitching rotation or starting rotation.

③ 7 relief pitchers, including 1 closer, who constitute the team's bullpen (named for the off-field area where pitchers warm up).

④ 1 backup catcher.

⑤ 5 backup infielders and backup outfielders, or players who can play multiple positions and are known as utility players.

4.2.2　Managers and coaches

The manager, or head coach, oversees the team's major strategic decisions, such as establishing the starting rotation and setting the lineup and the batting order before each game, and making substitutions during games—in particular, bringing in relief pitchers. Managers are typically assisted by two or more coaches; they may have specialized responsibilities, such as working with players on hitting, fielding, pitching, or strength and conditioning. At most levels of organized play, two coaches are stationed on the field when the team is at bat: the first base coach and the third base coach, who occupy designated coaches' boxes, just outside the foul lines. These coaches assist in the direction of baserunners, when the ball is in play, and relay tactical signals from the manager to batters and runners, during pauses in play. In contrast to many other team sports, baseball managers and coaches generally wear their team's uniforms; coaches must be in uniform to be allowed on the field to confer with players during a game.

4.2.3 Umpires

Any baseball game involves one or more umpires, who make rulings on the outcome of each play. At a minimum, one umpire will stand behind the catcher, to have a good view of the strike zone, and call balls and strikes. Additional umpires may be stationed near the other bases, thus making it easier to judge plays such as attempted force-outs and tag outs. In MLB, four umpires are used for each game, one near each base. In the playoffs, 6 umpires are used: one at each base and two in the outfield along the foul lines.

4.3 Field of play

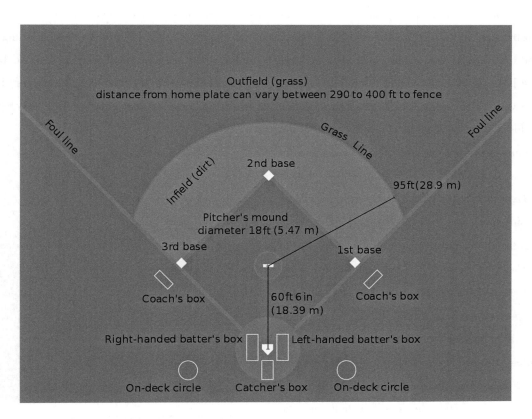

Figure 7.4 Diagram of a baseball field. By Wikimedia Commons

The starting point for much of the action on the field is the home plate (officially "home base"), a five-sided slab of white rubber. One side is 17 in (43.2 cm) long, the two adjacent sides are 8.5 in (21.6 cm). The remaining two sides are approximately 12 in (30.5 cm) and set at a right angle. The plate is set into the ground so that its surface is level with the field. The corner of the home plate where the two 11-inch sides meet at a right angle is at one corner of a 90 ft (27.43 m) square. The other three corners of the square, in counterclockwise order from the home plate, are called first, second, and third base. These bases are marked by canvas or rubber cushions, 18 in (45.7 cm) square and 3–5 in (7.6–12.7 cm) thick. Adjacent to each of the two parallel 8.5-inch sides is a batter's box.

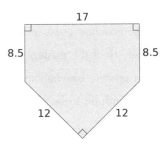

Figure 7.5 Specifications of home plate (inches)

All the bases, including home plate, lie entirely within fair territory. Thus, any batted ball that touches those bases must necessarily be ruled a fair ball.

Near the center of the square is an artificial hill known as the pitcher's mound, atop which is a white rubber slab known as the pitcher's plate, colloquially the "rubber".

The lines from home plate to first and third bases extend to the nearest fence, stand, or other obstruction and are called the foul lines. The portion of the playing field between (and including) the foul lines is fair territory; the rest is "foul territory". The area within the square formed by the bases is officially called the infield, though colloquially this term also includes fair territory in the vicinity of the square; fair territory outside the infield is known as the outfield. Most baseball fields are enclosed with a fence that marks the outer edge of the outfield. The fence is usually set at a distance ranging from 300 to 420 ft (91.4 to 128.0m) from the home plate. Most professional and college baseball fields have right and left foul poles which are about 440 to 500 ft (134.1 to 152.4 m) apart. These poles are at the intersection of the foul lines and the respective ends of the outfield fence, and unless otherwise specified within the ground rules, lie in fair territory. Thus, a batted ball that passes over the outfield wall in flight and touches the foul pole is a fair ball and the batter is awarded a home run.

Figure 7.6 2013 World Baseball Classic championship match. By Wikimedia

4.4 Equipment

4.4.1 Baseball

The baseball is about the size of an adult's fist, around 9 in (22.8 cm) in circumference. It has a rubber or cork center, wound in yarn and covered in white cowhide, with red stitching.

Figure 7.7 A baseball. By Wikipedia

4.4.2 Bat

The bat is a hitting tool, traditionally made of a single, solid piece of wood. Other materials are now commonly used for nonprofessional games. It is a hard round stick, about 2.5 in (6.4 cm) in diameter at the hitting end, tapering to a narrower handle and culminating in a knob. Bats used by adults are typically around 34 in (86.4 cm) long, and not longer than 42 in (106.7 cm).

4.4.3 Glove

The glove or mitt is a fielding tool, made of padded leather with webbing among the fingers. As an aid in catching and holding onto the ball, it takes various shapes to meet the specific needs of different fielding positions.

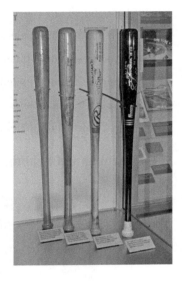

Figure 7.8 Baseball bats. By Dave Hogg

Figure 7.9 A custom-made Rolin baseball glove. By Wyk

4.4.4 Protective helmets

Protective helmets are also standard equipment for all batters.

Figure 7.10 A standard MLB batting helmet with a face protector. By Keith Allison

Section 5 Basic Tactics

Many of the pre-game and in-game strategic decisions in baseball revolve around a fundamental fact: in general, right-handed batters tend to be more successful against left-handed pitchers and, to an even greater degree, left-handed batters tend to be more successful against right-handed pitchers. A manager with several left-handed batters in the regular lineup, who knows the team will be facing a left-handed starting pitcher, may respond by starting one or more of the right-handed backups on the team's roster. During the late innings of a game, as relief pitchers and pinch hitters are brought in, the opposing manager will often go back and forth, trying to create favorable matchups with their substitutions. The manager of the fielding team tries to arrange same-handed pitcher-batter matchups and the manager of the batting team tries to arrange opposite-handed matchups. With a team that has the lead in the late innings, a manager may remove a starting position player—especially one whose turn at bat is not likely to come up again—for a more skillful fielder (known as a defensive substitution).

5.1 Pitching and fielding

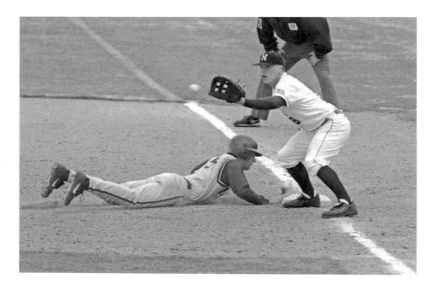

Figure 7.11 A first baseman receives a pickoff throw, as the runner dives back to first base.
By Brett A. Dawson

The tactical decision that precedes almost every play in a baseball game involves pitch selection. By gripping and then releasing the baseball in a certain manner, and by throwing it at a certain speed, pitchers can cause the baseball to break to either side, or downward, as it approaches the batter; thus creating differing pitches that can be selected. Among the resulting wide variety of pitches that may be thrown, the four basic types are the fastball, the changeup (or off-speed pitch), and two breaking balls—the curveball and the slider. Pitchers have different repertoires of pitches they are skillful at throwing. Conventionally, before each pitch, the catcher signals the pitcher what type of pitch to throw, as well as its general vertical or horizontal location. If there is disagreement on the selection, the pitcher may shake off the sign and the catcher will call for a different pitch.

With a runner on base and taking a lead, the pitcher may attempt a pickoff, a quick throw to a fielder covering the base to keep the runner's lead in check or, optimally, effect a tag out. Pickoff attempts, however, are subject to rules that severely restrict the pitcher's movements before and during the pickoff attempt. Violation of any one of these rules could result in the umpire calling a balk against the pitcher, which permits any runners on base to advance one base with impunity. If an attempted stolen base is anticipated, the catcher may call for a pitchout, a ball thrown deliberately off the plate, allowing the catcher to catch it while standing and throw it quickly to a base. Facing a batter with a strong tendency to hit to one side of the field, the fielding team may employ a shift, with most or all of the fielders moving to the left or right of their usual positions. With a runner on third base, the infielders may play in, moving closer to the home plate to improve the odds of throwing out the runner on a ground ball, though a sharply hit grounder is more likely to carry through a drawn-in infield.

5.2 Batting and baserunning

Figure 7.12   A player hits a pitch by swinging his bat. By Keith Allison

Several basic offensive tactics come into play with a runner on first base, including the fundamental choice of whether to attempt a steal of second base. The hit-and-run tactics are sometimes employed by a skillful contact hitter: the runner takes off with the pitch, drawing the shortstop or second baseman over to second base, creating a gap in the infield for the batter to poke the ball through. The sacrifice bunt, calls for the batter to focus on making soft contact with the ball, so that it rolls a short distance into the infield, allowing the runner to advance into scoring position as the batter is thrown out at first. A batter, particularly one who is a fast runner, may also attempt to bunt for a hit. A sacrifice bunt employed with a runner on third base, aimed at bringing that runner home, is known as a squeeze play. With a runner on third and fewer than two outs, a batter may instead concentrate on hitting a fly ball that, even if it is caught, it will be deep enough to allow the runner to tag up and score—a successful batter, in this case, gets credit for a sacrifice fly. In order to increase the chance of advancing a batter to first base via a walk, the manager will sometimes signal a batter who is ahead in the count (i.e., has more balls than strikes) to take, or not swing at, the next pitch. The batter's potential reward of reaching base (via a walk) exceeds the disadvantage if the next pitch is a strike.

Baseball Terms

Diamond /ˈdaɪəmənd/: The layout of the four bases in the infield. It's actually a square with 90 ft (27m) on each side, but from the stands, it resembles a parallelogram or "diamond".

Infield /ˈɪnfiːld/: A square that is 90 ft on each side with the corners being the four bases.

Outfield /ˈaʊtfiːld/: The part of a baseball field beyond the infield and between the foul lines.

Rubber /ˈrʌbə(r)/: The pitching plate on the mound. The pitcher must have one foot connected to the plate while pitching to the batter. The rubber is located 60 ft 6 in (18.4 m) from the home plate.

On Deck: A term used to refer to the next batter up in the inning. This person stands in a designated circular area and warms up before batting.

Bullpen /ˈbʊlpen/: Area designated for pitchers to warm up. Generally, it consists of two mounds and two home plates.

Starter /ˈstɑːtə(r)/: In baseball, a starter is the first pitcher in the game for each team. Starting pitchers are expected to pitch for a significant portion of the game, although their ability to do this depends on many factors, including effectiveness, stamina, health, and strategy.

Runner /ˈrʌnə(r)/: An offensive player who is advancing toward, touching, or returning to any base.

Designated Hitter: A designated hitter is a baseball player who bats in place of the pitcher when it is the pitcher's order of play. The DH does not have a fielding position.

Strike Zone: In baseball, the strike zone is the volume of space through which a pitch must pass in order to be called a strike even if the batter does not swing. The strike zone is defined as the volume of space above home plate and between the batter's knees and the midpoint of their torso. Whether a pitch passes through the zone is decided by an umpire, who is generally positioned behind the catcher.

At Bat: The offensive team's turn to bat the ball and score. Each player takes a turn at bat until three outs are made. Each Batter's opportunity at the plate is scored as an "at bat" for him.

Strike /straɪk/: A strike in baseball results when a batter swings at and misses a pitch, does not swing at a pitch in the strike zone, or hits a foul ball that is not caught by a fielder.

Ball: A pitch that misses the strike zone and is not swung at by the batter.

Called Game: A game suspended or ended by the umpire.

Bunt /bʌnt/: Bunt/short hit that is executed by letting the ball hit the bat (not swinging). It is used to surprise the fielders or to advance a runner.

Changeup: A slow-pitch thrown with the exact arm action as a fastball, designed to disrupt the timing of the hitter.

Curveball /kɜːvˌbɔːl/: In baseball, a curveball is a type of pitch thrown with a characteristic grip and hand movement that imparts forward spin to the ball, causing it to dive as it approaches the plate.

Fly Ball: A fly ball is a batted ball that goes high in the air in flights.

Forkball: The forkball is a type of pitch in baseball. Related to the split-finger fastball, the forkball is held between the first two fingers and thrown hard, snapping the wrist.

Knuckle Ball: A knuckleball or knuckler is a baseball pitch thrown to minimize the spin of the ball in flight, causing an erratic, unpredictable motion.

Double /ˈdʌbl/: A hit where the batter makes it safely to second base before the ball can be returned to the infield.

Grand Slam: A home run that is hit with a runner on every base. This hit scores 4 runs.

Intentional Walk: Four balls thrown on purpose to a batter advancing the hitter to first base. Generally, it is executed when first base is empty to set up a force play.

Green Light: Signal from the coach to hit the next good pitch, or a signal to a base runner that gives the runner the authority to decide when to attempt a steal.

Hit and Run: An offensive tactic whereby a baserunner (usually on first base) starts running as if to steal and the batter is obligated to swing at the pitch to try to drive the ball behind the runner to the right field.

Run down: A play used by fielders to tag out a runner caught between bases.

Force-out: A blockage is a situation in baseball in which a runner is out before reaching the base and the ball has been passed to the fielder on the base.

Run Batter in (RBI): A run batted in or runs batted in (RBI) is a statistic in baseball and softball that credits a batter for making a play that allows a run to be scored (except in certain situations such as when an error is made on the play). For example, if the batter bats a base hit which allows a teammate on a higher base to reach home and so score a run, then the batter gets credited with an RBI.

Strikeout /ˈstraɪkaʊt/: In baseball or softball, a strikeout (or strike-out) occurs when a batter accumulates three strikes during a time at bat. It usually means that the batter is out.

Wild Pitch: A wild pitch (WP) is charged to a pitcher when, in the opinion of the official scorer, a pitch is too high, too low, or too wide of home plate for the catcher to catch the ball with ordinary effort, and which allows one or more runners to advance or allows the batter to advance to first base, if it is a third strike with first base unoccupied. Neither a passed ball nor a wild pitch is charged as an error. It is a separate statistic.

Review Questions

1. How many fielders can each team field in a game?
2. What is a home run?
3. What is the international governing body of baseball?

Chapter 8

Gateball

Goals

1. Understand the development history of gateball
2. Master the major governing body and major events of gateball matches
3. Be familiar with gateball rules and professional terminology

Section 1   Introduction

Gateball is a team mallet sport inspired by croquet. It is a fast-paced, non-contact, highly strategic team game, which can be played by people of all ages and genders.

Gateball is played on a rectangular court 20 m (66 ft) long and 15 m (49 ft) wide. Each court has three gates and a goal pole. The game is played by two teams (red and white) of up to five players. Each player has a numbered ball corresponding to their order of play. The odd-numbered balls are red and the even-numbered balls are white. Teams score one point for hitting the ball through a gate and two points for hitting the goal pole according to the rules.

Figure 8.1   *A gateball match. By Julio D'ias*

Gateball was invented in Japan by Eji Suzuki in 1947. At the time there was a severe shortage of rubber needed to make balls used in many sports. Suzuki, who was working in the lumber industry in Hokkaido, realized that there was a ready supply of the wood used to make croquet balls and mallets. He revised the rules of croquet and created gateball as a game for young people.

Gateball first became popular in the late 1950s when a physical education instructor introduced gate ball to the women's societies and senior citizens' clubs in Kumamoto City. In 1962, the Kumamoto Gateball Association was formed and established a set of local rules. This version of the game became known nationally when it was demonstrated at a national fitness meet in Kumamoto in 1976. Soon after gate ball's popularity exploded as local government officials and representatives of senior citizens' organizations introduced the sport across the country.

Section 2　Major Governing Body

The **World Gateball Union** (**WGU**) is gateball's global umbrella organization, with members from 16 countries and regions. Gateball is played by more than 10 million people from more than 40 countries.

The Japanese Gateball Union (JGU) was founded in 1984. Under the leadership of its inaugural chairman, Ryoichi Sasakwa, JGU developed a unified set of rules and organized the first national conference. The following year, the JGU joined with 5 countries and regions, China, Korea, Brazil, United States of America, and Chinese Taipei, to form the World Gateball Union (WGU). The WGU has since been joined by Bolivia (1987), Paraguay (1987), Peru (1987), Argentina (1989), Canada (1989), Singapore (1994), Hong Kong, China (1998), Australia (2003), Macao, China (2005), Philippines (2012), and Indonesia (2013).

Section 3　Major Events

3.1　World Gateball Championships

The **World Gateball Championships** are held every four years. The first championship was played in Hokkaido in 1986 and involved teams from Brazil, China, Chinese Taipei, Japan, Korea, and the United States. Subsequent championships were held in Hawaii, US (1998); Toyama, Japan (2002); Jeju, South Korea (2006); Shanghai, China (2010); and 2014 Niigata (Japan) and other places.

3.2　World Games

In 2001, gateball was included as an exhibition event in the 6th World Games. The competition was held in Akita Prefecture in Japan and was attended by teams from China, Japan, South Korea, the USA, and Chinese Taipei. In the end, a team of mostly Japanese teenagers won.

Section 4　Rules

Gateball is played by two teams of up to five people on a rectangular field 20-25 m long and

15-20 m wide. The two teams use five balls each, either red or white depending on the team, and play in an alternating fashion between red and white balls numbered from 1 to 10. Each player plays the same ball throughout the game. At the beginning of the game the players, in order, place their ball in the designated "start area" and attempt to hit the ball through the first gate. If they successfully pass through the gate, they may play again. If the player misses the first gate, or their ball passes through the first gate but ends up outside of the court, they have pick up their ball and to try again in the second round. Since the 2015 rule change, a ball that goes through the first gate but ends up out of bounds is deemed to have passed the first gate but is an out-ball and will attempt to enter the court on their next turn from where the ball went out.

When stroking, if the ball hits another ball, this is called "touch". If both the stroker's ball and the touched ball remain within the inside line, the stroker shall step on the stroker's ball and place the other touched ball so that it is touching the stroker's ball, and hit the stroker's ball with the stick (this play is called a "spark"), sending the other touched ball off as the result of the impact. By passing through a gate or sparking the ball, the player receives another turn.

One point is given for every gate the ball passes in order and two points for hitting the goal pole. The winner is the team with the most points at the end of thirty minutes. The red team always gets to play first, and the white team has the final turn.

4.1 Gateball court

The gateball court consists of two parts, the inner field and the outer field. The inner field is rectangular, 20-25 m in length and 15-20 m in width. During the game, almost all the play is in the inner field. It is sometimes simply called "court" for this reason. The inner field is bounded by the inside line and it is surrounded by the outer field. The width of the outerfield is 50-100 cm. The rule book says the surface of the court should be flat and clear of any obstacles. There are many types of courts, launs, artificial launs, and clay as shown in Figure 8.2. You can choose either one.

The three gates and one goal pole are arranged in the inner field as shown in Figure 8.3. It is proportional to the original scale except for the goal pole. Each gate has its own numbers from one to three and is called the first, second, and third gate, respectively (or just Gate 1, 2, or 3). The inner width of the gate is 22 cm and the height is 19 cm. All gates should be perpendicular to each other.

There is a two-centimeter-wide goal pole in the center of the court. As its name suggests, if your ball hits the goal pole after it passes all three gates, your ball will make an "agari (finishing)" (agari is a Japanese word for finishing in a board game). The arrangement of the gates and a pole is very important.

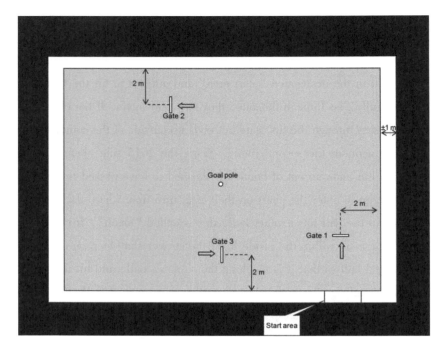

Figure 8. 2   Typical gateball court. By traditionalsports. org

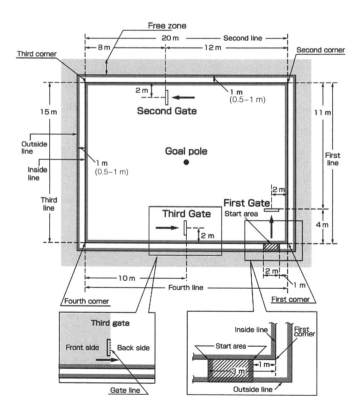

Figure 8. 3   The measurements of gateball court. By Official Gateball Rules

There are three gates and one goal pole in the court. The goal pole is located in the center of the court. The three gates are set parallel to the inside line as shown in Figure 8.3. The arrows near the gates represent the direction of passing them.

All gates and a goal pole should be firmly fixed. Square indicators should be attached to the gates so that players can recognize them easily.

Each gate has the direction of passing as shown in Figure 8.3. The side from which you can "pass" the gate is called the front side. The other side is called the back side. Although you can make your ball physically pass the gate from the back side, this is not a scoring play. Each corner or line also has a name. The corner nearest to the first gate is the first corner. The other three corners are called the second, third, or fourth corner and followed in an anticlockwise direction. The four inside lines are named the same way.

4.2 Equipment

Figure 8.4 Gateball equipment. By gateball. or

4.2.1 Mallet

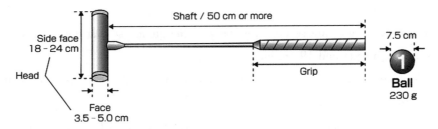

Figure 8.5 Stick by official gateball rules. By Official Gateball Rules

The stick shall consist of a head and a shaft forming a T-shaped instrument. Players hold the grip of a shaft and hit a ball with the face of a head.

The head is cylindrical in principle, with two faces running parallel to the shaft. The side face refers to the section of the stick that intersects with the shaft at a right angle. The face shall be a minimum 3.5 cm, and a maximum 5 cm, in diameter. The side face shall be 18-24 cm in length.

The shaft shall be stick-shaped and secured at the midpoint of the side face. The shaft shall be 50 cm or more in length, including the grip

4.2.2 Balls

The ball used shall be of an even spherical shape with a diameter of 7.5 cm (±0.7 mm) and a weight of 230 g (±10 g), made of synthetic resin. There shall be a total of 10 balls: 5 red balls and 5 white balls. The red balls shall be marked in white with the odd numbers "1", "3", "5", "7", and "9". The white balls shall be marked in red with the even numbers "2", "4", "6", "8", and "10". The ball number shall be 5 cm in height in principle, and be visibly marked in at least two locations on the ball.

Figure **8.6** *Ball. By Official Gateball Rules*

4.2.3 Gates and a goal pole

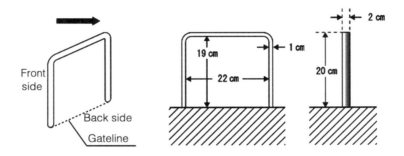

Figure **8.7** *Gates and a goal pole. By Official Gateball Rules*

The gates are upside-down U-shaped devices in a color that is easily identifiable on the court surface, which is a cylinder rod with a diameter of 1 cm (± 1 mm), and are placed in three locations on the court.

The two legs of the gate are secured vertically on the ground so that the inner space between the two legs is 22 cm wide and 19 cm high.

Goal poles consist of a cylinder rod with a diameter of 2 cm in a color that is easily identifiable on the court surface.

Goal poles must be placed in the center of the court and vertically in the ground with 20 cm of the pole above the surface of the ground.

Some poles can simply be placed on the ground when it is impossible to hammer them into the ground such as on artificial turf and on indoor courts.

4.2.4 Number cloth

Official Gateball Rules prescribe that players must wear the number indicating their playing order, and that it must be "10 cm

Figure **8.8** *Number Cloth By gateball. or*

or more in height", "a shape that is easily identified", and "must be placed on the chest and back, or chest only".

Section 5　Basic Tactics

When you spark teammates' ball, you make positive tactical choices about positioning, bearing in mind the playing order.

For example, the first team to pass a ball through gate 1 successfully (say with ball 1) will often place that ball between gate 2 and the boundary. That way, it is dangerous for the other team to try and touch without a ball going out, whilst if a ball from the other team (say ball 2) takes position to run gate 2 on its next turn, it can be touched by ball 1 and made use of, to benefit the first team. Instead of positioning in front of gate 2 therefore, ball 2 might go to guard the access to gate 3.

If you spark a ball from the opposing team, you might send it to where your team's balls can use it, bearing in mind the number sequence of those balls which are due to play before it. Alternatively, you might send it out of court, meaning it then needs to use its next turn just to come back into court, without being able to touch or to pass a gate.

Gateball Terms

Inner Field: A rectangular section of the court (field) that is 20–25 m long and 15–20 m wide, the outer edge of which is defined by the inside line.

Outer Field: A fixed area 1m in width, in principle, which forms a part of the court (field), the outer edge of which is the outside line and the inner edge of which is the inside line. The width can vary between 50 cm and 1 m.

Round /raʊnd/: The process of players number one through to ten playing their turn constitutes one round. The second round begins when player number one becomes the stroker for the second time.

Order /ˈɔːrdər/: The playing order of the strokers.

The Stroker's Ball: The ball's number is the same as the playing order number. For example, player number one's ball is therefore Ball number one.

Leading Team: The team playing with red balls, with odd numbers displayed in white, plays first.

Play Ball: A call by the chief referee to announce the start of the game.

Total Points/Team Points: The total number of points scored by each team at the end of the game.

Perfect Game: A game in which a team has scored 25 points.

Proper Play: The act of correctly stroking the ball, and the actions involved in realizing this.

Starting Point: The starting point for counting 10 seconds is either when the stroker is instructed to stroke, when the right for continuous stroke is gained, or when the right to spark is gained.

Abandonment of Rights: If a team announces its intention to abandon the game, or a team has less than five players at the start of the game, the team is seen as forfeiting the game, resulting in the other team winning by forfeit.

Passing Gate 1: Hit the ball from the start area and the ball goes through Gate 1.

Stroking /strəʊkɪŋ/: The stroker uses the face of the stick to stroke one's own stationary ball.

Pushing /pʊʃɪŋ/: A method of stroking in which the stroker uses the stick's face to push the ball forward, with the stick's face remaining in contact with his/her ball. Pushing is a stroking foul.

Sparking /ˌspɒrkɪŋ/: To move another ball as the result of the impact of stroking one's ball after the balls have been set. After a successful touch, and the stroker's ball and the touched ball have stopped moving as in-balls, the act of the stroker stepping on his/her ball so that the touched ball is in contact with his/her ball in the inner field, and stroking his/her ball so that the impact causes the other ball to move.

Touch /tʌtʃ/: A Touch occurs when the stroker's ball that is an in-ball is stroked and moves to touch another ball.

Contact /ˈkɑːntækt/: When a ball and a ball, a ball and a gate, or a ball and a goal pole are in contact with each other.

Ball Touch Foul: A foul in which a stroker touches a ball on the court for any reason other than that permitted by the game rules.

Out-ball Stroking Foul: A foul resulting from the stroker stroking an out-ball which ends up hitting another ball.

Call /kɔːl/: A referee gesturing and using his/her voice to convey, to the players and spectators, the progress of the game or his/her decision about a play or move.

Review Questions

1. What is gateball?
2. What is the international governing body for gateball?

Chapter 9

Ice Hockey

Goals

1. Understand the development history of ice hockey
2. Master the major governing body and major events of ice hockey matches
3. Be familiar with ice hockey game rules and professional terminology

Section 1   Introduction

Figure 9.1   International standard ice hockey rink of Nokia Arena in Tampere, Finland. By kallerna

Ice hockey, also known as hockey, is one of the collective ice sports with strong antagonism, which combines changeable skating skills with agile and skilled hockey skills. The players wear skates, slide with ice bars to fight for the ball, and the players use ice bars to hit the ball into the other team's goal. The winner is the one who scores more goals.

Ice hockey is the most popular in Canada, Eastern Europe, Northern Europe, and the United States. Ice hockey is the official national winter sport of Canada.

In addition, ice hockey is the most popular winter sport in Belarus, Croatia, the Czech Republic, Finland, Latvia, Russia, Slovakia, Sweden, and Switzerland. North America's

National Hockey League (NHL) is the highest level for men's ice hockey and the strongest professional ice hockey league in the world. The Kontinental Hockey League (KHL) is the highest league in Russia and much of Eastern Europe.

It is believed that Ice hockey has evolved from simple stick and ball games played in the 18th and 19th centuries in the United Kingdom and elsewhere. These games were brought to North America and several similar winter games using informal rules were developed, such as shinny and ice polo. The contemporary sport of ice hockey was developed in Canada, most notably in Montreal, where the first indoor hockey game was played on March 3, 1875. Some characteristics of that game, such as the length of the ice rink and the use of a puck, have been retained to this day. Amateur ice hockey leagues began in the 1880s, and professional ice hockey leagues originated around 1900. The Stanley Cup, emblematic of ice hockey club supremacy, was first awarded in 1893 to recognize the Canadian amateur champion and later became the championship trophy of the NHL. In the early 1900s, the Canadian rules were adopted by the Ligue Internationale de Hockey sur Glace, the precursor of the Interational Ice Hockey Federation (IIHF), and the sport was played for the first time at the Olympics during the 1920 Summer Olympics. Despite women having played since the beginning of the game, women's hockey was not professionally organized until much later, the first IIHF Women's World Championship being held in 1990 and being introduced into the Olympics in 1998. In international competitions, the national teams of six countries (the Big Six) predominate: Canada, Czech Republic, Finland, Russia, Sweden, and the United States.

Section 2 Major Governing Body

The **International Ice Hockey Federation (IIHF)** is a worldwide governing body for ice hockey. It is based in Zurich, Switzerland, and has 83 member countries.

The IIHF maintains the IIHF World Ranking based on international ice hockey tournaments. Rules of play for IIHF events differ from hockey in North America and the rules of the National Hockey League (NHL). Decisions of the IIHF can be appealed through the Court of Arbitration for Sport in Lausanne, Switzerland. The IIHF maintains its own hall of fame for international ice hockey. The IIHF Hall of Fame was founded in 1997, and has been located within the Hockey Hall of Fame since 1998.

Previously, the IIHF also managed the development of inline hockey; however, in June 2019, the IIHF announced that they would no longer govern inline hockey or organize the Inline Hockey World Championships.

Section 3   Major Events

3.1   National Hockey League

Figure 9.2   NHL faceoff. By Wikimedia

The **National Hockey League** (**NHL**) is a professional hockey league in North America, consisting of 32 teams, 25 in the United States and 7 in Canada. The teams are divided into two regions, East and West, each region is divided into three divisions, and the champions of the two regions compete for the Stanley Cup in the league finals each year. The Stanley Cup, the oldest professional sports trophy in North America, is awarded annually to the league playoff champion at the end of each season. The NHL is one of the major professional sports leagues in the United States and Canada and is considered to be the top-ranked professional ice hockey league in the world, with players from 17 countries as of the 2023–24 season. The International Ice Hockey Federation (IIHF) also views the Stanley Cup as one of the "most important championships available to the sport". The NHL is headquartered in Midtown Manhattan.

The National Hockey League was organized at the Windsor Hotel in Montreal on November 26, 1917, after the suspension of operations of its predecessor organization, the National Hockey Association (NHA), which had been founded in 1909 at Renfrew, Ontario. The NHL immediately took the NHA's place as one of the leagues that contested for the Stanley Cup in an annual interleague competition before a series of league mergers and dissolutions. In 1926, the NHL became the only league left competing for the Stanley Cup.

At its inception, the NHL had four teams, all in Canada, thus the adjective "National" in the league's name. The league expanded to the United States in 1924, when the Boston Bruins joined, and has since consisted of both American and Canadian teams. From 1942 to 1967, the league had only six teams, collectively (if not contemporaneously) nicknamed the "Original Six". The NHL added six new teams to double its size at the 1967 NHL expansion. The league then increased to 18 teams by 1974 and 21 teams in 1979. Between 1991 and 2000, the NHL further expanded to 30 teams. It added its 31st and 32nd teams in 2017 and 2021, respectively.

The NHL is the fifth-wealthiest professional sport league in the world by revenue, after the National Football League (NFL), the Major League Baseball (MLB), the National Basketball Association (NBA), and the English Premier League (EPL). The league's headquarters have been in Manhattan since 1989 when the head office moved from Montreal. There have been four league-wide work stoppages in NHL history, all occurring after 1992.

The NHL's regular season is typically held from October to April, with each team playing 82 games. Following the conclusion of the regular season, 16 teams advance to the Stanley Cup playoffs, a four-round tournament that runs into June to determine the league champion. Since the league's founding in 1917, the Montreal Canadiens have won the most combined NHL titles with 25, winning three NHL championship series before the league took full exclusivity of the Stanley Cup in 1926, and 22 Stanley Cups afterwards. The reigning league champion is the Vegas Golden Knights, who defeated the Florida Panthers in the 2023 Stanley Cup Finals.

3.2 Ice hockey at the Winter Olympic Games

Ice hockey tournaments have been staged at the Olympic Games since 1920. The men's tournament was introduced at the 1920 Summer Olympics and was transferred permanently to the Winter Olympic Games program in 1924, in France. The women's tournament was first held at the 1998 Winter Olympics.

3.3 Ice Hockey World Championships

The **Ice Hockey World Championships** are an annual international men's ice hockey tournament organized by the IIHF. First officially held at the 1920 Summer Olympics,

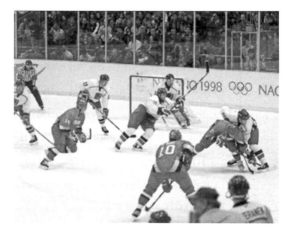

Figure 9.3 *The* 1998 *gold medal game between Russia and the Czech Republic was the first played between teams consisting mainly of NHL players. By Canadaolympic989*

it is the sport's highest-profile annual international tournament. The IIHF was created in 1908 while the European Championships, the precursor to the World Championships, were first held in

1910. The tournament held at the 1920 Summer Olympics is recognized as the first Ice Hockey World Championship. From 1920 to 1968, the Olympic hockey tournament was also considered the World Championship for that year.

3.4 The World Cup of Hockey

The **World Cup of Hockey** is an international ice hockey tournament. Inaugurated in 1996, it is the successor to the Canada Cup, which was held every 3 to 5 years from 1976 to 1991 and was the first international hockey championship to allow nations to field their top players. The World Cup has occurred thrice before on an irregular basis, with the United States winning in 1996 and Canada winning in 2004 and 2016. Following the 2016 tournament, it is uncertain if the series will be continued, after the cancellation of the 2020 tournament. The NHL will attempt to hold the next edition of the World Cup in 2025.

Section 4 Rules

4.1 Gameplay

Figure 9.4   VTB Arena is an example of an indoor ice hockey arena. By Oleg Bkhambri

While the general characteristics of the game remain constant, the exact rules depend on the particular code of play being used. The two most important codes are those of the IIHF and the NHL. Both of these codes, and others, originated from Canadian rules of ice hockey of the early 20th century.

Ice hockey is played on a hockey rink. During normal play, there are 6 players on ice skates on the ice per side, one of them being the goaltender. The objective of the game is to score goals by shooting a hard vulcanized rubber disc, the puck, into the opponent's goal net at the opposite end of the rink. The players use their sticks to pass or shoot the puck.

With certain restrictions, players may redirect the puck with any part of their body. Players may not hold the puck in their hands and are prohibited from using their hands to pass the puck to their teammates unless they are in the defensive zone.

Figure 9.5 *A standard ice hockey puck. By Matt Boulton*

Players however can knock a puck out of the air with their hands to themselves. Players are prohibited from kicking the puck into the opponent's goal, though unintentional redirections off the skate are permitted. Players may not intentionally bat the puck into the net with their hands.

Hockey is an off-side game, meaning that forward passes are allowed. Before the 1930s, hockey was an on-side game, meaning that only backward passes were allowed. Those rules favoured individual stick-handling as the key means of driving the puck forward. With the arrival of offside rules, the forward pass transformed hockey into a true team sport, where individual performance diminished in importance relative to team play, which could now be coordinated over the entire surface of the ice as opposed to merely rearward players.

The six players on each team are typically divided into three forwards, two defensemen, and one goaltender. The term skaters are typically used to describe all players who are not goaltenders. The forward positions consist of a center and two wingers: a left winger and a right winger. Forwards often play together as units or lines, with the same three forwards always playing together. The defensemen usually stay together as a pair generally divided between left and right. Left and right wingers or defensemen are generally positioned as such, based on the side on which they carry their sticks. A substitution of an entire unit at once is called a line change. Teams typically employ alternate sets of forward lines and defensive pairings when short-handed or on a power play. The goaltender stands in a usually blue, semi-circle called the crease in the defensive zone keeping pucks from going in. Substitutions are permitted at any time during the game, although during a stoppage of playing the home team is permitted the final change. When players are substituted during play, it is called changing on the fly. A new NHL rule added in the 2005 – 06 season prevents a team from changing their line after they ice the puck.

The boards surrounding the ice help keep the puck in play and they can also be used as tools to play the puck. Players are permitted to bodycheck opponents into the boards as a means of

Figure **9.6** *Players perform a line change. A line change is a substitution of an entire line at once.*
By Daniel Bowles

stopping progress. The referees, linesmen, and the outside of the goal are "in play" and do not cause a stoppage of the game when the puck or players are influenced (by either bouncing or colliding into them). Play can be stopped if the goal is knocked out of position. Play often proceeds for minutes without interruption. When play is stopped, it is restarted with a faceoff. Two players face each other and an official drops the puck to the ice, where the two players attempt to gain control of the puck. Markings (circles) on the ice indicate the locations for the faceoff and guide the positioning of players.

The three major rules of play in ice hockey that limit the movement of the puck are offside, icing, and the puck going out of play. A player is offside if he enters his opponent's zone before the puck itself. Under many situations, a player may not "ice the puck", which means shooting the puck all the way across both the center line and the opponent's goal line. The puck goes out of play whenever it goes past the perimeter of the ice rink (onto the player benches, over the glass, or onto the protective netting above the glass) and a stoppage of play is called by the officials using whistles. It also does not matter if the puck comes back onto the ice surface from those areas as the puck is considered dead once it leaves the perimeter of the rink. The referee may also blow the whistle for a stoppage in play if the puck is jammed along the boards when 2 or more players are battling for the puck for a long period of time, or if the puck is stuck on the back of either of the two nets for a period of time.

Under IIHF rules, each team may carry a maximum of 20 players and 2 goaltenders on their roster. NHL rules restrict the total number of players per game to 18, plus 2 goaltenders. In the

NHL, the players are usually divided into 4 lines of 3 forwards, and into 3 pairs of defenders. On occasion, teams may elect to substitute an extra defender for a forward. The 7th defender may play as a substitute defender who spend the game on the bench, or if a team chooses to play 4 lines then this 7th defender may see ice-time on the 4th line as a forward.

4.1.1 Periods and overtime

Figure 9.7 Scoreboard for a hockey game during the fourth period. By Sarah Connors

A professional game consists of three periods of 20 minutes, and the clock is running only when the puck is in play. The teams change ends after each period of play, including overtime. Recreational leagues and children's leagues often play shorter games, generally with three shorter periods of play.

If a tie occurs in tournament play, as well as in the NHL playoffs, North Americans favor sudden-death overtime, in which the teams continue to play 20-minute periods until a goal is scored. Up until the 1999–2000 season, regular-season NHL games were settled with a single 5-minute sudden-death period with 5 players (plus a goalie) per side, with both teams awarded one point in the standings in the event of a tie. With a goal, the winning team would be awarded two points and the losing team none (just as if they had lost in regulation). The total elapsed time from when the puck first drops, is about 2 hours and 20 minutes for a 60-minute game.

From the 1999–2000 to the 2003–04 seasons, the National Hockey League decided ties by playing a single 5-minute sudden-death overtime period with each team having four skaters per side (plus the goalie). In the event of a tie, each team would still receive one point in the standings but in the event of a victory the winning team would be awarded two points in the standings and the losing team one point. The idea was to discourage teams from playing for a tie since previously some teams might have preferred a tie and 1 point to risking a loss and zero points. The exception to this rule is that if a team opts to pull their goalie in exchange for an extra skater during overtime and is subsequently scored upon (an empty net goal), in which case the losing team receives no points for the overtime loss. Since the 2015–16 season, the single 5-minute sudden-death overtime session involves three skaters on each side. Since three skaters must always be on the ice in an NHL game, the consequences of penalties are slightly different from those during regulation play; any penalty during overtime that would result in a team losing a skater during regulation instead causes the other side to add a skater. Once the penalized team's penalty ends, the penalized skater exits the penalty box and the teams continue at 4-on-4 until the next stoppage of play, at which point the teams return to three skaters per side.

International play and several North American professional leagues, including the NHL (in the regular season), now use an overtime period identical to that from 1999–2000 to 2003–04 followed by a penalty shootout. If the score remains tied after an extra overtime period, the subsequent shootout consists of three players from each team taking penalty shots. After these 6 total shots, the team with more goals is awarded the victory. If the score is still tied, the shootout then proceeds to a sudden-death format. Regardless of the number of goals scored during the shootout by either team, the final score recorded will award the winning team one more goal than the score at the end of regulation time. In the NHL, if a game is decided in overtime or by a shootout, the winning team is awarded two points in the standings and the losing team is awarded one point. Ties no longer occur in the NHL.

Overtime in the NHL playoffs differs from the regular season. In the playoffs, there are no shootouts. If a game is tied after regulation, then a 20-minute period of 5-on-5 sudden-death overtime will be added. If the game is still tied after the overtime, another period is added until a team scores, which wins the match. Since 2019, the IIHF World Championships and the gold medal game in the Olympics have used the same format, but in a 3-on-3 format.

4.1.2 Penalties

In ice hockey, infractions of the rules lead to a play stoppage whereby the play is restarted at a faceoff. Some infractions result in a penalty on a player or team. In the simplest case, the offending player is sent to the penalty box and their team must play with one less player on the ice for a designated time. A minor penalty lasts for two minutes, a major penalty lasts for five minutes, and a double-minor penalty is two consecutive 2-minute penalties. A single minor penalty may be extended by 2 minutes for causing visible injury to the victimized player. This is usually when blood is drawn during high-sticking. Players may be also assessed personal extended penalties or game expulsions for misconduct in addition to the penalty or penalties their team must serve. The team that has been given a penalty is said to be playing short-handed while the opposing team is on a power play.

Figure **9.8** *An ice hockey player enters the penalty box.*
By Alex Micheu

A two-minute minor penalty is often charged for lesser infractions such as tripping, elbowing, roughing, high-sticking, delay of the game, too many players on the ice, boarding, illegal equipment, charging (leaping into an opponent or bodychecking him after taking more than two strides), holding, holding the stick (grabbing an opponent's stick), interference, hooking, slashing, kneeing, unsportsmanlike conduct (arguing a penalty call with referee, extremely vulgar or inappropriate verbal comments), "butt-ending" (striking an opponent with the knob of the stick), "spearing" (jabbing an opponent with the blade of the stick), or cross-checking. As of the 2005-06 season, a minor penalty is also assessed for diving, where a player embellishes or simulates an offense. More egregious fouls may be penalized by a four-minute double-minor penalty, particularly those that injure the victimized player. These penalties end either when the time runs out or when the other team scores during the power play. In the case of a goal scored during the first two minutes of a double-minor penalty, the first minor penalty expires, and the penalty clock of the second minor penalty is set down to two minutes upon a score.

Five-minute major penalties are called for especially violent instances of most minor infractions that result in intentional injury to an opponent, or when a minor penalty results in visible injury (such as bleeding), as well as for fighting. Major penalties are always served in full; they do not terminate on a goal scored by the other team. Major penalties assessed for fighting are typically offsetting, meaning neither team is short-handed and the players exit the

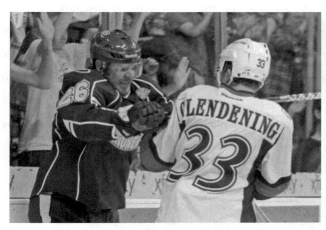 

Figure 9.9 (Left) A skater cross-checking his opponent, checking him with the shaft of his stick with two hands. By The AHL; (Right) A skater hooking his opponent, using his stick to restrain him. By mark6mauno

penalty box upon a stoppage of play following the expiration of their respective penalties. The foul of boarding (defined as "check[ing] an opponent in such a manner that causes the opponent to be thrown violently in the boards") is penalized either by a minor or major penalty at the discretion of the referee, based on the violent state of the hit. A minor or major penalty for boarding is often assessed when a player checks an opponent from behind and into the boards.

Some varieties of penalties do not require the offending team to play a man short. Concurrent five-minute major penalties in the NHL usually result from fighting. In the case of two players being assessed five-minute fighting majors, both the players serve five minutes without their team incurring a loss of player (both teams still have a full complement of players on the ice). This differs with two players from opposing sides getting minor penalties, at the same time or at any intersecting moment, resulting from more common infractions. In this case, both teams will have only four skating players (not counting the goaltender) until one or both penalties expire (if one penalty expires before the other, the opposing team gets a power play for the remainder of the time); this applies regardless of current pending penalties. However, in the NHL, a team always has at least three skaters on the ice. Thus, ten-minute misconduct penalties are served in full by the penalized player, but his team may immediately substitute another player on the ice unless a minor or major penalty is assessed in conjunction with the misconduct (a two-and-ten or five-and-ten). In this case, the team designates another player to serve the minor or major; both players go to the penalty box, but only the designee may not be replaced, and he is released upon the expiration of the two or five minutes, at which point the ten-minute misconduct begins. In addition, game misconducts are assessed for deliberate intent to inflict severe injury on an opponent (at the officials' discretion), or for a major penalty for a stick infraction or repeated major penalties. The offending player is ejected from the game and must immediately leave the playing surface (he does not sit in the penalty box); meanwhile, if an additional minor or major penalty is assessed, a designated player must serve out of that segment of the penalty in the box (similar to the above-mentioned "two-and-ten"). In some rare cases, a player may receive up to nineteen minutes in penalties for one string of plays. This could involve receiving a four-minute double-minor penalty, getting in a fight with an opposing player who retaliates, and then receiving a game misconduct after the fight. In this case, the player is ejected and two teammates must serve the double-minor and major penalties.

Figure 9.10 A skater taking a penalty shot, with a referee in the background. A referee may award a player with a penalty shot if they assess an infraction stopped the player from a clear scoring opportunity. By The Pancake of Heaven

A penalty shot is awarded to a player when the illegal actions of another player stop a clear scoring opportunity, most commonly when the player is on a breakaway. A penalty shot allows the obstructed player to pick up the puck on the center of the redline and attempt to score on the goalie with no other players on the ice, to compensate for the earlier missed scoring opportunity. A penalty shot is also awarded for a defender other than the goaltender covering the puck in the goal crease, a goaltender intentionally displacing his own goal posts during a breakaway to avoid a goal, a defender intentionally displacing his own goal posts when there is less than two minutes to play in regulation time or at any point during overtime, or a player or coach intentionally throwing a stick or other object at the puck or the puck carrier and the throwing action disrupts a shot or pass play.

Officials also stop play for puck movement violations, such as using one's hands to pass the puck in the offensive end, but no players are penalized for these offenses. The sole exceptions are deliberately falling on or gathering the puck to the body, carrying the puck in the hand, and shooting the puck out of play in one's defensive zone (all penalized two minutes for delay of game).

In the NHL, a unique penalty applies to the goalies. The goalies now are forbidden to play the puck in the "corners" of the rink near their own net. This will result in a two-minute penalty against the goalie's team. Only in the area in front of the goal line and immediately behind the net (marked by two red lines on either side of the net) can the goalie play the puck.

An additional rule that has never been a penalty, but was an infraction in the NHL before recent rule changes, is the two-line offside pass. Prior to the 2005–06 NHL season, play was stopped when a pass from inside a team's defending zone crossed the centre line, with a faceoff held in the defending zone of the offending team. Now, the centre line is no longer used in the NHL to determine a two-line pass infraction, a change that the IIHF adopted in 1998. Players are now able to pass the puck to teammates who are more than the blue and center ice red line away.

The NHL has taken steps to speed up the game of hockey and create a game of finesse, by reducing the number of illegal hits, fights, and "clutching and grabbing" that occurred in the past. Rules are now more strictly enforced, resulting in more penalties, which provides more protection to the players and facilitates more goals being scored. The governing body for the United States' amateur hockey has implemented many new rules to reduce the number of stick-on-body occurrences, as well as other detrimental and illegal facets of the game ("zero tolerance").

In men's hockey, but not in women's, a player may use his hip or shoulder to hit another player if the player has the puck or is the last to have touched it. This use of the hip and shoulder is called body checking. Not all physical contact is legal—in particular, hits from behind, hits to the head and most types of forceful stick-on-body contact are illegal.

A delayed penalty call occurs when an offense is committed by the team that does not have possession of the puck. In this circumstance the team with possession of the puck is allowed to complete the play; that is, play continues until a goal is scored, a player on the opposing team gains control of the puck, or the team in possession commits an infraction or penalty of their own. Because the team on which the penalty was called cannot control the puck without stopping play, it is impossible for them to score a goal. In these cases, the team in possession of the puck can pull the goalie for an extra attacker without fear of being scored on. However, it is possible for the controlling team to mishandle the puck into their own net. If a delayed penalty is signaled and the team in possession scores, the penalty is still assessed to the offending player, but not served. In 2012, this rule was changed by the United States' National Collegiate Athletic Association (NCAA) for college-level hockey. In college games, the penalty is still enforced even if the team in possession scores.

Figure 9.11 A referee calls a delayed penalty, which sees play continue until a goal is scored, or the opposing team regains control of the puck. By brapai

4.1.3　Officials

Figure 9.12 An official about to drop the puck during a faceoff. By Wikimedia

A typical game of ice hockey is governed by two to four officials on the ice, charged with enforcing the rules of the game. There are typically two linesmen who are mainly responsible for calling "offside" and "icing" violations, breaking up fights, and conducting faceoffs, and one or two referees, who call goals and all other penalties. Linesmen can, however, report to the referee (s) that a penalty should be assessed against an offending player in some situations. The restrictions on this practice vary depending on the governing rules. On-ice officials are assisted by off-ice officials who act as goal judges, timekeepers, and official scorers.

Figure 9.13 Officials working under a four-official system. Orange armbands are worn by the referees to distinguish them from the lineswomen.
By Bon hein

The most widespread system is the "three-man system", which uses one referee and two linesmen. A less commonly used system is the system of two referees and one linesman. This system is close to the regular three-man system except for a few procedure changes. Beginning with the National Hockey League, a number of leagues have implemented the "four-official system", where an additional referee is added to aid in the calling of penalties normally difficult to assess by one referee. The system has been used in every NHL game since 2001, at the IIHF World Championships, the Olympics, and in many professional and high-level amateur leagues in North America and Europe.

Officials are selected by the league they work for. Amateur hockey leagues use guidelines established by national organizing bodies as a basis for choosing their officiating staff. In North

America, the national organizing bodies Hockey Canada and USA Hockey approve officials according to their experience level as well as their ability to pass rules knowledge and skating ability tests. Hockey Canada has officiating levels I through VI. USA Hockey has officiating levels 1 through 4.

4.2 Hockey rinks

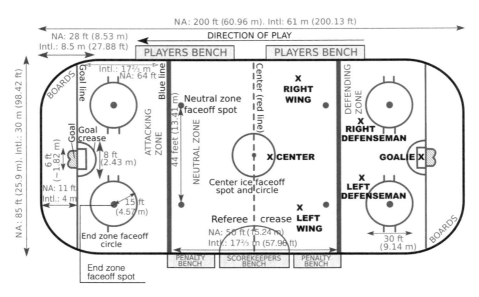

North American—NA; Internation—Intl.

Figure 9.14 Detailed diagram of an ice hockey rink. By Ysangkok

4.2.1 Dimensions

There are two standard sizes for hockey rinks: one used primarily in North America, also known as NHL size, and the other used in European and international competitions, also known as IIHF or Olympic size.

4.2.1.1 North American rinks

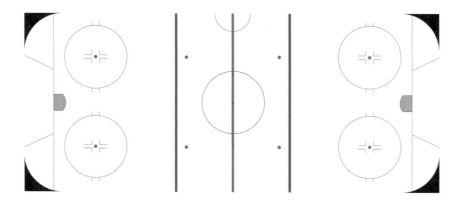

Figure 9.15 NHL Rink. By Юкатан

Most North American rinks follow the National Hockey League (NHL) specifications of 200 by 85 ft (60.96 m × 25.9 m) with a corner radius of 28 ft (8.5 m). Each goal line is 11 ft (3.4 m) from the end boards. NHL blue lines are 75 ft (22.9 m) from the end boards and 50 ft (15.2 m) apart.

4.2.1.2 International rinks

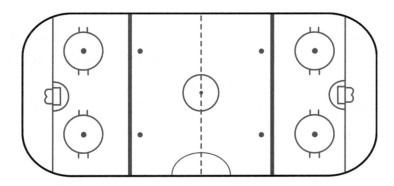

Figure 9.16   Traditional layout of an ice hockey rink surface. By Jecowa

Hockey rinks in the rest of the world follow the International Ice Hockey Federation (IIHF) specifications, which are 60.0 by 30.0 m (196.9 ft × 98.4 ft) with a corner radius of 8.5 m (27.9 ft). The two goal lines are 4.0 m (13.1 ft) from the end boards, and the blue lines are 22.86 m (75.0 ft) from the end boards.

4.2.2 Markings

4.2.2.1 Lines

The center line separates the ice in half crosswise. It is used to judge icing. It is a thick line, and in the NHL it must "contain regular interval markings of a uniform distinctive design, which will readily distinguish it from the two blue lines". It may also be used to judge two-line pass violations in leagues that use such a rule.

There are two thick blue lines that divide the rink into three parts, called zones. These two lines are used to judge if a player is offside. If an attacking player crosses the line into the other team's zone before the puck does, he is said to be offside.

Near each end of the rink, there is a thin red goal line spanning the width of the ice. It is used to judge goals and icing calls.

4.2.2.2 Faceoff spots and circles

There are 9 faceoff spots on a hockey rink. All faceoffs take place at these spots. There are two spots in each team's defensive zone, two at each end of the neutral zone, and one in the center of the rink.

There are faceoff circles around the center ice and end zone faceoff spots. There are hash marks painted on the ice near the end zone faceoff spots. The circles and hash marks show where players may legally position themselves during a faceoff or during in-game play.

Both the center faceoff spot and center faceoff circle are blue. The circle is 30 ft (9 m) in diameter, with an outline 2 in(5.1 cm) thick, and the faceoff spot is a solid blue circle 12 in (30 cm) in diameter. All of the other faceoff spots and circles are colored red.

4.2.2.3　Goal posts and nets

At each end of the ice, there is a goal consisting of a metal goal frame and a cloth net in which each team must place the puck to score. According to NHL and IIHF rules, the entire puck must cross the entire goal line in order to be counted as a goal. Under NHL rules concerning goal size (the same as IIHF rules), the opening of the goal is 72 in (180 cm) wide by 48 in (122 cm) tall, and the footprint of the goal is 40 in (100 cm) deep.

4.2.2.4　Goal crease

The goal area is a special area in front of the goal to allow the goalkeeper to keep the goal undisturbed.

According to the regulations of the IIHF, the specifications of the goal area are as follows: with the center point of the goal as the center of the circle, with a radius of 180 cm (71 in), a red line 5 cm (2 in) wide is drawn in front of the goal line in a semi-circle; the "L" shape, 15 cm(6 in) long and 5 cm (2 in) wide, is drawn at the two front corners inside the semicircle; the "L" is positioned 122 cm (48 in) forward from the goal line where it meets the semicircle. This area is usually blue to make it easier to see.

4.2.2.5　Referee's crease

The referee's crease is a semicircle 10 ft (3.0 m) in radius in front of the scorekeeper's bench. Under USA Hockey Rule 601(d)(5), any player entering or remaining in the referee's crease while the referee is reporting to or consulting with any game official may be assessed a misconduct penalty. The USA Hockey Casebook specifically states that the imposition of such a penalty would be unusual, and the player would typically first be asked to leave the referee's crease before the imposition of the penalty. The NHL has a similar rule, also calling for a misconduct penalty. Traditionally, captains and alternate captains are the only players allowed to approach the referee's crease.

4.2.3　Zones

The blue lines divide the rink into three zones. The central zone is called the neutral zone or simply center ice. The generic term for the outer zones is end zones, but they are more commonly referred to by terms relative to each team. The end zone in which a team is trying to score is called the attacking zone or offensive zone; the end zone in which the team's own goal net is

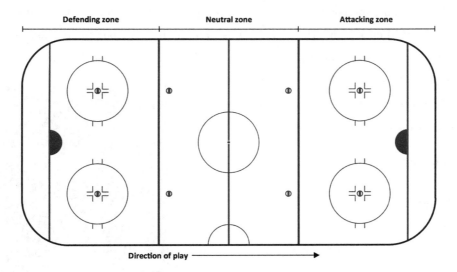

Figure 9.17 Zones of the rink. By Wikimedia

located is called the defending zone or defensive zone.

The blue line is considered part of whichever zone the puck is in. Therefore, if the puck is in the neutral zone, the blue line is part of the neutral zone. The puck must completely cross the blue line to be considered in the end zone. Once the puck is in the end zone, the blue line becomes part of that end zone. The puck must now completely cross the blue line in the other direction to be considered in the neutral zone again.

4.2.4 Boards

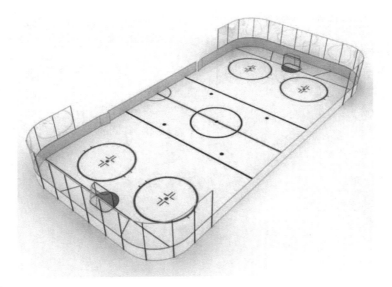

Figure 9.18 Boundary wall. By Wikimedia

In a hockey rink, the boards are the low walls that form the boundaries of the rink. They are 40-48 in (100-120 cm) high. The "side boards" are the boards along the two long sides of the rink. The half boards are the boards halfway between the goal line and the blue line. The sections of the rink located behind each goal are called the "end boards". The boards that are curved (near the ends of the rink) are called the "corner boards".

4.3 Equipment

4.3.1 Protective equipment

Since men's ice hockey is a full-contact sport, so body checks are allowed, and injuries are a common occurrence. Protective equipment is mandatory and is enforced in all competitive situations. This includes a helmet with either a visor or a full face mask, shoulder pads, elbow pads, mouth guards, protective gloves, heavily padded shorts (also known as hockey pants) or a girdle, a athletic cup (also known as a jock, for males; and a jill, for females), shin pads, skates, and (optionally) a neck protector.

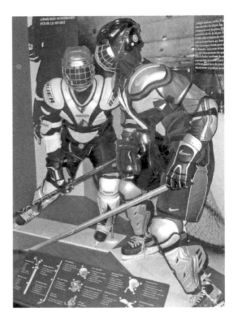

Figure **9.19** *Models with the protective equipment worn by ice hockey skaters, such as a helmet, shoulder pads, elbow pads, gloves, hockey pants, and shin guards. By Wafulz*

4.3.2 Equipment for goaltenders

Figure **9.20** *Equipment for goaltenders. By Fabien Perissinotto*

Goaltenders use different equipment. With hockey pucks approaching them at speeds of up to 100 mph (160.9 km/h) they must wear equipment with more protection. Goaltenders wear specialized goalie skates (these skates are built more for a movement side to side rather than forwards and backwards), a jock large leg pads (there are size restrictions in certain leagues), blocking glove, catching glove, a chest protector, a goalie mask, and a large jersey. Goaltenders' equipment has continually become larger and larger, leading to fewer goals in each game and many official rule changes.

4.3.3 Hockey skates

Hockey skates are optimized for physical acceleration, speed, and maneuverability. This includes rapid starts, stops, turns, and changes in skating direction. In addition, they must be rigid and tough to protect the skater's feet from contact with other skaters, sticks, pucks, boards, and the ice itself. Rigidity also improves the overall maneuverability of the skate. Blade length, thickness (width), curvature (rocker/radius front to back), and radius of hollow (across the blade width) are quite different from speed or figure

Figure 9.21   Ice hockey skates on ice. By Santeri Viinamäki

skates. Hockey players usually adjust these parameters based on their skill level, position, and body type. The blade width of most skates is about 0.125 inch (3.2 mm) thick.

4.3.4 Hockey stick

The hockey stick consists of a long, relatively wide, and slightly curved flat blade, attached to a shaft. The curve itself has a considerable impact on its performance. A deep curve makes it easier to lift the puck, while a shallow curve allows for easier backhand shots. The flex of the stick also impacts the performance. Typically, a less flexible stick is meant for a stronger player since the player is looking for the right balanced flex that allows the stick to flex easily while still having a strong "whip-back" which sends the puck flying at high speeds. It is quite distinct from sticks in other sports games and most suited to hitting and controlling the flat puck. Its unique shape

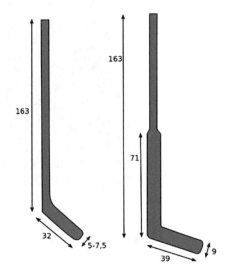

Figure 9.22   Typical hockey sticks, regular and goaltender, measurements in cm. By Ohkami

contributed to the early development of the game.

Section 5　Basic Tactics

5.1　Defensive tactics

Defensive ice hockey tactics vary from more active to more conservative styles of play. One distinction is between man-to-man oriented defensive systems, and zonal oriented defensive systems, though a lot of teams use a combination of the two. Defensive skills involve pass interception, shot blocking, and stick checking (in which an attempt is initiated by the stick of the defensive player to take away the puck or cut off the puck lane). Tactical points of emphasis in ice hockey defensive play are concepts like "managing gaps" (gap control), "boxing out" (not letting the offensive team go on the inside), and "staying on the right side" (of the puck). Another popular concept in ice hockey defensive tactics is that of playing a 200-foot game. A 200-foot game is a definition in ice hockey that describes a player's (usually a forward's) ability to have a strong presence in all three zones of an ice rink, which is standardized at 200 ft long.

Figure 9.23　Youths being taught how to properly deliver a check in ice hockey.
By Wikimedia

An important defensive tactic is checking—attempting to take the puck from an opponent or to remove the opponent from play. Stick checking, sweep checking, and poke checking are legal uses of the stick to obtain possession of the puck. The neutral zone trap is designed to isolate the puck carrier in the neutral zone preventing him from entering the offensive zone. Body checking is using one's shoulder or hip to strike an opponent who has the puck or who is the last to have touched it (the last person to have touched the puck is still legally "in possession" of it, so a penalty is generally called if he is checked more than two seconds after his last touch). Body checking is also a penalty in certain leagues in order to reduce the chance of injury to players. Often the term checking is used to refer to body checking, with its true definition generally only propagated among fans of the game.

5.2 Offensive tactics

Figure 9.24   The 2017 NHL Stanley Cup Playoffs at Verizon Center.
By Keith Allison

Offensive tactics include improving a team's position on the ice by advancing the puck out of one's zone towards the opponent's zone, progressively by gaining lines — first your own blue line, then the red line, and finally the opponent's blue line. NHL rules instated for the 2006 seasons redefined the offside rule to make the two-line pass legal: a player may pass the puck from behind his own blue line, past both that blue line and the center red line, to a player on the near side of the opponent's blue line. Offensive tactics are designed ultimately to score a goal by taking a shot. When a player purposely directs the puck towards the opponent's goal, he or she is said to "shoot" the puck.

A team that is losing by one or two goals in the last few minutes of play will often elect to pull the goalie; that is, to remove the goaltender and replace him or her with an extra attacker on the ice in the hope of gaining enough advantage to score a goal. However, it is an act of desperation, as it sometimes leads to the opposing team extending their lead by scoring a goal in the empty net.

One of the most important strategies for a team is their forecheck. Checking is the act of attacking the opposition in their defensive zone. Checking is an important part of the dump-and-chase strategy (i.e. shooting the puck into the offensive zone and then chasing after it). Each team will use its own unique system but the main ones are: 2-1-2, 1-2-2, and 1-4. The 2-1-2 is the most basic checking system where two forwards will go in deep and pressure the opposition's goalkeepers, the third forward stays high, and the two goalkeepers stay at the blue line. The 1-2-2 is a more conservative system where one forward pressures the puck carrier and the other two forwards cover the opposition's wingers, with the two goalkeepers staying at the blue line. The 1-4 is the most defensive checking system, referred to as the "neutral zone trap", where one forward will apply pressure to the puck carrier around the opposition's blue line and the other 4 players stand basically in a line by their blue line in hopes the opposition will skate into one of them. Another strategy is the left wing lock, which has two forwards pressure the puck and the left wing and the two goalkeepers stay at the blue line.

Figure 9.25 *Shea Weber winding up for a slapshot. By somegeekintn*

Figure 9.26 *A goalie heading to the bench in order to allow for an extra attacker. By Eric Kilby*

There are many other little tactics used in the game of hockey. Cycling moves the puck along the boards in the offensive zone to create a scoring chance by making defenders tired or moving them out of position. Pinching is when a defenseman pressures the opposition's winger in the offensive zone when they are breaking out, attempting to stop their attack and keep the puck in the offensive zone. A saucer pass is a pass used when an opposition's stick or body is in the passing lane. It is the act of raising the puck over the obstruction and having it land on a teammate's stick.

A deke, short for "decoy", is a feint with the body or stick to fool a defender or the goalie. Many modern players, such as Pavel Datsyuk, Sidney Crosby and Patrick Kane, have picked up the skill of "dangling", which is fancier decking and requires more stick-handling skills.

5.3 Fights

Figure 9.27 Fighting in ice hockey is officially prohibited in the rules, although it continues to be an established tradition in the sport in North America.
By ArtBrom

Although fighting is officially prohibited in the rules, it is not an uncommon occurrence at the professional level, and its prevalence has been both a target of criticism and a considerable draw for the sport. At the professional level in North America, fights are unofficial.

Enforcers and other players fight to demoralize the opposing players while exciting their own, as well as settling personal scores. A fight will also break out if one of the team's skilled players gets hit hard or someone receives what the team perceives as a dirty hit. The amateur game penalizes fisticuffs more harshly, as a player who receives a fighting major is also assessed at least a 10-minute misconduct penalty (in NCAA and some Junior leagues) or a game misconduct penalty and suspension (high school and younger, as well as some casual adult leagues). Crowds seem to like fighting in ice hockey and cheer when fighting erupts.

Ice hockey Terminology

Puck /pʌk/: The hard vulcanized rubber disc that players try to shoot past the goalie for a goal.

Rink /rɪŋk/: The playing surface of ice.

Attacking Zone: The zone where the opponent's goal is located.

Center Ice/Neutral Zone: Neutral area between the blue lines.

Defensive Zone: The zone or area closest to a team's goal.

Center Line: The red stripe that extends across the ice, midway between the goals.

Blue Lines: Lines that divide the rink into three zones: attacking, defending and neutral (center) zones.

Goal Crease: The shaded area directly in front of a hockey goal is called the crease. This is where a hockey goalie gets busy stopping goals, and where opposing players are prohibited from interfering with the goalie.

Goal Line: The two boundary lines located at each end of the field.

Board /bɔːrd/: The wooden wall surrounding the rink that keeps the puck in play.

Faceoff Spot: One of nine painted circles on the ice where a faceoff may occur. Two in each attacking/defending zone, two each near the corners of the neutral zone, and one at center ice.

Penalty Box: The area where a player sits to serve the time of a given penalty.

Dead Puck: A puck that flies out of the rink or that a player has caught in his hand.

Goal /goʊl/: One point scored when a puck goes among the goal posts from the stick of an attacking player and crosses the red line between the goal posts.

Empty Net Goal: A goal scored when the opposing goalkeeper is not on the ice.

Breakaway /ˈbrekəˈwe/: When a player controls the ball and moves forward, there is no other defender except the goalkeeper between him and the opposing goal line.

Checking /ˈtʃɛkɪŋ/: Using body contact to prevent an opposing player from gaining an advantageous position on the ice.

Hip Checking: A body checking in which a forceful thrust from the hip is used to knock an opponent against the boards or to the ice.

Back Checking: Checking an opponent while skating backwards towards one's own goal.

Deke /dɪk/: A player handles the puck or their movements in such a manner as to fool the opponent into moving.

Dump and Chase: An offensive means that the ball is directly hit across the opponent's blue line and dropped in the corner so that our players can fight for it. Such a strategy can quickly make our players enter the attacking zone.

Hat Trick: Three goals scored by a player in one game.

Minor Penalty: A two-minute penalty.

Major Penalty: A five-minute penalty.

Review Questions

1. What is the world governing body for ice hockey?
2. Please list three major international ice hockey events.

Chapter 10

Water Polo

Goals

1. Understand the development history of water polo
2. Master the major governing body and major events of water polo matches
3. Be familiar with water polo game rules and professional terminology

Section 1 Introduction

Figure 10.1 *Greece — Hungary WaterPolo match (World Junior Championship* 2004 *Naples , Italy).*
By Massimo Finizio

Water polo is a competitive team sport played in water between two teams of 7 players each. The game consists of four quarters in which the two teams attempt to score goals by throwing the ball into the opposing team's goal. The team with the most goals at the end of the game wins the match. Each team is made up of 6 field players and one goalkeeper. Excluding the goalkeeper, players participate in both offensive and defensive roles. Water polo is typically played in an all-deep pool so that players cannot touch the bottom.

A game of water polo mainly consists of the players swimming to move about the pool, treading water (mainly using the eggbeater kick), passing the ball, and shooting at the goal. Teamwork, tactical thinking and awareness are also highly important aspects of a game of water polo. Water polo is a highly physical and demanding sport and has frequently been cited as one of the most difficult sports to play.

Special equipment for water polo includes a water polo ball, a ball of varying colors which floats on the water; numbered and colored caps; and two goals, which either float in the water or are attached to the side of the pool.

The game is thought to have originated in Scotland in the mid-19th century as a sort of "water rugby". William Wilson is thought to have developed it in 1870s. The game thus developed with the formation of the London Water Polo League and has since expanded, becoming popular in parts of Europe, the United States, Brazil, China, Canada and Australia.

Section 2　Major Governing Body

World Aquatics, formerly known as FINA (French: Fédération Internationale de Natation; English: International Swimming Federation), is the international federation recognized by the International Olympic Committee (IOC) for administering international competitions in water sports. It is one of several international federations which administer a given sport or discipline for the IOC and the international community. It is based in Lausanne, Switzerland.

Founded as FINA in 1908, the federation was officially renamed World Aquatics in January 2023.

World Aquatics currently oversees competition in six aquatics sports: swimming, diving, high diving, artistic swimming, water polo, and open water swimming. World Aquatics also oversees "Masters" competition (for adults) in its disciplines.

FINA was founded on 19 July 1908 in the Manchester Hotel in London, at the end of the 1908 Summer Olympics. Eight national federations were responsible for the formation of FINA: Belgium, Denmark, Finland, France, Germany, Great Britain, Hungary and Sweden.

Section 3 Major Events

3.1 Water Polo at the Summer Olympics

Figure 10.2   Water polo at the 2004 Summer Olympics. By Vchristos

Water polo has been part of the Summer Olympics program since the second Games, in 1900. The women's water polo tournament was introduced for the 2000 Summer Olympics. Hungary has been the most successful country in men's tournaments, while the United States is the only team to win multiple times at the women's tournament since its introduction. Italy is the first and only country to win both the men's and women's water polo tournaments.

3.2 Water polo at the World Aquatics Championships

Water polo at the World Aquatics Championships is an international water polo tournament held every two years as part of the FINA World Aquatics Championships. The reigning champions of 2023 Fukuoka World Aquatics Championships are Hungary in men's and the Netherlands in women's competition.

3.3 FINA Men's Water Polo World Cup

The **FINA Men's Water Polo World Cup** is an international water polo tournament, organized by FINA and featuring eight men's national teams. It was established in 1979, initially taking place in odd years. Since 2002 it has been held every four years, in the even year between the Olympics.

3.4 FINA Water Polo World League

The **FINA Water Polo World League** is an international water polo league organized by FINA, which plays annually, typically from winter through to June. League play features continental tournaments for men and women, from which the top teams emerge to play in the championship tournament (the "Super Final") where the league champion team is crowned. Men's league play began in 2002, to capitalize on the increased worldwide popularity of water polo created by the 2000 Olympic Games, especially in Europe, North America and Australia. The women's league was added in 2004, based on growing interest in women's play. In October 2022, FINA announced that the tournament would be replaced with the FINA Water Polo World Cup and FINA Women's Water Polo World Cup from 2023 on.

3.5 European Water Polo Championship

The **European Water Polo Championship** is a sports competition for national water polo teams, currently held biannually and organized by the Ligue Européenne de Natation (LEN), the governing European aquatics federation. There are both men's and women's competitions.

The first European Water Polo Championship was held in 1926 in Budapest, Hungary, with just men's competition. The women for the first time competed in 1985 (Oslo, Norway) for the European title. The water polo tournament was part of the European Aquatics Championships up to and including 1997, and from 1999 the event was separated and got its own independent tournament.

3.6 LEN Champions League LEN

The **LEN Champions League** is the top-tier European professional water polo club competition with teams from up to 18 different countries.

It is organized by the Ligue Européenne de Natation (English: European Swimming League). The competition started in 1963 as the European Cup. A change of name and format occurred in 1996, with the competition being renamed Champions League and the final four system being established as the format of choice, for the first time during the 1996-97 LEN Champions League. From 2003 to 2011 the competition was named LEN Euro League (with the change of name being simply a re-branding) and from 2011 on LEN Champions League, its current name.

LEN Champions League is the most popular water polo league in the European continent. It has been won by 24 different clubs, 10 of which have won the title more than once. The most successful club in the competition is Pro Recco, which has won 11 titles by 2023.

Section 4 Rules

4.1 Number of players

Senior games consist of 7 players from each team (6 field players and a goalkeeper) that are allowed in the playing area of the pool during the game. FINA reduced the number of players in U20 (and younger) competitions that they sanction to 6 (5 field players and a goalkeeper) in 2014. If a player commits an exclusion (major) foul, then that team will play with one fewer player until the player is allowed to re-enter (typically 20 seconds). If a player commits a particularly violent act, such as striking a player, then the referee may signal a brutality foul, in which case that team is required to play with one fewer player in the water for 4 minutes, besides the culprit being ejected, i. e. they must leave the pool area and not return. Plus, the culprit may not be allowed to compete in a given number of future games depending on the governing body.

Players may be substituted in and out after goals, during timeouts, between quarters, and after injuries. During gameplay, players enter and exit in the corner of the pool (called the re-entry area), or in front of their goals. When play is stopped, they may enter or exit anywhere.

If at any time during playing a team has more players in the pool than they are allowed, a penalty is given to the opposing team. If a team starts with less than six outfield players, the referee may give a yellow card to the coach for allowing it to happen and give a major foul to the opposition on 6 m, if the 6th player then joins the game illegally.

A variation is Beach Water Polo, which has four players including the goalkeeper, a smaller field, and some other differing rules.

4.2 Caps

The two opposing teams must wear caps, which contrast:

with both (or either) goalkeepers' cap color,
with the other team's cap color, and
with the ball color.

In practice, one team usually wears dark caps and

Figure 10.3 *The field player's cap.*
By Wikimedia

the other white (usually white for the home team, and dark for the away team for FINA). Teams may choose to wear caps with different colors (e. g. their team colors). For instance, Australia's women's water polo team wears green caps.

For NFHS(National Federation of State High School Associations), CWPA(Collegiate Water Polo Association), and NCAA rules (United States) the home team is dark and the away team is white.

The water polo cap is used to protect the players' heads and ears, and the numbers on them (1-13) make them identifiable from afar, especially by the referee(s). Both goalies wear red or red-striped caps. The first-choice goalkeeper is usually marked "1" with the reserve being marked "13" (under FINA rules) or "1A" (under NCAA and NFHS rules).

4.3 Duration of the game

The game is divided into four periods; the length depends on the level of play. There is no overtime nor ties in international water polo, and games proceed to a shootout if a victor is required. At the collegiate level there are two straight 3-minute periods; and if still tied, multiple 3-minute golden goal overtime periods thereafter. Lower levels of play have different overtime rules depending on the organization. A 2-minute break follows every period (including overtime/shootout), but there's also a 5-minute halftime intermission.

Table 10.1 The Length of Each Period on Different Levels of Play

Level of play	Team level	Time each period/min	Authority
Olympics	National		FINA
FINA Water Polo World League	National	8	FINA
European Leagues	Club		LEN
Senior club play	Club	9	FINA
US College	Varsity	8	CWPA
US College	Club	7	CWPA
US High School	Varsity		NFHS
US High School	Junior Varsity	6	NFHS
US High School	Freshman/Sophomore	5~6	NFHS
USA Water Polo	14 and unders	5~7	USAWPR

4.4 Game and shot clock

The game clock is stopped when the ball is not in play (between a foul being committed and the free throw being taken, and between a goal being scored and the restart). As a result, the average quarter lasts around 12 minutes of real time. A team may not have possession of the ball for longer than 30 seconds without shooting for the goal unless an opponent commits an ejection foul. After 30 seconds, possession passes to the other team, and the shot clock is reset. The clock is also reset to 30 seconds after a goal or neutral throw, or penalty in which possession is exchanged.

However, if a team shoots the ball within the allotted time, and regains control of the ball (e.g. after a rebound from the goal post), the shot clock is reset to 20 seconds. It is also reset to 20 seconds after a major (exclusion) foul, corner throw, or rebound from a penalty throw if the attacking team retains possession.

The presence of a shot clock leads one of the key concepts in water polo: you do not need the ball. It will (eventually) come back to you, e.g. after a goal, a failed goal attempt, or at the end of the shot-clock period. So, it is not necessary to try to take the ball off your opponent, in an over-aggressive manner; as this risks a major foul, which gives your opponent another 20 seconds. You lose a player and they gain more time. So the art of defense is to "press" (i.e. occupation, irritateing, blocking an easy pass etc.) your opponent (without a major foul), slow down the play and wait for the ball.

4.5 Pool dimensions

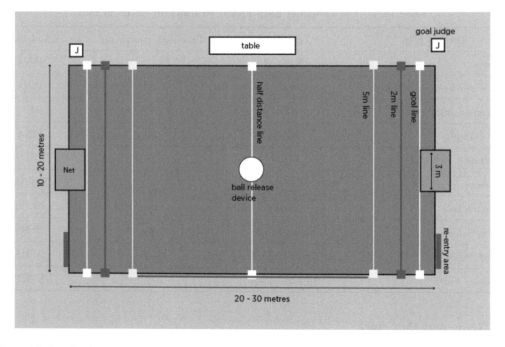

Figure 10.4 *The layout of a water polo pool showing the* **2m** *and* **5m** *markings (red and yellow), the halfway line (marked in white), a goal at either end and the length and width of the pool. By Jkwchui*

Dimensions of the water polo are not fixed and can vary between 20 m×10 m and 30 m × 20 m (FINA approved matches require a 30 m×20 m pool for men, and a 25 m×20 m pool for women), therefore short course pools can be used. The minimum water depth must be at least 1.8 m (6 ft), but this is often not the case due to the nature of the pool (as many have shallow ends). The goals are 3 m wide and 90 cm high.

The middle of the pool is designated by a white line. Before 2005, the pool was divided by 7- and 4-meter lines (distance out from the goal line). This has been merged into one 5-meter line since the 2005–06 season, and a "6-meter" line since the 2019–2020 season. The 6-meter line is marked by a yellow line. It was brought in by FINA in 2019, and related to the method of taking a free throw after an ordinary or exclusion foul. The "5 m" line is where penalties are shot and it is designated by a red line. The 2-meter line is designated with a red line, and no player of the attacking team can receive a ball inside this zone. Those have been in use since the 2020 Summer Olympics in 2021.

Water polo balls are generally yellow and of varying size and weight for juniors, women and men.

In a game, if the ball goes out of the playing area (or hits the edge of the pool and then falls back into the water), a free throw is given to the team that did not touch the ball last before it went out of play.

Also, the referee should not pick up the ball when it is at the side of the pool during a break in play, and hand it to the attacking team — as this can lead to an advantage to that team.

4.6 Beginning of play

In an all-deep water pool, the home team starts on the left side (looking across the pool from the scoring table). The teams change ends at halftime. In a pool with a shallow end, there is a toss of a coin to decide which team starts on which side. The teams change ends at the end of each quarter. At the start of each period and after every score, teams line up on their own goal line. The most common formation is for three players to go to each side of the goal, while the goalkeeper stays in the goal. If the ball is to be thrown into the center of the pool, the sprinter will often start in the goal, while the goalkeeper starts either in the goal as well, or to one side of the goal.

At the referee's whistle, both teams swim to the midpoint of the field (known as the "sprint" or the "swim-off") as the referee drops the ball onto the

Figure **10.5** *Swimoff or sprint to begin play. By Wpktsfs.*

water. Depending on the rules being played, this is either on the referee's side of the pool or in the center. In international competitions, the ball is normally placed in the middle of the pool and is supported with a floating ring. The first team to recover the ball becomes the attacker until a goal is scored or the defenders recover the ball.

Exceptionally, a foul may be given before either team reaches the ball. This usually occurs when a player uses the side to help themselves gain a speed advantage (i. e. by pulling on the side to move faster). In such scenarios, the non-offending team receives a free throw from the halfway line.

The swim-off occurs only at the start of periods and after scores. Thus it will either occur 2, 4 or 6 times in a match, depending on whether the match is in halves, quarters, or quarters and extends to extra time.

The referee (s) should check the players' nails before the start of play (to prevent scratching). Goggles and jewelry are not normally allowed.

4.7 Moving the ball

Figure 10.6 *Attacker* (7) *advancing the ball by dribbling. By Ryanjo*

Players can move the ball by throwing it to a teammate or swimming with the ball in front of them. Players are not allowed to push the ball underwater in order to keep it from an opponent, or push or hold an opposing player unless that player is holding the ball. If a player does push the ball underwater when it is in their possession, this is called "ball under" and will result in a "turnover" which means the offending player has to hand the ball over to the other team. It does not matter if the player holding the ball underwater is forced to do so by an opponent. The foul is still given against them.

Water polo is an intensely aggressive sport, so fouls are very common and result in a free throw during which the player cannot shoot at the goal unless outside the 6-meter line. If a foul is called outside the 6-meter line, the player may either shoot (in one movement, i. e. without faking), pass or continue swimming with the ball.

4.8 Scoring

A goal is scored if the ball completely passes between the goalposts and is underneath the crossbar. If a shot bounces off a goal post back into the field of play, and the ball is regained by the attacking team, the shot clock is reset (to 20 seconds), and play continues. If the shot goes outside the goal and touches the rope, or onto the deck (outside the field of play), a goal throw (to the defense) occurs, and the shot clock is reset (to 30 seconds). This has to be taken without delay (time limit not specified in rules). If the goalie, however, is the last to touch the ball before it goes out of play behind the goal line, or if a defender purposely sends the ball out, then the offense receives the ball for a "corner throw" on the 2-meter line. From a corner, which also has to be taken without delay (again a time limit not specified in the rules), the player can swim with the ball, shoot at a goal or pass. Goals are also scored if shots are taken before shot clock hits 0 and/or a game clock hits 00.0, provided the ball is free from the player's hands.

When the goalie blocks a shot, the defense may gain control of the ball, and make a long pass to a teammate who stayed on his offensive end of the pool when the rest of his team was defending. This is called cherry-picking or seagulling. This can occur as there is no offside rule in water polo, unlike football (soccer). So a defending player can "hang around" the opposition's goal.

The "own goal" concept also does not exist in water polo like football (soccer). But they do occur (rarely) and then the goal is awarded to the attacking player that last touched the ball.

4.9 Restart after a goal

After a goal is scored, the teams may line up anywhere within their own half of the pool. In practice, this is usually near the center of the pool. Play resumes when the referee signals for play to restart and the team not scoring the goal puts the ball into play by passing it backwards to a teammate.

4.10 Timeouts

Each team may call a variable (according to the rules being used) number of one 1-minute timeouts (USA/FINA) or 2-minute timeouts (NCAA/NFHS); and one timeout if the game goes into overtime/shoot-out. During gameplay, only the team in possession of the ball may call a timeout. Timeouts don't carry over to overtime/shoot-out. The penalty for calling a timeout during play without possession of the ball is a penalty foul going against the team. FINA Water polo rules allow for two timeouts for each team in a match. They can be taken in the same period.

Three short whistles are blown by the referee at 45 seconds (after a prompt from the scorers on the scoring table) during the timeout, and he/she waves the attacking players forward into the opponents' half. At 60 seconds, the ball is thrown to the goalkeeper (usually) on the halfway line, who can play the ball when another (single) long whistle is blown.

4.11 Substitutions

A substitute can enter the pool from any place during the intervals between quarters, after a goal has been scored, or during a timeout, and replace an injured player, but not after a penalty. If a substitution is made during play, the head of the player leaving should be visible in the re-entry area, before the player entering the pool can go under the rope. Neither can lift the rope.

4.12 Control over conduct

Water Polo referees utilize red and yellow cards when handling a bench conduct. A verbal warning may be issued depending on the severity of the infraction.

A yellow card may be issued at any point in the game and can be issued via a "walking yellow" in which the referee pulls a yellow card out without stopping live play. Following the issuance of a "walking yellow", at the next stoppage of play, the referee may pull the ball out to inform the table and a partner referee of the issuance of that card.

Figure **10.7** *A yellow card and a red card. By Wikimedia*

A red card can be issued to any team personnel (head and assistant coaches, team managers, players, and other officials with the team) or supporters. Following the issuance of a red card, the individual must leave the pool area, and have no further contact with the game (by any method). Red cards carry at least one-game suspension for the offender with a report being filed to the appropriate governing authority. A red card is also given to players acquiring their second yellow card.

4.13 Fouls

4.13.1 Ordinary fouls

Ordinary fouls occur when a player impedes or otherwise prevents the free movement of an opponent who is not holding the ball, but has it in or near their possession. The most common is when a player reaches over the shoulder of an opponent in order to knock the ball away while in the process hindering the opponent. Offensive players may be called for a foul by pushing off a

Figure **10.8** *Corner throw from the 2-meter line.*
By Wikimedia

defender to provide space for a pass or shot.

The referee indicates the foul with one short whistle blow and points one hand in the direction of the attacking team (standing roughly in line with the position of the foul), who retain possession. The attacker must make a free pass without undue delay (time period not specified in the rules) to another offensive player. If the foul has been committed outside the 6 m line, the offensive player can attempt a direct shot on goal, but the shot must be taken immediately and in one continuous motion (i.e. with no faking). If the offensive player fakes a shot and then shoots the ball, it is a turnover.

The defender (usually the one that has conceded the foul) has to back off (a distance not specified in the rules, but usually taken to be 1.5–2 m) to allow the free throw to be taken. In other words, they cannot simply hold their ground to block the offensive player. The defender, at a reasonable distance, can raise his arm to compete at the free throw. The throw (and all throws after infringements) has to be taken without delay. The maximum time period for this (also not stated in the rules) is usually taken to be about 3 seconds.

If the same defender repeatedly makes minor fouls, referees will exclude that player for 30 seconds. To avoid an ejection, the "hole" (center) defender may foul twice, and then have a wing defender switch with him so that the defense can continue to foul the "hole man" (center forward) without provoking an exclusion foul. The rule was altered to allow repeated fouls without exclusions, but is often still enforced by referees.

There are quite a few other infringements that lead to an ordinary foul, including standing if there is a shallow end, delaying taking a throw (free, goal or corner), taking a penalty throw incorrectly, touching the ball with two hands (if not the goalkeeper), simulating being fouled, time-wasting, and being within 2 m of the goal.

4.13.2 Major fouls

Figure 10.9 Defender (2) sinking attacker with the ball.
By Wikimedia

Major fouls (exclusion and penalty fouls) are committed when the defensive player "holds (especially with two hands), sinks or pulls back" (a key phrase in water polo) the offensive player. This includes swimming on the other player's legs or back, stopping the other player from swimming, or otherwise preventing the offensive player from preserving his advantage.

A referee signals a major foul by two short whistle bursts, then a long burst, and indicates that the player must leave the field of play and move to the penalty area for 20 seconds. The referee will first point to the player who commits the foul and will blow the whistle, then they will point to the ejection corner and blow the whistle again. The player must move to their re-entry area without impacting the natural gameplay and in reasonable time (or a penalty is given). A player that has been ejected thrice must sit out the rest of the match.

There are several other infringements that can lead to an exclusion foul:
- Sitting on the steps or side of the pool.
- Splashing an opponent in the face.
- Interfering with a free, goal or corner throw; this includes the defender failing to release the ball, or throwing or moving it away, or attempting to play the ball before it has left the hand of the thrower.

- Blocking a pass or shot with two hands inside 6 m; if the referee thinks that this action would have prevented a goal, a penalty can be awarded.
- After the change of possession, for a defending player to commit any foul anywhere in the attacking team's half of the pool; this is to prevent a foul before the attacker (or ball) has passed the halfway line.
- Kicking or striking an opponent (or showing an intent to); if this occurs within 6 m, a penalty throw is also awarded. The referee can decide to punish a kick or strike in this way, or with a misconduct or brutality foul (see later) depending on intent, and effect.
- For an excluded player to interfere with play, or not leave immediately. Another exclusion (personal) foul is recorded on that player, and a penalty is awarded.
- For an excluded player to re-enter (or substitute to enter) improperly, e.g., without a signal from the referee (or scoring table), or not from the re-entry area, or by affecting the alignment of the goal (e.g. by lifting the rope). They are excluded (again) but only one personal foul is recorded and a penalty is awarded (if the player's team is not in possession of the ball).
- For the defending goalkeeper to fail to take up the correct position at the taking of a penalty throw, having been ordered once to do so by the referee.

A brutality foul is called when a player kicks or strikes an opponent or official with malicious intent. For a brutality to be called, the strike must make contact with the player and must be with intent to injure. Otherwise, the player is punished with a misconduct foul, with substitution allowed after 20 seconds or a change of possession. The player who is charged with a brutality is red-carded; that team plays shorthanded for 4 minutes, and is forced to play with one fewer player than the other team for that duration. In addition to the exclusion, a penalty shot is also awarded to the opposing team if the foul occurs during actual play. Previously, the team who was charged with a brutality would be required to play the remainder of the game with one fewer player. All brutalities have to be reported by officials and further action may be taken by the relevant governing body. The action could include more games added to the one-game suspension.

A misconduct foul is an unsportsmanlike act; misconduct fouls include unacceptable language, violence or persistent fouls, taking part in the game after being excluded, or showing disrespect. The player is red-carded with substitution after 20 seconds has elapsed. There are two kinds of misconduct fouls that a player can incur. If the incident does not involve physical (or attempted) contact, the referee can impose a misconduct charge.

4.14 Five-meter penalty

If a defender commits a major foul within the 6-meter area that prevents a likely goal, the

Figure 10.10 Five-meter penalty shooting. By Иван Ђурчић

attacking team is awarded a penalty throw or shot. This is usually when the attacking player is impeded in taking a shot at goal, from behind or the side. According to the FINA rule changes in 2019, the referee no longer has any discretion in awarding a penalty (e.g., taking into account whether a goal was likely or not).

An attacking player lines up on the 5-meter line in front of the opposing goal. No other player may be in front of him or within 2 meters of his position. The defending goalkeeper must be between the goalposts. The referee signals with a whistle and by lowering his arm, and the player taking the penalty shot must immediately throw the ball with an uninterrupted motion toward the goal (i.e. without pumping or faking). The shooter's body can not at any time cross the 5-meter line until after the ball is released. If the shooter carries his body over the line and shoots, the result is a turn over. If the shot does not score and the ball stays in play, then play continues. Penalty shots are often successful, with 63.7% of shots being scored from them.

There are quite a few other infringements that can lead to a penalty: a player that has been excluded interfering with the game as they exit the pool, an excluded player entering the pool without a signal from the referee (or scoring table), a player or substitute exiting or entering the pool incorrectly (during game time, e.g., lifting the rope), a brutality foul, a coach or captain requesting a timeout when not in possession of the ball, and a coach delaying the return of the ball.

4.15 Overtime

4.15.1 FINA rules

If the score is tied at the end of regulation play, a penalty shootout will determine the winner. Five players and a goalkeeper are chosen by the coaches of each team. A player cannot be chosen if he/she is ineligible to play from receiving (i.e. 3 personal fouls or red carded).

Players shoot from the 5-meter line alternately at either end of the pool in turn until all five have taken a shot. If the score is still tied, the same players shoot alternately until one team misses and the other scores.

4.15.2 NCAA rules

Differing from FINA rules which require shootouts, NCAA rules require teams to play two three-minute overtime periods, and if still tied, play additional three-minute sudden-death periods until a team scores a goal and wins the game.

4.16 Equipment

4.16.1 Ball

Figure **10.11** *Water polo balls: old (left) and new designs (right).* ***By Antiflu***

A water polo ball is constructed of waterproof material to allow it to float on the water. The cover is textured to give players additional grip. The size of the ball is different for men's, women's and junior games.

4.16.2 Goals

Each side has a goal in the water polo game. These can either be put on the side of the pool, or in the pool using floaters.

4.16.3 Mouthguard

A mouthguard is not mandatory in most tournaments but is recommended.

4.16.4 Swimwear

Male water polo players wear either swim briefs or jammers (thigh-length trunks). Female players must wear a one-piece swimsuit. Suit-grabbing fouls are common, so players often wear tight-fitting suits, and may layer on several suits at a time for additional security. Many swimwear labels also sell specialized water polo suits that feature reinforced stitching and tougher fabric. Female water polo suits are generally one-piece outfits which do not have open backs, but zip securely up the back so as to not have straps that can be easily grabbed.

Figure **10.12** *Male swimwear (left) and Female swimwear (right). By Hy Crutchett*

4.17 Positions

There are seven players in the water from each team at one time. There are six players that play out and one goalkeeper. Unlike most common team sports, there is little positional play; field players will often fill several positions throughout the game as situations demand. These positions usually consist of a center forward, a center back, two wing players and two drivers. Players who are skilled in all positions of offense or defense are called utility players. Utility players tend to come off the bench, though this is not absolute. Certain body types are more suited for particular positions, and left-handed players are especially coveted on the right-hand side of the field, allowing teams to launch two-sided attacks.

4.17.1 Offense

The offensive positions include one center forward (also called "2-meter man", located on or near the 2-meter line, roughly in the center of the goal), two wings (located on or near the 2-meter line, just outside of the goal posts, respectively), two drivers (also called "flats", located on or near the 5-meter line, roughly at the goal posts), and one "point" (usually just behind the 5-meter line, roughly in the center of the goal), positioned farthest from the goal. The wings, drivers and point are often called the perimeter players; while the hole set directs play. There is a typical numbering system for these positions in U.S. NCAA men's division one polo. Beginning with the offensive wing to the opposing goalie's right side is called one. The flat in a counterclockwise from one is called two. Moving along in the same direction the point player is three, the next flat is four, the final wing is five, and the hole set is six. Additionally, the position in which a player is can give advantages based on a player's handedness, to improve a shooting or passing angle (for example, the right wing is often left-handed).

The center sets up in front of the opposing team's goalie and scores the most individually (especially during lower-level play where flats do not have the required strength to effectively shoot from outside or to penetrate and then pass to teammates like the point guard in basketball, or center midfield player in soccer). The center's position nearest to the goal allows explosive shots from close range.

4.17.2 Defense

Defensive positions are often the same, but just switched from offense to defense. For example, the center forward or hole set, who directs the attack on offense, on defense is known as "hole D" (also known as set guard, hole guard, hole check, pit defense or two-meter defense), and guards the opposing team's center forward (also called the hole). Defense can be played man-to-man or in zones, such as a 2-4 (four defenders along the goal line). It can also be played as a combination of the two in what is known as an "M drop" defense, in which the point defender moves away ("sloughs off") his man into a zone in order to better defend the center position. In this defense, the two-wing defenders split the area furthest from the goal, allowing them a clearer lane for the counter-attack if their team recovers the ball.

4.17.3 Goalkeeper

Figure 10.13 Goalkeeper blocking a shot. By Juan Fernández

The goalkeeper has the main role of blocking shots against the goal as well as guiding and informing their defense of imposing threats and gaps in the defense. The goalkeeper usually begins the offensive play by passing the ball across the pool to an attacker. It is not unusual for a goalkeeper to make an assisting pass to a goal on a breakaway.

The goalkeeper is given several privileges above those of the other players, but only within the 5-meter area in front of their own goal:
- The ability to punch the ball with a clenched fist.
- The ability to touch the ball with two hands.

In general, a foul that would cause an ejection of a field player might bring on a 5 m shot on the goalkeeper. Also, if a goalkeeper pushes the ball underwater, the action will not be punished with a turnover like with field players, but with a penalty shot.

Section 5 Basic Strategies

5.1 Offense strategy

5.1.1 Player positioning

The most basic positional setup is known as a "3-3", so called because there are two lines in front of the opponent's goal. Another setup, used more by professional teams, is known as an "arc", "umbrella", or "mushroom"; perimeter players form the shape of an arc around the goal, with the hole set as the handle or stalk. Yet another option for the offensive set is called a 4-2 or double hole; there are two center forward offensive players in front of the goal. Double hole is most often used in "man-up" situations, or when the defense has only one skilled "hole D", or to draw in a defender and then pass out to a perimeter player for a shot ("kick out").

5.1.2 Advancing the ball

When the offense takes possession of the ball, the strategy is to advance the ball down the field of play and to score a goal. Players can move the ball by throwing it to a teammate or swimming with the ball in front of them (dribbling). If an attacker uses his/her arm to push away a defending player and free up space for a pass or shot, the referee will rule a turnover and the defence will take possession of the ball. If an attacker advances inside the 2-meter line without the ball or before the ball is inside the 2-meter area, they are ruled offside and the ball is turned over to the defense. This is often overlooked if the attacker is well to the side of the pool or when the ball is at the other side of the pool.

5.1.3 Setting the ball

The key to the offense is to accurately pass (or "set") the ball into the center forward or hole set, positioned directly in front of the goal ("the hole"). Any field player may throw the hole set a "wet pass". A wet pass is one that hits the water just outside the hole set's reach. A dry pass may also be used. This is where the hole set receives the ball directly in his hand and then attempts a shot at the cage. This pass is much more difficult because if the pass is not properly caught, the officials will be likely to call an offensive foul resulting in a change of ball possession. The hole set attempts to take possession of the ball (after a wet pass), to shoot at the goal, or to draw a foul from his defender. A minor foul is called if his defender (called the "hole D") attempts to impede movement before the hole set has possession. The referee indicates the foul with one short whistle blow and points one hand to the spot of the foul and the other hand in the direction of the attack of the team to whom the free throw has been awarded. The hole set then has a "reasonable amount of time" (typically about three seconds; there is no FINA rule on this issue) to re-commence play by making a free pass to one of the other players. The defensive team cannot hinder the hole set until the free throw has been taken, but the hole set cannot shoot a goal once the foul has been awarded until the ball has been played by at least one other player. If the hole set attempts a goal without the free throw, the goal is not counted and the defense takes possession of the ball, unless the shot is made outside the 5-meter line. As soon as the hole set has a free pass, the other attacking players attempt to swim (or drive) away from their defenders towards the goal. The players at the flat position will attempt to set a screen (also known as a pick) for the driver. If a driver gets free from a defender, the player calls for the pass from the hole set and attempts a shot at the goal.

5.1.4 Man-up (6 on 5)

Figure 10.14 A classic 4-2 man-up situation. By Prisonblues

If a defender interferes with a free throw, holds or sinks an attacker who is not in possession or splashes water into the face of an opponent, the defensive player is excluded from the game for

20 seconds, known as a "kick out" or an ejection. The attacking team typically positions 4 players on the 2-meter line, and 2 players on 5-meter line (4-2), passing the ball around until an open player attempts a shot. Other formations include a 3-3 (two lines of three attackers each) or arc (attackers make an arc in front of the goal and one offensive player sits in the "hole" or "pit" in front of the goal). The 5 defending players try to pressure the attackers, block shots and prevent a goal from being scored for the 20 seconds while they are a player down. The other defenders can only block the ball with one hand to help the goalkeeper. The defensive player is allowed to return immediately if the offense scores, or if the defense recovers the ball before the 20 seconds expires.

5.2　Defense strategy

Figure 10.15　*Water polo defense*: *A defender may only hold, block or pull an opponent who is touching or holding the ball. By LauraHale*

On defense, the players work to regain possession of the ball and to prevent a goal in their own net. The defense attempts to knock away or steal the ball from the offense or to commit a foul in order to stop an offensive player from taking a goal shot. The defender attempts to stay between the attacker and the goal, a position known as inside water.

5.2.1　Goalkeeper's defense strategy

Even with good backup from the rest of the defenders, stopping attacks can prove very difficult if the goalkeeper remains in the middle of the goal. The most defensible position is along a semicircular line connecting the goal posts and extending out in the center. Depending on the ball carrier's location, the goalkeeper is positioned along that semicircle roughly a meter out of the goal to reduce the attacker's shooting angle. The goalkeeper stops using their hands to tread water when the opponent enters at about the 7-meter mark and starts to lift their upper body using the eggbeater technique to prepare to block the shot. Finally, the goalkeeper tries to block the ball down, which is often hard for the longer reaches, but prevents an offensive rebound and second shot. As is the case with other defensive players, a goalkeeper who aggressively fouls an attacker in position to score can be charged with a penalty shot for the other team. The goalkeeper can also be ejected for twenty seconds if a major foul is committed. Also, inside the 5-meter mark, the goalie can swing at the ball with a closed fist without being penalized.

5.2.2 Advantage rule

If an offensive player, such as the center forward, has possession of the ball in front of the goal, the defensive player tries to steal the ball or to keep the center forward from shooting or passing. If the defender cannot achieve these aims, he/she may commit a foul intentionally. The hole set then is given a free throw but must pass off the ball to another offensive player, rather than making a direct shot at the goal. Defensive perimeter players may also intentionally cause a minor foul and then move toward the goal, away from their attacker, who must take a free throw. This technique, called sloughing, allows the defense an opportunity to double-team the hole set and possibly steal the inbound pass. The referee may refrain from declaring a foul, if in his judgment this would give an advantage to the offender's team. This is known as the Advantage Rule.

Water Polo Terminology

Field Player: A player other than the goalkeeper.

Driver /ˈdraɪvə/: A perimeter player in the 3-3 offense, positioned on either side of the point or center forward, who attempts to swim toward the goal to escape their defender, receive the ball and score.

Perimeter Player: The 5 offensive positions, other than the center forward, i.e. wings, drivers and point. The perimeter players interchange their positions several times during a single offensive play.

Period /ˈpɪriəd/: The game is divided into four periods; the length depends on the level of play.

2-Meter Line: The line at each end of the pool crossing 2 meters in front of the goal, designated by a red mark on the edge of the pool. The edge of the playing area from the 2-meter mark to the goal line is a red line.

Re-entry Area: Area at each end of the pool near each team bench, designated by a red line, where players may enter and exit the playing area for substitution or exclusion penalties.

Dead Time: The time between the whistle after a foul, which stops the clock, and the resetting of the clock after the ball returns to play.

Passing Lane: The path between the player with the ball and his/her teammate to whom he/she intends to pass.

Neutral Throw: Similar to a jump ball in basketball; the referee drops the ball between players from each team.

Advantage Rule: Permiting the referee to refrain from calling a foul if, in his/her opinion, the foul would be an advantage to the offending team.

Free Throw: The method of putting the ball in play after the team is awarded the ball by the referee. It must be taken from the spot where the infraction occurred (or anywhere behind that point) unless otherwise specified. The free throw can be taken by any player, and they may pass or dribble the ball. They cannot shoot on net unless the foul occurred outside the 5-meter zone.

Eggbeater Kick: A kicking stroke used for stability and support in treading water, similar to an alternating breaststroke kick.

Dribbling /ˈdrɪblɪŋ/: Swimming while controlling the ball in front of the head.

Dry Pass: A pass made where the ball is caught without touching the water.

Wet Pass: A deliberate pass into the water, just out of reach of the intended teammate and his/her defender. The receiving player can then lunge towards the ball and out of the water to make a shot or pass.

Backhand Pass: A pass or shot in which the ball carrier flips the ball directly behind him/her.

Wet Shot: A shot that is attempted while the ball is touching the water, usually a quick, wrist shot.

Lob Shot: A high-arcing shot that is intended to fall above the goalie's hands and below the crossbar.

Corner Throw: Awarded when the goalkeeper deflects the ball out of bounds, or a defensive player intentionally sends the ball over the back line.

Bunny Shot: A goal that's scored by a hard shot aimed at, or close to, the goalie's head.

Cherry Picking: A player stays on their offensive end of the pool when the rest of their team is defending, waiting for a turnover, often resulting in a long pass and uncontested goal.

Ball under: A technical foul that occurs when a player holds the ball underwater while being held or tackled by an opponent.

Penalty Shot: A free shot taken by an offensive player upon the referee's whistle from the 5-meter line. Awarded for a foul occurred inside the 5-meter line preventing a goal.

Press /pres/: The most commonly used defensive strategy, a man-to-man defense.

Counter Attack: An offensive strategy that tries to give the offense an advantage by quickly moving the ball down the pool after a turnover.

Double Post: An offensive strategy that uses 2 attackers on the 2-meter line in front of the opponent's goal, with one positioned in front of each goal post.

Drop /drɑːp/: Defenders swim back to the center of the pool to block passes and shots by advancing attackers, while a defender presses the ball carrier to cause a hurried pass.

Ordinary or Minor Foul: The referee signals with one short whistle blow and points one hand to the spot of the foul and the other hand in the direction of the team that gains possession. Play continues immediately.

Exclusion or Major Foul: A referee signals a major foul by two short whistle bursts and indicates that the player must leave the field without impacting play and move to the penalty area for 20 seconds.

3-3 Offense: A basic positional offense composed of two lines containing 3 players each: point and two drivers along the 5-meter line, and wings and center forward along the 2-meter line.

4-2 Offense: The team on offense positions 4 players on the 2-meter line, and 2 players on 5-meter line. It is commonly used in man-up situations.

Review Questions

1. What is the world governing body for water polo?
2. Please list three major international water polo events.

第一章

足　球

学习目标

1. 了解足球的发展历史
2. 掌握足球赛事的主要管理机构和重要赛事
3. 熟悉足球比赛规则和专业术语

第一节　概　述

图 1.1　2010 年世界杯比赛期间，南非约翰内斯堡的足球城体育场（作者 Steve Evans）

足球主要专指英式足球（soccer）或美式足球（football），官方名称为协会足球（association football），是一项集体运动，在两队之间进行比赛，两队各有 11 名球员，主要是用脚控制球在一个矩形场地上进行的运动。比赛的目标是通过移动球,将球射入由对方防守的长方形球门,争取比对方进球更多。传统上,比赛有两个 45 分钟的半场,比赛总时间为 90 分钟。足球是世界上最受欢迎的运动,据估计,在 200 多个国家和地区活跃着 2.5 亿名球员。

足球比赛是根据《足球竞赛规则》(Laws of the Game)进行的,这是一套自 1863 年起生效的规则,自 1886 年以来一直由国际足球协会理事会(IFAB)维护。足球的周长为 68～70 厘米(27～28 英寸)。两队比赛的目标是将球射入对方的球门(门柱之间、横梁下以及越过球门线),从而得分。比赛时,球员主要使用脚,但也可以使用除了手或手臂之外身体的任何部位来控球、击球或传球。只有守门员在禁区内可以使用手和手臂。比赛结束时,进球多的球队赢得比赛。在某些情况下,进球可能会被判无效,比如越位判罚或进球前的犯规。根据比赛的形式,进球数相等可能导致平局、加时赛或者点球决胜。

国际上,足球由国际足联(FIFA)管理。国际足联下辖 6 个大洲的足球联合会:亚洲足球联合会(AFC),非洲足球联合会(CAF),中北美洲和加勒比足球联合会(CONCACAF)、南美洲足球联合会(CONMEBOL)、大洋洲足球联合会(OFC)和欧洲足球协会联盟(UEFA)。在这些联盟中,成立于 1916 年的南美洲足联是最古老的一个。国家足球协会(如英格兰足球总会或中国足球协会)负责管理本国的职业和业余足球比赛,并根据《足球竞赛规则》协调比赛。水平最高和最负盛名的国际足球比赛是国际足联世界杯(FIFA World Cup),也称国际足联男足世界杯(FIFA Men's World Cup),以及国际足联女足世界杯(FIFA Women's World Cup)。男子足球世界杯是世界上观看人数最多的体育赛事,超过了奥运会。欧洲足球俱乐部中最负盛名的两项比赛是欧洲冠军联赛,也称欧洲男子冠军联赛,以及欧洲女子冠军联赛,它们吸引了全世界众多的电视观众。自 2009 年以来,欧洲男子冠军联赛的决赛一直是世界上最受关注的年度体育赛事。

图 1.2　左图是雅典国家考古博物馆展出的一块公元前 375—400 年的古代石雕上的一个埃皮斯基罗斯球员;右图是 12 世纪中国宋朝的孩子们在玩蹴鞠(左图来源:维基共享资源)(右图作者 苏汉臣)

中国竞技游戏蹴鞠(字面意思是"踢球")类似于现代英式足球。蹴鞠选手可以使用除手以外的任何身体部位,目的是将球从开口踢进网中。在汉代(公元前206年—公元220年),蹴鞠比赛被标准化并建立了规则。其他东亚地区的游戏包括日本的 *kemari* 和韩国的 *chuk-guk*,都受到了蹴鞠的影响。*Kemari* 起源于公元600年后的飞鸟时代,它是一种仪式性的比赛,而不是竞技性的比赛,比赛中要踢 *mari*,一种由动物皮制成的球。在北美,*pasuckuakohowog* 是阿尔冈琴人玩的一种球类游戏,被描述为"与当时欧洲的民间足球几乎一模一样,都是把球踢进球门"。

英式足球本身并没有久远的历史。尽管足球与世界各地的其他球类运动有相似之处,但国际足联表示,足球与欧洲以外的古代运动没有任何历史联系。英格兰足球的历史至少可以追溯到公元8世纪。现代足球的规则是基于19世纪中期对英国公立学校中各种形式足球进行的标准化。

第二节 主要管理机构

国际足球联合会,缩写为FIFA,是国际英式足球、沙滩足球和五人制足球的管理机构。国际足球联合会成立于1904年,负责监督比利时、丹麦、法国、德国、荷兰、西班牙(以马德里足球俱乐部为代表)、瑞典和瑞士等国家协会之间的国际比赛。总部设在瑞士苏黎世,目前有211个国家协会成员,这些国家协会还必须是世界上6个区域联合会之一的成员:非洲足球联合会、亚洲足球联合会、欧洲足球协会联盟、中北美洲和加勒比足球联合会、大洋洲足球联合会和南美洲足球联合会。

国际足联在其组织章程中概述了几个目标,包括发展国际足球协会,努力确保每个人都能接触到足球,倡导诚信和公平竞争。国际足联负责组织和推广英式足球的主要国际比赛,特别是1930年开始的世界杯和1991年开始的女足世界杯。国际足联并不单独制定《足球竞赛规则》,制定比赛规则是由国际足球联合理事会负责。国际足联作为国际足球联合理事会的成员适用并执行所有国际足联的比赛规则。所有国际足联比赛的收入都来自赞助;2022年,国际足联收入超过58亿美元,2019—2022年周期结束时净收入为12亿美元,现金储备超过39亿美元。

第三节 重要赛事

3.1 国际足联世界杯

国际足联世界杯,通常简称"世界杯",是一项国际足球协会比赛,由国际足球联合会(FIFA)成员中的成年男子国家队参加,国际足联是足球运动的全球管理机构。自1930年首届赛事以来,除了1942年和1946年因第二次世界大战而中断外,每四年举办一次。卫冕冠军是阿根廷国家足球队,他们在2022年赢得了他们的第三个世界杯冠军。

比赛从资格赛阶段开始,在前三年进行,以确定哪些球队有资格进入决赛阶段。在决赛阶段,32支队伍将在一个月的时间里在主办国的赛场争夺冠军。主办国将自动获得进入决赛阶段的资格。国际足球联合会计划把2026年的世界杯决赛阶段参赛名额增加到48支球队。

世界杯自1930年创立以来,到2022年,已经举办了22场决赛,共有80支国家队参加了比赛。8支国家队赢得了世界杯。巴西取得了5次冠军,是唯一一支参加过所有世界杯决赛的球队。其他世界杯冠军是德国和意大利,各获得4次冠军;阿根廷,获

图1.3　2018年7月15日,世界杯决赛结束后,法国足球运动员奥斯曼·登巴姆萨伊勒斯手持世界杯奖杯(作者 Антон Зайцев)

得3次冠军;法国队和首届冠军乌拉圭队各获2次冠军;英格兰和西班牙各获得1次冠军。

世界杯是世界上最负盛名的足球赛事,也是世界上最受欢迎和关注的单项体育赛事。2018年世界杯的观众人数估计为35.7亿,接近全球人口的一半;而2022年世界杯的观众人数估计为50亿,其中约有15亿人观看了决赛。

17个国家举办过世界杯,最近的一次是卡塔尔,它主办了2022年的世界杯。2026年世界杯将由加拿大、美国和墨西哥联合主办,这将使墨西哥成为第一个举办过3届世界杯的国家。

3.2　国际足联女足世界杯

国际足联女足世界杯是一项国际足球比赛,由国际足球的管理机构国际足联(FIFA)成员中的女子成年国家队参加。自1991年首届国际足联女足世界杯在中国举办以来,该项赛事每四年举行一次,在男子世界杯之后一年举行。按照世界杯目前的赛制,各国国家队将在三年的预选赛阶段争夺剩余的31个席位。主办国的球队自动进入决赛阶段。世界杯决赛阶段在主办国的比赛场地进行,为期一个月左右。

在前9届国际足联女足世界杯的比赛中,共有5支国家队夺冠。美国曾4次夺冠,其他冠军分别是德国、日本、挪威和西班牙。德国获得2次冠军,日本、挪威和西班牙各获1次冠军。

目前为止,共有8个国家举办过女足世界杯。中国和美国各举办过2次世界杯,澳大利亚、加拿大、法国、德国、新西兰和瑞典各举办过一次。

2023年的女足世界杯由澳大利亚和新西兰主办,这是第一次在南半球举行女足世界杯,也是第一次由两个国家合办的女足世界杯。

图1.4　2019年女足世界杯决赛亚历克斯·摩根和斯蒂芬妮·范德格拉特在比赛中对抗（作者 Holly Cheng）

3.3　奥运会足球比赛

除了1896年（首届奥运会）和1932年（试图推广新的国际足联世界杯）之外，夏季奥运会男子足球比赛一直是每届夏季奥运会的比赛项目。1996年亚特兰大奥运会，女子足球被列入正式比赛项目。

为了避免与世界杯竞争，国际足联以各种方式限制精英球员参加奥运会男子足球比赛：目前，参加男子比赛的球队必须由23岁以下的球员组成，但允许每队有3个例外。

相比之下，奥运会女足比赛是一项完全高水平的国际比赛，其声望仅次于国际足联女足世界杯。

3.4　欧洲足球锦标赛

欧洲足球锦标赛（UEFA European Football Championship，简称"欧锦赛"，也称"欧洲杯"），是由欧洲足球协会联盟（UEFA）组织的主要足球锦标赛。这项比赛由欧足联成员国的成年男子国家队参加，决定欧洲大陆的冠军。欧洲足球锦标赛是继FIFA世界杯之后世界上收视率第二高的足球锦标赛。2012年欧洲杯决赛吸引了全球约3亿观众观看。自1960年以来，欧洲杯每四年举行一次，但

图1.5　2012年西班牙足球运动员费尔南多·托雷斯、胡安·马塔和塞尔希奥·拉莫斯庆祝赢得欧洲杯冠军（图片来源：Football.ua）

2020 年除外,当时因欧洲新型冠状病毒感染疫情比赛推迟到 2021 年举行,但保留了"2020年欧洲杯"(Euro 2020)的名称。欧洲足球锦标赛原定在国际足联世界杯之间的偶数年举行,最初被称为欧洲国家杯(European Nations' Cup),直到 1968 年改为现名。自 1996 年起,单项赛事被命名为"欧洲杯[年份]"。

在进入之前,除主办国(自动获得参赛资格)外的所有球队都要参加预选赛。直到 2016 年,冠军得主可以参加下一年的国际足联联合会杯(FIFA Confederations Cup),但不是必须参加。从 2020 年起,冠军球队将参加南美洲-欧洲冠军杯(CONMEBOL-UEFA Cup of Champions)的比赛。

前 16 届欧洲杯共有 10 支国家队夺冠：德国和西班牙各获 3 次冠军；意大利和法国各获 2 次冠军；苏联、捷克斯洛伐克、荷兰、丹麦、希腊和葡萄牙各获 1 次冠军。迄今为止,西班牙队是唯一一支连续获得冠军的球队,分别在 2008 年和 2012 年获得了冠军。

3.5 国际足联联合会杯

国际足联联合会杯(FIFA Confederations Cup)是国际足联为男子国家队举办的国际足球锦标赛,每四年举行一次。赛事由六大洲锦标赛(亚洲足联、非洲足联、中北美洲及加勒比海足联、南美足联、大洋洲足联和欧洲足联)的冠军以及当时的国际足联世界杯冠军和主办国共同角逐,参赛队伍总数达到 8 支。

2001 年至 2017 年(2003 年除外),联合会杯在次年将要举办世界杯的国家举行,作为更大规模的世界杯的测试赛。

2019 年 3 月,国际足联证实将不再举办联合会杯,取而代之的是国际足联俱乐部世界杯(FIFA Club World Cup)。

3.6 欧洲冠军联赛

欧洲冠军联赛(UEFA Champions League),历史上被称为欧洲杯(European Cup),在世界范围内大多缩写为 UCL,是由欧洲足球协会联盟组织的年度俱乐部足球比赛。该赛事由欧洲顶级俱乐部参赛,通过小组循环赛决定获胜者,以获得参加两回合淘汰赛和单回合决赛的资格。欧洲冠军联赛是世界上最受关注的俱乐部比赛,也是第三大最受关注的足球比赛,仅次于国际足联世界杯和欧洲足球锦标赛。它是世界上最负盛名的足球锦标赛之一,也是欧洲足球中最负盛名的俱乐部比赛,由国家联赛冠军(对一些国家来说,还有一个或多个亚军)参加。

欧洲冠军联赛始创于 1955 年,当时被称为"欧洲俱乐部冠军杯"(法语：Coupe des Clubs Champions Européens),通常被称为欧洲冠军杯(英语：European Cup)。最初,该赛事以直接淘汰制形式进行,只对欧洲国内联赛的冠军开放,冠军队被视为欧洲足球俱乐部的冠军。随后在 1991 年增设了小组循环赛环节,并于 1992 年改为现在的名称。1997—1998 赛季开始,某些国家可以派出多支球队参赛。欧洲冠军联赛后来扩大了参赛规模,目前,虽然大多数欧洲国家联赛仍然只能派出他们的冠军参赛,但实力最强的联赛最多可以派出4支球队参赛。大部分在本国联赛中排名第二的俱乐部,没有资格参加欧洲冠军联赛,但有资格参加第二级别的欧洲联赛(UEFA Europa League),以及从2021年起举办的第三级别的欧洲协会联赛(UEFA Europa Conference League)。

　　按照目前的赛制,欧洲冠军联赛从6月下旬开始,分为预选赛、3轮资格赛和1轮附加赛,全部比赛采用两回合赛制。6支晋级球队进入小组赛,与提前晋级的26支球队会合。32支球队被分成8组,每组4支球队进行双循环小组赛。8个小组冠军和8个小组亚军进入淘汰赛阶段,决赛将在5月底或6月初进行。冠军联赛的冠军自动获得资格参加下一年欧洲冠军联赛、欧洲超级杯,国际足联世俱杯以及从2024年开始的新的国际足联洲际杯(FIFA Intercontinental Cup)(洲际杯用以取代之前的世俱杯)。

　　在欧冠历史上,西班牙俱乐部以19次获得冠军居于榜首,其次是英格兰15次和意大利12次。英格兰有6支俱乐部获得过冠军,拥有最多的冠军球队。迄今为止,共有23家俱乐部获得过冠军,其中13家获得过一次以上冠军,8家成功卫冕。截至2023年,皇家马德里是欧洲杯历史上最成功的俱乐部,曾14次夺冠。曼城在2023年的决赛中以1比0击败国际米兰,获得了他们的第一个欧冠冠军。

第四节　比　赛　规　则

4.1　比赛方法

　　足球比赛是按照一套比赛规则《足球竞赛规则》进行的。比赛时,两队各有11名队员,球员要将球踢进对方的球门(门柱之间和横梁之下)来得分。比赛结束时进球多的球队获

图1.6　开球。除开球队员外的其他球员必须在本队的半场内,对方球员不得在直径10码的中圈内
(作者 Michael Barera)

胜；如果两队的进球数相等，则比赛为平局。每支球队由一名队长领导，根据比赛规则，队长只有一项官方职责：在开球或罚点球之前，代表本队进行抛硬币。

足球比赛最基本的规则是守门员以外的球员在比赛过程中不能故意用手或胳膊控制球，尽管他们在掷界外球时必须用手。球员通常用脚来移动球，但也可以用除了手和手臂以外的身体任何部位（尤其是用前额"顶"球）控球。在正常的比赛中，所有的球员都可以自由地在球场的任何方向上踢球和移动，但是球员不能把球传给越位的队友。

在比赛过程中，球员试图通过运球、传球和射门等方式来控球并创造进球机会，而对方球员可以试图通过拦截传球或抢断来获得控球权；在此期间，双方选手之间的身体接触是受到限制的。除天气、场地问题、球员受伤等因素外，足球比赛一般是连续流畅的，只有当足球出界、裁判员判罚球员犯规等情况时，比赛才会停止。比赛暂停后，将按照具体规定重新开始。

图 1.7　一名队员用滑铲动作使对手失去对球的控制（作者 D League）

在职业级别的比赛中，大多数比赛只产生少量的进球。例如，2005—2006 赛季的英超联赛平均每场进球只有 2.48 个。比赛规则中没有明确规定除守门员以外的球员位置，但一些特定的位置已经在长期的比赛中形成。大体来说，球员位置包括三种主要类型：前锋，主要负责进球；后卫，专门阻止对手得分；中场球员，抢断对手的球、控球并将球传给本方的前锋。这些位置上的球员被称为场上球员，以区别于守门员。

球员位置可以根据队员处于场上不同区域的时间进一步细分。例如，有中后卫和左右前卫之分。10 名场上球员可以任意组合安排，每个位置上的球员数量决定了球队的比赛风格。一个阵型中，如果前锋人数多，后卫人数少，则是倾向于进攻性的打法；而反之则倾向于更慢、更具防守性的打法。比赛对球员的移动没有限制，球员可以任意切换位置，但球员在比赛中的大部分时间都在一个特定的位置上。球队球员的布局被称为阵型，确定球队的阵型和战术通常是球队主教练的权利。

4.2 选手、装备和裁判

每队最多由 11 名球员组成(不包括替补球员),其中必须有一名守门员。比赛规则规定比赛时一个队伍最低人数为 7 人。守门员是唯一可以用手或胳膊触球的球员,前提是守门员必须在本队球门前的禁区内。尽管主教练策略性地安排了场上球员(非守门员)到各个位置,但足球规则并未对这些位置进行定义或要求。

球员需要穿戴的基本装备包括球衫、短裤、球袜、球鞋和符合要求的护胫。医学专家和专业人士强烈建议男性运动员使用运动护裆和防护罩。头盔不是必需的基本装备,但球员可以通过佩戴头盔来保护头部免受伤害。比赛过程中禁止选手佩戴或使用任何对自己或其他选手有危险的物品,如珠宝或手表。守门员的服装必须容易与其他球员和比赛官员的服装进行区分。

图 1.8 裁判在足球比赛中执裁
(图片来源:thetelf)

球员在比赛过程中可以被替换,大多数国际和国内联赛允许的最大替换人数是 90 分钟内替换 3 人,如果比赛进入加时赛,每队允许多换一人,但在其他比赛或友谊赛中允许替换的人数可能有所不同。换人的常见原因包括球员受伤、疲劳、效率低下、战术改变或在一场势均力敌的比赛快结束时故意浪费时间。在标准的成人比赛中,被替换下场的球员不得再参加比赛。国际足球协会建议"如果任何一队球员少于 7 人,比赛不应继续进行"。弃权比赛比分的决定权属于各个足球协会。

比赛由一名主裁判执裁,他"在被指派作为主裁的比赛中,有绝对的权力来执行比赛规则"(规则第 5 条),主裁判的决定是最终结果。主裁判由两名助理裁判协助执裁。在许多高水平的比赛中,还有一名第四裁判协助主裁判,必要时可以替换其他裁判。

球门线技术用于判断球是否整体越过了球门线,从而确定是否进球得分。视频助理裁判(VAR)也越来越多地出现在高水平比赛中,通过视频回放来帮助裁判们纠正明显的错误。比赛中有 4 种判罚可以进行视频回放:判罚红牌或黄牌时认错人、判罚进球以及进球过程中是否有违规行为、直接红牌判罚以及点球判罚。

4.3 足球

足球是圆形的,周长在 68~70 cm(27~28 in)之

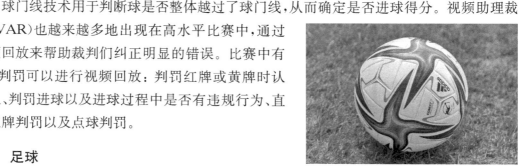

图 1.9 一个典型的足球
(作者 Steffen Prößdorf)

间,重量在 410~450 g(14~16 oz)之间,海平面压力在 0.6~1.1 标准大气压①(8.5~15.6 lb/in²)之间。以前,足球是由几块缝在一起的皮革表面,再加上一个用于加压的乳胶气囊构成的,但现代各级别比赛使用的足球都是用合成材料制成的。

4.4 足球场

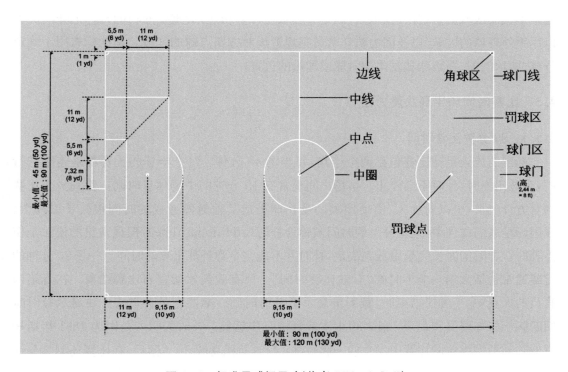

图 1.10　标准足球场尺寸(作者 Bildersindtoll)

由于足球比赛规则是在英格兰制定的,因此最初足球比赛规则是由国际足球联合会理事会内部的 4 个英国足球协会管理,足球场的标准尺寸最初也是用英制单位表示。目前的足球比赛规则规定用近似的公制单位来表示足球场的尺寸(在后面的括号内用英制单位表示)。而在英国等使用公制历史相对较短的英语国家(或只是部分使用公制),英制单位仍然很流行。

国际成人足球比赛的球场长度为 100~110 m(110~120 yd),宽度为 64~75 m(70~80 yd)。非国际比赛的场地长度范围是 90~120 m(100~130 yd),宽度范围是 45~90 m(50~100 yd),但场地不能是正方形。2008 年,国际足球联合会理事会批准将 105 m(115 yd)长,68 m(74 yd)宽作为国际比赛的标准球场尺寸,但这一决定后来被搁置,从未真正执行过。

足球场较长的边界线是边线,较短的边界线(放置球门的线)是球门线。每条球门线的中间都有一个长方形的球门,位于两条边线中间。球门立柱的内缘间距必须为 7.32 m

---

① 1 标准大气压＝1.01×10⁵ Pa。

(24 ft),球门柱支撑的水平横梁的下沿距离地面必须为 2.44 m(8 ft)。球网通常放在球门后面,但规则中没有对其作具体规定。

禁区在球门前方,这一区域以四条线为标志,第一条线是球门线。从球门立柱出发,沿球门线向两侧延伸 16.5 m(18 yd)处,向场内画两条 16.5 m(18 yd)长与球门线垂直的线。这就是第二条和第三条线。再通过一条直线将它们连接起来,这是第四条线。这四条线围起来形成的区域就是禁区(罚球区)。这个区域有许多功能,最重要的功能是标记守门员可以用手处理球的区域,以及因为防守队员犯规造成对方罚点球的区域。其他标志用于确定开球、踢球门球、罚点球和发角球时球或球员的位置。

4.5 比赛时间和平局决胜方法

4.5.1 90分钟正常时间

标准的成人足球比赛包括两个半场,每半场 45 分钟。每个半场的比赛都是连续进行的,当球出界时,计时不会停止。半场之间通常有 15 分钟的中场休息时间。裁判员是比赛的官方计时员,可以对换人、需要照顾的受伤球员或其他暂停造成的时间损失予以补偿。在国际足联的文件中,这个补上的时间被称为补时(additional time),但最常见的说法是伤停补时。补时的时长完全由裁判决定,补时并不能完全弥补球出界的时间。一场 90 分钟的比赛通常包括大约一个小时的"有效比赛时间"。只有裁判才能宣布比赛结束。在有第四官员的比赛中,半场快结束时,裁判员会示意补时时间。第四官员会举着一块显示补时时间的牌子告知球员和观众。补时可由主裁判进一步延长。补时的引入是因为 1891 年斯托克城和阿斯顿维拉的比赛中发生的一起事件:当时斯托克城 0∶1 落后,在比赛还剩 2 分钟时,斯托克城获得了一个点球,可是维拉队门将把球踢出了场外,当球被取回时,90 分钟已经到了,比赛结束了。此后,规则规定任何半场的持续时间都要延长至罚点球或重罚点球结束,任何比赛都不能在罚点球前结束。

4.5.2 平局决胜方法

在联赛中,比赛可能以平局结束。在需要决出胜者的淘汰赛中,可以采用多种方法来打破这种僵局,例如有些比赛可能会采用重赛。在规定时间结束后打成平局的比赛可以进入加时赛,加时赛包括另外两个 15 分钟的半场。如果加时赛结束后仍然是平局,一些比赛允许使用点球决胜(在正式的《足球竞赛规则》中被称为"从罚球点踢球")来决定哪支球队进入下一阶段的比赛。在补时阶段进的球计入比赛的最后得分,但点球决胜只用于决定球队是否进入下一轮比赛(点球决胜进球不计入最终比分)。

在采用两回合赛制的比赛中,每个队在主场比赛一次,两场比赛的总成绩决定哪一支球队晋级下一轮。在总进球数相等的情况下,客场进球规则可以用来决定赢家。在这种情况下,赢家是在客场比赛中进球数较多的球队。如果结果仍然相等,就需要进行加时赛或点球决胜。

图 1.11　如果比赛打成平局,大多数淘汰赛都采用点球决胜(作者 rayand)

4.6　活球和死球

图 1.12　一名球员发任意球,对方球员排成人墙试图阻挡球(作者 Neier)

根据比赛规则,比赛的两种基本状态是活球状态和死球状态。从每个半场比赛的开球到半场结束,球一直处于活球状态,除非球出界或比赛被裁判叫停。根据成为死球的方式,可通过 8 种方法重新开始比赛:

① 开球:在对方球队进球后开球,或在每半场比赛开始时开球。

② 界外球:当球越过边线时,如果一方队员最后触球,将判给对方发界外球。

③ 球门球：当球完全越过球门线而没有进球，并且是进攻方的球员最后触球，将判给防守方踢球门球。

④ 角球：在没有进球的情况下，球完全越过球门线，且最后一次由防守队员触球，将判给进攻队角球。

⑤ 间接任意球：在"比较轻微的"犯规、某些技术犯规或在没有发生具体犯规的情况下，在停止比赛以警告或罚下球员时，判给对方球队间接任意球。间接任意球不能直接得分（在球没有先碰到另一名球员的情况下）。

⑥ 直接任意球：在某些"严重"犯规后判给被犯规球队直接任意球。直接任意球可以直接进球得分。

⑦ 罚点球：在对方禁区内被防守方犯规的球队获得罚点球机会。

⑧ 坠球：当裁判因球员严重受伤、外界干扰或球有缺陷等原因停止比赛时，通过坠球重新开始比赛。

4.7 违规行为

4.7.1 场上违规

球员在比赛中做出违反《足球竞赛规则》的行为时，就会构成犯规。《足球竞赛规则》第 12 条列出了构成犯规的行为。故意手球、绊倒对手或推搡对手都属于"严重犯规"，根据犯规发生的地点，可判罚直接任意球或点球。其他犯规可罚间接任意球。

图 1.13 出示黄牌表示警告，被出示红牌的队员要被罚出场。红黄牌在 1970 年世界杯上首次亮相，并一直沿用至今（图片来源：维基百科）

主裁可以对场上球员或替补队员的违规行为处以警告（黄牌）或罚下（红牌）的处罚。在同一场比赛中，第二张黄牌将导致红牌，红牌将导致球员被罚下场。被出示黄牌的球员将被"记录"，裁判会在官方笔记本上记下该球员的名字。如果一名球员被罚下场，则不得安排替补球员替换其位置，该球员也不得参加后续比赛。违规行为随时可能发生，虽然规则列出了构成违规行为的情况，但其定义很广泛，特别是"违反体育道德行为"的描写可以用来解释大多数违反体育精神的行为，即使有些行为没有被列入具体的犯规内容中。主裁可以向场上球员、替补球员或被替换球员出示黄牌或红牌。非球员，如主教练和后勤人员不能被出示黄牌或红牌，但如果他们不能以负责任的方式行事，可能会被驱逐出技术区。

足球比赛的"有利原则"是指如果对被犯规的球队有利，为了维护比赛的流畅性，裁判可以允许比赛继续进行，而不吹犯规。如果在"几秒钟"内预期的优势没有出现，主裁判可以对最初的犯规进行处罚。即使一个犯规行为未因有利原则而受到处罚，在下次比赛停止时，犯规者仍可能因不当行为而受到处罚。

主裁对于所有球场上的问题的决定都是最终结果。在比赛结束后，即使后来的证据表明判罚(包括裁定进球/进球无效)是错误的,比赛的比分也不能被更改。

4.7.2 场外违规

除了足球运动的总体管理,足球协会和比赛组织者还在足球运动更广泛方面促进良好的行为,处理诸如对媒体的评论、俱乐部的财务管理、兴奋剂、年龄欺诈和假球等问题。大多数比赛会对被罚下的球员强制禁赛。在球场上,如果发生被认为是非常严重的(如种族歧视的指控)事件,则可能会导致赛事管理者决定施加比红牌更严厉的处罚。如果俱乐部认为裁判判决不正确或过于严厉,一些协会允许对球员在场上受到的禁赛提出上诉。

对违规行为的处罚可以针对个人,也可以针对整个俱乐部。处罚可能包括罚款、扣分(在联赛中),甚至取消比赛资格。例如,英格兰足球联赛(English Football League)对任何违反财务管理规定的球队扣12分。其他的行政处罚包括判罚比赛弃权。弃权的球队将被判技术上的失败;弃权球队的对手将被判技术上的胜利。

第五节 基 本 战 术

虽然足球看起来是一项相对简单的运动,但只是其规则和基本比赛方式简单。比赛的策略可能相当复杂,尤其是在职业比赛和世界杯等高水平比赛中。

5.1 基本进攻战术

比赛中,拥有控球权的球队进行进攻。在进攻时,球队可能会采取多种不同的战术或策略,具体取决于当时参加比赛的球员以及球员的技术水平和类型。

所有足球运动员都应该采用的进攻策略之一是传球和移动(Passing and Moving)。这意味着球员永远不应该在进攻时停滞不前。每当球员控球时,他们都需要传球或运球。只是原地不动肯定会失去控球权。这也适用于控球球员附近的任何进攻球员。他们应该始终移动寻找空位,并为队友提供传球路线。

另一个好的策略是传球,然后快速移动到靠近球门的另一个空位。继续移动并创造传球路线可能会使防守方处于劣势。

转换进攻(Switch the Attack)也是一个好的进攻策略。这是向球场上防守球员较少的另一个区域的长传,可能会向本方球门方向回传球,也可能会向球场另一侧横传。这使得进攻队有机会重新集结,形成新的进攻机会。

一些进攻球队会使用控球(Possession Ball)战术。这是指球队试图长时间保持控球。他们可能会在没有明显进攻的情况下左右传球。在一场漫长的足球比赛中,这是一个很好的策略。传球比运球或追球要省力得多。防守的足球队会比进攻的球队用更多的体力去追球。当进攻队领先并想要休息一下时,这也是一个很好的策略。

5.2 基本防守战术

没有控球权的球队是防守队。良好的团队防守对于赢得任何足球比赛都至关重要。防守不仅仅是守门员的工作,也是所有十一名球员的工作。

一支优秀的防守球队需要学会沟通并形成防御进攻的屏障。球和球门之间应始终保持有一或两名球员。其他球员应该防守住其他进攻球员,以确保他们无法获得短距离射门的机会。这通常称为"盯人"(marking)。

对于防守球员来说,迫使控球球员向边线移动是一个好主意。通过封堵正确的角度和转动身体,防守球员可以引导进攻球员到边线。这使得进攻方很难获得良好的射门机会或获得良好的传球角度。这也可能导致他们在边线处丢球,从而使防守方夺回控球权。

有些球队有一名球员称为"清道夫"。这是一名防守球员,位置通常比其他防守队员稍深一些。清道夫在后场游走,寻找抢断或"清扫"任何突破防守的球。

防守还可以用两名球员围困控球球员,防止他们传球并抢断球。这可能是一个有风险但值得一试的战术。

防守应该充分利用足球比赛越位规则。通过协调最后一道防线并跟踪进攻球员的位置,防守可以使进攻球员陷于越位位置并导致失误。

足球术语

FIFA /ˈfiːfə/:国际足联的首字母缩写,国际足联是足球运动的国际管理机构,总部设在瑞士。

联合会:负责本地区足球事务的组织。

足球场:进行足球比赛的场地。

中点:在场地中央标明的开球点。

角旗:标示球场四个角的旗帜。

边线:是指比赛场地较长的边界线。

球门线:位于场地两端的两条边界线。

球门区:球门前的矩形区域,也因其尺寸被称为6码区域。

禁区:球门前的长方形区域,守门员可以在里面处理球。禁区也因其尺寸被称为18码区域。

罚球点:距球门线12码处指定罚点球的罚球点。

远门柱:离球较远一侧的门柱。

近门柱:离球较近的门柱。

裁判员:负责比赛的裁判员。

前锋:是指将球向前推进到对手的球门区以创造得分机会的球员。

边锋:是指在球场两侧踢球的进攻球员。

中场：是指负责串联前锋和后卫的球员。

后卫：是指阻止对方进攻队员进球的防守球员。

守门员：是指专门负责防守最后一道防线的球员，在球门区域时被允许用手控球。

清道夫：是足球比赛中承担特定防守任务的拖后中卫的别称。其职责是只守不攻，执行单一的补位防守任务，负责防守守门员之前的最后一道防线。

开球：开球在每半场比赛开始时和进球后，从球场中心位置进行。

点球：当防守方在大禁区内犯规时，判罚点球。点球时，进攻方只能派一名球员踢球，防守方也只能派一名守门员防守。

角球：是指由进攻队员在球场角球区开出的任意球。当防守队员触碰到球，并使球越过底线时，判罚角球。

任意球：是一种在足球比赛中发生犯规后重新开始比赛的方法，属于定位球的一种。任意球包括直接任意球和间接任意球两种形式。

直接任意球：可以由主罚任意球的球员直接进球的任意球。

间接任意球：不能由主罚任意球的球员直接进球的任意球。

球门球：当进攻队将球踢过门线时，防守队将获得踢球门球的机会。球门球可以由任何球员来踢，但通常是由守门员踢。

运球：球员在跑步时保持对球的控制。

射门：是指球员踢球、头球或任何企图把球射进球门得分的行为。

头球：用头传球或控球。

掷界外球：在球越过边线后掷界外球。掷界外球的球员必须双脚在边线上或边线后，必须与地面保持接触，并且必须用双手从头后掷界外球。界外球不能直接得分。

脚尖踢球：用脚尖来踢球。

后脚跟踢球：一种传球或射门的动作，指球员用脚跟将球向后推给另一名球员或踢进球门。

抽射：是指用一只脚在半空中踢球的动作。

倒钩：一种令人惊叹的动作，运动员腾空而起的后空翻，将球向后踢过头顶。这个动作的名字来源于他们的腿就像踩自行车一样的动作。

弧线球：一种使球产生旋转的踢球技术，运动员使用这种技术踢球可以使球在空中弧线飞行。

回传球：是指球员向己方球门方向传球，通常传给守门员。这是一种以重新开始比赛为目的的防守动作。

直塞球：是指进攻方利用直线传球穿透对方防守阵型的一种传球方式。

铲球：铲球是防守球员在单脚触球前沿球场表面滑行的拦截动作。

抢断：用脚把球从对手的控制中夺走。

越位：如果一名进攻球员在队友传球的一瞬间，比球和倒数第二名防守方球员更靠近对方的球门线,这名球员就处于越位位置。如果接球球员在本方半场,就不属于越位。在越位发生的地方,对方球队将获得一个间接任意球。

造越位:是指在进攻方传球前的瞬间,防守方球员快速全线压上,使进攻方球员处于越位位置。

一脚传球:指球员第一次触球时就把球传给对方。

撞墙式二过一:是指进攻时的一种过人战术,即形成两人过一人局面时,二人一传一切,接球者一次出球,使传来的球像撞在墙上快速反弹一样,从而加快过人速度。

人盯人防守:一名防守队员针对一名进攻队员进行连续跟踪防守的防守战术。

区域联防:一种防守战术,每个球员负责防守一个区域的球场,而不是固定防守对方一位球员。

犯规:任何违规的比赛行为。

阻挡犯规:是指用身体阻挡对手的行为,将被判罚间接任意球。

黄牌:对于轻微的犯规,裁判会出示黄牌以示警告。

红牌:当球员严重犯规或在同一场比赛中被出示两张黄牌时,将被出示红牌并罚下。被罚下的球员不可替换。

练 习

1. 足球运动的国际管理机构是什么?
2. 请列举三个主要国际足球赛事。
3. 标准足球比赛场地的长度和宽度分别是多少米?
4. 古代足球运动起源于哪个国家?被称作什么?

第二章

篮 球

学习目标

1. 了解篮球的发展历史
2. 掌握篮球赛事的主要管理机构和重要赛事
3. 熟悉篮球比赛规则和专业术语

第一节 概 述

图 2.1 室内篮球场(作者 Max12Max)

篮球是一项集体运动,由两队组成,通常每队五名球员,两支球队在一个长方形的篮球场上互相对抗,比赛的主要目的是将球投入对手的篮筐,同时阻止对方球员将球投入本方的篮筐。三分线内的投篮分值为2分,三分线后的投篮分值为3分。犯规后,比赛计时停止,球员犯规或被指定技术犯规,将给予对方1次、2次或3次分值为1分的罚球。在比赛结束时得分较多的一方获胜,如果比赛结束后双方比分持平,则必须延长比赛时间(加时赛)。

球员通过边走或边跑动拍球(运球),或把球传给队友这两种方式向前推进球,这两种推进球的方式都需要相当高的技术。进攻时,球员可以使用各种投篮方式——上篮、跳投或扣篮等;防守时,球员可以抢断球、拦截传球或者封盖;进攻或防守队员都可以抢篮板球,即抢夺没有投中、从篮筐或篮板上反弹的球。在没有运球的情况下抬起或移动自己的枢轴脚、带球跑或者用双手持球然后继续运球,都是违例行为。

在篮球比赛中,每队有 5 名球员上场,分为 5 个位置:身高最高的球员通常是中锋;第二高和最强壮的通常是大前锋;一个稍矮但更敏捷的球员通常是小前锋;最矮的球员或最好的控球手通常是得分后卫和控球后卫,控球后卫通过组织进攻和防守(球员的位置)来实施教练的比赛战术。在非正式的比赛中球员可以进行三对三、二对二和一对一的比赛。

1891 年,美国马萨诸塞州斯普林菲尔德的加拿大裔美国体育老师詹姆斯·奈史密斯发明了篮球,现已发展成为世界上最受欢迎和观众人数最多的运动之一。无论从受欢迎程度、薪资、人才还是竞争水平来看,美国职业篮球联赛(National Basketball Association,NBA)是世界上最重要的职业篮球联盟(其大部分人才来自美国大学篮球队)。在北美以外地区,国家联赛的顶级俱乐部才有资格参加欧洲篮球联赛和美洲冠军篮球联赛等洲际锦标赛。国际篮联篮球世界杯和奥运会男子篮球比赛是这项运动的主要国际赛事,吸引了来自世界各地的顶尖国家篮球队参赛。每个大洲都为国家队举办地区性赛事,比如欧洲男子篮球锦标赛和国际篮联美洲杯篮球赛。

国际篮联女篮世界杯和奥运会女篮比赛由来自各大洲锦标赛选拔的顶尖国家队参加。北美的主要联赛是美国女子篮球职业联赛(Women's National Basketball Association,WNBA)[美国全国大学体育协会(National Collegiate Athletic Association,NCAA)的女子一级篮球锦标赛也很受欢迎],而欧洲实力最强的俱乐部都会参加欧洲女子篮球联赛。

第二节 主要管理机构

图 2.2 位于瑞士米村的国际篮联总部(作者 Richard Ruilliart)

国际篮球联合会（International Basketball Federation，FIBA）是一个国际性的篮球运动组织，管理全球篮球运动，由世界各国的篮球协会组成，总部设于瑞士米村，原名是国际业余篮球联合会（Federation Internationale de Basketball Amateur，FIBA）。1989年该组织去掉了名字中的"业余"一词，保留了首字母缩略词，"BA"现在代表篮球英文的前两个字母。

国际篮球联合会负责制定国际篮球规则、制定篮球比赛用的篮球场和篮球规格（例如：篮球筐的高度、篮球场的长宽度、禁区的大小、三分线的距离和比赛用球等）、控制球员在国家间的流动、任命国际篮球比赛执法的裁判和举办大型篮球赛事。1932年成立至今，共有213个会员国家。自1989年起，分为5个地区委员会，专责处理该地区篮球事务，分别是：非洲地区委员会、美洲地区委员会、亚洲地区委员会、欧洲地区委员会和大洋洲地区委员会。

国际篮联组织由国际奥委会（International Olympic Committe，IOC）批准的男子和女子国际篮联世界奥运会篮球资格赛（FIBA World Olympic Qualifying Tournament）和夏季奥运会篮球赛事。国际篮联篮球世界杯是每四年举行一次的男子国家队世界锦标赛，各队争夺奈史密斯奖杯，该奖杯以篮球的发明者——加拿大裔美国人詹姆斯·奈史密斯的名字命名。篮球世界杯的比赛组织结构与国际足联世界杯类似，但不完全相同；1970年到2014年期间，这两个比赛都在同一年举行，但从2019年开始，篮球世界杯改至国际足联世界杯之后的一年举行。国际篮联女篮世界杯也是每四年举行一次；1986年到2014年期间，它与男子比赛于同一年在不同国家举行。

第三节　重要赛事

3.1　奥运会篮球比赛

自1936年以来，奥运会篮球比赛一直是一项男子运动。在被纳入正式比赛项目之前，篮球在1904年作为表演项目出现。女子篮球在1976年夏季奥运会上首次亮相。国际篮联组织男子和女子国际篮联世界奥运会篮球资格赛和夏季奥运会篮球比赛，这些比赛都得到了国际奥委会的批准。

美国是迄今为止在奥运会篮球项目上最成功的国家，美国男子篮球队在参加的19次奥运会篮球比赛中赢得了16次冠军，其中包括从1936年到1968年的七连冠。美国女队在参加的10次奥运会篮球比赛中，赢得了8次冠军，其中包括从1996年到2020年的七连冠。除了美国，阿根廷是目前唯一一个在奥运会男子和女子篮球比赛中都获得过冠军的国家。此外，已经不存在的国家苏联、南斯拉夫和独联体队也赢得过冠军。

2017年6月9日，国际奥委会执行委员会宣布，从2020年日本东京夏季奥运会开始，3×3篮球成为正式的奥运会项目，分为男子组和女子组进行比赛。

3.2　国际篮联篮球世界杯

国际篮联篮球世界杯(FIBA Basketball World Cup),也被称为"国际篮联世界杯"(FIBA World Cup of Basketball/FIBA World Cup),在1950年至2010年期间被称为国际篮联世界锦标赛(FIBA World Championship),是一项由国际篮球联合会(FIBA)成员国的成年男子国家队参加的国际篮球赛事。国际篮联是篮球运动的全球管理机构。篮球世界杯堪称国际篮联的旗舰赛事。

国际篮联世界杯的比赛组织结构与国际足联世界杯类似,在1970年至2014年期间,这两项赛事都是在同一年举行。女队的平行赛事,现称为国际篮联女篮世界杯,也是每四年举行一次。1986年至2014年期间,男子和女子篮球世界杯于同一年在不同国家举行。目前的赛制规定由32支球队在主办国的场馆争夺冠军,获胜的球队将获得奈史密斯奖杯(Naismith Trophy),该奖杯于1967年首次颁发。

继2014年国际篮联男子和女子锦标赛之后,男子篮球世界杯被安排在新的四年周期,以避免与FIFA世界杯在时间上发生冲突。男子篮球世界杯于2019年举行,也就是FIFA世界杯之后的一年。"国际篮联女子世界锦标赛"在2014年之后更名为"国际篮联女子篮球世界杯",将保持之前的4年周期,与FIFA世界杯同一年举行比赛。

1994年在加拿大举行的国际篮联世界锦标赛是第一次允许现役美国NBA球员参加的世界杯锦标赛,这些现役球员都已经参加了正式的NBA常规赛。此后,所有的国际篮联世界锦标赛/世界杯赛都被认为是完全职业水平的比赛。

3.3　国际篮联女子篮球世界杯

国际篮联女子篮球世界杯(FIBA Women's Basketball World Cup),也称为"女子篮球世界杯"(Basket World Cup for Women)或简称"国际篮联女篮世界杯"(FIBA Women's World Cup),是每四年举行一次的女子国家队国际篮球赛事,由国际篮球联合会创建。首届比赛于1953年在智利举行,距离第一届男子世界锦标赛已经过去了3年。在其早期历史的大部分时间里,它不是与男子锦标赛在同一年举行的,直到1967年才获得四年一次的固定周期。1983年的比赛结束后,国际篮联改变了比赛安排,将女子比赛安排在偶数年的非奥运年举行,1970年的男子比赛也是如此。

女篮世界杯以前被称为国际篮联世界女子锦标赛(FIBA World Championship for Women),自2018年起改为现名。从1986年到2014年,该赛事与国际篮联男子篮球世界杯在同一年举行,但在不同的国家举行。在2014年的比赛之后,男子世界杯被重新安排在一个新的4年周期举行(最近一次是2019年),以避免与男子足球世界杯在时间上发生冲突;但女子世界杯仍然是同样的4年周期,与男子足球世界杯在同一年举行,决赛在足球世界杯结束几个月后举行。

3.4　美国职业篮球联赛

图 2.3　1991 年 3 月 28 日,芝加哥公牛队对阵新泽西网队（作者 The Eloquent Peasant）

　　美国职业篮球联赛,也称为国家篮球协会（NBA）是北美的一个职业篮球联赛。该联赛由 30 支球队组成（29 支美国球队,1 支加拿大球队）,是美国和加拿大四大职业体育联赛之一,是世界上首屈一指的男子职业篮球联赛。

　　协会于 1946 年 6 月 6 日在纽约市成立,原名全美篮球协会（Basketball Association of America,BAA）。1949 年 8 月 3 日,在与国家篮球联盟（National Basketball League,NBL）合并后,美国篮球协会更名为国家篮球协会（NBA）,联盟的几个国际和个人团队办公室都设在总部曼哈顿中城之外。

　　在北美,按收入计算,NBA 是仅次于美国国家橄榄球联盟（National Football League,NFL）和美国职业棒球大联盟（Major League Baseball,MLB）的第三富有的职业体育联盟,在世界上排名前四。截至 2020 年,按每位球员的平均年薪计算,NBA 球员是世界上收入最高的运动员。

　　目前的联盟组织将 30 支球队分为两个联盟：东部联盟（Eastern Conference）和西部联盟（Western Conference）;而每个联盟各由三个分区组成,每个分区有 5 支球队。目前的分区赛制是在 2004—2005 赛季引入的,大多数球队都在美国的东半部：13 支球队在东部时区,9 支在中部时区,3 支在山区,5 支在太平洋时区。NBA 常规赛从 10 月持续到次年 4 月,季后赛一直延续到 6 月。

　　在常规赛中,每支球队要打 82 场比赛,主客场各 41 场。一支球队一年要面对本赛区的对手 4 次（16 场）。每支球队与同联盟其他两个赛区的 6 支球队进行 4 次（24 场）比赛,其余 4 支球队进行 3 次（12 场）比赛。最后,每支球队与另一个联盟的所有球队各打两场（30 场）

比赛。

从 2023—2024 赛季开始，常规赛包括季中锦标赛（in-season tournament），其中所有比赛（决赛除外）都将计入常规赛。

NBA 季后赛在常规赛结束后的 4 月开始，每个联盟的前八名的球队，无论分区排位如何，都将争夺联赛的总冠军。

季后赛采用锦标赛的形式。每支球队在七局四胜制的系列赛中对阵对手，第一个赢得 4 场比赛的球队进入下一轮，而另一支球队则被淘汰出季后赛。在下一轮比赛中，获胜的队伍将对阵同一联盟的另一支晋级队伍。每个联盟除一支球队外，其余球队均被淘汰出季后赛。

季后赛的最后一轮是在两个联盟的胜者之间进行七局四胜制的系列赛，被称为 NBA 总决赛（NBA Finals），每年 6 月举行（有时，系列赛将在 5 月底开始）。NBA 总决赛冠军将获得拉里·奥布莱恩总冠军奖杯（Larry O'Brien Championship Trophy）。获胜球队的每位球员和主要贡献者，包括教练和总经理，都会获得一枚总冠军戒指。

第四节 比 赛 规 则

篮球比赛的目的是通过从上方将篮球投进对手的篮筐，同时阻止对手投篮得分，从而得分超过对手。以这种方式得分的尝试被称为投篮。一次成功的投篮可得两分，如果在国际比赛中从距离篮筐 6.75 m（22 ft 2 in）的三分线外投篮，在 NBA 比赛中从距离篮筐 7.24 m（23 ft 9 in）的三分线以外投篮，一次成功的投篮可得三分。在被犯规后，从罚球线投篮可以获得一分。当一个球队通过投篮或罚球得分后，未得分的球队在本方场地端线外的一个点上发界外球，重新开始比赛。

4.1 比赛规则

国际篮联的比赛分为 4 节，每节 10 分钟；美国男篮职业联赛的比赛则是每节 12 分钟；美国大学男子比赛采用两个 20 分钟的半场，大学女子比赛采用 4 节，每节 10 分钟；大多数美国高中校队比赛采用 4 节，每节 8 分钟，比赛时间因州而异。根据国际篮联、美国男篮职业联赛和美国大学生篮球联赛（NCAA）的规定，半场休息时间为 15 分钟；美国高中则为 10 分钟。加时赛，除高中为 4 分钟外，都是 5 分钟。球队在下半场交换场地。设定的比赛时间是实际的比赛时间；当比赛停止时，计时钟停止。因此，完成比赛时间通常需要比设定的时间长得多，通常是 2 小时左右。

每队五名球员同时上场，换人没有次数限制，但只能在比赛停止时进行换人。每个球队都有一名教练，负责监督球队的发展和制定比赛战术，以及其他团队人员，如助理教练、经理、统计员、医生和训练员。

不论男队或女队，标准的比赛服包括一条短裤和一件运动衫，比赛服的正面和背面都印有独特的、清晰可见的号码。运动员穿着能够提供额外脚踝支撑的高帮篮球鞋。一般来说,队服上印的都是球队、球员的名字,在北美以外的地区,还印有赞助商的名字。

为了与球员进行短暂的会面,在教练的要求下(有时是 NBA 的强制要求),有限次数的暂停和计时钟停止是允许的。暂停时间通常不超过 1 分钟(在 NBA 是 100 秒),除非电视转播需要插播广告。

比赛是由一名总裁判(在 NBA 中被称为 crew chief),1~2 个裁判(在 NBA 中被称为 referees)、计时员与记录员(table officials)控制。在美国男篮职业联赛、大学比赛、和许多高中的比赛中,球场上总共有 3 名裁判。计时员与记分员负责记录每队的得分、计时、个人和球队犯规、换人、球权指示器和投篮计时器。

4.2 违例

篮球可以通过球员投篮、球员之间传球、抛、拍、滚或运球(球员边跑边使球触地弹回手中)的方式向对方篮筐推进。

比赛时,篮球必须保持在球场范围内,造成球出界的球队将失去控球权。如果球触及边界线,或触及界外的任何球员或物体,即为出界。

球员在不带球的情况下可以走的步数是有限制的,如超过限制会导致走步违例(traveling)。球员停止运球后,不能继续运球。双手触球被认为是停止运球,这一违例也被称为二次运球(double dribble)。在运球过程中,球员不能将手放在球的底部携带球,这个动作被称为翻腕违例(carrying the ball)。一支球队,一旦在前场掌握了控球权,就不能将球回传给后场队员。违反这些规则将导致失去控球权。

篮球不能用脚踢,也不能用拳头击打。对于进攻队员,违反这些规则将导致失去控球权;在防守方面,大多数联赛会重新设定投篮时间,让进攻方发界外球。

把球推进过半场是有时间限制的,国际篮联和美国职业篮球协会的规定是 8 秒;一次进攻时间,国际篮联和美国职业篮球协会的规定是 24 秒;被严密防守时的最长持球时间是 5 秒;在罚球(或"关键")区内停留的最长时间是 3 秒。这些规则旨在促进更多的进攻。

此外,球员在阻止对手投球得分或帮助队友投篮得分方面也有限制。妨碍中篮(goaltending)是指防守队员触碰到一个向下飞向篮筐的球;而与之相关的篮上干扰(basket interference)违例则是触碰到篮筐边上或篮筐上方的球,或者球员将手从篮筐下面伸过篮筐。

图 2.4 佐兰·德拉季奇(右)接触卡尔·英格利希犯规(作者 Carlos Delgado)

4.3 犯规

试图通过某些方式的身体接触不公平地使对手处于不利地位的行为属于违规,被称为侵人犯规(personal foul),这是防守球员最常见的违规行为;然而,进攻球员也同样会违规。被犯规的球员将会得到一次罚界外球的机会;或者在投篮被犯规时得到一次或多次罚球,这取决于投篮是否成功。在距离篮筐 15 ft(4.6 m)的罚球线上罚球可得 1 分。

裁判负责判断球员的身体接触是否违规,有时判罚会引起争议。对于犯规的判罚会因比赛、联赛和裁判的不同而不同。

第二类犯规被称为技术犯规(technical fouls),比赛时球队或球员可能会被指控违反各种规则,包括没有在记分簿上正确记录球员,或违反体育精神的行为。这些违规行为会导致 1~2 次罚球,罚球可以由在场的 5 名球员中的任何一人来执行。重复犯规可能导致取消犯规球员比赛资格。因为过度或不必要的身体接触导致的明显犯规被称为故意犯规(intentional foul);在美国男篮职业联赛中被称为恶意犯规(flagrant foul)。在国际篮联和美国大学生篮球联赛的女子篮球比赛中,被驱逐出场的犯规被称为取消比赛资格的犯规(disqualifying foul)。

图 2.5 裁判判罚犯规
(图片来源:Wikipedia)

在美国男篮职业联赛、美国大学生篮球联赛的女篮比赛和国际篮球比赛中,如果一支球队在一段时间内(一节或 1 半场)的犯规次数超过了一定的数量,对方球队在这段时间内所受到的所有非投篮犯规都会得到 1 或 2 次罚球,罚球次数取决于联盟的规定。在美国大学男篮和高中男女篮球比赛中,如果一个队在半场内累计 7 次犯规,对方将得到一次罚球机会,如果第一次罚球命中,将得到第二次罚球机会,这被称为"追加罚球(one-and-one)"。如果一方在半场内犯规超过 10 次,那么在半场剩余的时间里,任何犯规都会导致对方得到 2 次罚球。

当球队罚球时,对手不得干扰罚球队员,也不得试图重新获得控球权,直到最后一次或可能的最后一次罚球出手。

当一支球队犯规次数达到一定数量后,另一支球队会获得额外的罚球(bonus)"。在记分牌上,通常用一个指示灯显示"罚球"("Bonus" or "Penalty"),并有一个发光的方向箭头或圆点指示:当对方犯规时,该队将获得罚球(一些记分牌还显示了犯规次数)。

在两次罚球的情况下,如果一支球队第一次罚球未中,对方必须等到第二次罚球完成后才能试图收回控球权并继续比赛。

如果一名球员在投篮时被犯规,导致投篮没中,该球员将获得与投篮得分相等的罚球机会。如果一名球员在投 2 分球时被犯规,将得到 2 次罚篮机会;投 3 分球时被犯规,将会

图 2.6 当因技术犯规而罚球时，只有罚球队员(此图中为安德烈·伊万诺夫)被允许进入延长的罚球线下面的区域(作者 Artem Korzhimanov)

得到 3 次罚篮机会。

如果一名球员在投篮时被犯规，且投篮成功通常该球员将获得 1 分的额外罚球机会，这种情况被称为"打三分"或"打四分"(或者更通俗地说，"加罚一球")，因为在犯规时得了 2 分或 3 分，并得到额外的 1 分罚球。

4.4 比赛装备

篮球比赛中必要的装备是篮球和篮球场：一个两端各有一个篮筐的平坦的长方形篮球场。比赛级别的篮球场要求使用更多的设备，如比赛时钟、计分表、记分牌、球权箭头和哨声控制的停表系统。

4.4.1 篮球场

国际比赛的标准篮球场长 28 m(92 ft)，宽 15 m(49 ft)。美国男篮职业联赛(NBA)和美国大学生篮球联赛(NCAA)的球场是 29 m×15 m(94 ft×50 ft)。大多数球场都是木地板，通常采用枫木板，木板的长边与篮球场的长边平行。主队的名字和标志通常画在中圈或其周围。

4.4.2 篮筐

篮筐是一个直径 46 cm(18 in)的钢圈，篮筐下方装有篮网，篮筐固定在篮板上，篮板的尺寸为 1.8 m×1.1 m(6 ft×3.5 ft)，在球场的两端各有一个篮筐。篮板上的白框高 46 cm(18 in)，宽 61 cm(2 ft)。

在几乎所有级别的比赛中，篮筐的上沿距离地面都是 10 ft(3.05 m)，篮筐在底线内 4 ft

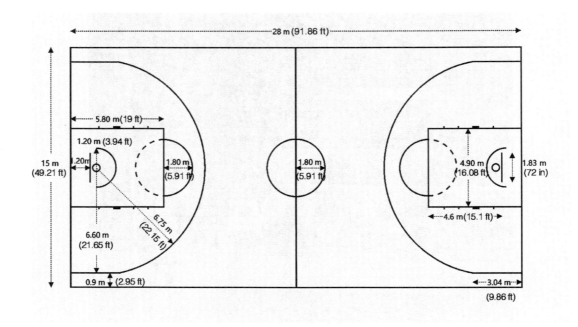

图 2.7 篮球场（作者 Lencer）

(1.22 m)处。球场和篮板的尺寸可能会有所不同,但篮筐的正确高度是非常重要的,因为几英寸的偏差就会对投篮产生非常不利的影响。球网必须"在球穿过篮筐时产生短暂阻碍作用",从而有助于从视觉上确认球穿过了篮筐。篮网阻碍球还有另一个好处,就是减慢球的下落速度,使得篮板球不会跑得太远。

4.4.3 篮球

篮球的尺寸也有具体规定。官方规定的男子篮球比赛用球为 7 号球或 295 球,周长为 29.5 in(75 cm),重 22 oz(623.69 g)。女子篮球比赛用球为 6 号或"285 球",周长为 28.5 in (72 cm),重 20 oz(567 g)。3×3 篮球是半场 3 对 3 比赛的正式版本,所有比赛(男子、女子和混合队)都使用同一种专用球,这种球的周长与 6 号球相同,重量与 7 号球相同。

图 2.8 篮球正穿过篮筐（作者 Class Kerelin Molina）

图 2.9 传统的八片式篮球（作者 Reisio）

第五节 常用技术

5.1 位置

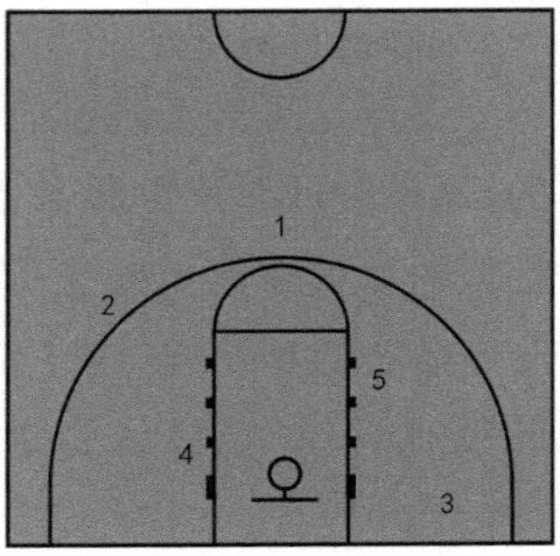

尽管篮球比赛规则没有明确规定球员的场上位置,但球员位置已经成为篮球运动的一部分。在篮球发展的早期,球队通常设置两个后卫、两个前锋和一个中锋;之后,一些特定的位置有所变化。就目前的趋势而言,包括迈克·沙舍夫斯基(Mike Krzyzewski)在内的许多顶级教练都提倡无位置篮球的理念:如果球员的技术允许,大个子球员可以自由地在外线投篮和运球。常见的篮球位置包括:

控球后卫(Point guard,俗称"1号位置"):是球队中速度最快的球员,通过控球组织球队的进攻,并确保球在正确的时间传给正确的球员。

1—控球后卫;2—得分后卫;3—小前锋;4—大前锋;5—中锋。

图 2.10 进攻区域内的球员位置(图片来源:Wikipedia)

得分后卫(Shooting guard,俗称"2号位置"):在进攻端创造大量的投篮机会,主要是远距离投篮;防守对方最好的外线球员。

小前锋(Small forward,俗称"3号位置"):通常主要通过切入篮下和运球突破得分;防守时,拼抢篮板和进行抢断,但有时会打得更加积极。

大前锋(Power forward,俗称"4号位置"):经常背对篮筐进攻;防守时,在篮下(区域联防)或对抗对方的大前锋(人盯人防守)。

中锋(Center,俗称"5号位置"):进攻时,利用身高和身材优势得分;防守时负责近距离保护篮筐或者抢篮板球。

上述篮球位置不是一成不变的。对于今天的大多数球队来说,得分后卫和小前锋有着非常相似的职责,他们通常被称为边锋(wings),大前锋和中锋也被称为内线球员(post players)。虽然大多数球队将两名球员称为后卫,两名称为前锋,一名称为中锋,但在某些情况下,球队会用不同的名称来称呼他们。

5.2 投篮

投篮是通过将球投进篮筐来得分的行为,其方法因球员和具体情境而异。

通常情况下,投篮是指球员面对篮筐,双脚亦指向篮筐,将球放在略高于头部的优势手(投篮臂)的指尖上,同时用另一只手支撑球的一侧,随后跳跃(虽然不总是)并伸出投篮臂来投球。而所谓的随球动作(follow-through)是指投篮的手臂完全伸展,手腕完全弯曲的动作在球投出后保持一会。球员们可以通过使球平稳地下旋来缓冲它对篮筐的冲击力。不同球员对理想的投篮轨迹认知不同,但一般建议以适当的弧度投出。球员可以直接把球投入篮筐,也可以利用篮板改变球的方向使球入筐。

使用上述姿势时,最常见的两种投篮方式是原地投篮和跳投。在做这两种投篮动作之前,都要先做一个下蹲动作,这可以提升肌肉的负荷能力,从而增加投篮的力量。原地投篮时,投篮选手采用站立姿势,投球时双脚都不离开地面,这种投篮方式通常用于罚球。而对于跳投而言,投球是在半空中进行的,球在接近起跳的最高点被释放。这会为球提供更大的力量和更长的飞行距离,并使投篮者能超过防守队员的高度进行投篮。但如果在脚回到地面之前没有投球,则被认为是一个走步违例(traveling violation)。

上篮(layup)是另一种常见的投篮方式。这种投篮方式要求球员朝篮筐移动,并把球"向上"抛入篮筐中,通常不接触篮板(不接触篮板,低手投球的方式称为挑篮)。最受观众欢迎且命中率最高的投篮方式是扣篮(slam dunk)。扣篮时,球员跳得很高,向下扣球,同时手接触到篮筐。

图 2.11　近距离跳投
(图片来源:Wikimedia)

与上篮相比,一种很少见的投篮方式是"不可思议的投篮(circus shot)"。"不可思议的投篮"是指一种投篮命中率很低的投篮方式,当投篮者失去平衡、腾空而起、摔倒或背对篮筐时,通过翻转、举起、由下向上抛或向篮筐方向扔的高难度的投篮方式。向后投篮(back-shot)是指球员背对篮筐时的投篮,可以用优势手投篮,也可以用另一只手投篮,但是这种投篮成功率很低。

一个完全没有碰到篮筐和篮板的投篮被称为三不沾(air ball)。一个特别糟糕的投篮,或者只碰到篮板的投篮,被戏称为"砖头"。滞空时间(hang time)是指球员起跳后在空中停留的时间长度,无论是扣篮、上篮还是跳投。

5.3　篮板球

抢篮板球的目的是在投篮或罚球未命中,球从篮筐或篮板上弹起时,成功地获得控球权。篮板球在比赛中起着重要作用,因为大多数控球都是在球队投球未中的情况下结束的。篮板球分为两类:进

图 2.12　一名球员抢到进攻篮板
(作者 Tony The Tiger)

攻篮板球，即球被进攻方抢回，不改变控球权；防守篮板球，即防守方获得控球权。大部分篮板球都被防守方抢到，因为防守的球队往往处于更有利的位置来争抢篮板球。

5.4 传球

传球（pass）是球员之间传递篮球的一种方式，大多数传球都伴随着向前迈一步的动作以增加传球的力量，并通过双手的随球动作来确保传球的准确性。

主要的传球方式是胸前传球（chest pass），球直接从传球者的胸前传到接球者的胸部位置。正确的胸前传球包括一个快速的拇指外翻动作，以增加球的飞行速度，让防守队员几乎没有时间作出反应。

另一种传球方式是击地传球（bounce pass）。传球者将球从自己的胸前推出，传向距离接球者三分之二处的地面，使球轻快地反弹向接球者。击地传球比胸前传球需要更长的时间来完成，但也更难被对方球员拦截（故意踢球是违例行为）。因此，在场上较为拥挤，或需要绕过防守队员时，球员们常常会选择使用击地传球这一方式。

过顶传球（overhead pass）是指将球越过防守队员的一种传球方式，传球队员将球举过头顶传递给队友。

快攻传球（outlet pass）是指在球队得到防守篮板球后，向前传球发动快攻。快攻传球是抢到防守篮板球之后的第一次传球。

好的传球最关键的一点就是难以被拦截。优秀的传球者可以非常准确地传球，并且他们确切地知道其他队友喜欢在哪里接球。有一种特殊的传球方式是传球队员在传球时不看接球的队友，这就是所谓的"盲传"（no-look pass）。

另一种先进的传球方式是背后传球（behind-the-back pass），顾名思义，是指传球者的背后把球传给队友的一种技巧。虽然有些球员可以有效地进行这样的传球，但许多教练不鼓励盲传或背后传球。因为他们认为这些传球方式难以控制，更容易导致失误或违例。

5.5 运球

运球（Dribbling）是一种用一只手连续地使球击地弹起的动作，是球员带球的必要步骤。运球时，球员不是用手拍球，而是用指尖将球推向地面，这样能够更好地控制球。

当运球经过对手时，运球队员应该用离对手较远的手运球，使防守球员难以碰到球。因此，对球员来说，能够熟练地使用左右手运球是非常重要的。

图 2.13　一名球员（左）背身单打卡住一位防守队员（作者 Damon J. Moritz）

优秀的运球队员（或控球队员）倾向于降低重心进行运球，从而缩短球从地面反弹到手的距离，使防守队员难以"抢断"球。优秀的控球队员经常在背后、两腿之间运球，并突然改变方向，使运球模式更难以预测，更难以防守。这种运球方式被称为变向运球过人（crossover），是运球过人最有效的方式。

技术娴熟的球员可以在不看篮球的情况下运球，利用运球动作或余光来跟踪球的位置。由于不必把注意力集中在球上，球员可以搜寻队友位置或寻找得分良机，同时避免被对手抢断的风险。

5.6 盖帽

在篮球比赛中，当进攻球员投篮出手后，防守队员通过用手触球，成功改变球的运行轨迹的动作，被称为盖帽（block）。在几乎所有形式的比赛中，在球处于抛物线下降的路径时触球是违规的，称为妨碍中篮（goaltending）。在美国职业篮球联赛和美国大学生篮球联赛的男子篮球比赛中，当投篮过程中篮球触碰到篮板，或球的任何部分尚处于篮筐正上方时，进行盖帽动作将被视为违规。根据国际规则，若球处于抛物线下

图 2.14　盖帽（图片来源：Wikimedia）

降阶段且尚未触及篮筐，或已触碰篮板但未达到篮筐，此时进行盖帽同样被视为违规。然而，当球击中篮筐后，再次触球是合规的，不再被视为一个盖帽。

为了成功盖帽，球员必须能够跃升至一个比投篮出手点更高的位置。因此，身高可以成为盖帽的优势，个子较高的大前锋或中锋通常比个子较矮的后卫队员拥有更多的盖帽机会。然而，如果有好的时机和足够高的垂直跳跃能力，那么即使是较矮的球员也可以完成有效的盖帽。

第六节　基本战术

篮球比赛中，主要有两种防守战术：区域联防（zone defense）和人盯人防守（man-to-man defense）。在区域联防战术中，每位球员被指定负责防守球场的特定区域。这种战术通常能创造出双人包夹防守的机会，即所谓的"陷阱"（trap）。在人盯人防守战术中，每个防守队员防守一个特定的对手。

进攻战术更加多样化，通常包括有计划的传球和无球球员的移动。进攻球员在无球情况下快速移动以获得有利位置的动作被称为切入（cut）。进攻球员为阻止对手防守队友而采取的合规动作，即挡住防守者的移动路线使队友从他旁边切入，称为掩护（screen or pick)。这两种战术在挡拆(pick and roll)战术中被结合在一起,即球员先进行掩护,转身切到篮下,伺机接传球,然后上篮得分,或执行下一个战术。掩护和切入在进攻中非常重要;可以形成快速的传球和集体合作,最后形成一次成功的投篮。球队通常有多个进攻战术,以确保他们的行动不被预测。在球场上,控球后卫通常负责向其他队员指示比赛战术。

篮球术语

中锋:中锋是篮球比赛阵容中的五个位置之一,一般都由队中最高的球员担任,主要负责得分、抢篮板球和篮下防守。

小前锋:篮球比赛阵容中的五个位置之一。小前锋通常是最全能的球员,通常是场上第三高的球员。

大前锋:又译为强力前锋,通常是球场上第二高的球员,扮演与中锋相似的角色。

控球后卫:有时也称组织后卫,是篮球比赛阵容中的一个固定位置。控球后卫是球场上最矮的球员和最好的控球队员,负责组织球队的进攻。

得分后卫:篮球比赛阵容中的五个位置之一,得分后卫通常是球队最好的得分手和第二矮的球员。

肘区:是指罚球线的两端与三秒区相交的位置。

低位:篮筐底部两侧的球场区域。

高位:罚球线两端到罚球区顶部的球场区域。

罚球区:即三秒区,罚球线内的一个区域,在篮筐前划出的一个半圆形区域。

罚球线:是指距离篮板的垂线15 ft,与底线平行的一条线,罚球选手从那里投篮。

篮板:是指与篮筐相连接的木制或玻璃纤维材质的方形板。

投篮计时钟:一种计时器,旨在通过要求在计时器到期前完成投篮,来提高进攻速度(从而提高得分频率);如果球没有接触到篮筐或进入篮筐,则称为投篮时间犯规,这将导致投篮队失去控球权。在 NBA、WNBA 和 FIBA 比赛中,时间限制是 24 秒。

跳球:比赛双方2名球员跳起争抢一个由主裁判抛到他们中间上空的篮球。

上篮:是指进攻球员在跑动中将球投进篮筐的进攻动作。

长传:是指进攻队在抢到后场篮板球后的第一次传球,试图通过长传以最快的速度完成进攻。

篮板球:在投篮不中以后,两支球队任一方的球员抢得控球权,记为篮板球。

打板投篮:是指球员投篮时,球碰到篮球后击中篮筐边缘或直接进网。

空心篮:是指投篮命中的篮球只碰到篮网,没有碰到篮筐,发出"刷"的一声。

三不沾球:是指一个没有被封盖的投篮,完全没有碰到篮筐、篮圈和篮板。

空中接力:是一种进攻方式,一名球员传球给在篮筐附近的队友,队友跳起来,在空中接住球,在触地前扣篮或投篮。

切入：是指一种进攻技巧，一名没有控球的球员使用特定的动作从球场的一个位置移动到另一个位置，其主要目的是创造空间并摆脱防守获得空位。

卡位：是指通过扩大身体姿势和张开手臂，用身体作为一道屏障，来争取占据一个比对手更有利的篮板位置。

掩护：进攻球员站在队友和防守球员之间，为队友在空位投篮创造机会。

挡拆：是指进攻方无球球员用自己的身体挡住防守球员前进方向，该无球球员只能采用静立姿势来进行挡拆，否则会被判进攻犯规或移动挡拆犯规。

盖帽：是指在篮球比赛中，当进攻球员投篮出手后，防守球员通过触球或阻挡来改变球的运动轨迹，从而阻止对方进球。

助攻：如果一个球员将球传给队友，队友接球后直接得分，在技术统计表上为该传球球员记录一次助攻。

失误：是指在普通比赛中或因违反规则受到处罚而失去控球权。

三秒违例：是指进攻球员站在三秒区内超过三秒。

二次运球：球员使用两只手同时运球，或者是在运球停止之后又重新开始运球，即为二次运球，属于一种违例行为。

走步：或叫带球走，是指比赛时违规移动中枢脚，没有保持住轴心脚而倒在地板上，或走三步或更多步而没有运球的动作。

进攻犯规：是指进攻队员的犯规。

带球撞人：是一种进攻犯规，当持球队员撞向一个没有移动的防守队员时，就会被判罚带球撞人。

假摔：球员在与对手很少或没有身体接触的情况下故意或夸张地摔倒，目的是造成对手个人犯规。

罚球：是指在篮球比赛中，由于对手犯规而在罚球线后进行无阻碍投篮。

加罚一球：是指投篮手得分时因对手犯规而获得罚球，尤指命中后的罚球。

背打战术：是指球员在低位拿球背向篮筐的一种进攻战术。

快攻：一种进攻战术，一支球队试图尽可能快地推进球并得分，使对手没有时间进行有效防守。快攻通常在抢断或盖帽后进行。

人盯人防守：是指每个球员防守一名对手球员的防守战术。

区域联防：是一种防守战术，每个防守队员负责防守球场的一个区域，并且必须防守任何进入该区域的对手。

全场紧逼：是一种防守战术，在对手传球之前及之后，持续紧盯对手，以增加对手压力，经常在进攻方还没进入防守方半场之前，在对方半场就进行紧逼防守。可能会采取人盯人防守或是区域联防，形成区域紧逼。有时会试图阻止对手在后场或中场发界外球，并阻拦干扰发球球员。

练 习

1. 篮球运动的国际管理机构是什么？
2. 篮球运动起源于哪个国家和哪一年？
3. 篮球比赛中球员在场上的主要位置有哪些？

第三章

草地曲棍球

学习目标

1. 了解曲棍球的发展历史
2. 掌握曲棍球赛事的主要管理机构和重要赛事
3. 熟悉曲棍球比赛规则和专业术语

第一节 概　　述

图 3.1　2018 年夏季青年奥运会上的曲棍球比赛（作者 BugWarp）

草地曲棍球（Field hockey），或简称曲棍球（hockey），是一项以标准曲棍球形式构成的集体运动，每队共有 11 名球员，由 10 名场上球员和 1 名守门员组成。比赛时，两队必须在球场上移动曲棍球，使用曲棍将球击向对方的射门圈，然后再将其射入球门。比赛结束时，进球较多的队获胜。比赛在草地、洒水草皮、人造草皮或室内木板场地上进行。

这项现代运动起源于 19 世纪英国的公立学校，现在在全球范围内流行。管理机构是国际曲棍球联合会（FIH）。在国际比赛中，包括奥运会（Olympic Games）、世界杯（World Cup）、FIH 职业联赛（FIH Pro League）、青少年世界杯（Junior World Cup）以及过去的世界联赛（World League）和冠军杯（Champions Trophy），都包括男子和女子的比赛。许多国家举办大量的青少年、成年和大师俱乐部比赛。国际曲棍球联合会还负责组织曲棍球规则委员会,并制定比赛规则。

在一些国家,草地曲棍球是一种很普遍的曲棍球运动形式,简称为"hockey"。"草地曲棍球"(field hockey)一词主要在加拿大和美国使用,在那里"曲棍球"(hockey)更多是指冰球(ice hockey)。在瑞典,人们使用"landhockey"这个词。草地曲棍球的一种流行的变体是室内曲棍球(indoor field hockey),它在许多方面有所不同,但仍然具有草地曲棍球的主要特点。

第二节　主要管理机构

国际曲棍球联合会(International Hockey Federation,FIH)是草地曲棍球和室内曲棍球运动的国际管理机构,其总部设在瑞士洛桑。国际曲棍球联合会负责曲棍球的主要国际比赛,特别是曲棍球世界杯(Hockey World Cup)。

国际曲棍球联合会于1924年1月7日由保罗·莱奥泰(Paul Léautey)在巴黎成立,他担任第一任主席,以回应曲棍球在1924年夏季奥运会项目中被取消的问题,此前,巴黎奥组委因该项目没有国际组织而拒绝设立曲棍球项目。7个创始成员国是奥地利、比利时、捷克斯洛伐克、法国、匈牙利、西班牙和瑞士。

国际女子曲棍球协会联合会(International Federation of Women's Hockey Associations,IFWHA)于1927年由澳大利亚、丹麦、英格兰、爱尔兰、苏格兰、南非、美国和威尔士发起成立。1982年,国际曲棍球联合会与国际女子曲棍球联合会合并。

第三节　重要赛事

3.1　奥运会曲棍球比赛

图3.2　2008年夏季奥运会曲棍球比赛(德国女队对阵中国女队)(作者 Andre Kiwitz)

1908年的伦敦奥运会上,曲棍球作为男子比赛项目被引入奥运会,当时有6支球队参加,其中有4支来自大不列颠及爱尔兰联合王国。

1924年巴黎奥运会由于曲棍球没有国际性管理机构而取消了该项比赛。同年国际曲棍球联合会成立以应对曲棍球运动被取消的问题。在下一届奥运会(1928年阿姆斯特丹奥运会)上曲棍球重新成为奥运会比赛项目。

国际奥委会在1980年的夏季奥运会上首次引入了女子曲棍球项目。1976年蒙特利尔奥运会,曲棍球比赛首次在人造草坪上举行。

在1988年奥运会之前,这项比赛是邀请赛,但国际曲棍球联合会自1992年奥运会以来引入了资格赛制度。荷兰队以18枚奖牌(6金、6银、6铜)领跑奖牌榜。印度在金牌数量上处于领先位置。

3.2 世界杯曲棍球赛

男子曲棍球世界杯(Men's FIH Hockey World Cup)是由国际曲棍球联合会组织的一项国际草地曲棍球赛事。这项赛事始于1971年,每四年举办一次,在两届夏季奥运会之间举行。巴基斯坦是最成功的球队,曾4次赢得世界杯冠军;荷兰、澳大利亚和德国各获得3次冠军;比利时和印度各赢得过一次冠军。2018年世界杯参赛队伍扩大到16支。

女子曲棍球世界杯(Women's FIH Hockey World Cup)是一项国际女子草地曲棍球赛事,其资格赛和决赛阶段的形式与男子相似,自1974年以来一直举办。自1982年国际曲棍球联合会与国际女子曲棍球协会联合会合并以来,该比赛一直由国际曲棍球联合会组织。自1986年以来,它每四年定期举行一次,与男子比赛同年举行。

世界杯曲棍球赛分为资格赛和决赛两个阶段。每个阶段的比赛形式是一样的。

自1977年以来,资格赛阶段一直是曲棍球世界杯的一部分。所有参赛队伍都将参加资格赛。参赛队伍分成2个或2个以上的组别,争夺决赛的入场券。排名前两名的球队将自动获得参赛资格,其余席位将由季后赛决出。

决赛阶段将由洲际冠军和其他有资格的球队参加。有时它还由夏季奥运会曲棍球比赛的冠军或洲际亚军参加。各队再次分组,进行循环赛。分组是根据当前的FIH世界排名确定的。

3.3 FIH职业联赛

FIH男子职业联赛(Men's FIH Pro League)是由国际曲棍球联合会组织的一项国际男子曲棍球比赛,取代了男子曲棍球联合会世界联赛(Men's FIH Hockey World League)。这项比赛同时也是世界杯曲棍球赛和奥运会的预选赛。第一届比赛于2019年举行。9支队伍获得了4年的参赛资格。

FIH女子职业联赛(Women's FIH Pro League)是由国际曲棍球联合会组织的一项国际女子曲棍球比赛,取代了女子曲棍球联合会世界联赛(Women's FIH Hockey World

League)。这项比赛也是世界杯曲棍球赛和奥运会的预选赛。第一届比赛于 2019 年举行。9 支队伍获得了 4 年的参赛资格。

联赛中,9 支男子和女子球队参加双循环赛,从 10 月到次年 6 月进行主客场比赛,赛季结束时排名第一的球队赢得联赛冠军。从 2022—2023 赛季开始,赛季末排名垫底的球队将被降级,取而代之的是男子 FIH 国家杯(Men's FIH Nations Cup)/女子 FIH 国家杯(Women's FIH Nations Cup)的冠军。

第四节 比赛规则

4.1 概述

曲棍球的户外比赛场地是一块长 91.4 m、宽 55 m 的光滑平坦的场地。2 支队伍各由 11 名队员组成,进行时长为 70 分钟的比赛。每队的 11 名队员中有 1 名是守门员,每个运动员手持一根曲棍,用曲棍来移动曲棍球。曲棍长约 1 yd,重约 1.5 lb。曲棍的一端是较细的圆形把手(像扫帚柄),曲棍的底部用来击球的一端呈刀刃状,一面是平的,另一面通常是圆的。曲棍球是一个硬质的塑料球,在比赛中,运动员运球,并在队友间传球,而对手则试图抢得控球权。曲棍球的大小与棒球相似,但是比棒球更大、更重、更硬。虽然曲棍球的比赛战术和策略与足球非常相似,但曲棍球运动具有独特性:控球的球员不能使用身体、装备或队友来掩护、拉扯或以其他方式阻挡对手触球。这需要运动员具有专业的运球、传球和接球技术。比赛中,两队都试图运球或传球进入射门区,然后将球射进球门得分。射门区的形状很像字母"D"。只有当进攻方从射门区内合规地击球(推球、推击球、铲击球、大力击球、垫射)时,才能得分。比赛结束时,进球较多的球队获胜。

4.2 比赛

比赛由 2 名场上裁判员执裁。传统上,每个裁判员通常负责一半的场地,大致按对角线划分。场上裁判员通常由记录台技术人员协助,包括计时员和记录员。

在比赛开始前,要抛硬币,获胜的队长可以选边或选择开球。自 2017 年起,比赛分为 4 节,每节 15 分钟,每节比赛后休息 2 分钟,中场休息 15 分钟然后交换场地。在每一节比赛开始时,以及进球后,比赛从中场传球开始。开球前,所有球员必须在本队所在半场(传球的球员除外),球可以沿地面向任何方向开出。两队分别

图 3.3 一名弗吉尼亚骑士队的球员正在传球
(作者 Jack Marion)

在上下半场开球,进球后,丢球的球队拥有开球权。双方球队在中场休息时交换场地。

比赛时,场上球员们只能用曲棍的正面击球。使用曲棍的背面击球属于违规行为,对方将获得球权。只要在抢断时没有接触控球队员或对方的球棒,抢断就是允许的(如果在不可避免会进行身体接触的位置抢断,且之后发生了身体接触,这种行为可能被处罚)。此外,控球球员不允许故意使用身体推开防守队员。

场上球员不能用脚踢球,但如果球意外地击中了脚,并且球员没有从接触中获利,那么这种接触就不会受到处罚。

阻碍通常发生在三种情况下:当防守队员挡在持球球员和球之间以阻碍他们控球;当防守队员的球棒伸到进攻队员的球棒与球之间或与进攻队员的球棒或身体接触时;以及当阻碍对方球员抢断队友的球时,也会被判阻碍犯规(称为第三方阻碍)。

当球完全越过边线(在边线上仍算作界内)时,由对方一名队员发边线球,将球击回球场。球必须放在边线上,击球的位置要尽可能靠近球出界的位置。如果进攻队员将球击出底线,则判给防守方一个 16 yd(15 m)球。进攻方在距离对方底线 16 yd 范围内的犯规也可判 16 yd 球。

4.3 球员位置

球员的场上位置不是固定不变的,在比赛过程中会经常发生变化。每支球队最多可以上场 11 名球员,通常会设置前锋、中场和后卫(边后卫)的场上位置,球员的位置随着频繁的攻防转换而前后移动。球队可以采用不同的人员安排:

- 设置一名守门员。守门员穿着与其他队员不同颜色的球衣,并配备全套防护装备,包括头盔、护腿和护脚;
- 不设置守门员,只有场上球员。没有球员有守门员特权,也没有球员穿不同颜色的球衣;在防守短角球(penalty corner)或射门时,除面罩外,球员不得佩戴防护头盔。

4.3.1 比赛阵型

由于曲棍球具有非常动态的比赛特点,因此很难将场上位置等同于足球比赛中常见的静态阵型。虽然场上位置通常分为边后卫、中卫、中场或前锋,但对球员来说,了解场上的每个位置是很重要的。例如,我们经常会看到一个中卫出现位置重叠,并最终出现在进攻位置上,而中场和前锋则需要重新调整位置以填补他们留下的空间。像这样在前后位置之间移动的情况,在所有位置都非常普遍。

4.3.2 守门员

当球在射门区内,穿着全套防护装备的守门员在防守时,可以用球棒、脚、护脚或护腿来推动球;也

图 3.4 守门员菲利普·诺伊塞尔全力以赴防守球门(作者 Neusserf)

可以用球棒、脚、护脚、护腿或身体的任何其他部位来停球或使球向任何方向偏转,包括越过后防线。场上队员可以使用他们的曲棍,但他们不允许用脚和腿推动球、停球或使球向任何方向偏转,包括越过后防线。然而,无论是守门员还是拥有守门员特权的球员,都不允许使用他们所穿的防护装备对其他球员构成危险。

守门员或有守门员特权的球员都不能压在球上,但是,他们可以用手臂、手或身体的任何其他部位把球推开。故意压在球上将导致判罚点球,而如果裁判认为守门员意外压在球上(例如球卡在他们的防护装备中),则判罚短角球。

当球在他们防守的射门区外时,守门员或有守门员特权的球员只允许用他们的曲棍击球。此外,守门员或有守门员特权的戴着头盔的球员,在其防守半场的 23 m 区域外不得参加比赛,罚点球时除外。守门员在任何时候都必须佩戴防护头盔,罚点球时除外。

4.4 定位球

4.4.1 任意球

当犯规行为发生在射门区外时,将判罚任意球。被犯规的一方获得任意球,罚球时,可以朝任何方向击球、推球或挑球。罚任意球时只能通过推击(flick)或铲击(scoop)将球挑起,不能通过大力击球将球挑起。罚任意球必须在犯规地点的控球距离(playing distance)内进行,罚球时,球必须处于静止状态,对手必须退到离球 5 m(5.5 yd)以外的地方。

如上所述,如果进攻球员在射门区外犯规,

图 3.5　边线击球(作者 Dimitri Aguero)

或者进攻球员造成球越过后防线,则判给防守方 15 m 球。在距离射门区 5 m 范围内罚任意球时,包括罚任意球的球员在内的所有人都必须距离射门区至少 5 m;除罚任意球的球员外的所有人都必须距离球至少 5 m。如果进攻方在防守方 23 m(25 yd)线内罚任意球,球必须在射门区外移动至少 5 m 的距离才能进入射门区。

4.4.2 长角球

如果是防守队员无意造成球出后防线,进攻方将获得在 23 m 线上的一次任意球,称为长角球(long corner);如果是故意导致球出后防线,将判罚短角球(penalty corner)。这一任意球由进攻方在 23 m 线上的一个点罚球,该点与球出界的位置一致。

4.4.3 短角球

以下情况判罚短角球:

1. 一名防守队员在射门区内犯规,而这个犯规并不能阻止对方进球的可能性;
2. 防守队员在射门区内对无控球或无机会控球的对手故意犯规;

图 3.6　2012 年伦敦奥运会中国队对韩国队的短角球（图片来源：The Hammer）

3. 防守队员在射门区外，但在本方 23 m 线内故意犯规；
4. 防守队员故意造成球出本方的后防线；
5. 在本方射门区内，球卡在防守队员的衣服或装备里。

罚短角球时，5 名防守队员（通常包括守门员）站在后防线后面，球距离最近的门柱至少 10 码。防守队的所有其他球员必须在中线之外，即不在他们自己的半场，直到球进入比赛状态。一名进攻队员从球门任何一侧 10 米的标记处罚出短角球（射门区半径为 14.63 m），其他进攻队员站在射门区外。罚球队员将球推或击打给射门区外的其他进攻队员，比赛重新开始；在进攻队员射门得分之前，球必须先经过射门区外，然后再进入射门区内。

出于安全考虑，如果短角球的第一次射门是击球，在其越过球门线时，高度不得超过 460 mm（球门"后挡板"的高度）。然而，如果球被认为低于后挡板高度，那么另一名球员（防守球员或进攻球员）随后可以将球偏转到这个高度以上，前提是这种偏转不会导致危险。扫击（slap stroke）（扫击是曲棍贴于地面或靠近地面击球的动作）被归类为击球，因此，第一次射门如果采用扫击也必须低于后挡板的高度。

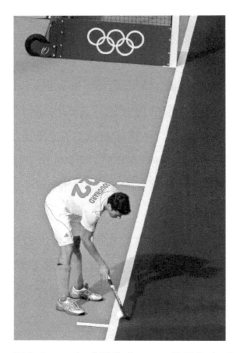

图 3.7　一名球员将在 10 m 处罚短角球。上面的 5 m 标线为防守队员可以站的最近位置（图片来源：Rega Photography）

罚短角球时,如果第一次射门是推球(push)、推击球(flick)或铲击球(scoop),特别是拖射(drag flick),只要该射门不会对任何对手构成危险,就允许该射门高于后挡板的高度。拖射之所以得到广泛应用和发展,是因为它摆脱了第一次使用击球(hit)射门时受到的高度限制,使得技术好的球员同样可以拖射出像其他人击球(hit)动作一样的大力拖射。

4.4.4 点球

图 3.8　点球:由进攻方在罚球点面对守门员进行的一次罚球　　(作者 Dimitri Aguero)

当防守队员在射门区内犯规(无论是意外或其他情况),阻止了一个可能的进球;或者在射门区内故意犯规;或者在罚短角球时,防守队员多次过早从后防线进入场内,都会被判点球。罚点球是在射门区内由一名进攻员在距离球门 6.4 m 的罚球点上面对守门员进行的。罚球队员只能用推球、推击球或铲击球的方式射门一次。如果球被扑出,比赛以 15 m 球(15 m hit)重新开始。如果球进了,比赛按正常方式重新开始。

4.5　危险动作和挑高球

根据国际曲棍球联合会发布的《曲棍球竞赛规则(2015)》,判断危险球(dangerously played ball)只有两个标准:第一个标准是造成对手的合规躲避行为(合规躲避行为由裁判裁定)。第二个标准是在对手距离球不足 5 m 的情况下,挑起球击中对手膝盖以上的部位,属于危险球。这是专门针对短角球射门的规则,但通常适用于整个比赛和球场的所有部分,尽管不完全一致。

在关于危险球的规则中没有提到球的速度。在某些情况下,击中球员膝盖以上的球可能不会被判罚,这取决于裁判的判断。例如,一个刺断(jab tackle)可能会意外地挑起球,近距离击中对手膝盖以上的部位,但在裁判看来,因为球速很慢,不会构成危险。相反,在裁判看来,球近距离高速击中对手,虽然低于膝盖高度,可能会被认为是危险或鲁莽的行为,特别是当前锋可以选择更安全的击球方式时。

如果一个球被挑得很高,将会落向附近的对手中间,则会被认为具有潜在危险,比赛可能因此而停止。一个挑起的高球落向一个空旷的空间中的一个队员,这时,如果一个对手移动到接球队员 5 m 以内的范围内,球在被控制到地面之前就存在潜在的危险——这条规则通常不会被严格执行;允许距离通常只是指控球距离(playing distance),一般 2~3 m 的范围,以及在接球队员接到球时对手被允许接近球的距离。比赛中,执行规则的灵活性通常是基于裁判对球员技术的判断,也就是对比赛水平的判断。为了维持比赛的流畅性,在《国际曲联曲棍球竞赛规则(2015)》(FIH Rules of Hockey 2015)和《2015 年国际曲联裁判简报》(FIH Umpires' Briefings 2015)通常要求裁判非必要不进行判罚。裁判具有最终决定权。

"落球"(falling ball)一词对于可能被称为侵犯犯规(encroaching offenses)的情况很重要。一般来说,只有当对方的球员正在接一个被挑至高于头部(尽管规则中没有规定高度)的球,并且球正在下落,这时侵犯对方接球球员才会被视为犯规。

一般来说,即使一方有潜在危险的行为,如果对手没有因此受到不利的影响,或者显然没有因此受伤而无法继续比赛,那么发生潜在危险行为的一方也不会受到处罚。在任何犯规情形中(包括危险行为),如果裁判根据有利原则(advantage)允许比赛继续进行,在该段比赛结束后,可以对犯规的一方判罚侵人犯规(personal penalty),即警告或停赛,而不是判罚球队罚球(team penalty),如任意球或短角球(然而,一旦裁判根据有利原则让比赛继续进行,就不能叫停比赛并判罚球队罚球)。

将球挑过对方的曲棍(或贴于地面的身体)不构成犯规,前提是考虑到对方的安全且没有危险。例如,一个技术娴熟的进攻队员会把球挑过防守球员的球棍或俯卧的身体,然后过掉他们;但是如果进攻球员把球挑到防守球员的身体上,这几乎肯定会被认为是危险球。

用曲棍把球弹起来,甚至边弹球边跑都不违反规则,只要这不会导致与试图抢断的对手发生潜在的危险冲突。例如,两名球员同时试图在空中抢球,可能会被认为是一种危险的情况,很可能是第一个把球挑起来的球员,或边弹起球边跑的球员会被判罚违规。

危险动作规则也适用于在接近球、击球(取代了曾经被称为"曲棍"的规则,该规则曾经禁止在任何比赛中将球棒的任何部分举过肩膀。这一限制已经被取消,但仍然不应该以危及对手的方式使用球棒)或试图抢断球(与绊倒、阻碍和阻挡有关的犯规)时对曲棍的使用。裁判员对使用球棒击打对手的处罚通常要比对冲撞、阻碍和阻挡等犯规行为严厉得多,尽管后者在发生时,尤其是当它们属于故意犯规时,也会得到严厉的处罚。

图 3.9 绿牌(警告并暂停 2 分钟);黄牌(根据犯规程度停赛 5/10 分钟);红牌(永久停赛)(图片来源:Wikipedia)

4.6 警告和离场

曲棍球采用三级罚牌系统,表示警告和停赛:

当被出示绿牌时,球员必须离场 2 分钟,任何进一步的违规行为都将导致补判罚黄牌或红牌。

黄牌表示判罚暂时离场，类似于冰球比赛判罚犯规球员去受罚席（penalty box）。持续时间由出示黄牌的裁判决定，被出示黄牌的球员必须进入预先由裁判或该国的地方/州/国家协会确定的场地区域。大多数裁判员会判罚暂时离场至少 5 分钟；最长时间由裁判根据犯规严重程度酌情决定，例如，第二次黄牌或第一次因危险动作导致的黄牌可能会被判罚 10 分钟（在某些比赛形式下，包括室内比赛，根据当地规则，暂时罚出场的时间会缩短。）然而，如果判罚暂时离场的时间长于比赛剩余时间，则有可能将该球员罚出场。

与足球比赛一样，红牌是一种取消本场比赛资格的处罚，没有替补，通常会导致球员被禁赛一段时间或一定数量的比赛（这取决于当地的比赛条件，而不是曲棍球规则）。球员也必须离开球场和周围区域。

如果教练被罚离场，根据地方规则，一名本队球员可能必须在比赛的剩余时间内离开球场。

图 3.10　宾夕法尼亚州的一名曲棍球运动员被出示绿牌（作者 Cathi Alloway）

除了颜色外，曲棍球罚牌的形状也不同，所以很容易辨认。绿牌通常是三角形的，黄牌是长方形的，红牌是圆形的。

与足球不同，一名球员可能会收到不止一张绿牌或黄牌。然而，球员不能因为同样的犯规行为而被判罚同样的牌（例如，因危险动作收到两张黄牌），对于第二次同样的犯规行为，必须给一张更严重的牌。如果因为不同的犯规行为而得到第二张黄牌（例如，因故意踩踏得到第一张黄牌，之后因为危险动作得到第二张黄牌），那么暂时离场的时间将比第一次暂时离场的时间长得多。

如果任意球在进攻区 23 m 范围内，裁判可以在判罚任意球后，因为犯规方不服从裁判或其他不当行为将该任意球升级为短角球。

4.7　得分

各队的目标是将球送入射门区，然后在射门区内通过击球、推球或推击球将球射入球门，从而得分。60 分钟比赛结束后，进球多的队获胜。对于非成年人的比赛，或者一些锦标赛，比赛时间可能会缩短。如果比赛采用倒计时进攻时钟，就像冰球比赛那样，那么在比赛结束前，只有当球完全越过球门线并进入球门时，才算进球，而不是在球离开球棒射门时。

如果比赛结束时比分相同，则根据比赛形式，要么宣布平局（draw），要么进入加时赛（extra time），或者进行点球决胜（penalty shoot-out）。在许多比赛（例如常规的俱乐部比赛，或者奥运会或世界杯等国际曲棍球联合会官方锦标赛中的预选赛）中，平局的成绩仍然有效，并计入比赛总成绩。国际曲棍球联合会官方锦标赛规则规定，自 2013 年 3 月起，当排名赛（classification match）打平需要决胜局时，不再有加时赛，直接进入点球大战。然而，许多协会都遵循以前的比赛程序，包括两节各 7.5 分钟的"金球制"（golden goal）加时赛，在加时赛里，只要一支球队得分，比赛就结束了。

加时赛有很多不同的形式，具体形式取决于联赛或锦标赛的规则。在美国大学比赛中，加时赛采用 10 分钟的七人"金球制"加时赛，每队有 7 名球员。如果比分仍相同，比赛将进入一对一比赛（one-on-one competition），每队选择 5 名球员从 23 m（25 yd）线运球至射门区射门。在将球保持在界内的情况下，球员有八秒的时间向守门员把守的球门射门。一轮比赛在进球、球出界、犯规（犯规后以罚点球、推击球或一对一比赛结束而告终）或时间截止后结束。如果仍然是平局，则进行更多轮比赛，直到一支球队得分为止。

4.8　比赛场地

4.8.1　曲棍球场

曲棍球场是一个 91.4 m × 55 m（100.0 yd × 60.1 yd）的矩形场地。两端各有一个高 2.14 m（7 ft）、宽 3.66 m（12 ft）的球门，两条距离底线 22.90 m（25 yd）的线（通常称为 23 m 线或 25 yd 线），以及一条位于场地中间的中线。在距离球门中心 6.40 m（7 yd）处有一个直径为 0.15 m（6 in）的点，称为点球点。射门区弧线距离基线 15 m（16 yd）。

4.8.2　球门

曲棍球的球门由两根立柱组成，在顶部用一根横梁连接起来，当球通过门柱时，球会被球网接住。门柱和横梁必须使用白色的矩形柱子制成，宽 51 mm，厚 51～76 mm。曲棍球的球门还包括一个离地面 50 cm 的侧板和背板。背板的宽度与球门的宽度一样，为 3.66 m（12.0 ft），侧板深度为 1.2 m（3 ft 11 in）。

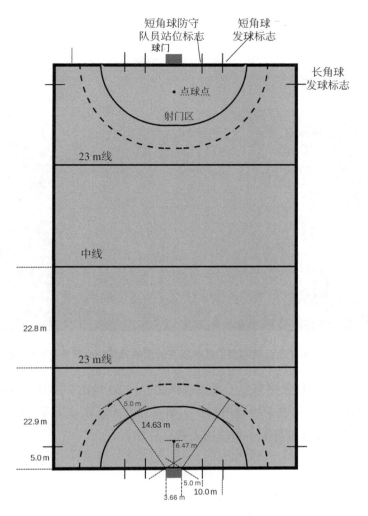

图 3.11 曲棍球场地示意图(图片来源：Hockey field.svg)

图 3.12 曲棍球门(图片来源：sportsequip.co.uk)

4.8.3 球场地面

图 3.13 2000 年夏季奥运会期间悉尼奥林匹克公园曲棍球中心球场(作者 Jimmy Harris)

历史上,这项运动是在天然草皮上发展起来的。在 20 世纪 70 年代早期,人造草皮开始被用于曲棍球比赛,1976 年在蒙特利尔举行了第一届在人造草皮上举行的奥运会。现在所有国际比赛和大多数国家比赛都必须使用人造草皮球场。

4.9 比赛装备

4.9.1 曲棍球

标准曲棍球是硬质圆球,由实心塑料制成(有的内部是软木芯),通常为白色,也可以是任何颜色,只要与比赛场地颜色形成鲜明对比即可。球的直径为 71.3～74.8 mm(2.81～2.94 in),质量为 156～163 g(5.5～5.7 oz)。球的表面通常布满凹痕,以减少漂滑现象,漂滑现象可能会导致球在潮湿表面上的速度不一致。

图 3.14 曲棍球和 5 法郎硬币(作者 Clément Bucco)

4.9.2 曲棍

每位球员携带一根曲棍,长度通常在 80～95 cm(31～37 in)之间;还可以使用更短或更长的曲棍。曲棍的长度取决于球员的个人身高:曲棍的顶部通常到达球员的臀部,较高的球员通常拥有更长的曲棍。守门员可以使用专用曲棍,也可以使用普通的曲棍。专门的守门员曲棍在末端有另一条曲线,以增加其表面积来阻挡球。

曲棍传统上是由木头制成的，但现在也经常用玻璃纤维、凯夫拉尔或碳纤维复合材料制成。曲棍是禁止使用金属材料的，因为如果曲棍折断，锋利的边缘可能会造成伤害。曲棍有一个圆形的手柄，底部有一个J形钩，左边是平的（当向下看手柄，钩子朝上时）。所有的曲棍必须是右手使用的；左手使用的曲棍是被禁止的。

传统上，从曲棍正面的顶部到底部有一个轻微的弧线（称为弓或耙），另一个曲线从"跟部"边缘到手柄顶部（通常是手柄部分插入球杆头部所形成的角度），这有助于球杆头在击球时瞄准球，使击球更容易、更准确。

4.9.3 守门员装备

2007年的《曲棍球竞赛规则》在守门员的规定方面发生了重大变化。装备齐全的守门员必须佩戴头盔、护腿和护脚，并且像其他球员一样，必须携带一根曲棍。守门员可以使用场上球员的曲棍或专用的守门员曲棍，前提是曲棍的尺寸符合规则。通常，曲棍球守门员还穿着大量的附加防护装备，包括护胸、带衬垫的短裤、厚厚的衬垫护手、护裆、护颈和护臂。守门员不得越过23 m线，唯一的例外是当比赛时钟暂停时，守门员要去球场另一端罚点球。守门员也可以在罚点球时摘下头盔。虽然守门员可以用脚和手解围球，但与场上球员一样，他们只能使用曲棍的一侧。只要是为了解围而不是针对球员，守门员就允许滑铲。

图 3.15　曲棍　（作者 Martin Conlon）

图 3.16　守门员用手套扑救。其身上是曲棍球守门员的典型装备（图片来源：Wikimedia）

现在，球队甚至可以拥有全部11名场上球员，而不设守门员。在这种情况下，任何球员都不得佩戴头盔或其他守门员装备，也不得使用曲棍以外任何身体部位击球。这种人员配备形式可以提供战术优势。例如,比赛剩余时间很短,但比分落后的情况下,在场球员数量的增加可以提升落后队获胜的概率;或者在没有守门员或没有守门员装备的情况下仍然可以进行比赛。

第五节 基本战术

与足球和许多其他集体项目一样,曲棍球运动的基本战术是在某一时刻在场上的特定区域中形成以多打少的局面。当控球时,进攻队员通过人数优势进行传球,使防守球员远离球而无法进行有效的抢断,并进一步利用这种人数优势来赢得时间和创造充分的空间用于射门得分。当对手控球时,人数优势可以用来隔离和引导控球的对手,并控制传球路线,以便通过拦截或抢断以获得控球权。技术高超的球员有时在面对多个对手时,仍然可以控制住球并成功传球或射门,但这往往比快速的、较早的传球消耗更多的体能。

如果球队在整个比赛过程中保持沟通,根据与球的关系,每名球员都有其相应的不同职责。根据球员与球的关系,场上球员分为:持球球员(进攻方);紧逼球员(防守方)、辅助球员和跑位球员。

球员在场上移动球的主要方法有:(a) 传球(passing);(b) 推球(pushing)并把球控制在身体的前面或右侧跑动;(c) 运球(dribbling);球员用曲棍控制球并朝各个方向移动以躲避对手。传球时,可以用推击动作(pushing stroke),即球员用手腕使曲棍头与球接触,并用曲棍头推球;"推击球"(flick)或"铲击球"(scoop)",与推击球类似,但多了手臂和腿的动作,以及将球挑离地面的旋转动作;"击球"(hit),即挥棍击球且与球接触的动作通常非常有力,使球以超过 70 mph(110 km/h)的速度被推进。为了产生强有力的击球,通常是为了长传或射门,曲棍会被举得很高,并以最大力量挥棍击球,这种击球有时被称为"重击球"(drive)。

抢断(Tackle)是指通过将曲棍放在球的路径上或用曲棍头或曲棍柄直接打在球上。为了提高抢断的效率,球员通常会将整根曲棍水平地靠近地面,从而形成更宽的障碍。为了避免被抢断,控球队员要么使用推球、推击球或击球方式将球传给队友,要么使用假动作来过掉抢断球员。

近年来,短角球(penalty corner)作为进球的机会变得越来越重要,特别是随着拖掷球(drag flick)的技术发展。通过拖掷球或击球射门为射门留出时间的短角球战术涉及各种复杂的战术配合,包括在向球门偏转之前的多次传球,但最常见的射门方法是直接的推击球或击球射门。

对于最高水平的比赛而言,曲棍球是一项快速移动、高技术的运动,球员通过带着曲棍快速移动、快速准确的传球和大力的击球,试图保持控球权并将球射向球门。曲棍球比赛不允许有身体接触的抢断和其他身体阻碍的方式,使用的一些战术类似于足球,但球速更快。

随着 2009 年对 23 m 区域内进攻方任意球规则的修改,向射门区内大力击球的常用战术被禁止。尽管在更高水平的比赛中,这种战术被认为是有战术风险的,创造得分的概率也很低,但还是有一定的效果,可以通过大力击球使球落到防守球员的脚上,或者造成球从防守球员的曲棍危险地向上反弹来获得短角球。国际曲棍球联合会认为这是一种危险的做法,很容易导致球在射门区内发生向上的反弹,从而造成伤害,因为在发任意球时,射门区内常常很拥挤,因此禁止了这种做法。

曲棍球术语

场上队员：比赛中守门员以外的选手。

前锋：是指以为球队进球为主要任务的锋线球员。

边锋：是指活动范围在球场两侧边线附近的锋线球员。

中锋：是指占据进攻区域中路并射门的进攻位置,通常被称为"前锋"。

中场队员：是指负责中场位置的球员,既负责进攻,也负责防守。他们的任务是接到防守端的球,然后把球传给进攻端。

内线队员：一种前锋或中场位置,当一条线上有3名以上球员时,该球员位于或接近场地的中心位置。

后卫：防守端的球员,主要是防止对方前锋得分。

争球：用来在球权不明确时重新开始比赛。球被放置在双方2名面对面站立的球员之间,他们必须用球棍在球上方轻敲三次后开始比赛。

中圈内发球：是指在每半场比赛开始时或一支球队在被对手进球后进行的发球。

短角球：当防守方在射门区内犯规,或者防守方故意造成球出底线时,进攻方将获得短角球。罚球时,球被放置在距离最近的门柱11 yd(10 ft)的后防线上,由进攻方球员将球传给在射门区外的队友进行射门。

长角球：进攻方在离底线5 yd的边线上的一个任意球。当防守方将球击过后防线时,就会判给进攻方长角球。

点球：在曲棍球比赛中,罚点球是最严厉的处罚。造成点球的原因有两种,一是当犯规行为阻止了某一进球机会,二是防守队员在射门区内故意犯规。

16 yd/15 m 球：是指进攻方造成球出底线后,防守方在离球门线16 yd处的一次击球。

推球入界：当一方球员将球击出界外后,对方球队在边线上罚任意球。

拖挪球：是一种进攻技术,主要在短角球中使用,包括两个主要组成部分,即铲击球和推击球。这项技术包括跑动,然后利用身体转动有力地向球门"抛球"的动作。

推击球：用曲棍快速地把球从地面举挑到空中,球的高度不能高于比赛场地18 ft。

铲击球：指运用手腕力量,使用曲棍头抽击或撞击球体,将球击打离开地面的一种击球技术。

推球：是指一个球员用推的动作沿着地面移动球的动作。

横扫击球：球员以横扫的动作将曲棍低挥到草皮上击球。

挥击球：球员利用手臂和腰部力量，由后向前挥棍将球击出的方法。其特点是力量大、球速快、运行距离长。

印度式运球：在使用人造草皮后流行起来的一种运球方式，一种通过在球上转动曲棍来左右移动球的运球方式。

阻挡：是指一名球员用球棒或身体阻挡或阻止另一名球员击球，是一种犯规行为。

球棍干扰：使用球棍击打对方球棍的犯规，无论是有意还是无意。

抢断：一名防守球员为阻止另一名进攻球员控球而采取的动作。

危险动作：指任何可能导致受伤行为的犯规，比如推搡、绊人、球棍干扰或对距离不到 5 yd 的对手打高球。

射门区：是指一个像大写"D"的半圆形区域。射门区弧距离每个门柱 16 yd，并由一条短直线连接。进攻球员必须在这个区域内才能得分。它也被称为"D"。

练 习

1. 曲棍球运动的国际管理机构是什么？
2. 曲棍球的球一般是由什么制成的？

第四章

手 球

学习目标

1. 了解手球的发展历史
2. 掌握手球赛事的管理机构和重要赛事
3. 熟悉手球比赛规则和专业术语

第一节 概 述

图 4.1　一场手球比赛正在德国曼海姆的 SAP 室内球场进行（作者 D. roller, saparena）

手球是一项集体运动，两队各 7 名队员（2 名场上队员和 1 名守门员）用手传球，目的是将球掷进对方的球门。一场标准的手球比赛包括上半场和下半场，各 30 分钟，进球多的球队获胜。

现代手球比赛的场地尺寸为 40 m×20 m（131 ft×66 ft），两条端线中间各有一个球门。球门周围有一个 6 m（20 ft）区，只有防守方守门员可以进入；进攻队员必须从球门区外射门或从球门区外"鱼跃"进射门区射门才能得分。手球比赛通常在室内进行，而室外手球的形式主要有室外手球（field handball）、捷克手球（Czech handball，在过去更常见）和沙滩手球（beach handball）。手球比赛的特点是速度快、得分高。现在的职业比赛中，每个球队通常能进 20～35 个球；但在几十年前，经常会出现进球很少的比赛。在比赛中，球员可能会上演帽子戏法(hat tricks)。防守球员可以通过身体接触来阻止进攻球员接近球门。手球比赛没有强制要求选手佩戴防护装备,但球员可以佩戴柔软的防护带、护垫和护齿。

19世纪末,手球的比赛规则在丹麦制定成文。1917年10月29日,现代手球比赛规则在柏林公布,这一天也被认为是手球运动的诞生日,此后比赛规则又经过数次修订。同年,德国举行了第一场正式的手球比赛。在现代规则下,第一场国际男子手球比赛于1925年举行;第一场国际女子手球比赛于1930年举行。在1936年的柏林夏季奥运会上,男子手球首次作为室外项目出现;在1972年的慕尼黑夏季奥运会上,男子手球作为室内项目出现。从此,男子手球比赛就成了奥运会的正式比赛项目。1976年夏季奥运会增加了女子手球项目。

手球运动在欧洲最受欢迎,自1938年以来,在男子世锦赛上,欧洲国家几乎囊括了所有奖牌,仅有一枚奖牌被非欧洲国家夺得。在女子世锦赛上,只有两个非欧洲国家赢得了冠军——韩国和巴西。该项运动在东亚、北非和南美部分地区也很受欢迎。

第二节 主要管理机构

国际手球联合会(International Handball Federation,IHF)是手球和沙滩手球的管理机构。国际手球联合会负责组织和举办重要的国际手球比赛,特别是始于1938年的国际手球联合会世界男子手球锦标赛(IHF World Men's Handball Championship)和始于1957年的国际手球联合会世界女子手球锦标赛(IHF World Women's Handball Championship)。

国际手球联合会(IHF)成立于1946年,负责监管国际比赛,总部设在巴塞尔,目前有210个国家联合会。每个成员国还必须是6个区域联合会之一的成员:非洲手球联合会、亚洲手球联合会、欧洲手球联合会、北美和加勒比地区手球联合会、大洋洲手球联合会和中南美洲手球联合会。

第三节 重要赛事

3.1 奥运会手球比赛

夏季奥运会手球项目指的是2种不同的运动项目。在1936年柏林夏季奥运会上,室外男子手球项目被引入,但之后就被取消了。在1952年的奥运会上,室外手球被列为表演项目。1972年夏季奥运会也是在德国举办,男子(室内)手球项目被引入。1976年蒙特利尔夏季奥运会引入了女子手球项目。

3.2 世界手球锦标赛

自1938年以来,国际手球联合会一直在室内举办世界男子手球锦标赛(IHF Men's

图 4.2 夏季奥运会手球比赛(来源：Wikipedia)

Handball World Championship)。

第一届室内男子手球锦标赛于 1938 年在德国举行,共有来自欧洲的 4 支球队参加,每支球队由 7 名球员组成,他们通过循环赛的方式决出冠军。直到 16 年后,第二届世界锦标赛才在瑞典举行。纵观世界锦标赛的历史,欧洲球队一直占据着主导地位,直到 2015 年才有非欧国家卡塔尔获得奖牌。多年来,世界锦标赛的组织发生了变化。最初,预赛和正赛都有小组赛,但自 1995 年以来,预赛之后采用淘汰制。

世界女子手球锦标赛(IHF Women's Handball World Championship)自 1957 年起由国际手球联合会举办。除了 1995 年韩国作为第一支非欧洲球队夺冠和 2013 年巴西作为第一支美洲球队夺冠外,其他冠军都由欧洲球队夺得。最大的赢家是俄罗斯和挪威,截至 2023 年底他们各获得 4 次冠军。

第一届世界女子手球锦标赛共有 9 支球队参加,从 2021 年开始,参加球队逐步增加到 32 支。1977 年引入了 B 级锦标赛,后来在 1986 年引入了 C 级锦标赛,作为真正的锦标赛或称为 A 级锦标赛的资格赛。1993 年,B 级和 C 级锦标赛作为资格赛的制度被目前基于各大洲联合会的资格赛制度所取代。

从 1978 年到 1990 年,世界女子手球锦标赛每隔 4 年举行一次,与奥运会间隔举行(1976 的年夏季奥运会引入了女子手球比赛)。从 1993 年起,每两年举行一次。前五届比赛在夏季或初秋举行,其余的都在 11 月或 12 月举行。

3.3 欧洲手球锦标赛

欧洲男子手球锦标赛(European Men's Handball Championship)是欧洲成年男子手球国家队的官方比赛,自 1994 年以来每两年举行一次,在世界锦标赛(World Championship)之间的偶数年举行。除了为欧洲冠军加冕外,该锦标赛还作为奥运会和世界锦标赛的资格赛。到 2023 年底,最成功的球队是瑞典队,他们赢得了五次冠军,而西班牙赢得的奖牌最多。

欧洲女子手球锦标赛(European Women's Handball Championship)是欧洲成年女子手球国家队的官方比赛,每两年举行一次。除了为欧洲冠军加冕外,该锦标赛还作为奥运会和世界锦标赛的资格赛。截至2022年12月,挪威获得过9次冠军,丹麦获得过3次冠军,匈牙利、黑山和法国各获得过1次冠军。

1946年,8个欧洲国家成立了国际手球联合会,尽管非欧洲国家参加了世界手球锦标赛,但奖牌一直由欧洲国家包揽。欧洲手球联合会(European Handball Federation)成立于1991年。1995年世界手球锦标赛从4年一次改为2年一次,欧洲手球联合会开始了自己的锦标赛——这也是世界手球锦标赛的地区预选赛。

3.4 北美加勒比手球锦标赛

北美加勒比男子手球锦标赛(North American and the Caribbean Men's Handball Championship)是北美和加勒比地区男子国家手球队的正式比赛。该锦标赛除了为冠军队伍加冕,同时也是泛美手球锦标赛(Pan American Handball Championship)的资格赛。从2020年开始,该锦标赛成为国际手球联合会世界男子手球锦标赛的资格赛。

北美加勒比女子手球锦标赛(North American and the Caribbean Women's Handball Championship)是北美和加勒比地区女子国家手球球队的官方比赛。该锦标赛除了为冠军队伍加冕,同时也是泛美手球锦标赛的资格赛。从2019年开始,该锦标赛成为国际手球联合会世界女子手球锦标赛的资格赛。

第四节 比赛规则

4.1 概述

两队各7名球员(6名场上球员和1名守门员)上场,试图通过将球打进对方的球门来得分。在处理球时,球员受以下限制:

① 接到球后,球员可以传球、控球或射门。

② 球员不允许用脚触球,只有守门员在球门区内可以用脚触球。

③ 球员接到球后,必须运球(与篮球运球不同)。在不进行运球的情况下,球员最多只能在不超过3秒的时间内做出不超过3步的移动。

④ 除防守方守门员外,任何进攻或防守队员均不得进入球门区(距离球门6 m以内)。在球门区内的射门或传球必须在触地之前完成才有效。守门员可以到球门区外,但不允许用手拿球越过球门区边界。

⑤ 当守门员站在球门区内时,本方队员不能将球传给守门员。

当进攻球员跃入球门区域时,就会出现明显的得分机会。例如,一名进攻球员可能会在球门区内接到传球,然后在触地前射门或传球。当一名采用鱼跃进攻的队员传给另一名鱼跃进攻的队友时,得分机会就会更大。

4.2 持续时间

一场标准的比赛有两个30分钟的半场,中间有10分钟或15分钟的中场休息(在锦标赛和奥运会中)。中场休息时,两支球队在交换场地的同时也互换替补席(bench)。对青少年来说,半场比赛的时间会缩短——12~15岁组别为25分钟,8~11岁组别为20分钟;尽管一些国家联合会在执行时可能与官方指南有所不同。

如果在一场比赛(如锦标赛)中必须决出胜负,并且在常规时间之后以平局结束,则最多有2个加时赛,每个加时赛由2个连续的5分钟半场组成,中间有1分钟的休息时间。如果仍不能决出胜负,则通过点球大战(best-of-five)来决出胜负(五局三胜制;如果仍然是平局,则继续增加点球回合,直到一方获胜)。

裁判员可自行决定暂停,典型的原因是受伤、停赛或球场清洁,如更换守门员。

自2012年起,每支球队每场比赛有3次暂停机会(半场最多2次),每次暂停1分钟。只有控球的队才有叫暂停的权利,参赛队代表必须在计时员的工作台上出示标有黑色T的绿卡。计时员随即发出声音信号停止计时。在2012年之前,每支球队每半场只允许暂停一次。为了能够叫暂停,加时赛和点球大战算作下半场的延伸。

4.3 裁判

手球比赛由两名权力相等的裁判执裁。一些国家手球管理机构允许在特殊情况下,比如有裁判临时生病的情况下,只设置一名裁判。如果发生两个裁判员意见不一致的情况,则比赛将进行短暂的暂停,以便双方进行协商并达成一致意见;若已作出判罚,则以两者中更为严厉的判罚作为最终决定。裁判有义务"根据他们对事实的观察"作出决定。裁判的

图4.3 裁判员(身穿蓝色短袖衬衫)位于球队两侧(图片来源:Wikipedia)

判决是最终的，只有在他们不遵守规则的情况下，球队才有权提出上诉。

两个裁判的站位要使所有队员们都在他们的观察视野之内。他们站在对角线上，以便每个人都能观察到一条边线。根据他们的站位，一个被称为场地裁判（field referee），另一个被称为球门裁判（goal referee）。裁判员位置根据攻守的转换自动切换，他们实际上大约每10分钟交换一次位置（长换），每5分钟交换一次边（短换）。

国际手球联合会规定了18种裁判手势，以便与球员和随队官员进行快速的视觉交流。出示黄牌表示警告；出示红牌意味着取消比赛资格；如果取消比赛资格并伴有书面报告（report），则会被出示蓝牌。裁判也会用鸣哨来示意犯规或重新开始比赛。

裁判由一名记分员（scorekeeper）和一名计时员（timekeeper）协助，他们分别负责记录进球和暂停，或开始和停止计时等官方事务。他们也会密切关注替补席，如果发现换人错误，会立刻通知裁判。他们的工作台位于两队的换人区之间。

4.4　场上队员、守门员和随队官员

每队由7名场上队员和7名替补队员组成。场上必须有一名守门员，服装与场上其他球员不同。在比赛过程中，可以在任何时间以任何数量替换球员。换人在换人线上进行，不需要事先通知裁判。

一些国家的手球管理机构，如德国手球联合会（DHB），规定青年队只有在控球型或暂停期间才允许换人。这个限制是为了防止球队过早形成专业化的进攻型球员或防守型球员。

4.4.1　场上队员

场上球员可以用膝关节以上（包括膝盖）的任何身体部位触球。和其他集体运动一样，手球的接球和运球是有区别的。持球队员只能静止站立3秒钟，并且只能走3步，随后必须进行投球、传球或运球。任何时候走三步以上都是走步（traveling），会导致失误（turnover）。球员可以根据需要多次运球（不过，传球更快，是首选的进攻方法），只要每次运球时手只接触球的顶部。持球（carrying）是完全禁止的，会导致失误。运球停止后，球员有权再持球3秒或走3步，然后必须传球或射门，进一步持球或运球将导致二次运球（double dribble）失误和对方罚任意球（free throw）。其他进攻违规的行为包括持球撞人（charging）和违规掩护（setting an illegal screen）。

4.4.2　守门员

只有守门员可以在球门区内自由活动，但持球或带球时不得离开球门区。在球门区内，他们可以出于防守目的，使用包括脚在内的任何身体部位触球（其他动作则需遵守与场上球员相同的规则限制）。守门员可以以场上队员身份参与队友的正常比赛，如果球队选择使用这种战术以期在进攻人数上超过防守球员，守门员可以被一名常规场上球员替换。在2015年之前，被指定为守门员的场上球员必须穿上与守门员球衣颜色相同的背心或围衣以便能被识别。为了使比赛更具进攻性，规则进行了一项变更，现在允许任何球员替换守门员，而无需成为指定守门员。这条规则首次在2015年12月举行的世界女子手球锦标赛

图 4.4　一名女队员在罚 7 m 球(作者 Armin Kuebelbeck)

中使用,此后在 2016 年 1 月的欧洲男子手球锦标赛和 2016 年奥运会男女比赛中使用。这项规则的修改导致了空门进球的急剧增加。

与足球等其他项目不同的是,如果守门员将球挡出底线,他们的球队将会保持控球权。然后,守门员通过在球门区内掷球门球(goalkeeper throw),使比赛重新开始。在罚点球时,若球员故意将球掷向没有移动的守门员的头部,该行为将导致红牌处罚,直接取消该球员的比赛资格(disqualification)。在常规比赛中,只要球员掷球时没有对手阻挡犯规(obstruction),击中没有移动的守门员的头部将导致停赛两分钟(two-minute suspension)。

在本方球门区(D-zone)之外,守门员被视为普通场上球员,必须遵守场上球员的规则;在禁区外抓住或拦截对方球员将面临直接被取消比赛资格的风险。守门员不得带球返回球门区。传球给本方守门员是违例行为。

4.4.3　随队官员

每队最多允许 4 名随队官员坐在替补席上,随队官员既不是运动员也不是替补队员。必须有一名随队官员作为球队指定代表,通常是该队的领队(team manager)。自 2012 年起,球队代表最多可以叫 3 次球队暂停(每半场最多 2 次),需向记分员、计时员和裁判员提出申请(在此之前,每半场 1 次);加时赛和点球大战被视为下半场的延伸。其他官员通常包括队医或管理人员。没有裁判员的允许,任何官员都不能进入比赛场地。

4.5　球

手球是圆形的,由皮革或合成材料制成,不允许表面存在反光或过于光滑的情况。由于手球是由单手控制,其官方尺寸会根据参赛球队的年龄和性别

图 4.5　3 号手球
(作者 Armin Kuebelbeck)

而有所不同。

表 4.1 手球官方尺寸

尺寸	组别	周长/cm	重量/g
1	8 岁以上少年	50～52	290～330
2	14 岁以上女子,12 岁以上男子	54～56	325～375
3	16 岁以上男子	58～60	425～475

4.6 定点球

裁判可在进球、球出界、失误或暂停后判给一方一个特殊的掷球。所有特殊掷球都要求掷球球员在特定位置进行,并对所有其他球员的位置进行限制。部分特殊掷球在执行前,必须等待裁判的哨声作为开始信号。

4.6.1 开球

开球(throw-off)在球场中央进行。掷球队员必须一只脚触到中线,所有其他进攻队员必须留在自己的半场,直到裁判鸣哨重新开始比赛。防守队员必须与掷球队员保持至少 3 m 的距离,直到球离开他的手。在每个半场的开始和对方球队得分后进行开球,开球必须得到裁判的批准。

现代手球引入了"快速开球"(fast throw-off)的概念,也就是说,一旦罚球队达到罚球要求,裁判将立即重新开始比赛。许多球队利用这一规则,在对手形成稳固的防线之前轻松得分。

4.6.2 掷界外球

当一方的球完全越过边线或触碰到天花板时,对方球队将获得一次掷界外球(throw-in)的机会。如果球出底线,只有当防守队场上队员(field player)造成出界时才判界外球。罚球队员掷球时要将一只脚放在球出界处的边线上。所有防守球员必须离罚球队员至少 3 m(9.8 ft),但允许紧贴本方球门线站位,即使该位置距离罚球队员不到 3 m。

4.6.3 掷球门球

如果球在没有受到防守方犯规阻挡(interference)的情况下出了底线,或被防守方守门员扑救出底线,或者进攻方违反了球门区规则,则判给防守方球门球。这是最常见的球权转换。随后,守门员可以从球门区内的任何地方掷球,重新开始比赛。

4.6.4 掷任意球

裁判暂停比赛后,通过一个任意球(free throw)重新开始比赛。如果犯规发生在对方任意球线(free-throw line)外,则从造成犯规的地点掷任意球;如果犯规发生在对方任意球线内,则在离犯规位置最近的任意球线上掷任意球。手球比赛中的任意球相当于足球比赛中的任意球。然而，对于防守方来说，犯规造成对方罚任意球通常不会被视为不良的体育精神，而且犯规造成对方罚任意球本身并不会导致重大的劣势（特别是在对手被警告消极比赛（passive play）期间，获得罚任意球不会取消警告，而射门则会取消。）。罚球队员可以尝试直接射门，但是，如果防守队已经组织好了防守，直接射门的成功率会很低。然而，如果裁判判罚了任意球，而此时半场或全场比赛结束，则通常会尝试直接射门，偶尔也会进球。

4.6.5 掷 7 m 球

图 4.6　掷 7 m 球　（作者 Frank）

在场上任何地方，当明显的得分机会被对方队员、球队官员或观众违规阻止时，判罚掷 7 m 球（seven-meter throw）。不管因何种理由，如果裁判中断了一个合规的得分机会，也会判罚 7 m 球。掷球时，掷球队员站在 7 m（23 ft）线后，只有守方守门员一个人守门。守门员必须与 7 m 线保持 3 m（9.8 ft）的距离，不能超过地板上的守门员限制线（goalkeeper's restraining line）。任意球发出前，所有其他球员必须留在任意球线后，防守方场上球员必须与 7 m 线保持 3 m 距离。掷球队员必须等待裁判鸣哨后才能掷球。7 m 球相当于足球比赛中的点球；然而，7 m 球更为常见，通常会在一场比赛中出现多次。

4.7　犯规与个人处罚

给予犯规球员的处罚（penalties）要比判罚任意球严厉得多，将会以累进的形式处罚犯规球员。这些处罚主要针对的是针对对手而非球的行为，如搂抱（reaching around）、拉人（holding）、推人（pushing）、绊人（tripping）、撞人（jumping into），以及从球员侧面、背后接

图4.7 手球比赛中出示黄牌(作者 Armin Kuebelbeck)

触或阻碍对手进攻的行为,这些均被视为违规,并将受到处罚。任何阻止明显得分机会的犯规行为将会导致判罚给对方7 m点球。

通常情况下,裁判会对犯规行为出示黄牌进行警告;但是,如果身体接触特别危险,比如击打对手的头部、颈部或喉咙,裁判可以不警告,而是判罚立刻停赛2分钟(two-minute suspension)。球员在被出示黄牌之前会被警告一次;如果球员累计3张黄牌,他们就有被红牌罚下的风险。

红牌将导致该队员被驱逐出场(ejection),犯规队一名球员必须被罚2分钟退场(two-minute penalty)。球员可能会因为特别严厉的判罚而直接吃到红牌。例如,在快攻中任何背后的接触都会被出示红牌;任何故意伤害对手的行为也会被出示红牌。被出示红牌的球员必须完全离开比赛区域。在2分钟退场处罚结束后,被取消比赛资格(disqualification)的球员可以被另一名球员替换。教练员或随队官员也可以被累进处罚。任何被罚2分钟退场的教练或官员都必须让本队一名球员退场2分钟;然而,这名球员并不是被处罚的对象,他可以再次上场,因为处罚的目的是被处罚球队比对方少一名球员。

无论裁判出于何种原因将球判给对手,持球的球员必须迅速放下球,否则将面临2分钟退场的风险。此外,用手势或言语质疑裁判的判罚,以及对裁判的判罚提出异议,通常都有可能被出示黄牌。如果被罚出场的球员继续抗议,不直接走到替补席,或者如果裁判认为其故意拖延比赛时间,那么该球员将面临2张黄牌的风险。违例换人(在换人区外换人;或替补队员过早进场)是被禁止的,会面临黄牌的风险。

4.8 比赛场地

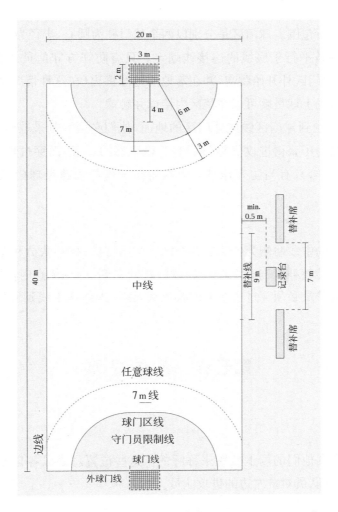

图 4.8　手球场地示意图　（图片来源：handballfield.svg）

手球在 40 m×20 m(131 ft 2.80 in×65 ft 7.40 in)的场地上进行，两端的中心各有一个球门。球门周围是一个近似半圆形的区域，称为球门区(zone or crease)，球门区线距离球门 6 m。距离球门 9 m 的一条近似半圆形的虚线是任意球线(free-throw line)。球场上每条线都是它所包围区域的一部分，这意味着中线(middle line)同时属于两个半场。

4.8.1　球门

球门高 2 m，宽 3 m。它们必须牢固地用螺栓固定在地板上或后面的墙上。

门柱和横梁必须由相同的材料（如木材或铝材）制成，门柱和横梁的横截面为边长 8 cm(3 in)的正方形。从比赛场地可见的横梁的 3 个面必须交替地涂上两种对比鲜明的颜色，这两种颜色都必须与背景颜色区别明显。同一场地的两个球门颜色必须一致。

球门上必须挂一个网,以确保在正常情况下,掷进球门的球不会立即弹出或穿过球门。

4.8.2 球门区

球门被球门区所包围。球门区是分别以两个球门柱为圆心,半径为 6 m,从底线开始的四分之一圆以及一条平行于底线的连接线划定。只有防守方守门员才允许进入球门区。然而,只要球员在球门区外开始跳起,并在落地前把球掷出(在这种情况下,只要球离手,就允许落在禁区内),场上球员就可以在禁区内接球并触球。

如果无球球员触到球门区线或球门区的地面,他们必须立刻采取最直接的路径离开。如果一名进攻球员为了获得进攻优势(例如,获得更好的位置)而穿过禁区,他们的球队就会失去控球权。同样,只有当防守球员为了获得防守优势而违反球门区规则时才会受到处罚。

4.8.3 替补区

在一条边线外的中线两侧为各队的替补区。球队官员、替补队员和退场队员必须在此区域内等候。球队的替补区与球队防守的球门在同一侧;中场休息时,替补区互换。任何进入或离开比赛的球员必须穿过边线上的换人线,该换人线从中线延伸到球队一侧 4.5 m (15 ft)。

第五节 基 本 战 术

5.1 阵型

球员通常是根据他们的场上位置来称呼的。这些位置总是以各自守门员的视角来表示,因此右边的防守队员对抗左边的进攻队员。

5.1.1 进攻阵型

① 左、右边锋(Left and right wingman)。这些球员通常速度很快,擅长控球和从球门区外横向跳起,以便获得更好的射门角度。球队通常会让右手球员占据左侧位置,反之亦然。

② 左、右内锋(Left and right backcourt)。这些球员通常是通过高高跳起,越过防守球员来射门。因此,这些位置适合身材高大并且射门有力的球员。

③ 中后卫(Center backcourt)。这个位置上的球员需要有丰富的经验,他的作用是控球和组织进攻,相当于篮球比赛中的控球后卫。

④ 中锋(Pivot)。中锋通常混入对方防守球员中,做挡拆,试图破坏防守球员的阵型。这个位置对跳跃能力的要求最低,但对控球和体力要求很高。

有时球队会采用双中锋的进攻阵型。

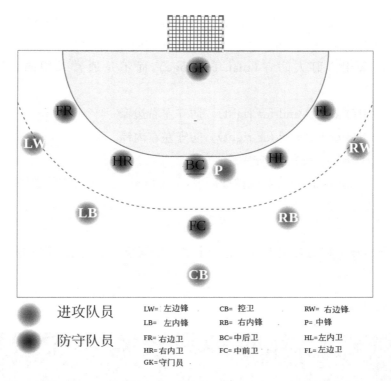

图 4.9 5-1 防守阵型中进攻方(红色)和防守方(蓝色)的位置(作者 Kuebi)

5.1.2 防守阵型

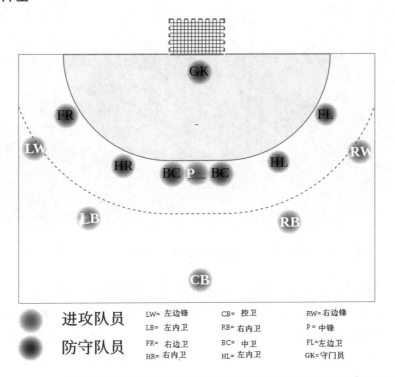

图 4.10 6-0 防守阵型中进攻方(红色)和防守方(蓝色)的位置 (作者 kuebi)

防守阵型有很多变化，通常被描述为 $n:m$ 阵型，其中 n 是在球门线防守的球员数量，m 是更具进攻性的防守球员数量。例外是 3：2：1 的防守阵型和 $n+m$ 阵型（例如 5+1），其中 m 名球员采用人盯人防守（man coverage），而不是通常采用的区域防守（zone coverage）。

① 左、右边卫（Far left and far right）。防守左右边锋。
② 左、右内卫（Far left and far right）。防守左右内锋。
③ 中后卫（Back center）。防守中锋。
④ 中前卫（Front center）。对应控球后卫，也可以对应一个特定的后场球员。

5.2 进攻打法

进攻时，所有场上球员都位于防守方的半场。根据攻击的速度，可以分为三波进攻，成功率依次降低：

5.2.1 第一波进攻

图 4.11　女子手球——快攻中的跳投　（作者 Armin Kuebelbeck）

第一波进攻的特点是在球门周围没有防守球员。成功的机会非常大，因为球员在射门时没有阻碍。这样的进攻通常发生在对方传球被拦截或抢断之后，如果防守队能够迅速展开进攻的话。通常由左边卫（far left）或右边卫（far right）尝试发动进攻，因为他们靠近边线，防守的任务不是很重。一旦对手出现失误，他们会立刻冲向对方球门，并在中途接球。因此，这些位置通常由速度快的球员负责。

5.2.2 第二波进攻

如果第一波进攻不成功,且一些防守球员在球门区周围占据了位置,第二波进攻就会开始:剩下的进攻球员通过快速传球向前推进,争取在局部人数上超过撤退的防守球员。如果一名进攻球员设法到达球门区边缘或在这个位置接球,防守球员就无法通过合规的手段阻挡他射门。从这个位置进行射门,成功的机会很大。随着"快发"(fast throw-off)规则的出现,第二波进攻变得更加重要。

5.2.3 第三波进攻

图 4.12　男子手球——跳起射门　(作者 Kuebi)

第二波进攻的时间很短,因为防守队员会堵住球门区周围的防守漏洞。在第三波进攻中,进攻球员使用标准化的进攻模式,通常包括传中和后场球员之间的传球,这些球员要么试图通过空档把球传给他们的中锋,然后中锋从球门区外跳起射门(jumping shot),要么通过传球配合引诱防守球员离开边锋。

当所有防守球员回到球门区,并且到达他们的习惯防守位置,第三波进攻演变为常规的进攻。一些球队会替换上专门的进攻球员。然而,这意味着,如果对方球队能够迅速转守为攻,这些球员必须扮演防守角色。进攻节奏快的球队善于在转守为攻时发起快攻。

比赛中,如果进攻球队没有取得足够的进展(最终射门),裁判可以判罚进攻队消极比赛(passive play)(自 1995 年以来,规则规定在此情况下裁判将通过高举一只手发出提前警告,表明进攻队应该尽快射门),然后将控球权移交给另一支球队。当裁判把手举起进行警告后,如果射门以及犯规导致黄牌或罚2分钟,将标志着新一轮进攻开始,裁判将会把手放下;但是,如果射门被防守方封堵或者进攻方正常地罚任意球,裁判不会把手放下。这条规则是为了防止进攻球队无限期地拖延比赛。

5.3 防守打法

通常的防守阵型包括6-0阵型,所有的防守队员在6 m(20 ft)线和9 m(30 ft)线之间排成一排,形成一道人墙;5-1阵型,是指一名球员在9 m(30 ft)线外游弋,通常负责防守中锋,而其他5名球员则在6 m(20 ft)线上站成一排;很少见的4-2阵型,前面有2个防守球员时。速度快的球队也会尝试3-3阵型,一种接近于人盯人的阵型。不同国家球队的防守阵型差异很大,反映了每个国家的比赛风格。6-0阵型有时被称为"平面防守"(flat defense),而所有其他阵型通常被称为"进攻型防守"(offensive defense)。

手球术语

场上球员/普通球员:除守门员外,在场上比赛的队员被称为场上球员或普通球员。

守门员:当对手试图射门时防守球门的球员。守门员被允许在球门区内活动。

开球:开球在球场中央进行。掷球队员必须用一只脚站在中线上,所有其他进攻队员必须留在自己的半场,直到裁判鸣哨重新开始比赛。防守队员必须与掷球队员保持至少3 m的距离,直到球离开他的手。在每个半场的开始和对方球队得分后进行开球,开球必须得到裁判的批准。

掷球门球:当进攻队员将球踢出对方底线,且最后触球的是进攻队员或防守守门员时,即判给防守队一次掷球门球。

掷界外球:当球出边线后,防守队在球出边线的位置掷界外球。掷球队员必须将一只脚站在边线上以完成单手掷球。所有对方队员必须保持离球3 m的距离。

掷角球:进攻球员用任意一只手从球场的角球区掷球。在防守球员将球打过本方底线或打到球门两侧时,进攻方队员将得到一个角球。

掷任意球:在比赛中,当一方犯规时,判给对方球队掷任意球,从距离球门9 m的任意球线外掷出。

掷7 m球:是指从距离球门7 m的标记处射门。罚球时,一名球员被指派通过直接掷球方式射门得分。

鱼跃射门:是一种从6 m线外跳入球门区的射门方式,要求在不接触6 m线的情况下完成射门。

裁判员掷球:在手球比赛中,因一些原因导致比赛中断后,裁判员为恢复比赛而进行的掷球。

警告(黄牌):像足球比赛一样,手球裁判有权对球员发出警告。若球员第二次受到警告,则将会被罚离场2分钟,该球员所在球队必须在少一人的情况下继续比赛;如果同一名球员获得第二张黄牌,将被再判罚离场2分钟;而如果同一名球员获得第三次黄牌警告,则将会被出示红牌并取消比赛资格。被取消比赛资格的球员所在的球队必须在接下来的2分钟内减少一人,2分钟之后才能补充一名球员上场。

取消资格(红牌): 被取消资格的球员必须离开球场和替补席,但球队可以在2分钟停赛结束后替换该球员。

驱逐离场: 严重违规会被驱逐离场,类似于足球比赛中的红牌。被驱逐离场的队员所在的球队在剩下的比赛中会少一名队员。

练 习

1. 在国际锦标赛和奥运会中,手球比赛有几个30分钟的半场?
2. 手球运动的国际管理机构是什么?
3. 近代手球运动最早起源于哪个洲?

第五章 美式橄榄球

> **学习目标**
> 1. 了解美式橄榄球的发展历史
> 2. 掌握美式橄榄球赛事的主要管理机构和重要赛事
> 3. 熟悉美式橄榄球比赛规则和专业术语

第一节 概 述

美式橄榄球（American football），在美国和加拿大简称为橄榄球（football），也被称为烤盘足球（gridiron football），是一项集体运动，比赛由两队各11名球员在一个长方形的场地上进行，两端各有一个球门。进攻方，即拥有椭圆形橄榄球的球队，试图通过带球跑动或传球向前推进；而防守方，即无球的球队，旨在阻止进攻方的前进，并试图取得控球权。进攻方必须在4次进攻（down）中前进至少10 yd，如果失败了，他们就把球权交给防守方，但如果成功了，就会得到新的4次进攻机会继续进攻。得分主要是通过将球推进到对方的达阵区，也称端区（end zone）达阵得分（touchdown）或将球踢过对方的球门柱（goalposts）得分。比赛结束时得分较多的球队获胜。

图5.1 巴拿马城埃米利奥罗约体育场
（作者 Pedro Arenas）

美式橄榄球发源于足球和英式橄榄球运动，在美国发展而成。第一场美式橄榄球比赛于1869年11月6日在罗格斯大学和普林斯顿大学之间进行，比赛的规则是根据当时的足球规则制定的。从1880年起，"美式橄榄球之父"沃尔特·坎普（Walter Camp）制定了一系列规则变更，确立了（裆下后传）发球（snap）、争球线（line of scrimmage）、11人队和档（down）的概念。后来的规则变化使向前传球（forward pass）合法化，创造了中立区（neutral zone），并规定了橄榄球的大小和形状。美式橄榄球与加拿大橄榄球联系密切，平行发展（尽管他们的规则发展独立于坎普的规则）。美式橄榄球区别于英式橄榄球和足球的大部分特征也存在于加拿大橄榄球中。这两项运动被认为是烤盘足球（gridiron football）的主要形式。

就转播收视率而言，美式橄榄球是美国最受欢迎的运动。最流行的比赛形式是职业橄榄球比赛和大学橄榄球比赛，其他主要比赛级别是高中和青少年橄榄球比赛。截至 2022 年，美国有近 104 万名高中运动员参加美式橄榄球运动，另有 81 000 名大学运动员在全国大学生体育协会（National Collegiate Athletic Association，NCAA）和全国大学校际体育协会（National Association of Intercollegiate Athletics，NAIA）参加美式橄榄球运动。美国国家橄榄球联盟（NFL）的平均上座率是世界上所有职业体育联盟中最高的。其冠军赛"超级碗"（Super Bowl）是全球收视率最高的俱乐部体育赛事之一。2022 年，该联盟的年收入约为 186 亿美元，使其成为世界上最有价值的体育联盟。全球范围内还有其他职业和业余美式橄榄球联赛，但这项运动在世界上的普及度远不如棒球或篮球等其他美国运动；这项运动在北美其他地区、欧洲、巴西和日本拥有越来越多的追随者。

第二节　主要管理机构

2.1　国际美式橄榄球联合会

国际美式橄榄球联合会（International Federation of American Football，IFAF）是美式橄榄球的国际管理机构。国际美式橄榄球联合会负责监督所有接触式和非接触式业余国际比赛的组织和推广，包括每四年举办一次的 IFAF 美式橄榄球世界锦标赛（IFAF World Championship of American Football）。IFAF 于 2003 年成为国际单项体育联合会总会（Global Association of International Sports Federations，GAISF）临时成员，并于 2005 年成为正式成员。该组织的总部位于法兰西岛大区的拉库尔讷夫法国公社（French commune of La Courneuve）。

国际美式橄榄球联合会（IFAF）的分支机构遍布世界各地，截至 2024 年 5 月，拥有 75 个成员：IFAF 非洲：12 个；IFAF 美洲：16 个；IFAF 亚洲：13 个；IFAF 欧洲：29 个；IFAF 大洋洲：5 个。

2.2　美国橄榄球协会

美国橄榄球协会（USA Football）是美国美式橄榄球运动的管理机构，是国际美式橄榄球联合会（IFAF）的成员，也是美国奥林匹克与残疾人奥林匹克委员会（United States Olympic & Paralympic Committee）认可的体育组织。美国橄榄球协会选拔和组织美国男子国家队和美国女子国家队去参加国际美式橄榄球联合会批准的国际比赛。

美国橄榄球协会是一个独立的非营利组织，总部位于印第安纳州印第安纳波利斯（Indianapolis，Indiana），其使命包括设计和提供一流的美式橄榄球教育、发展和比赛项目，包括美式橄榄球和腰旗橄榄球。美国橄榄球协会与医学、儿童权益倡导以及体育领域的领导者合作，支持青少年、高中生和其他业余球员获得积极的橄榄球体验。

美国橄榄球协会于2002年由全国橄榄球联盟（National Football League，NFL）和全国橄榄球联盟球员协会（National Football League Players Association，NFLPA）资助成立。

第三节　重要赛事

3.1　IFAF世界美式橄榄球锦标赛

IFAF世界美式橄榄球锦标赛（也称为"IFAF世界杯"）是一项国际美式橄榄球赛事，每四年举办一次，由代表成员国的球队参加。该项赛事由该运动的国际管理机构——国际美式橄榄球联合会（IFAF）主办。71个国家拥有美式橄榄球国家队。

在2011年的锦标赛中，8支球队参加了比赛，分为两组，每组4支球队（1999年和2007年有6支球队；2003年有4支球队；2015年有7支球队）。首轮比赛采用小组循环赛形式，每支球队互相比赛一次。然而，与小组赛结束后的淘汰赛不同，各组战绩最好的球队进行金牌争夺战，各组第二名争夺铜牌，第三名球队争夺第五名，第四名的球队争夺第七名，这样就保证了每支球队都有四场比赛。

东道国球队和卫冕冠军自动获得IFAF世界美式橄榄球锦标赛席位。欧洲美式足球锦标赛（European Championship of American football）的冠亚军都获得了参赛资格。来自泛美美式橄榄球联合会（Pan American Federation of American Football）的2支球队获得了席位，亚洲美式足球联合会（Asian Federation of American Football）和大洋洲美式足球联合会（Oceania Federation of American Football）各有一支球队获得了席位。

2019年锦标赛（推迟到2023年，然后又推迟到2025年举行），赛事将扩大到12支球队。参赛队伍将被分为4组，每组3支球队。每支球队将与该组的其他两支球队各进行一次比赛，总共进行两场小组赛。接下来，将进入第二轮的排名赛并争夺奖牌。

由于美式橄榄球在美国的受欢迎程度远高于世界其他任何地方，因此美国队在前两届比赛中都没有派出队伍参加。美国在之后的三届比赛中派出了队伍，但由于球员入选资格标准极其严格，因此美国的大多数美式橄榄球运动员没有资格入选该队。尽管有这些限制，美国队还是赢得了他们参加的全部三届世界锦标赛冠军。同样，加拿大直到2011年才参加比赛，并在该届比赛中紧随美国队之后获得第二名。

3.2　全国橄榄球联盟联赛（NFL）

全国橄榄球联盟（National Football League，NFL）是美国的职业美式橄榄球联赛。全国橄榄球联盟被分为美国橄榄球联合会（AFC）和国家橄榄球联合会（NFC），每个联合会有16支球队，共32支球队；此外每个联合会又被划分成东南西北4个分区，每个分区由4支球队组成。NFL 是美国和加拿大主要的职业体育联盟之一，也是世界上职业水平最高的美式橄榄球联盟。

每个 NFL 赛季都会在每年的 8 月开始为期 3 周的季前赛（preseason），随后从 9 月初到第二年 1 月初举行为期 18 周的常规赛（regular season），每支球队都会打 17 场比赛，并有一个轮空周。常规赛结束后，每个联合会的 7 支球队，包括 4 支分区冠军队和 4 支外卡球队（wild card teams），得以晋级全国橄榄球联盟季后赛，NFL 的季后赛为单淘汰赛（single-elimination tournament），两个联合会的获胜者将在次年二月的超级碗（Super Bowl）中争夺赛季的总冠军。

全国橄榄球联盟成立于 1920 年，当时名为美国职业橄榄球协会（American Professional Football Association，APFA），并在 1922 年赛季更名为"全国橄榄球联盟"（National Football League，NFL）。最初联盟通过赛季末排名决定冠军归属，1933 年赛季开始，全国橄榄球联盟施行了季后赛制度，并一直持续到 1966 年。在 NFL 与竞争对手美国橄榄球联盟（American Football League，AFL）合并后，首届超级碗比赛于 1967 年首次进行，目的是在两个联合会最好的球队之间决出冠军，并从 1970 年开始作为全赛季的总冠军之战持续至今。

从营收层面上来看，NFL 是世界上最赚钱的体育联盟，同时拥有众多非常富有的俱乐部。NFL 是世界上平均上座人数最高的职业体育联盟（2023 年平均每场 69 582 人），同时也是美国最受欢迎的体育联盟。作为赛季冠军争夺战的超级碗是世界上最受关注的俱乐部体育赛事之一，比赛的电视转播收视率一直居高不下。NFL 的总部位于曼哈顿中城。

绿湾包装工队（Green Bay Packers）是获得 NFL 总冠军次数最多的球队，总共获得 13 次，其中包括超级碗时代之前的 9 次冠军以及超级碗设立后的 4 次冠军。自从超级碗设立以来，新英格兰爱国者队（New England Patriots）和匹兹堡钢人队（Pittsburgh Steelers）都获得 6 次冠军，并列成为赢得超级碗次数最多的球队。

3.3　NCAA 第一级别美式橄榄球碗赛分区

美国大学体育协会（NCAA）第一级别橄榄球碗赛分区（NCAA Division I Football Bowl Subdivision，FBS），以前称为 I-A 级，是美国大学橄榄球的最高级别球赛。FBS 由美国大学体育协会（NCAA）中最大的学校组成，截至 2024 赛季，FBS 共有 10 个联盟和 134 所学校。

大学橄榄球是美国大部分地区最受欢迎的观赏性运动之一，顶尖学校的年收入可达数千万美元。顶级的 FBS 球队会吸引成千上万的球迷前来观看比赛，美国 15 座容量最大的体育场都是 FBS 球队的主场或主办 FBS 橄榄球比赛。自 2021 年 7 月 1 日起，大学运动员可以因使用其姓名、图像和肖像而获得报酬。在此之前，大学只能向球员提供非金钱补偿，例如用于支付学费、住宿费和书本费的体育奖学金。

FBS 赛季开始于 8 月底或 9 月初,结束于 1 月的大学橄榄球季后赛全国冠军赛（College Football Playoff National Championship）。大多数 FBS 球队每年要打 12 场常规赛,其中 8～9 场比赛是对阵分区对手。FBS 的所有 10 个分区都会举行分区冠军赛,以决出分区冠军。每支球队理论上可以参加联盟比赛、非联盟比赛、一场联盟冠军赛以及最多两场碗赛(如果被大学橄榄球季后赛委员会评为全国前四名的大学球队)。只有 4 支季后赛球队有资格在季后赛中参加 2 场碗赛,而不是像其余球队只参加一场碗赛;只有 2 场季后赛半决赛的获胜者才能在大学橄榄球季后赛全国冠军赛（College Football Playoff National Championship）中相遇时参加第 15 场比赛。

第四节　比赛规则

4.1　球队和位置

橄榄球比赛在 2 支球队之间进行,每支球队有 11 名球员,上场人数超过 11 人将受到处罚。球队可以在每档(down)进攻之间替换任意数量的球员,这种球员分组轮换的规则(platoon system)取代了原来的有限替换球员的规则,导致球队使用专门的进攻组(offensive unit)、防守组(defensive unit)和特勤(special teams unit)组进行比赛。正式球员名单(active roster)上允许的球员人数因联赛而异:美国全国橄榄球联盟(NFL)的球队名单有 53 名球员,而 NCAA 第一级别允许球队在冠军赛分区(Football Championship Subdivision,FCS)中拥有 63 名奖学金球员,在碗赛分区(FBS)中拥有 85 名奖学金球员。

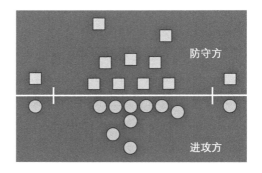

图 5.2　典型的发球前阵型图。进攻方(红色)以 I 型阵型排列,而防守方(蓝色)以 4-3 阵型排列。两种阵型都是合规的(作者 Killervogel5)

橄榄球比赛中,每个球员必须有一个 1～99 之间的球衣号码(uniform number),有些球队可能会"退役"某些号码,不再使用这些号码。美国全国橄榄球联盟(NFL)球队必须按照联盟批准的编号系统为其球员编号,任何例外情况都必须得到联盟专员(commissioner)的批准。

尽管这项运动几乎都是男性参与,但女性也有资格参加高中、大学和职业橄榄球比赛。从来没有女性曾参加过美国全国橄榄球联盟(NFL),但曾有女性参加过高中和大学橄榄球比赛。根据美国体育与健身产业协会的数据,2018 年,参加非营利性组织波普华纳小学者(Pop Warner Little Scholars)组织的青少年橄榄球运动的 225 000 名球员中有 1 100 名是女孩,而在 550 万参加橄榄球比赛的美国人中,约有 11% 是女性。

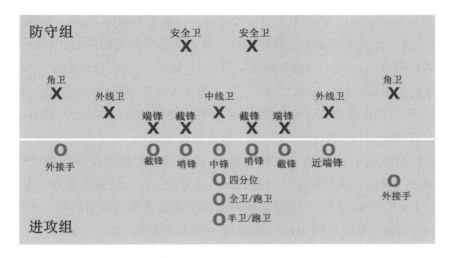

图 5.3　进攻时的 I 阵型和防守时的 4-3 阵型　（作者 Kainaw）

4.1.1　进攻组（进攻队）

图 5.4　基尔波罗的海飓风队四分卫位于中间位置，准备发球　（作者 BalticHurricanes）

进攻组的作用是将橄榄球向前推进，最终目标是达阵得分（touchdown）。

进攻队必须排成合规的阵型（formation）才能发球。如果后场超过 4 名球员或进攻线上编号 50～79 的球员少于 5 名，则进攻阵型被视为违规。球员可以临时排在与他们的号码不一致的位置，只要他们立即向裁判报告，然后裁判通知防守队这一变化。在球被发出（snap）之前，除中锋（center）外，任何球队的球员均不得在中立区（neutral zone）排队或越过中立区。内线进攻队员在球开出之前不得移动。

主要的后场位置是四分卫（quarterback，QB）、半卫或后卫（halfback/tailback，HB/

TB)和全卫（fullback,FB）。四分卫是进攻的领导者。要么是四分卫,要么是教练负责指挥比赛。四分卫通常会在球队排队之前告知其他进攻队员所采用的阵型。四分卫排在中锋身后接球,然后传球（handoff）、抛球（throw）给跑卫、前锋,或自己持球冲锋。

半卫,也称跑卫（running back）或后卫,其主要职责是持球跑阵（running play）,有时也担任接球手。全卫的体型往往比半卫高大,主要充当拦截队员（blocker）,但有时在短距离或靠近球门线的情况下充当跑卫。他们很少担任接球手。

攻击线锋（offensive line）由几名球员组成,他们的主要职责是阻止防守线球员拦截（tackle）持球的跑阵队员或在传球时擒抱（sack）四分卫。攻击线锋的领导者是中锋,他负责将球传给四分卫、阻截对手,并确保其他锋线队员在比赛期间各尽其职。中锋两侧是哨锋（offensive guard）,截锋（offensive tackle）在哨锋外侧排列。

主要的接球手是外接手（wide receiver,WR）和近端锋（tight ends,TE）。外接手在争球线上（line of scrimmage）或附近排成一排,在争球线外分开。外接手的主要目标是接住四分卫的传球,但他们也可能在跑阵过程中充当诱饵或阻截队员。近端锋在截锋（offensive tackle）外侧排列,既充当接球手又充当阻截队员。

4.1.2　防守组（防守队）

图 5.5　达拉斯牛仔队的防守队员迫使休斯敦德州人队的跑卫阿里安·福斯特掉球
(作者 AJ Guel)

防守组的作用是通过拦截持球队员或迫使对手失误（turnover）,如造成被抄截（interception）或掉球（fumble）,来阻止进攻方得分。

防守线锋（defensive line,DL）由防守端锋（defensive ends,DE）和防守截锋（defensive tackles,DT）组成。防守端锋排列在防线两端,而防守截锋则排列在防守端锋之间的内侧。防守端锋和防守截锋的主要职责分别是阻止对手在外线和内线的跑阵,在四分卫传球时,向他施压,并占据防线以便线卫（linebackers）突破。

图5.6 汉堡海魔队的角卫布伦特·格莱姆斯抄截了一次传球
（作者 Torsten Bolten）

线卫在防守线锋后面但在防守后卫（defensive backfield）前面排列，分为两种类型：中线卫（middle linebacker，MLB）和外线卫（outside linebacker，OLB）。鉴于他们在进攻后场的有利位置，线卫往往充当防守组的领导者并指挥防守。他们的职责包括防守跑阵、向四分卫施压以及在对方传球时抢断对方的后卫、外接手和近端锋。

防守后卫通常称为第二防线，由角卫（cornerback，CB）和安全卫（safety，S）组成。安全卫本身又分为自由卫（free safety，FS）和强卫（strong safety，SS）。角卫在防守阵型外侧排列，通常与接球手相对，以便对他们进行防守。安全卫在角卫之间排列，但位于防守后卫后面较远的地方。安全卫往往被视为"最后一道防线"，负责阻止深度传球和跑阵突破（breakout）。

4.1.3 特勤组（特勤队）

图5.7 匹兹堡钢人队的踢球员杰夫·里德执行开球
（作者 Joey Gannon）

特勤组(special teams unit)负责所有的踢球(kick)动作。进攻方的特勤组执行射门得分(field-goal-attempts)、弃踢(punt)和开球(kickoff),而对方球队的防守组则致力于阻截或回击。

射门得分和达阵后加分(point-after-touchdown)组有3个特定位置:踢球员(placekicker,K/PK)、扶球手(holder,H)和长开球手(long snapper,LS)。长开球手的任务是将球传给扶球手,扶球手接住球并为踢球手摆放好球。开球时通常没有扶球手扶球,因为球是从发球台(tee)上踢的;然而,在某些情况下可以使用扶球手,例如如果风阻止球在发球台上保持直立。接球组(receiving team)中接球的球员称为开球回攻手(kickoff returner)。

专门负责弃踢的球员是弃踢手(punter,P)、长开球手、护球手(upback)和阻跑员(gunner,G)。长开球手将球直接传给弃踢手,然后弃踢手将球抛出,在球落地之前踢出。阻跑员在罚球线外分开排队,沿着球场奔跑,目标是拦截弃踢回攻手(punt returner,PR),即接住弃踢球的球员。护球手在争球线后面不远的地方排列,为弃踢手提供额外的保护。

4.2 得分

图 5.8 海军学院海校生队球员(深色球衣)达阵得分,塔尔萨大学金色飓风队一名防守队员(白色球衣)在一旁看着。得分线由橙色的标柱标记(作者 Christop)

在橄榄球比赛中,比赛结束时得分较多的球队获胜。橄榄球比赛中有多种得分方式。达阵(touchdown)可得六分,是美式橄榄球中最有价值的得分方式。当进攻方球员带球进入对方达阵区(end zone)或者在达阵区中合规地接住了传来的球(前提是落地之前没有被擒抱而推出达阵区或掉球),即为成功达阵。得分的一方可以获得一次达阵后加分[point(s)-after-touchdown,PAT]或者转换(conversion)的进攻机会。通常是从对方的 2 yd 或 3 yd 线(取决于比赛的水平)进行加踢或转换。如果达阵后加分是通过踢定位球(place kick)或落地球(drop kick)穿过球门柱得分,则得 1 分,通常称为一分加踢或附加分(extra point);如果达阵后加分是通过普通的达阵得分,则得 2 分,称为 2 分转换(two-point conversion)。一般来说,达阵后加分几乎都会成功,而两分转换的风险更大,失败的可能性也更高;因此,一分加踢比 2 分转换更为常见。

通过踢定位球或落地球,使球穿过球门立柱并越过防守方球门横梁,这样的射门得 3 分。实际上,几乎所有射门尝试都是通过定位球完成的。虽然落地球在橄榄球运动的早期很常见,但现代橄榄球的形状使得踢出可靠的落地球变得困难。美国全国橄榄球联盟上一次成功的通过落地球得分是在 2006 年,在此之前的一次成功的落地球是在 1941 年。在射门得分或达阵后加分成功后,得分队必须将球权交给对手。

当进攻队员在自己的达阵区内被擒抱或掉球时,由防守一方得 2 分,称为安全分(safety)。此外,让对手获得安全分的球队必须通过任意球(free kick)将球踢给得分球队。

4.3 橄榄球场与装备

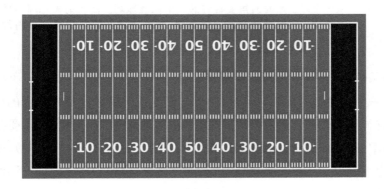

图 5.9 现代美式橄榄球场示意图(作者 Xyzzy n)

橄榄球比赛场地为矩形,长 120 yd(109.7 m)、宽 53⅓ yd(48.76 m)。较长的边界称为边线(sideline),较短的边界称为底线(end line)。底线前的标示线称为球门线(goal line),两球门线之间的距离为 100 yd(91.44 m)。得分的区域位于底线与球门线之间 10 yd(9.144 m)宽的区域,叫做达阵区(end zone),也称为底线区或端区。

在边线与得分线和底线交会处的内角放置达阵柱(weighted pylon)。球场上的白线表示到达阵区的距离。码标线(inbound lines or hash marks)是短的平行线,标记 1 yd(0.914 4 m)的增量。每隔 5 yd(4.57 m)标划一条横贯球场的分码线(yard line)。在球场的两端各划一条一码宽的线,在职业比赛中这条线标划在 2 yd 线的中间,在大学比赛中标划在 3 yd 线的中间。球场两侧每隔 10 yd 标示一个数字,显示与最近的得分线的距离(以 yd 为单位)。

球门柱(goalpost/upright)位于两条底线的中心。球门立柱由一根横杆相连,横杆距地面 10 ft(3.0 m)。在职业和大学比赛中,球门立柱相距 18.6 ft(5.64 m);在高中比赛中,立柱相距 23.4 ft(7.11 m)。职业比赛球场上的立柱垂直高度为 35 ft(11 m);大学球场至少 10 yd(9.144 m);高中球场至少 10 ft(3.0 m)。球门柱的底部安装有防护垫,每个立柱的顶

图 5.10 从一个端区后面的角度看到的一个橄榄球场。高大的黄色球门柱标志着球必须经过两个球门柱之间，才能成功射门得分或得到附加分
（作者 Clstds）

端通常系有一条橙色丝带，作为风向及风力指示。

橄榄球是一个椭圆形的皮革球，类似于英式或澳式橄榄球比赛中使用的球。为了容纳压缩空气，在皮革外壳内的人造橡胶出现之前，猪的膀胱被广泛使用，以承受挤压力。在所有级别的比赛中，橄榄球被充气至每平方英寸 12.5～13.5 磅（86～93 kPa），或略低于一个大气压，重量为 14～15 oz（396.9～425.3 g）；除此之外，确切的尺寸根据不同级别的比赛略有不同。在职业比赛中，球的长轴为 11～11.25 in（28～29 cm），长周长为 28～28.5 in（71～72 cm），短周长为 21～21.25 in（53.4～54 cm）；在大学和高中比赛中，球的长轴为 10.875～11.437 5 in（27.6～29.1 cm），长周长为 27.75～28.5 in（70～72 cm），短周长为 20.75～21.25 in（52.7～54 cm）。

4.4　持续时间和暂停

职业橄榄球比赛和大学橄榄球比赛的时长为 60 分钟，分为各 30 分钟的两个半场和每节 15 分钟的四节。第一节和第二节为上半场，第三节和第四节为下半场；高中橄榄球比赛时长为 48 分钟，也分四节进行，每节各 12 分钟。两个半场之间有中场休息（halftime）时间，第一节和第三节之后有短暂的休息。比赛开始前，裁判和双方队长在中场抛硬币（coin toss）。客队（visiting team）可以猜"正面"（heads）或"反面"（tails）；抛硬币的获胜者可以选择接球（receive）或者开球（kick off），或者选边，他们也可以将选择权推迟（defer）到下半场。除非抛硬币获胜的一方决定推迟选择，否则输的一方只能选择获胜队未选择的选项——接球、开球或选边来开始下半场。大多数抛硬币获胜的球队会选择接球或推迟选择，因为选择开球的话，对方球队就会知道如何选边。球队在第一节和第三节后交换场地。

如果一节比赛的时间结束时一档进攻正在进行中,则比赛将继续进行,直到这档进攻结束为止。如果比赛期间发生犯规,而比赛时间已到,则该节可能会通过不限时间十码进攻(untimed down)的方式延长。

由于比赛暂停,比赛实际持续时间比规定的时间要长——美国全国橄榄球联盟(NFL)的比赛平均持续 3 个小时多一点。橄榄球比赛时间是通过比赛时钟(game clock)来计时的。计时员负责根据相应官员的指示启动、停止和操作比赛时钟。独立的进攻时钟(play clock)用于显示进攻方距离必须开始比赛所剩的时间。在比赛中出现行政暂停后,进攻时钟设置为 25 秒;而当比赛继续进行且没有此类中断时,进攻时钟设置为 40 秒。如果进攻方未能在进攻时钟显示"00"之前开始比赛,则进攻方将被判拖延比赛犯规(delay of game foul)。

4.5 推进球和档

图 5.11　卡罗莱纳黑豹队四分卫杰克·德尔霍姆(17 号)正在向前传球　　(作者 Tomasland)

进攻队可以通过两种主要方式推进球:跑阵(running)和传球(passing)。在典型的比赛中,中锋从两腿之间将球向后传给四分卫(quarterback),这一过程称为"开球"(snap)。然后四分卫递传或抛球给跑卫、前锋,或自己持球冲锋。当持球球员被擒抱或出界或传球没被接住而落在地上时,比赛结束。只有当传球者位于争球线后面时,才能合规地向前传球(forward pass);每档进攻只能进行一次向前传球。与英式橄榄球一样,球员也可以在比赛过程中随时向后传球(pass the ball backward)。在美国全国橄榄球联盟中,如果跑阵球员的头盔脱落,比赛也会立即停止。

进攻队有 4 次进攻机会向前(防守方的达阵区)推进 10 yd,每次机会称为一个"档"(down,即被对方拦截放倒一次)。当进攻一方成功在四档内累积推进了 10 yd(或超过),便可再次获得继续进攻的四档。如果未能推进 10 yd,则球权将交给防守方。在大多数情况下,如果进攻方到了第四档进攻,他们会采用弃踢(punt),将球踢给对手,迫使对手从更远的地方开始发动进攻;如果他们在射门范围内(field goal range),他们可能会尝试射门得分。一组裁判(工作人员)负责跟踪进攻和测量推进的距离。电视转播时,赛场上会显示一条黄线,向观众展示首攻线。

4.6 踢法

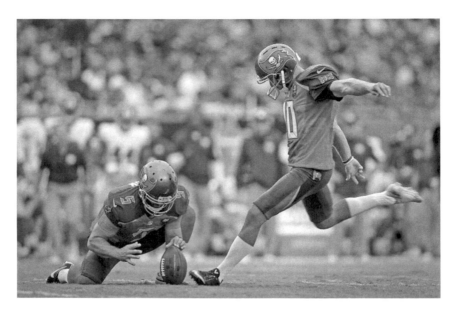

图5.12 坦帕湾海盗队的踢球员康纳·巴斯即将从扶球手手中将球踢向球门。这是射门得分或一分加踢的标准方法(作者 Ned T. Johns)

橄榄球比赛中有两种踢法:一种是争球踢(scrimmage kick),由进攻球队在任意档在争球线后或争球线上进行;另一种是任意球(free kick)。任意球包括开球(kickoff)(在第一节、第三节和加时赛开始,以及在尝试射门或射门得分之后进行)和安全踢(safety kick)(在获得安全分之后进行)。

在职业和大学橄榄球比赛中,开球时,球被放置在踢球队的35 yd线上;在高中比赛中,球被放置在40 yd线上。球员可以踢落地球(drop kick),也可以踢定位球(place kick)。如果选择踢定位球,则可以将球放在地面或球座(tee)上;在两种情况下都可以使用扶球手(holder)。进行安全踢时,踢球队从本方20 yd线上踢出,可以弃踢、踢落地球或踢定位球,但在职业比赛中不得使用球座。防守队(receiving team)的任何成员都可以接球或推进球。一旦球被踢出至少10 yd并接触地面,或被防守队的任何队员触碰,踢球队就可以重新抢回控球权。

争球踢包括三种类型,分别是踢定位球、踢落地球和弃踢。只有踢定位球和落地球才能得分。踢定位球是用于得分的标准方法,因为橄榄球的尖头形状使得踢球员很难踢出可靠的落地球。争球踢开始后,只有在争球线后面接住或抢回球时,踢球队才能带球向前推进。如果球被踢球方在攻防线前方触碰或抢得,球在被接触的地点变为死球(dead ball)。踢球队不得干扰接球手接球。接球队可以选择发出安全接球(fair catch)的手势,这将禁止防守方阻截(block)或擒抱(tackle)接球手。球一旦被接住,比赛即告结束,球不得向前推进。

4.7 裁判和犯规

裁判员负责执行比赛规则并监控比赛计时。所有裁判员都带哨子,穿黑白条纹衬衫,戴黑色帽子,主裁除外,主裁带白色的帽子。每个裁判都携带一面加重黄旗(weighted yellow flag),用以将其扔到地上以表示发生犯规(foul)。发现多次犯规的裁判将扔掉帽子作为第二个信号。女性可以担任裁判员;莎拉·托马斯(Sarah Thomas)于 2015 年成为 NFL 第一位女性裁判。场上的 7 名裁判(标准裁判组为 7 人;大学及以下级别的比赛使用较少的裁判)各自承担着不同的职责:

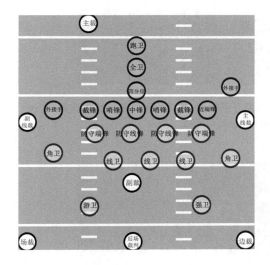

图 5.13 传统的 7 人制裁判系统(白色)与典型的进攻阵型(蓝色)和防守阵型(红色)的相对位置图(作者 Zzyzx11)

图 5.14 裁判员在中场会面
(作者 Belinda Hankins Miller)

主裁判(referee)位于进攻后卫的后方和侧面。主裁负责监督和控制比赛,判定得分(score)和进攻推进码数(down number)以及在裁判中拥有对规则的最终解释权。主裁宣布所有处罚,并与犯规球队队长讨论违规情况,监控对四分卫的违规攻击,提出首攻测量要求,并在球员被驱逐时通知主教练。主裁站在四分卫传球手臂一侧。在大多数比赛中,主裁负责在争球踢(scrimmage kick)前放置橄榄球。

副裁判(umpire)位于防守后场,但在 NFL 中,副裁判的位置在队形的另一侧,与主裁的位置相对。副裁判沿着争球线监视比赛,以确保开球前场上的进攻球员不超过 11 人,并且没有攻击线锋(offensive line)在传球时违规进入前场(illegally downfield)。副裁判会监控攻击线锋和防守线锋之间的接触,并判罚大部分的阻挡(holding)犯规。副裁判负责记录暂停次数、掷硬币获胜者和比赛得分。他们还在攻防线附近涉及球权的情况下协助主裁,确定球员装备是否合规,如果在雨中进行比赛时,在开球前负责将湿球擦干。

图 5.15　裁判们用链尺测量第一次进攻的距离。球离杆子很近,表示第一次进攻没有达到 10 yd
(作者 BrokenSphere)

图 5.16　2008 年 11 月 16 日,旧金山 49 人队与圣路易斯公羊队的比赛中,后裁判李·戴尔准备拿起罚球旗
(作者 BrokenSphere)

后场裁判（back judge）位于防守后场较后的位置，在副裁判后方。后场裁判负责确保防守队在场上的球员不超过 11 人，并判定接球是否合法、射门或一分加踢是不是好球以及是不发生传球干扰（pass interference）违规。如果不使用目视的进攻时钟（play clock），后场裁判要负责进攻时间，即控制每次进攻之间的时间。

主线裁（head linesman/down judge）位于争球线的一端。主线裁负责观察任何争球线犯规和手球犯规行为，并协助副线裁（line judge）进行对于违规换位或违规移动的判罚。主线裁还负责对其所在一侧的出界情况进行裁决，监督链尺工作人员（chain crew）的工作，并在鸣哨结束比赛时标记跑阵队员的前进进度。

边裁（side judge）位于主线裁 20 yd 处。边裁的职责与场裁（field judge）一样。在射门和一分加踢时，边裁位于副裁判的侧面。

副线裁（line judge）位于攻防线的末端，与主裁相对，负责监督球员的替换、弃踢时的争球线以及比赛时间。每节结束时，副线裁将通知主裁判，并在中场休息还剩 5 分钟时通知主队主教练。在 NFL 中，当半场还剩 2 分钟时，副线裁判也会提醒主裁判。如果比赛时钟出现故障或无法操作，副线裁将成为官方计时员。

场裁（field judge）位于副线裁 20 yd 处。场裁监视和控制进攻时钟，统计场上防守球员的数量，并观察进攻球员的进攻传球干扰和手球犯规行为。场裁还对接球（catch）、抢回球（recovery）、球员出界时的地点以及非法触碰越过攻防线的掉球（fumble）做出裁决。在射门和一分加踢时，场裁位于后场裁判对面的球门柱下方。

中央裁判是仅在大学橄榄球顶级联赛中使用的第八名裁判。中央裁判站在主裁判的旁边，就像 NFL 中副裁判的做法一样。中央裁判负责在每次进攻后放置橄榄球，并承担许多与主裁判员相同的职责，但宣布判罚除外。

图 5.17　链尺工作人员　（作者 Rickyrab）

图 5.18　首次进攻标示　（作者 DoubleBlue）

另一组裁判，即链尺工作人员（chain crew），负责移动链尺（chain）。这些链尺由两根大棍子组成，棍子之间有一条 10 yd 长的链条，用于测量第一档进攻的距离。比赛期间，链

279

尺工作人员会留在场边,但如果裁判要求,他们会短暂地将链尺带到场上进行测量。典型的链尺工作人员团队至少有3人——2名成员分别握住一根长棍,第三名成员握住进攻位置标记(down marker)。进攻位置标记是一根带有刻度的长棍,每次进攻后都会转动以指示当前是第几次进攻,并且通常会移动到球停止的大致位置。链尺系统已经使用了100多年,被认为是一种精确的距离测量方法,很少受到任何一方的批评。

第五节 基本战术

战术在美式足球中起着至关重要的作用。为了赢得比赛,两支球队都精心策划了比赛的各个方面。这包括决定阵型,为特定位置选择球员,分配每个球员在进攻和防守上的角色和指示。

在整个比赛过程中,每个团队都在不断调整自己的策略,以应对对方的优势和劣势。他们尝试不同的方法来智胜或压制对手。在进攻方面,球队的目标是通过触地得分和射门得分,同时对对方的防守策略保持警惕。在防守方面,目标是防止进攻得分,以及试图拦截球和把场上形势转向对他们有利的方向。

战术包括:假跑真传(play-action pass)、假传真跑的延迟交递(delayed hand-off)、伴传实跑(draw play)、掩护传球(screen pass)、四分卫短传跑锋等战术。无论采取何种战术,进攻方场上行动主要分为以下两种:集体前移(line move forward),一般是要跑阵(running play);集体后移(line move backward),一般是要传球(passing play)。

一般来说,跑阵战术比传球战术更为安全。不过,也有一些较为保守的传球及较为冒险的跑阵。为了欺骗对手,有些传球会摆出一副跑阵的样子,反之亦然。美式橄榄球有很多计谋,例如有时进攻方会排出踢球的阵型,但又突然尝试去传球或持球冲锋。成功的高风险计谋都会让球迷们看得兴奋不已。当然,如果对手已经洞悉了计谋,亦会为球队带来不幸的结果。

美式橄榄球术语

进攻组(进攻队):进攻组的作用是将橄榄球向前推进,最终目标是达阵得分。

攻击线锋:由5个人组成的人墙,为4分卫和持球队员提供掩护和保护。每条攻击线都有1名中锋(负责发球),2名哨锋和2名截锋。

防守组(防守队):防守的作用是通过拦截持球者或迫使对方失误(抄截或失球)来防止进攻得分。

防守线锋:防守线锋由1名或2名防守截锋和2名防守端锋组成,防守端锋在防守截锋外侧活动。防守线锋与线卫协作,试图控制争球线。

后场/后卫:美式橄榄球场上争球线后的区域。后场(backfield)或进攻型后场(offensive backfield)也可以指在争球线后开始进攻的队员,通常包括场上的任何后卫,如四分卫、跑卫和全卫。

特勤组：是指那些负责特殊任务（主要指踢球）时上场的球员们。他们负责开球、弃踢、任意球和射门。通常由第二和第三阵容球员组成。

聚商：场上的11名球员在比赛间隙聚在一起讨论比赛策略。

档：持球的一队（进攻方）有4次进攻机会向前（防守方的端区）推进10 yd，每次机会称为一个"档"（down，即被对方拦截放倒一次）。如果没有做到这一点，必须把球权交给对手，通常是在第四次进攻时用脚踢。

达阵区：也称底线区、端区，球场两端各10 yd长的区域。当持球队员进入达阵区时，就可以触地得分。如果持球时在自己的端区内被阻截，对方会得到一个安全球。

达阵：当持球队员越过对手的得分线，当球员在对方的达阵区接住球时，或者当防守队员在对方的端区抢得一个掉落的球时，称为达阵，得6分。

一分加踢：也称为达阵后加分或附加分，达阵之后，得分队将获得一次额外的进攻机会，将球放在对方的2 yd或3 yd线上（取决于不同联赛的规则），得分队把球踢进门柱之内，得1分，称为达阵后加分（point after touchdown，PAT），或称为一分加踢或附加分（extra point，XP）。

安全分：防守方通过在对手的达阵区擒抱控球的进攻球员而获得的得分，得2分。

攻防线：一条假想的线，从进攻结束时放置球的地方延伸到场地的两边。在球再次投入比赛之前，进攻队和防守队都不能越过攻防线。

第二防线：4名防守队员，他们负责防守传球，并在线卫后面和在接球手对面的边角处列队。

发球：由中锋将球（在两腿之间抛）传给四分卫、射门时传给扶球员或弃踢员的动作。当球发出后，球正式进入比赛状态，比赛开始。

开球：使球进入比赛状态的任意球（防守队不能进行阻截）。开球是在第一节和第三节开始时以及每次达阵和射门得分后进行的。

射门：得分为3分的射门，可以在场上的任何位置进行，但通常在距门柱40 yd的范围内进行。和一分加踢一样，踢出的球必须越过横梁，并在两个门柱之间，才算进球。

弃踢：球员将球抛出，在球落向脚时踢一脚。当进攻方无法向前推进10 yd，必须将控球权交给防守方时，通常会在第四次进攻时弃踢。

递传：一个球员把球交给另一个球员的动作。传球通常发生在四分卫和跑卫之间。

冲球：也称为跑阵，通过持球向前跑而不是传球来推进球。

擒杀：防守队员在攻防线后擒抱摔倒四分卫，造成码数损失。

抄截：被防守队员接住的传球，结束进攻队员的控球。

安全接球：当球员弃踢回攻时，他挥手示意，发出安全接球的信号后，这个球员不能带球跑，那些试图擒抱他的防守队员也不能碰他。

不成功传球：因为没有接球手能接住而掉在地上的向前的传球，或者接球手掉在地上或接出界外的传球。

掉球：带球队员在进攻结束前,掉落了球或者被打掉,丧失了对球的控制权。首个抢得球权的球员被称为完成了一次"救球",其所属球队获得进攻权。

回攻：在交换球权后,如踢球或拦截后,将球向对方场地推进的动作。

练 习

1. 美式橄榄球比赛中每个队各上场几名队员？
2. 列举出三个美式橄榄球的专业术语。
3. 哪个美式橄榄球赛事是世界上收视率最高的体育赛事之一？

第六章

马　　球

> **学习目标**
> 1. 了解马球的发展历史
> 2. 掌握马球赛事的主要管理机构和重要赛事
> 3. 熟悉马球比赛规则和专业术语

第一节　概　　述

马球是一种骑马的球类运动，是一项传统的场地运动，也是世界上最古老的集体运动之一。该运动的理念是通过使用长柄木槌将一个小而硬的球击入对手的球门得分。这种运动通常持续1~2个小时，分成若干节（"chukkas"或"chukkers"）进行。每队有4名骑手。

马球被称为"帝王的运动"。在古代，它是骑手和上流社会所热衷的一项观赏性运动，并经常得到赞助。这项运动的概念及其变体可以追溯到公元前6世纪—公元1世纪，起源于游牧的伊朗人玩的马术游戏。这项运动最初是波斯骑兵部队（通常是皇家卫队或其他精锐部队）的训练项目。一个著名的例子是萨拉丁，他作为一名技艺高超的马球运动员而闻名，这项运动有助于他的军事训练。现在，马球运动在全世界都很流行，国际马球联合会有100多个成员国，有16个国家参加了职业马球比赛。此外，马球曾在1900—1936年期间成为奥运会比赛项目。

图6.1　公元706年，唐朝朝臣在马背上打马球（图片来源：Wikimedia）

竞技场马球比赛是室内、半室外比赛的变种，规则类似，每队有3名骑手。比赛场地是较小的封闭场地，通常由压实的沙子或细砂石铺成。比赛通常在室内进行。由于空间的限制，竞技场马球有更多的机动性，使用的是一个充气球，比场地马球中使用的硬实心球稍大。骑手们使用标准的球棍，也可以选择稍微大一点的球棍。

第二节 主要管理机构

国际马球联合会(Federation of International Polo,FIP)是由国际奥林匹克委员会正式承认的代表马球运动的国际联合会。它成立于1982年,由11个国家马球协会的代表建立,目前代表着90多个国家的国家马球协会。国际马球联合会的主要目标是提高马球这项重要运动的国际形象和地位。

国际马球联合会(FIP)的使命是在全球范围内推广马球运动,以捍卫和确保公平竞争和道德操守;目的是在比赛期间及赛后,在比赛场地和任何马球运动员见面的地方培养具有绅士风度的体育态度,推动构建一个伟大的世界马球大家庭。

第三节 重要赛事

3.1 世界马球锦标赛

图6.2 2011年阿根廷世界马球锦标赛(作者 Emanuel Agustin Lorenzoni Macchi)

世界马球锦标赛(World Polo Championship)是国家间的马球比赛。该赛事由马球运动的管理机构国际马球联合会(FIP)组织,由国家队参赛。对球员的性别没有限制。首届世界马球锦标赛于1987年由阿根廷主办,现在每三到四年举办一次。

参赛队伍的等级之和不得超过14。正是由于这一规定,与其他运动不同,顶尖水平的运动员不能参加世界马球锦标赛。

3.2　竞技场马球欧洲锦标赛

竞技场马球欧洲锦标赛是一项由 4 支国际球队参加的锦标赛。这些球队都是国家队，由各自的国家联合会（都是国际马球联合会成员）提名。比赛的级别是每队 10～12 级（竞技场差点），比赛分为 4 节（Chukkers）进行。

3.3　雪地马球世界杯邀请赛

雪地马球世界杯邀请赛是一项雪地马球邀请赛，始于 2012 年，每年在中国天津大都会马球俱乐部举行。

世界马球联合会（FIP）举办的雪地马球世界杯邀请赛，是其在全球范围内推广这项运动、提升该运动的形象和地位的一个里程碑。

雪地马球在平坦压实的雪地或结冰的湖面上进行，比赛速度与对身体素质的要求与传统场地马球相同，但由于比赛场地较小，被认为具有更快的比赛进程。得益于球场边缘的高侧板，雪地马球观众还可以更近距离地观看比赛。

3.4　超级国家杯

超级国家杯（FIP Super Nations Cup）是世界上级别最高的国际赛事之一，在中国天津的天津金鼎大都会马球俱乐部举行。来自世界马球运动领先国家的 4 支职业球队参加了这场 24 级的比赛。

3.5　大使杯

在国际马球联合会成立的几年内，有 19 个国家签署了协议，还有 10 个临时成员。招募新成员国的主要方式是一系列的比赛，后来被称为"大使杯"。这些比赛最初是国际马球联合会成员和合作者之间的比赛，因此比赛不存在参赛资格的问题。最初的计划是在世界各地举行马球赛事，结识国际马球联合会的所有朋友和合作者，并邀请新人打马球，将马球推广到世界各地。

第一届大使杯其中一场比赛是在莫斯科举行的，目的是复兴这项在 1918 年俄国革命中被废除的运动。由于没有场地，这场比赛是在马戏团帐篷里进行的室内马球比赛。组织这项赛事付出了很多艰苦的努力，但从那以后，马球运动又开始在俄罗斯流行起来，而且还在不断发展。

第四节　比 赛 规 则

马球的规则旨在保障选手和马匹的安全。比赛由裁判员监督。当发生犯规时，裁判会吹哨，并给予犯规队员处罚。马球的战术是建立在"球行线"基础上的，这是一条想象中的线,是沿着球的运动路线的延伸线。依据球线,制定了球员安全接近球的规则。每当球改变方向时,"球行线"就会随之改变。击球的球员通常有通行权,其他球员不允许越过该球员前面的球行线。当球员接近球时,他们行进在球行线的两侧,让两侧的球员都有机会接触到球。在不造成危险的情况下,球员可以越过球行线。大多数犯规和处罚都与球员违规地越过球行线或影响通行权有关。当球员的球行线在他的右侧时,他有通行权。"冲撞"是指一名球员利用自己的马通过与对手的马有并肩的接触,将对手的马推离球行线。

防守队员有各种机会让他们的球队获得控球权。他们可以把对手推到线外,或者从对手那里抢断球。另一种常见的防守战术叫做"勾杆"。当一名球员挥杆击球时,他的对手可以用球杆勾住正在击球球员的球杆来阻止他挥杆。球员只有在挥杆的一侧或对手的正后方时才能进行勾杆。球员不得故意用球杆碰触其他选手、其他选手的马具或马。不安全的勾杆是犯规行为,将导致被判点球。例如,球员越过对手的马试图勾杆是犯规行为。

另一种基本的防守战术叫做冲撞或挤出球行线。这和冰球的身体阻挡很像。在挤出球行线的行动中,球员骑着他们的马与对手的坐骑并排,以使对手远离球。这种战术必须正确执行,以免危及马匹或运动员的安全。接触的角度必须是安全的,不能使马匹失去平衡,或以任何方式伤害到马匹。两名沿球行线前进并互相挤着对方的球员有优先于任何方向来的球员的通行权。

像曲棍球、冰球或篮球一样,马球中的犯规是指违反比赛规则的潜在危险行为。对于新手观众来说,犯规可能很难辨别。罚球的判罚取决于犯规的严重程度和犯规位置。马球场上的白线表示中场的位置以及 60 yd,40 yd 和 30 yd 的罚球位置。

每年由每个国家的马球协会审查和公布官方规则和对规则的解释。大多数较小的协会都遵守英国马球运动的国家管理机构赫灵汉姆马球协会(Hurlingham Polo Association)和美国马球协会(United States Polo Association)的规则。

4.1 室外马球

室外马球比赛持续大约 1.5～2 小时,包括 4～8 节(chukkas),每节 7 分钟,球员在比赛期间或 2 节之间可以换坐骑。在每七分钟一节结束时,比赛再继续 30 秒或直到死球,以先到者为准。每节之间有 3 分钟的休息时间,中场休息 5 分钟。比赛是连续的,只有在违反规则、马具(装备)破损、马或选手受伤时才会停止。比赛目标是将球打入球门得分,在球门内,无论球飞得多高都有效。如果球偏离了球门,防守队可以在球越过球门线的地方获得一次原地罚球,从而使比赛重新开始。

4.2 室内和竞技场马球

竞技场马球的规则和室外马球一样,但是体能消耗没有室外马球运动员那么高。它是

图 6.3　2007 年东南亚运动会马球比赛印度尼西亚队对阵泰国队（作者 Dirgayuza Setiawan）

在一个 300 ft×150 ft(91 m×46 m)的封闭竞技场中进行的,和其他马术运动的场地一样;最小尺寸为 150 ft×75 ft(46 m×23 m)。美国有许多竞技场马球俱乐部,主要的马球俱乐部(包括圣巴巴拉马球和网球俱乐部)都有定期举行的竞技场马球比赛项目。室外和室内比赛的区别主要在如下方面:速度(室外更快)、身体素质(室内/竞技场要求更高)、球的大小(室内更大)、球门的大小(因为竞技场更小,所以球门更小),以及一些处罚。在美国和加拿大,大学马球是竞技场马球;在英国,大学马球是室内外兼而有之。

竞技场马球的形式包括沙滩马球和牛仔马球。沙滩马球在许多国家由 3 人一队在沙地上进行;牛仔马球几乎只在美国西部由 5 人一队在泥地上进行。

另一种现代变体是雪地马球,在平整的雪地或冰冻的湖面上进行。雪地马球的形式因场地的不同而不同,每队一般由 3 名队员组成,通常使用颜色鲜艳的塑料球。

4.3　比赛场地

比赛场地是 300 yd×160 yd(270 m×150 m),面积约为 6 个足球场或 9 个美式橄榄球场(10 英亩),而竞技场马球场地规格是 96 m×46 m。比赛场地使用经过精心维护、仔细修剪的草皮,能够为比赛提供一个安全、可靠的比赛场地。球门设置在场地两端中间,球门柱相距 8 yd。马球场地的表面需要仔细和持续的维护,以保持良好的比赛条件。在比赛中场休息时,观众被邀请到球场上参加一项被称为"踩草皮"的马球传统活动,这不仅有助于恢复被马蹄破坏形成的土堆(草皮),而且还为观众提供了四处走动和社交的机会。

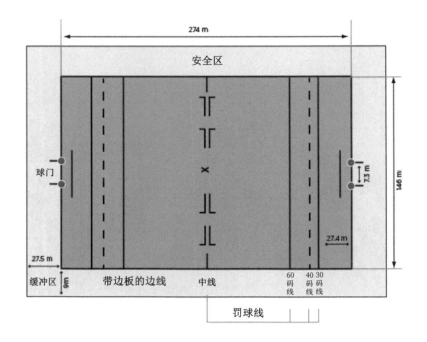

图6.4 马球场地尺寸(图片来源：Wikipedia)

4.4 马球马

马球比赛使用的坐骑被称为"马球小马"（尽管"小马"一词纯粹是传统的叫法），是一匹全尺寸的马。它们的马肩高从14.2～16手(58～64 in,147～163 cm)不等,重900～1 100 lb(410～500 kg)。马球马的挑选要考虑马的爆发速度、耐力、敏捷性和机动性。马的性情至关重要：马必须在压力下保持敏捷的反应,不能变得兴奋或难以控制。此外,马需要足够的智力以了解现场发生的事情,跟上比赛节奏,了解其他队员、其他马匹以及可能发生的变化。许多马球马是纯种马或纯种马的杂交品种。它们经过训练,使骑手可以一只手握着缰绳,并根据骑

图6.5 马球马(图片来源：Wikimedia)

手的腿和体重提示作出反应,以便向前移动、转弯和停止。一匹训练有素的马能平稳而迅速地驮着骑手奔向马球。对球队来说,马可以占到球员技术和球队净值的60%～75%。

马球马的训练通常从3岁开始,持续大约6个月到2年。大多数马在5岁左右达到完全的身体成熟,小马在6岁或7岁左右达到运动能力和训练的顶峰。如果没有任何意外,马球马可能有能力比赛到18～20岁。

每个队员必须有不止一匹马,以允许疲惫的坐骑被体力充沛的坐骑替代,替换马球马可以在任何时候进行。在低级别比赛中,球员的马球马可能有 2～3 匹(马在重新使用之前至少要休息一节时间),在中等级别比赛中可能有 4 匹或更多的马(每节至少有 1 匹),在最高水平的比赛中甚至更多。

4.5 选手

图 6.6 阿根廷马球公开赛(作者 Roger Schultz)

每队由 4 名骑手组成,可组成男女混合队。

每个位置上的球员都有特定的职责:

① 1 号是场上进攻最集中的位置。1 号位通常会对位对方的 4 号位,通常是队里的新秀;

② 2 号球员在进攻中扮演着重要的角色,要么自己突破并得分,要么传给 1 号球员并在他们身后突破。在防守端,他们要对位对方的 3 号球员(通常是对方最好的球员)。考虑到这个位置的难度,球队中最好的球员打 2 号位并不罕见(只要有另一个强壮的球员可以打 3 号位);

③ 3 号是战术领袖,必须是一个长传有力的击球手,能给 2 号和 1 号传球,同时保持稳固的防守。球队中最好的球员通常是 3 号球员,通常拥有最高的级别;

④ 4 号是主要的防守球员。他们可以在球场上的任何地方移动,通常试图阻止得分。4 号球员专注防守,让 3 号球员可以尝试更多的进攻,因为他们知道如果他们丢球,会有 4 号球员进行防守;

⑤ 马球必须用右手打,以防止正面碰撞。

4.6 比赛装备

4.6.1 队员和坐骑的安全装备

各个主办方对装备的详细规定各不相同,但都是为了球员和坐骑的安全。

强制性装备包括有帽带的防护头盔,所有球员都要戴上。这种头盔必须符合当地认可的安全标准,PAS015(英国),NOCSAE(美国)。护脸器通常与头盔是一体的。

图 6.7 马球带护脸头盔(作者 Montanabw)　　图 6.8 戴着护膝的马球运动员(作者 Trebaxus)

在正式比赛期间,马球靴和护膝在英国是强制性的装备,并且建议在任何地方的所有比赛中都穿马球靴。英国还建议佩戴护目镜、护肘和护齿。此外,各队的球衣需要能区分球员所在球队,而不能像裁判服那样有黑白相间的条纹。

正式比赛时穿白色马球裤。通常,马球手套的作用是防止缰绳和马球杆对手的伤害。

不允许携带任何可能伤害马匹的装备,例如某些马刺或鞭子。

4.6.2 球

现代室外马球是由高强度塑料制成的。历史上,它们是由竹子、皮革覆盖的软木、硬橡胶和多年的柳根制成的。最初,英国人使用的是涂成白色的皮革板球。

室外马球的标准直径为 3~3.5 in(7.6~8.9 cm),重量为 99~130 g(3.5~4.5 oz)。

塑料球是在 20 世纪 70 年代引入的,它们不易破损,而且便宜得多。

室内和竞技场马球由皮革覆盖,充气,直径约为 4.5 in(11 cm)。

图 6.9 马球杆和马球(作者 Montanabw)

球的周长必须不能小于 12.5 in(32 cm)或大于 15 in(38 cm)。重量不得少于 170 g(6.0 oz)或多于 182 g(6.4 oz)。在 70 °F(21 ℃)时,从 9 in(2.7 m)的高处落到混凝土地面上进行回弹测试时,在制造商规定的膨胀率下,回弹应最小为 54 in(140 cm),最大为 64 in(160 cm)。这种球的特点是又硬又有良好的弹性。

4.6.3 马球杆

图 6.10　马球杆(图片来源：Wikimedia)

马球杆包括一个带有橡胶包裹手柄的藤杆，一个被称为吊带的环形皮带(用来缠绕在拇指上)，和一个木制的雪茄形杆头。马球杆是用玛瑙藤制成的(不是空心的竹子)，尽管现在有一小部分马球杆是用复合材料制成的。复合材料通常不被顶级选手所青睐，因为复合材料马球杆的杆不能像传统的藤条球杆那样吸收振动。杆头通常由一种叫做涕巴(tepa)的硬木制成，大约 9.25 in 长。杆头的重量是 160~240 g(5.6~8.5 oz)，这取决于选手的喜好和使用的木材类型，而杆的重量和灵活性可以根据选手的喜好而变化。对于经验丰富的球员来说，杆头的重量是一个重要的考虑因素。女选手通常比男选手使用更轻的马球杆。对于一些马球运动员来说，马球杆的长度取决于马的大小：马越高，球杆就越长。然而，有些选手更喜欢使用单一长度的球杆，而不管马的高度。不管怎样，骑不同高度的马需要骑手进行一些调整。马球杆的可变长度通常在 127 cm(50 in)到 134 cm(53 in)之间。马球杆(mallet)这个词只在美式英语中使用，而英式英语更喜欢用马球棍(polo stick)这个词。球是用杆头的宽边击打，而不是用它又圆又平的两端击打。

4.6.4 马鞍

马球鞍为英式风格，与马身紧密接触，类似跳鞍(尽管大多数马球鞍在鞍坯下没有襟翼)。有些选手不使用鞍毯。马鞍有一个平坦的座位，没有膝盖支撑；骑手采用前倾座椅和封闭的膝围，与传统盛装舞步不同。通常会加一块胸革带，附在前部钢坯上。由于必须使

图 6.11　马球马鞍(来源：Wikimedia)

用站立式的鞍,因此,为了安全起见,胸甲是必要的。系带通常由颈带支撑,许多马鞍也有肚带。马镫铁比大多数马镫都重,马镫皮带也更宽更厚,以增加运动员站在马镫上时的安全性。马球马的腿从膝盖以下到脚掌都用马球绷带包裹着,以尽量减少疼痛。跳靴(前开)或马靴有时与马球绷带一起使用,以增加保护。通常,这些绷带与球队的颜色相匹配。马球马的鬃毛通常是弯曲的,它的尾巴被截断或编成辫子,这样就不会钩住骑手的马球杆。

马球马使用双缰绳,以提高信号的准确性。衔铁通常是口衔或大勒衔。在这两种情况下,口衔或柄缰绳是骑手手中的底部缰绳,而小勒缰是顶部缰绳。如果使用口衔,除了调教笼头外,还会有一个垂鼻勒,以固定索具。两套缰绳可以交替使用。

第五节　基本战术

5.1　骑手与马匹的协调性

骑手与马匹的协调性是马球运动中最关键的因素。骑手必须能够精确地指挥马匹,尤其是在快速改变方向或加速争夺球时。骑手和马需要经过长期的训练才能建立理解、信任和协作。

5.2　战术定位

在马球运动中,定位就是一切。球员需要知道如何移动,确保自己和球队拥有合适的空间。优秀的球员善于快速浏览比赛并确定他们应该在哪里协助进攻或防守。

5.3 团队合作和沟通

沟通和协调程度较高的团队获胜的机会更大。球员之间使用手势和语言交流可以帮助突破对手的防御并组织有效的攻击。

5.4 防守站位

球员必须意识到自己的防守角色,无论是保护队友还是追逐对方球员。知道何时向控球球员施压以及何时留守球门进行防守至关重要。

5.5 快速进攻

快速由守转攻是成功球队的关键特征之一。球队最好在对手重新组织防守之前快速转移球并冲向球门。

马球术语

缰绳：这些缰绳从骑手的手里穿过衔铁到马鞍的一侧,增加了杠杆作用,能够控制强壮的马匹,使马的头保持向下。

衔铁：这是一种在侧边的圆形衔铁,把马头向上拉,马就会停下来。

大勒衔：这是由一根杆子和链子组成的衔铁,把马头向下拉,马就会停下来。

马领缰：这是从马笼头到马腰的带子,它能防止马头撞到骑手。检查马领缰非常重要,不能太松,也不能太紧。在马放松状态下,马领缰应该沿着马脖子下面的轮廓垂下。

肚带：肚带是在马肚子下面,把马鞍固定在马上的带子。肚带应该系紧,只能允许有两个手指能够在里面滑动。上马前要确定肚带已经系紧。

掷球入界：比赛开始或恢复前,裁判将球掷入两队之间。

出界：当一个球越过边线或边线板,这时候裁判在两队之间再扔一个球。出界球不允许暂停。

界外球：如果一方在进攻中把球打过对方的底线,防守方则从己方底线原地罚球继续比赛。

安全罚球：如果防守方将球击出本方底线,则进攻方在正对球出界点的 60 yd (约 54.86 m)线处罚球。它相当于足球中的角球,在罚球时,任何后卫必须离球超过 30 yd。

局：也称为节,一场马球比赛中有 6 局(竞技场马球和低球门马球有 4 局),每局持续 7 分钟,加时赛最多 30 秒。如果在 30 秒内,球撞到边板或出界,或者裁判吹响哨子,则一局结束。除非双方打成平手,否则第 6 局不允许加时赛,此时将进行第 7 局,直到打进一球。骑手骑着不同的马参加每局比赛,尽管他们可以让马休息一两局,然后再骑着这匹马比赛。

边板：比赛分为"有边板"和"无边板",不过那些有观众的比赛通常都有边板,以保持球在球场中,避免发生任何意外。边板高度不得超过 28 cm,且只能沿着场地边线设置。

球行线： 是指当球被击出后，从击球点到马球运动轨迹的一条延伸线。这条球线非常重要，骑手不能穿越这条线。如果骑手穿越了这条线，就会造成一个非常危险的犯规。

反手： 马的左侧。

正手： 马的右侧。

颈下击球： 从马的脖子下面进行的击球。

走斜： 马球比赛与判断角度息息相关。应避免在球场上直线奔跑。相反，在场地上向右侧移动，这样队友能够把球传给你。在某些情况下，如果左路有空位，那么球也可以传给左路。马球应该以斜线的方式从一端向边板移动。

挤靠： 比赛中，两名骑手可以相互接触并将对方推离球线，以防止对方击球。挤靠主要依靠马来进行，球员也可以使用身体，但不能用肘部。

冲撞： 一名球员可被允许骑向另一名球员的球线以阻碍其击球。冲撞的角度必须很小，不能超过45度，而且马跑得越快，冲撞的角度越小。

勾杆： 球员把自己的球杆挡在对方击球的路线上，破坏对方的击球。不能隔马来钩杆，这是个非常危险的犯规。

练 习

1. 什么是马球运动？
2. 马球比赛分为几局？

第七章

棒　　球

学习目标

1. 了解棒球运动的发展历史
2. 掌握棒球运动的管理机构和重要赛事
3. 熟悉棒球运动的比赛规则和专业术语

第一节　概　　述

图 7.1　芬威公园——波士顿红袜队的主场(作者 Kevin Read)

棒球是一种用球棒击球的运动,攻守两队轮流进攻和防守。当防守队的一名球员(投手)将球投给进攻队的一名试图用球棒击球的球员(击球手)时,比赛就开始了。进攻方(击球队)的目标是把球打入赛场,然后击球员跑垒,按照逆时针方向跑过 4 个垒"得分"。防守方的目标是防止击球手跑垒,防止跑垒员绕垒前进。当跑垒员按顺序合规地绕垒前进并触碰到本垒板（球员作为击球手开启比赛的地方）时，就可以得分。到比赛结束时得分多的队获胜。

进攻队的首要目标是让队员安全上一垒。进攻队中未被"出局"的一垒队员可以尝试以跑垒员的身份进入下一垒，可以立即进垒，也可以在队友轮流击球时进垒。防守队试图通过迫使击球手或跑垒员"出局"（离开赛场）的方式来阻止对手得分。投手和外野手都有办法让进攻队的球员出局。双方球队在击球和防守之间来回切换；一旦防守队记录3次出局，进攻队的进攻就结束了。每队轮流进攻一局。一场比赛通常由9局组成，在比赛结束时得分较多的队获胜。如果在9局结束时比分打平，通常会进行加时赛。棒球比赛没有设置时限，大多数比赛在第9局结束。

棒球是由18世纪中期英国老式球棒击球运动演变而来的。这项运动是由移民带到北美的，他们在那里发展了现代版本的棒球运动。19世纪后期，棒球被广泛认为是美国的国家运动。棒球在北美、中美洲和南美洲的部分地区、加勒比海和东亚（特别是在日本、韩国和中国台湾地区）很受欢迎。

在美国和加拿大，美国职业棒球大联盟（Major League Baseball，MLB）的球队为国家联盟（National League，NL）和美国联盟（American League，AL），每一个联盟都分为3个区：东部、西部和中部。美国职业棒球大联盟的冠军由世界职业棒球大赛（World Series，WS）的季后赛决定。日本的顶级联赛同样分为中部联赛和太平洋联赛，古巴则分为西部联赛和东部联赛。由世界棒垒球总会（World Baseball Softball Confederation，WBSC）组织的世界棒球经典赛（World Baseball Classic，WBC）是这项运动的主要国际比赛，吸引了来自世界各地的顶级国家队参赛。

第二节　主要管理机构

2.1　世界棒垒球总会

世界棒垒球总会（WBSC）是棒球和垒球运动的国际管理机构。国际棒球联合会（International Baseball Federation，IBAF）和国际垒球联合会（International Softball Federation，ISF）分别是以前的棒球和垒球的国际管理机构，于2013年合并成立了世界棒垒球总会。在世界棒垒球总会的组织架构下，国际棒球联合会和国际垒球联合会现在分别是世界棒垒球总会的棒球分部和垒球分部。每个分部由一个执行理事会管理，而世界棒垒球总会则由一个执行委员会管理。

世界棒垒球总会，总部位于瑞士皮伊（Pully），在2013年9月8日举行的第125届国际奥委会会议上被国际奥林匹克委员会批准为棒球和垒球运动的全球唯一管理机构。

世界棒垒球总会在亚洲、非洲、美洲、欧洲和大洋洲的136个国家和地区拥有190个会员。职业棒球组织和青少年组织也包括在内，并以非正式会员作为世界棒垒球总会的一个分支。

作为公认的棒球和垒球管理机构,世界棒垒球总会负责监督所有国际比赛,并对以国家队身份参加的所有竞赛、锦标赛和世界锦标赛拥有专有权,这些权利也适用于奥运会。从 1992 年到 2008 年,棒球一直是奥运会比赛项目,之后退出了奥运会,在 2020 年又回到了奥运会。世界棒垒球总会会员拥有组织和选拔国家队的权利。世界棒垒球总会及其成员在每个成员国对棒球运动进行批准和管理的独家权力适用于在 136 个国家和地区建立的会员协会。

2.2 美国职业棒球大联盟

美国职业棒球大联盟(MLB)是一个职业棒球组织。美国职业棒球大联盟是美国和加拿大的主要职业体育联盟之一,由 30 支球队组成,其中 29 支来自美国,1 支来自加拿大;30 支球队平均分配给国家联盟(NL)和美国联盟(AL)。国家联盟和美国联盟分别成立于 1876 年和 1901 年。两个联盟在 1903 年达成合作协议,使美国职业棒球大联盟成为世界上历史最悠久的主要职业体育联盟。他们在法律上一直是独立的实体,直到 2000 年才合并为一个由棒球专员领导的单一组织。美国职业棒球大联盟的总部设在曼哈顿中城。

第三节 重要赛事

3.1 奥运会棒球项目

棒球在 1904 年夏季奥运会上作为非正式项目首次亮相,在 1992 年夏季奥运会上成为正式的奥运会项目。棒球是 1992—2008 年奥运会的比赛项目,后来从夏季奥运会项目中退出,于 2020 年恢复。奥运会棒球比赛由世界棒垒球总会(WBSC)负责管理。

3.2 世界棒球经典赛

世界棒球经典赛(WBC)是由国际棒球联合会(IBAF)批准的国际棒球锦标赛,从 2006 年开始举办至 2013 年;2013 年之后改由世界棒垒球总会(WBSC)与美国职业棒球大联盟(MLB)合作负责。举行世界棒球经典赛是由美国职业棒球大联盟(MLB)、美国职业棒球大联盟球员协会(Major League Baseball Players Association,MLBPA)以及世界各地的其他职业棒球联盟及其球员协会向国际棒球联合会(IBAF)提出的建议。它是世界棒垒球总会(WBSC)批准的两项主要高水平棒球锦标赛之一,另外一项是 12 强赛(Premier12),但世界棒球经典赛是唯一一项授予获胜者"世界冠军"头衔的比赛。

这项赛事是第一个允许由世界各地主要联盟的职业球员组成的国家队参赛的赛事,包括来自美国职业棒球大联盟的球员。除了为世界上最优秀的棒球运动员提供一个代表各自国家参赛的平台外,世界棒球经典赛的创立还旨在进一步在全球推广棒球运动。

3.3 世界棒球 12 强赛

世界棒球 12 强赛（WBSC Premier12）是由世界棒垒球总会（WBSC）组织的国际棒球锦标赛，由世界上排名最高的 12 支国家棒球队参赛。第一届比赛于 2015 年 11 月举行。第二届世界棒球 12 强赛，于 2019 年 11 月举行，同时作为 2020 年夏季奥运会棒球比赛的预选赛，有 2 支球队获得了参赛资格。

3.4 女子棒球世界杯

世界杯女子棒球赛（Women's Baseball World Cup）是一项国际棒球锦标赛，来自世界各地的女子国家棒球队参加比赛。2012 年的比赛得到了国际棒球联合会（IBAF）的批准；在 2013 年国际棒球联合会 IBAF 与国际垒球联合会（ISF）合并后，随后的比赛由世界棒垒球总会（WBSC）批准。在前 8 届比赛中，美国队 2 次夺冠，日本队在 2008 年、2010 年、2012 年、2014 年、2016 年和 2018 年连续 6 次夺冠。

第四节 比 赛 规 则

4.1 比赛

图 7.2　等待投球的击球手、捕手和裁判　（图片来源：Wikimedia）

棒球比赛在两队之间进行，每队由 9 名队员组成，两队轮流进攻（击球和跑垒）和防守（投球和接防）。两轮比赛，一个队进攻一次，一个队防守一次，构成一局。一场比赛由 9 局组成（高中级别比赛打 7 局；大学、职业棒球小联盟以及从 2020 赛季开始的美国职业棒球大联盟3个级别的一日"连赛2场"也打7局;少年棒球联盟比赛打6局)。每局上半场由一队(通常是客队)击球;另一支球队(通常是主队)在每局的下半场击球。比赛的目标是比对手得更多的分。进攻方的队员按顺序触碰位于正方形棒球场地的4个垒,试图得分。击球员的任务是将球击出之后,从本垒起跑,按照逆时针方向安全到达下一垒位,经过一垒、二垒和三垒,最终回到本垒,从而得分。防守队试图通过造成进攻方队员出局,来阻止进攻方队员跑垒得分。当进攻方3人出局时,两队在接下来的比赛中互换进攻与防守。在9局比赛后,如果双方的比分打平,则进行加时赛来决出胜负。许多业余比赛,特别是无组织的比赛,球员的数量和局数会有所不同。

4.2 人员

4.2.1 球员

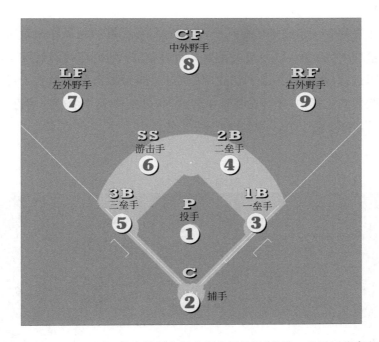

图7.3 棒球场上的防守位置,带有缩写和记分员位置编号(非统一编号)(作者 Michael J)

棒球花名册上的球员人数会因为不同联赛和比赛组织水平而有所不同。一个美国职业棒球大联盟(MLB)球队的花名册上有26名球员,每名球员都有特定的责任。典型的球员名单如下:

① 8名各个位置的先发野手:1名捕手、4名内野手和3名外野手。
② 5名轮值的先发投手。
③ 7名替补投手,包括一名终结者,组成球队的替补投手练习区(因作为投手热身的场外区域而得名)。
④ 1名替补捕手。

⑤ 5名替补内野手和替补外野手，或者可以打多个位置的全能球员。

4.2.2 主教练和教练

主教练负责球队的主要战略决策，例如在每场比赛前确定先发投手、比赛阵容和击球手上场顺序，以及在比赛中的换人，特别是替补投手的替换。主教练通常由两名或更多教练协助；教练们各有专门的职责，比如和球员一起练习击打、防守、投球或进行力量和身体训练。在大多数正式的比赛中，当球队击球时，有两名教练在场上：一垒教练和三垒教练。他们分别站在位于界外线外的教练区。在比赛中，这些教练负责为跑垒员进行指导，并在比赛暂停时将主教练的战术意图传达给击球手和跑垒员。与许多其他集体运动不同，棒球主教练和教练通常穿着球队的队服；在比赛时，教练员必须穿着球队的队服才能在场上与球员进行交流。

4.2.3 裁判员

任何棒球比赛都有一名或多名裁判员，他们对每场比赛的结果作出裁决。至少要有一名裁判员站在接球手的后面，以便更好地观察好球区，来判罚坏球和好球。额外的裁判可能会在其他垒附近，以便更容易地判罚比赛，如对试图封杀出局和触杀出局的判罚。在美国职业棒球大联盟的比赛中，每场比赛有4名裁判，分别位于4个垒的附近。在季后赛中，使用6名裁判员：每个垒1名，外野沿界外线2名。

4.3 棒球场

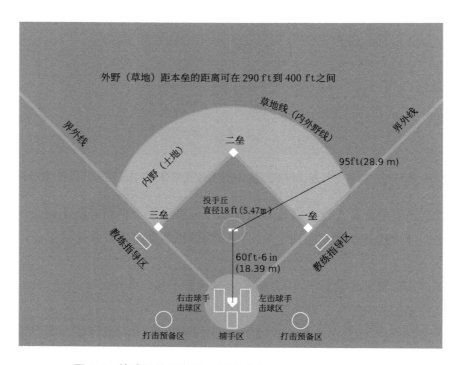

图7.4 棒球场的示意图 （图片来源：Wikimedia Commons）

本垒板（正式的名称是"本垒"）是球场上大部分比赛行动的起点。本垒板是一块五边形白色橡胶板，一条边的边长是 17 in(43 cm)；该边的两条相邻边的长度是 8.5 in(21.6 cm)，其余两条边形成一个直角，边长大约是 12 in(30.5 cm)。本垒板被固定在地面上，表面与球场表面保持水平。本垒板的两个边长为 12 in 的边相交形成的直角位于边长为 90 in(27.43 m)正方形的一个角上。从本垒开始按逆时针方向排列，正方形的其他三个角分别被称为一垒、二垒和三垒。一、二、三垒

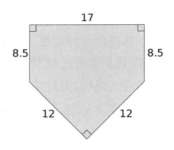

图 7.5　本垒板规格(in)

是由 18 in(45.7 cm)见方，3～5 in(7.6～12.7 cm)厚的帆布或橡胶制成的垒包。在本垒板两条 8.5 in 的平行边的两侧各有一个击球区。

所有的垒，包括本垒，都完全位于界内区。因此，任何击中这些垒的球都必须被判定为界内球。

靠近正方形场地中心的地方是一座人造小土堆，被称为投手丘，上面有一块白色的橡胶板，被称为投手板。

从本垒到一垒和三垒连线的延伸线（延伸到最近的栅栏、看台或其他障碍物），被称为界外线。界外线之间（包括界外线）的球场部分为界内区；其余的部分都是"界外区"。由垒包组成的正方形区域被称为内野（或内场），这个术语在口语中也包括正方形场地附近的界内区域；内野以外的界内区域称为外野（或外场）。大多数棒球场都用围栏围起来，作为外野的外缘边界。围栏通常设置在距离本垒板 300～420 ft(90～130 m)的位置上。大多数职业棒球场和大学棒球场都设有左右两个界外柱，相距约 440～500 ft(130～150 m)。界外柱位于界外线和外野围栏两端

图 7.6　2013 年世界棒球经典冠军赛
（图片来源：Wikimedia）

的交会处，除非规则另有规定，否则界外柱位于界内区域。因此，如果一个击出的球在飞过外野围栏时碰到界外柱，属于界内球，击球手被判本垒打。

4.4　比赛装备

4.4.1　棒球

棒球和成年人的拳头差不多大，周长约 9 in(23 cm)。球的内部是橡胶或软木，用纱线缠绕，外面覆盖着白色的牛皮，用红色的线缝制。

图 7.7　棒球
（图片来源：Wikipedia）

301

4.4.2 球棒

球棒是一种击球工具,传统上是由一块坚固的木头制成的,而现在非专业比赛通常使用其他材料的球棒。球棒是一根坚硬的圆棍,击打端直径约为 2.5 in(6.4 cm),手柄从击打端往下逐渐变细,顶端有一个圆形凸起。成年人使用的球棒通常长约 34 in(86.4 cm),最长不超过 42 in(106.7 cm)。

4.4.3 棒球手套

棒球手套是一种接球工具,由皮革制成,内有衬垫,手指之间有带子相连。作为接球和抓球的辅助工具,棒球手套有各种形状,以满足不同接球位置的特定需要。

4.4.4 防护头盔

防护头盔是所有击球手的标准装备。

图 7.8 球棒 (作者 Dave Hogg)

图 7.9 定制的罗林棒球手套(作者 Wyk)

图 7.10 带面罩的标准 MLB 棒球头盔 (作者 Keith Allison)

第五节 基本战术

在棒球比赛中,许多赛前和赛时的战略决策都围绕着一个基本事实:一般来说,右手击球手在对抗左手投手时往往更有优势;而左手击球手在对抗右手投手时往往优势更大。如果主教练安排的常规阵容中有几个左手击球手,当他知道球队将面对一个左手先发投手时,在球队的名单中,他可能会先发一个或多个右手替补击球手来应对。在比赛的最后几局,当替补投手和替补击球手上场时,对方的主教练通常会不断换人,试图用他们的替补球员创造有利的对位。防守队的主教练试图安排同手投手与击球手对位;进攻队的主教练试图安排与投球手相反手的击球手进行对位。当一支球队在最后一局领先时,主教练可能会换下一名首发球员(尤其是那些不太可能再上场的球员),换上一名技术更娴熟的外野手(即防守替补)。

5.1 投球和接防

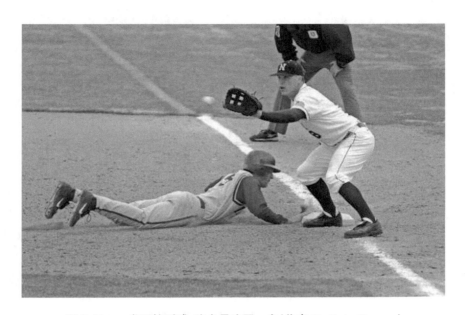

图 7.11 一垒手接到球,跑垒员跑回一垒(作者 Brett A. Dawson)

在棒球比赛中,几乎每一场比赛之前在制定比赛战术时都会涉及投球方式的选择。通过以一定的方式抓握并释放棒球,并使球在出手时达到一定的速度,投手可以使棒球在接近击球手时向两侧或向下变换方向;因此,投球手可以选择不同的投球方式。在各种各样的投球中有 4 种基本类型:快速球、变速球(或慢速球)和两种变向球——曲线球和滑球。投手们都掌握不同的投球技巧。按照惯例,在每次投球之前,捕手会示意投球手该投哪种类型的球,以及球的垂直和水平位置。如果在选择上有分歧,投球手可能会挥手表示不同意,捕手会示意发另一个类型的球。

当跑垒员上垒并取得领先时,投球手可能会尝试一个牵制球,即投出一个快速球给守垒的外野手,以控制提前离垒的跑垒员,理想情况下可以打出一个触杀出局。然而,在打牵制球之前和打牵制球的过程中,投球手的动作受到规则的严格限制。违反规则中的任何一条都可能导致裁判判罚投手犯规,进而允许任何垒上的跑垒员前进一垒。如果预料到有人企图盗垒,捕手可以要求投手投出坏球(pitchout)——故意从板上扔下的球,让捕手站着接住球,然后迅速投到垒上。如果面对一个倾向于往球场一侧击球的击球手,防守队可能会选择换人,让大多数或所有的外野手从他们的常规位置向左或向右移动。当跑垒员在三垒时,内野手可能会采取近迫防守策略,移动到距离离本垒更近的地方,以提高通过滚地球触杀跑垒员出局的概率,尽管一个被大力击中的滚地球更有可能穿过内野区。

5.2　击球和跑垒

图 7.12　球员挥动球棒击球(作者 Keith Allison)

一垒上的跑垒员有几种基本的进攻战术，包括选择是否在二垒盗垒。棒球比赛中(很少三振出局的)经验丰富的击球手有时也会采用打带跑战术：由技术娴熟的击球手触击，跑垒员趁机起跑，吸引短投手或二垒手跑到二垒，在内野留下空档，让击球手把球击穿。牺牲短打战术要求击球手柔和地击球，使球滚出一小段距离进入内野，让跑垒员在击球手出局的情况下进入得分位置。击球手，尤其是跑得快的击球手，也可能试图击出一记安打。用牺牲短打让跑垒员上三垒，目的是把跑垒员送回本垒得分，这被称为强迫取分。当跑垒员在三垒且少于两人出局时，击球手可能会转而集中精力打一个高飞牺牲打(sacrifice fly)，即使球被接住，也会有足够的时间让跑垒员触垒得分。在打出高飞牺牲打，并且跑垒员成功回到本垒得分的情况下，击球员将获得一个一分打点(run batted in)。为了增加击球手自由上一垒的机会，主教练有时会向在计数中领先的击球手(即坏球数多于好球数)发出信号，让他接下一球或不挥棒。如果下一个球是好球，击球手获得自由上一垒的机会很大。

棒球术语

(棒球场)内场：内场中 4 个垒的布局，实际上是一个边长为 90 ft(27.4 m)的正方形，但从看台上看，像一个平行四边形或"菱形"。

内野：90 in 见方的区域，4 个边角是 4 个垒。

外野：棒球场内野和界外线之间的部分。

投手板：投手丘上的投手板。投手向击球手投球时，必须有一只脚与投手板接触。投手板距本垒 60 ft 6 in(18.4 m)。

打击预备区：是指在一局中的下一个击球手。这个击球手站在指定的圆形区域，在击球前进行热身。

替补投手练习区：投手热身的地方，一般由两个投手丘和两个本垒组成。

先发投手：是每队在比赛中的第一个投手。先发投手被期望在比赛的大部分时间里投球，尽管他们的能力取决于许多因素，包括效率、耐力、健康状况和策略。

跑垒员：是指向任何垒位前进、触碰或返回垒位的进攻队员。

指定击球手：是指在棒球比赛中，按照打序轮到投手进攻时，代替投手上场击球的击球手。指定击球手专职击球，不需要防守。

好球区：是指即使击球手不挥棒，球也必须经过的区域，这种球才能被称为好球。好球区被定义为本垒板以上以及击球手膝盖和躯干中点之间的空间。一个球是否穿过好球区是由裁判认定的，裁判通常站在接球手的后面。

打数：指的是一个击球手的上场次数。每个球员轮流击球，直到 3 人出局。每个击球手在本垒上的机会都被记为"at bat"。

好球：是指在棒球比赛中，当击球手挥棒打偏了一个球，没有挥棒打好球区里的球，或者打了一个界外球而没有被外野手接住。

坏球："坏球"是指投手合规直接通过"好球区"而又未被击球员挥击的球。

提前结束比赛：在棒球比赛中，由裁判根据某种理由提前结束比赛的情况。

触击/短打：是指在棒球比赛中，击球员不挥棒并将球棒横握，有意轻轻用球棒触球而使球在内野缓慢滚动的击球，是一种用来使外野手意想不到或使跑垒员前进的打法。

变速球：一种慢速投球，用手臂的准确动作投出快速球，目的是扰乱击球手对击球时机的判断。

曲线球：曲线球是棒球比赛中的一种投球方式，具有独特的握力和手部动作，使球向前旋转，并在接近本垒板时向下俯冲。

飞球：被击出的在空中飞得很高的球。

指叉球：是棒球球路的一种。将食指与中指叉开夹住球，利用投快速球的动作以及两根手指的力量将球投出，球在本垒板前会下沉，影响击球员的击球。

蝴蝶球：又称指关节球、不旋转球。是棒球中的一种球路，一种特殊的变化球，球速不快，目的是尽量减少球在飞行中的旋转，从而导致不稳定、不可预测的运动。

二垒安打：击球手在球返回内野前安全到达二垒的一击。

满垒本垒打：是指击球员在满垒时(也就是一垒、二垒、三垒都有跑垒员时)打出的本垒打，可一次得到 4 分。

故意保送上垒：故意向击球手投出 4 个坏球，使击球手进到一垒。通常在一垒无人的情况下执行这个战术，以形成一个强迫进垒。

开绿灯：是指教练暗示击球员击打下一个好球，或暗示跑垒员可以自己决定何时尝试偷垒。

打带跑：一种进攻战术，当跑垒员（通常在一垒）开始跑动，有偷垒的迹象，击球手有义务进行挥棒击球，试图把球从击球手身后击到右外野，一般击球手多会故意将球往地上打。

夹杀：外野手用来在两垒之间触杀跑垒员的战术。

封杀出局：是指跑垒员在尚未到达下一个垒包时，球已传到该垒包的防守者，使跑垒员出局的情形。

打点：是指棒球和垒球中的一项统计数据，它将得分归功于击球手的击球（某些情况除外，例如在比赛中出现失误）。例如，如果击球手击出一记安打，使得在更高垒上的队友可以到达本垒，从而得一分，那么击球手就会得到一分打点。

三振：是指在棒球比赛中，击球手经裁判判定获得3个好球后，记一出局。另外，三振作为投手的统计数据。击球手被判定三振出局之时，投球手即可获记一次夺三振。

暴投：当官方记分员认为一个球离本垒太高、太低或太偏，捕手无法通过正常防守行为接住球，从而使一名或多名跑垒员有机会向前推进时，投手就会被判为暴投；如果这是第三个打击，且一垒无人占据，将允许击球手前进到一垒。捕手漏接球和暴投都不算作失误，这是一个单独的统计数据。

练 习

1. 在一局比赛中，每个球队能派出几名防守球员？
2. 什么是本垒打？
3. 棒球运动的国际管理机构是什么？

第八章

门　球

> **学习目标**
> 1. 了解门球运动的发展历史
> 2. 掌握门球运动的管理机构和重要赛事
> 3. 熟悉门球运动的比赛规则和专业术语

第一节　概　述

门球是一个受槌球启发的集体木槌运动。它具有节奏快、非接触、高度战略性的特点，所有年龄和性别的人都可以参与。

门球是在长 20 m(66 ft)，宽 15 m(49 ft)的长方形场地上进行的。每个球场有 3 个门和 1 个柱。比赛在两队(红队和白队)之间进行，每队最多 5 名球员。每个球员都有一个与他们的比赛顺序相对应的编号球，奇数球是红色的，偶数球是白色的。根据规则，球队击球通过球门得 1 分，击中球门杆得 2 分。

图 8.1　门球比赛
(作者 Julio D'ias)

门球是 1947 年由铃木荣治在日本发明的。当时，制造许多运动项目使用的球所需的橡胶严重短缺。铃木当时在北海道的木材行业工作，他意识到制作槌球和木槌的木材供应充足，便修改了槌球的规则，并发明了门球作为年轻人的游戏。

门球在 20 世纪 50 年代末开始流行，当时一位体育教练将门球介绍给了熊本市的妇女协会和老年人俱乐部。1962 年，熊本门球协会成立，并制定了一套地方规则。1976 年，在熊本举行的全国健身大会上，这种版本的游戏闻名全国。不久之后，随着地方政府官员和老年组织的代表在全国范围内推广这项运动，迅速提升了门球的受欢迎程度。

第二节 主要管理机构

世界门球联盟(World Gateball Union,WGU)是门球的全球性组织,成员来自16个国家和地区。目前有来自40多个国家的1 000多万人打门球。

日本门球联盟(Japanese Gateball Union,JGU)成立于1984年。在首任主席笹川良一的领导下,日本大学制定了一套统一的规则,并组织了第一次全国会议。次年,世界门球联盟与中国、韩国、巴西、美国和中国台北5个国家和地区联合成立了世界门球联盟(WGU)。此后,玻利维亚(1987年)、巴拉圭(1987年)、秘鲁(1987年)、阿根廷(1989年)、加拿大(1989年)、新加坡(1994年)、中国香港(1998年)、澳大利亚(2003年)、中国澳门(2005年)、菲律宾(2012年)和印度尼西亚(2013年)相继加入了世界门球联盟。

第三节 重 要 赛 事

3.1 世界门球锦标赛

世界门球锦标赛(World Gateball Championships)每四年举行一次。1986年,第一届锦标赛在北海道举行,参赛队伍来自巴西、中国、中国台北、日本、韩国和美国。随后的锦标赛在美国夏威夷(1998年)、日本富山(2002)、韩国济州岛(2006)、中国上海(2010)和日本新潟(2014年)等地举行。

3.2 世界比赛

2001年,门球作为表演赛项目被列入第六届世界运动会(World Games)。比赛在日本秋田县举行,来自中国、日本、韩国、美国和中国台北的队伍参加了比赛。最终,一支主要由日本青少年组成的球队获胜。

第四节 比 赛 规 则

门球是在长20~25 m,宽15~20 m的长方形场地上,在两队(每队最多5人)之间进行比赛。两队各使用5个球,根据球队的不同,一方用红球,另一方用白球。红球和白球交替使用,编号从1~10。每个球员在比赛中都用自己的同一个球。在比赛开始时,击球员按顺序将球放在指定的"开球区",并尝试将球击过第一个门。如果球成功地通过了球门,他们就可以再打一次。如果球没通过第一个门,或者他们的球通过了第一个门,但最终落在了球场外,他们就得捡起球,并在第二轮中再次尝试通过第一个门。自2015年规则变更以来,一个穿过第一个门但最终出界的球被认为已经通过了第一个门,但它是一个出界球,在下一个回合,需要从球出界的地方击球进入场地。

击球时,如果自球碰到了另一个球,叫作"撞击"。如果自球和被撞他球都停留在比赛线内,击球者应踩在自球上,将他球与自球贴靠,并用球棒击打自球(这种打法称为"闪击"),将他球击出。如果击球员使球通过一个门或打出闪击,他将获得另一个击球机会。

球按顺序通过一个门得一分,最后撞击,球撞得分柱(goal pole)可得 2 分。在 30 min 的比赛结束时,得分较多的球队获胜。红队总是先上场,白队打最后的一轮。

4.1 门球场地

门球场由内场(inner field)和外场(outer field)两部分组成。内场呈矩形,长 20~25 m,宽 15~20 m。在比赛中,几乎所有的比赛都在内场进行。因此,门球场有时被简称为"球场"("court")。内场以内线为界,外场围绕着内场。外场的宽度为 50~100 cm。规则手册规定,球场的表面应该平整,没有任何障碍物。有许多类型的球场,草坪、人造草坪和土场地,可以任选其一(图 8.2)。

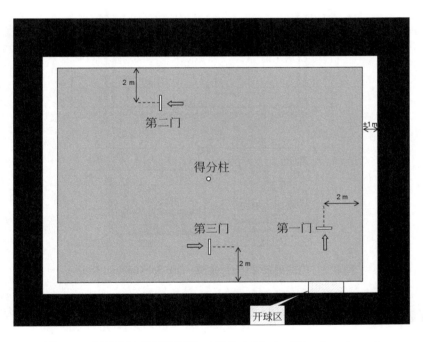

图 8.2　典型的门球场示意图　(图片来源:traditionalsports.org)

内场设置有三个门和一个得分柱。每个门都有自己的编号,从 1~3,分别称为第一、第二和第三门(或只是门 1、2 或 3)。门的内宽 22 cm,高 19 cm。所有的门都应该互相垂直。

球场中央有 1 个 2 cm 宽的球柱。顾名思义,如果球在通过所有 3 个门后击中了得分柱,就完成了一个"agari"(agari 是一个日语单词,表示成功完成)。门和得分柱的设置非常重要。

场上有3个球门和1个得分柱。得分柱位于球场的中央,3个门与内线平行(图8.3)。球门旁的箭头代表通过它们的方向。

所有球门和得分柱都应固定牢固。方形数字指示牌应该安装在球门上,便于球员识别球门。

每个门都有通过的方向(图8.3),可以"通过"球门的那一面被称为前面,另一面叫作后面。虽然可以让球从后面通过球门,但这样是不能得分的。每个角和每条线都有各自的名称,离第一门最近的角称为第一角,另外3个角分别称为第二、第三和第四角,沿逆时针方向排列。4条内线的命名方式相同。

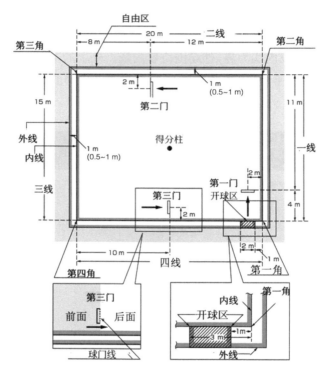

图8.3 门球场尺寸(图片来源:Official Gateball Rules)

4.2 比赛装备

图8.4 门球装备(图片来源:gateball.or)

4.2.1 球槌

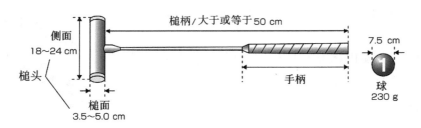

图 8.5 球槌 （图片来源：Official Gateball Rules）

球槌由槌头（head）和槌柄（shaft）组成，形成一个 T 字形。

球员握住手柄（grip），用槌头的面（face）击球槌头原则上为圆柱形，两个面（face）平行于槌柄。侧面（side face）是指与槌柄成直角相交的球槌部分。槌面直径最小 3.5 cm，最大 5.0 cm。侧面长度为 18～24 cm。

槌柄应呈棒状，并固定在槌头侧面中点处。槌柄的长度应大于或等于 50 cm，包括手柄。

4.2.2 球

使用的球应为直径 7.5 cm（±0.7 cm）、重量 230 g（±10 g）、表面光滑的圆形球，由合成树脂制成。一共有 10 个球：5 个红球，5 个白球。红球用白色标记奇数"1""3""5""7"和"9"；白球用红色标记偶数"2""4""6""8"和"10"。球号高度原则上为 5 cm，并在球上至少 2 个位置明显地标记出来。

图 8.6 球
（图片来源：Official Gateball Rules）

4.2.3 球门和得分柱

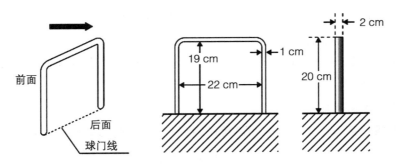

图 8.7 球门和得分柱 （图片来源：Official Gateball Rules）

球门由直径为 1 cm（±1 mm）的圆柱形金属棒制成，为倒置的 U 型装置，颜色要易于在球场上被识别，分别放置在球场上的 3 个位置。

球门的 2 根立柱垂直固定在地面上，2 根立柱之间的内部空间为 22 cm 宽，19 cm 高。

得分柱是直径 2 cm(±1 mm)的圆柱体,得分柱的颜色要易于在球场上被识别。

得分柱必须放置在场地中央,垂直于地面,门柱高于地面 20 cm。

在人造草坪和室内球场等无法将门柱插入地面时,可以使用直接放置在地面上的球门。

4.2.4 号码布

门球规则规定,球员必须佩戴表明其比赛顺序的号码,号码的高度必须在 10 cm 或以上,形状易于辨认,必须佩戴在胸前和背后,或仅佩戴在胸前。

图 8.8 号码布
(图片来源:gateball.or)

第五节 基本策略

当你闪击队友的球时,你会在位置上作出积极的战术选择,同时牢记比赛顺序。

例如,第一个成功将球传过 1 号门的球队(例如使用球 1)通常会将球放置在 2 号门和边界之间。这样,对方球队在没有球出界的情况下尝试触球是危险的,而如果对方球队的球(例如球 2)在下一回合进入 2 号门,则可能会被球触及 1 并加以利用,使第一支队伍受益。因此,球 2 可能会去防守通往 3 号门的通道,而不是位于 2 号门前面。

如果您闪击了对方球队的球,您可以将其送到您球队的球可以使用它的地方,同时记住在该球之前要比赛的球的编号顺序。或者,您可以将其送出球场,这意味着它需要使用下一个回合才能回到球场,而无法击中或通过大门。

门球术语

内场:长 20~25 m,宽 15~20 m 的长方形场地,由内线界定。

外场:一般是宽度为 1 m 的固定区域,构成场地的一部分,外缘为外线,内缘为内线。宽度从 50 cm 到 1 m 不等。

轮:从 1 号到 10 号选手轮流进行比赛的过程构成一轮。第二轮比赛开始时,1 号球员第二次成为击球手。

顺序:击球手的比赛顺序。

击球手用球:是指与比赛编号相同的球,例如,1 号球员的球就是 1 号球。

先发队:先发队用红色球,球上印有白色奇数,首先击球。

开球:裁判长宣布比赛开始的叫法。

总分/队分:每队在比赛结束时的总得分。

完美比赛:一支球队得到 25 分的比赛。

正确打法:正确击球的行为,以及实现这一行为所涉及的动作。

起始点:是指计算 10 秒的起始点。当击球手被指示开始击球时,当获得连续击球的权利时,或当获得闪击的权利时开始计时。

放弃权利：如果一支队伍宣布放弃比赛,或者一支队伍在比赛开始时人数少于5人,那么该队伍将被视为放弃比赛,导致另一支队伍因弃权而获胜。

通过1号门：从开球区击球,球通过1号门。

击球：击球者用球棒的正面击打自己静止的球。

推球：一种击球的方法,击球者用球槌向前推球,而球槌的面与球保持接触。推球是一种击球犯规。

闪击：在一次成功的触球后,击球手的球和被触球都停止了作为界内球的运动,击球手踩在他的球上,使被触球与他的球在内场接触,并抚摸他的球,使撞击引起另一个球运动。

撞击：是指当击球手的球是界内球时被槌击,在移动过程中触碰到另一个球。

贴靠：球与球、球与门或球与门柱相互接触的状态。

触球犯规：击球者在球场上因比赛规则允许以外的任何原因触球而造成的犯规。

界外击球犯规：由于击球者触碰一个界外球而击中另一个球,因此被判定为犯规。

判罚：裁判员用手势和声音向运动员和观众传达比赛的进度或对比赛或行动的决定。

练 习

1. 什么是门球运动?
2. 门球运动的国际管理机构是什么?

第九章

冰　　球

> **学习目标**
>
> 1. 了解冰球的发展历史
> 2. 掌握冰球赛事的主要管理机构和重要赛事
> 3. 熟悉冰球比赛规则和专业术语

第一节　概　　述

图 9.1　芬兰坦佩雷诺基亚竞技场的国际标准冰球场　（作者 Kallerna）

冰球（ice hockey）又称冰上曲棍球，是一项对抗性很强的集体冰上运动，它结合了多变的滑冰技巧和敏捷熟练的冰球技巧。队员们穿着溜冰鞋，滑冰的同时用冰球杆抢球，并用冰球杆把球击进对方的球门。进球较多的一方赢得比赛。

冰球在加拿大、东欧、北欧和美国最受欢迎，也是加拿大官方的全国性冬季运动。

此外，在白俄罗斯、克罗地亚、捷克、芬兰、拉脱维亚、俄罗斯、斯洛伐克、瑞典和瑞士，冰球是最受欢迎的冬季运动。国家冰球联盟（National Hockey League，NHL）是男子冰球的最高水平联盟，也是世界上最强的职业冰球联赛。大陆冰球联赛（Kontinental Hockey League，KHL）是俄罗斯和东欧大部分地区的最高水平联赛。

冰球被认为是从 18 世纪和 19 世纪在英国及其他地区进行的简单棍棒击球运动演变而来的。这些运动被带到北美，并发展出了一些类似的使用非正式规则的冬季运动，如马球和冰球。当代冰球运动是从加拿大发展起来的，尤其是蒙特利尔，1875 年 3 月 3 日在那里举行了第一场室内冰球比赛。那场比赛的一些特点，如冰球场的长度和冰球的使用，一直保留到今天。业余冰球联赛始于19世纪80年代，职业冰球联赛大约起源于1900年。斯坦利杯（Stanley Cup）是冰球俱乐部至高无上的荣誉，1893年首次颁发给加拿大业余冠军，后来成为国家冰球联盟的冠军奖杯。20世纪初，加拿大的规则被国际冰上曲棍球联盟（Ligue Internationale de Hockey sur Glace）即国际冰球联合会（International Ice Hockey Federation，IIHF）的前身采用。1920年，这项运动首次出现在夏季奥运会上。尽管在冰球运动发展的初期就有女性参与，但很久以后，女子冰球才被专业地组织起来。1990年举行了第一届国际冰球联合会世界女子冰球锦标赛（IIHF Women's Ice Hockey World Champions），1998年女子冰球被引入奥运会。在国际比赛中，6个国家的冰球国家队（the Big Six）占主导地位，这6个国家分别是加拿大、捷克、芬兰、俄罗斯、瑞典和美国。

第二节 主要管理机构

国际冰球联合会（IIHF）是一个全球性的冰球管理机构。总部设在瑞士苏黎世，拥有83个成员国。

国际冰球联合会（IIHF）根据国际冰球锦标赛的成绩进行世界排名。国际冰球联合会的比赛规则不同于北美冰球和北美国家冰球联盟联赛（National Hockey League，NHL）的比赛规则，且其各项决定可以通过瑞士洛桑体育仲裁法庭提出上诉。国际冰球联合会拥有自己的国际冰球名人堂。国际冰球联合会名人堂（IIHF Hall of Fame）创立于1997年，自1998年以来一直坐落于冰球名人堂（Hockey Hall of Fame）内。

在此之前，国际冰球联合会还负责管理轮滑曲棍球（inline hockey）的发展；然而，在2019年6月，国际冰球联合会宣布它们将不再管理轮滑曲棍球或组织轮滑曲棍球世界锦标赛。

第三节 重要赛事

3.1 国家冰球联盟联赛

国家冰球联盟（NHL）是北美的职业冰球联盟，由32支球队组成，其中25支在美国，7支在加拿大。队伍共分成东、西2个大区，每个大区各分为3个分区，每年东西两区的冠军会在联盟总决赛中争夺斯坦利杯。斯坦利杯是北美最古老的职业体育奖杯，每年在赛季结束时颁发给联盟季后赛冠军。国家冰球联盟是美国和加拿大的主要职业体育联盟之一，被认为是世界上级别最高的职业冰球联赛，截至2023—2024赛季，有来自17个国家的球员参加联赛。国际冰球联合会（IIHF）也将斯坦利杯视为"这项运动中最重要的冠军赛"之一。联盟总部在曼哈顿中城。

国家冰球联盟于1917年11月26日在蒙特利尔的温莎酒店成立，其前身是1909年在安大略省伦弗鲁（Renfrew）成立的国家冰球协会（NHA）。在一系列的联盟合并和解散之

图 9.2　国家冰球联盟联赛开球（图片来源：Wikimedia）

际，NHL 立即取代了 NHA 的位置，成为每年争夺斯坦利杯的联盟之一。到 1926 年，国家冰球联盟成为唯一一个争夺斯坦利杯的联盟。

在成立之初，国家冰球联盟有 4 支球队，都在加拿大，因此在联盟的名字中有"国家"这个词。1924 年，随着波士顿棕熊队的加入，联盟扩展到美国，此后一直由美国和加拿大的球队组成。1942—1967 年，联盟只有 6 支球队，一起被称为"原始六队"。在 1967 年的扩张中，国家冰球联盟增加了 6 支新球队，使其规模翻了一番。到 1974 年，联盟增加到 18 支球队；1979 年，增加到 21 支球队。1991—2000 年间，国家冰球联盟进一步扩大到 30 支球队。2017 年和 2021 年分别增加了第 31 支和第 32 支球队。

按收入计算，国家冰球联盟是世界上第五富有的职业体育联盟。仅次于美国国家橄榄球联盟（NFL）、美国职业棒球大联盟（MLB）、美国国家篮球协会（NBA）和英超联赛（EPL）。1989 年，联盟总部从蒙特利尔搬到了曼哈顿。NHL 历史上有四次全联盟范围的停工，都发生在 1992 年之后。

国家冰球联盟的常规赛通常在 10 月至次年 4 月举行，每支球队打 82 场比赛。常规赛结束后，16 支球队进入斯坦利杯季后赛，经过 4 轮比赛决出联赛冠军，比赛要一直持续到 6 月。自 1917 年联盟成立以来，蒙特利尔加拿大人队赢得了最多的 NHL 冠军，共 25 次，在联盟于 1926 年获得斯坦利杯完全专营权之前赢得了 3 次 NHL 冠军系列赛，之后又赢得了 22 次斯坦利杯。卫冕联赛冠军是维加斯黄金骑士队在 2023 年的斯坦利杯决赛中，他们队击败了佛罗里达美洲豹队。

图 9.3　1998 年俄罗斯和捷克之间的金牌争夺战是第一次主要由 NHL 球员组成的球队之间的比赛（作者 Canadaolympic989）

3.2 冬季奥运会冰球比赛

自1920年以来,冰球比赛一直是奥运会的比赛项目。男子比赛在1920年夏季奥运会上被引入,并在1924年法国冬季奥运会上被永久转为冬季奥运会项目。女子比赛在1998年冬季奥运会上首次举行。

3.3 世界冰球锦标赛

世界冰球锦标赛(Ice Hockey World Championships)是由国际冰球联合会(IIHF)组织的年度世界男子冰球锦标赛,在1920年夏季奥运会上首次正式举行,是这项运动最引人注目的年度国际锦标赛。国际冰球联合会成立于1908年,而世界锦标赛的前身欧洲锦标赛(European Championships)于1910年首次举行。在1920年夏季奥运会上举行的比赛被认为是第一届冰球世界锦标赛。1920—1968年,奥运会冰球锦标赛也被认为是当年的世界锦标赛。

3.4 冰球世界杯

冰球世界杯(World Cup of Hockey)是一项国际冰球锦标赛,它于1996年成立,是加拿大杯的继任者。加拿大杯从1976年到1991年每3~5年举行一次,是第一个允许各国派出顶级球员的国际冰球锦标赛。世界杯此前曾不定期举办过3次,1996年美国夺冠,2004年和2016年加拿大夺冠。在2016年的比赛之后,2020年的比赛取消了。这个系列赛是否会继续下去还不确定,但国家冰球联盟将尝试在2025年举办下一届世界杯。

第四节 比赛规则

4.1 比赛方法

图9.4 VTB竞技场是一个室内冰球馆 (作者 Oleg Bkhambri)

虽然冰球比赛的一般特征保持不变,但确切的规则取决于不同赛事所使用的特定比赛规则(code of play)。两个最重要的比赛规则是国际冰球联合会(IIHF)和北美职业冰球联赛(NHL)的比赛规则。这两个规则以及其他规则均源自20世纪初加拿大的冰球规则。

冰球比赛在冰球场上进行。在正常比赛中,每队有6名穿着滑冰鞋的球员,其中一名是守门员。比赛的目标是通过将一个硬硫化橡胶圆盘——冰球(puck)射入对手的球门来得分。球员们用冰球杆(stick)传球或射门。

在某些限制下,球员可以用身体的任何部位改变冰球的方向。球员不得将冰球拿在手中,也不得用手将冰球传给队友,除非他们在防守区内。然而,球员可以用手将冰球从空中击落。禁止球员将冰球踢入对方球门,但球员无意地通过冰鞋碰进球门是被允许的。球员不得故意用手将冰球击入球门。

冰球是一项有越位规则的比赛(off-side game),这意味着向前传球是被允许的。在20世纪30年代之前,冰球是一项没有越位的比赛(on-side game),这意味着

图9.5 标准的冰球
(作者 Matt Boulton)

只允许向后传球。这些规则倾向于个人用球杆控球作为推动冰球前进的关键手段。随着越位规则的实施,向前传球使得冰球变成了一项真正的集体运动,个人表现在其中的重要性相较于集体合作有所降低。现在,球员可以在整个冰面上进行配合,而不再局限于仅与后方的球员配合。

每支球队的6名球员通常分为3名前锋、2名后卫和1名守门员。术语"滑冰者"(skaters)通常是指所有非守门员的球员。前锋位置由1个中锋和2个边锋组成:一个左翼和一个右翼。前锋经常以组合或锋线形式进攻,同样的3个前锋总是一起配合。后卫通常

图9.6 球员们正在进行换线,换线是指一次替换一组队员(作者 Daniel Bowles)

是一对，一般分为左后卫和右后卫。左右边锋或左右后卫的位置通常取决于他们是哪只手拿球杆。一次替换整个组称为换线。当人手不足或处于优势局面时，球队通常采用不同的锋线和防守组合。守门员站在半圆形区域（通常为蓝色，称为防守区域的球门区）阻止对方射门得分。在比赛中可以随时换人，但在比赛暂停期间，主队可以进行最后的换人。当球员在比赛中被换下时，被称为即时换人。在 2005—2006 赛季，国家冰球联盟（NHL）增加了一条新规则：禁止球队在打底板球后换人。

围在冰面上的界板可以帮助冰球保持在比赛状态，它们也可以被用作冰球比赛的工具。运动员被允许利用身体冲撞将对手撞到界板上，以此阻止对手前进。裁判、边裁和球门外侧都是"比赛中的一部分"，当冰球或球员受到他们的影响（造成球弹起或发生碰撞）时，不会导致比赛停止。如果球门被撞得偏离了位置，比赛可以停止。比赛通常持续几分钟不间断。当比赛停止时，比赛将以争球重新开始。2 名球员面对面，1 名裁判将冰球扔到冰上，2 名球员争夺冰球的控制权。冰面上的标记（圆圈）指示了争球的位置和球员的站位。

冰球比赛中限制冰球移动的三大规则是越位、底板球和球出界。如果一名球员比冰球先进入对手的区域，他就越位了。在许多情况下，球员可能不会"长射"（ice the puck），即把冰球打过中线和对手的球门线。当冰球越过冰场的边界（落在球员的板凳上、落在玻璃上或落在玻璃上的防护网）时，裁判就会鸣哨宣布比赛停止。即使冰球从这些区域反弹回到球场上也无效，因为冰球一旦离开冰球场的边线就被认为是死球。当 2 名或 2 名以上的球员长时间争夺冰球，导致冰球被卡在界板边缘，或者冰球被卡在任何一方的球门网后方一段时间时，裁判也可以鸣哨暂停比赛。

根据国际冰球联合会（IIHF）的规定，每支球队最多可拥有 20 名球员和 2 名守门员。国家冰球联盟（NHL）规则将每场比赛的总人数限制在 18 人，外加 2 名守门员。在国家冰球联盟中，球员通常分成 4 组进攻线（每组 3 名前锋）和 3 对后卫。有时，球队可能会选择用 1 名后卫代替 1 名前锋。第 7 名后卫可以作为替补后卫，在替补席上度过比赛；或者如果球队选择打 4 线，第 7 名后卫可以在第 4 线作为前锋出场。

4.1.1 局和加时赛

一场职业比赛分为 3 局，每局 20 分钟，计时器只在冰球进入比赛状态时计时。每局比赛结束后（包括加时赛），2 队都要交换比赛场地。休闲联赛和儿童联赛比赛时间较短，通常进行时长较短的 3 局比赛。

如果在锦标赛比赛（tournament play）以及 NHL 季后赛（playoffs）中出现平局，北美人倾向于采用突然死亡加时赛（sudden-death overtime），即 2 支球队继续进行 20 min 的比赛，直到进球为止。直到 1999—2000 赛季，NHL 常规赛的结果均由每队 5 名球员（包括 1 名守门员）的单场 5 分钟突然死亡加时赛决定，如果出现平局，两队在积分榜上各得 1 分。如果有进球，获胜的球队将获得 2 分，而失败的球队则不会获得任何积分（就像在常规赛中输球一样）。一场 60 分钟的比赛，从冰球第一次落地开始的总时间大约是 2 小时 20 分钟。

从 1999—2000 赛季到 2003—2004 赛季，国家冰球联盟（NHL）是通过一场 5 min 的突

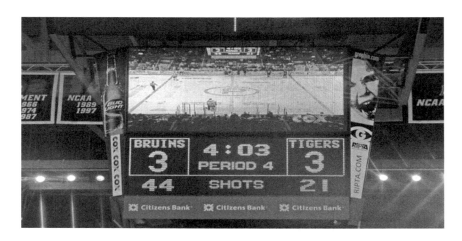

图 9.7　第四节比赛的记分牌(作者 Sarah Connors)

然死亡加时赛来决定平局结果,每支球队出 4 名球员(加上守门员)。如果出现平局,每支球队仍将在积分榜上获得 1 分;如果分出胜负,获胜队将在积分榜上获得 2 分,而失败的球队将在积分榜上获得一分。这个规定是为了阻止球队打平局,因为以前有些球队可能更愿意平局得 1 分,而不愿冒着输球得 0 分的风险。此规则的例外情况是,如果一支球队在加时赛期间选择撤下守门员以换取一名额外的场上队员,并随后被对手得分(空门进球),在这种情况下,输掉的球队不会获得积分。自 2015—2016 赛季以来,单场 5 min 的突然死亡加时赛中,每方上场 3 名场上队员。由于 NHL 比赛中必须始终有 3 名场上球员在场,因此判罚与常规赛中的判罚略有不同;在常规赛中导致减少 1 名队员的处罚,在加时赛期间则会导致另一方增加 1 名队员。一旦被罚下场队员的罚时结束,就会离开处罚室(penalty box)回到球场,双方继续以 4 对 4(4-on-4)比赛,直到下一次比赛暂停,此时球队恢复到每队 3 名球员。

国际比赛和一些北美职业联赛,包括北美职业冰球联赛(NHL)常规赛,现在都采用加时赛,与 1999—2000 赛季到 2003—2004 赛季的加时赛相同,加时赛之后是点球大战。如果在加时赛后比分仍然持平,则随后进行的点球大战,由 2 队各派出 3 名球员罚点球。在总共 6 次点球之后,进球较多的球队获胜。如果比分仍然是平局,那么点球大战就会进入突然死亡的形式。无论双方在点球大战中进了多少球,最终获胜队的进球数将比常规时间结束时的分数多出 1 个进球。在北美职业冰球联赛中,如果一场比赛是通过加时赛或点球决胜,获胜队在积分榜上得 2 分,失败队得 1 分。北美职业冰球联赛不再会出现平局。

北美职业冰球联赛季后赛与常规赛的加时赛不同。在季后赛中没有点球大战。常规赛中,如果比赛结束后打成平局,将增加 20 分钟的 5 对 5 突然死亡加时赛。如果加时赛结束后双方仍打成平手,则再打一个 20 分钟的加时赛,直到一方得分为止。自 2019 年以来,国际冰球联合会世界锦标赛(IIHF World Championships)和奥运会金牌争夺战的加时赛都使用这种赛制,但采用 3 对 3 的形式。

4.1.2 处罚

图 9.8　一名冰球运动员进入处罚室(作者 Alex Micheu)

在冰球比赛中,违规会导致比赛暂停,通过争球使比赛重新开始。有些违规行为会导致球员或球队受到处罚。在最简单的情况下,犯规队员会被送到处罚室,并且犯规球员的球队必须在一定的时间内以少一人的阵容继续比赛。小罚(minor penalty)2 分钟,大罚(major penalty)5 分钟,双重小罚(double-minor penalty)是指连续 2 次罚时 2 分钟。如果对受害球员造成明显伤害,则一次小罚可以延长 2 分钟。这通常是因为举杆过肩犯规造成了球员出血的情况。除了罚球以及犯规球员的球队必须受到的处罚外,球员还可能因不当行为而受到个人延长处罚(personal extended penalties)或驱逐出场(expulsion)。受到处罚的球队在比赛中会少一人,而对方球队则处于以多打少(power play)的局面。

对于较轻的违规行为判处 2 分钟小罚,这些较轻的违规行为包括:例如绊人(tripping)、肘击(elbowing)、动作粗暴(roughing)、举杆过肩(high-sticking)、拖延比赛(delay of the game)、冰上球员过多、墙板冲撞(boarding)、违规装备(illegal equipment)、进攻冲撞(charging,跳向对手或跨两步后身体冲撞对手)、抱人(holding)、抓杆(holding the stick,抓住对手的球杆)、无球干扰(interference)、勾人(hooking)、用杆打人(slashing)、用膝撞人(kneeing)、违反体育道德的行为(unsportsmanlike conduct,与裁判争论点球、极其粗俗或不恰当的口头评论)、"杆柄杵人"(butt-ending)、用杆刃刺人(spearing)或横杆推挡(cross-checking)。从 2005—2006 赛季开始,假摔(diving)也会被判小罚,即球员夸大或模仿犯规的行为。更严重的犯规可能会受到 2 分钟双重小罚(double-minor penalty)的处罚,特别是那些导致球员受伤的犯规。这些处罚会在比赛时间结束或对手球队在以多打少得分时结束。如果在双重小罚的前 2 分钟内进球,则第一个小罚到期,第二个小罚将在得分后开始计时2分钟。

图9.9 （左）一名球员双手拿着球杆阻挡对手，造成横杆推挡犯规（作者 The AHL）；（右）一名球员用他的球杆勾住他的对手，造成勾人犯规（作者 mark6mauno）

对于大多数故意导致对手受伤的轻微违规行为，特别是暴力违规行为，或者当小罚导致明显伤害（例如流血）时，又或者是发生打架行为的情况下，会判罚5分钟的大罚。大罚总是全额执行；不会因对方队进球而终止比赛。因打架（fighting）而受到的大罚通常是相互抵消，这意味着2支球队人数仍然一样，并且球员在各自的处罚期满后，在暂停比赛时离开处罚室（penalty box）。墙板冲撞犯规（boarding，是指冲撞对手，导致对手被猛烈地撞到墙板上），由裁判员根据撞击的暴力程度酌情决定处以小罚或大罚。球员因墙板冲撞犯规受到小罚或大罚通常是因为从背后把对手冲撞向墙板。

有些处罚并不会导致犯规球队少1人。北美职业冰球联赛（NHL）中2个人同时被判罚的5分钟大罚，通常是由打架造成的。如果2名球员因打架被判罚5分钟大罚，则这2名球员均离场5分钟，而他们的球队不会缺少球员（2队在场上仍然满员比赛）。这与双方的2名球员同时或在不同时间因更常见的违规行为而受到小罚不同。在后一种情况下，2队将只有4名场上球员（不包括守门员），直到1个或2个球员处罚到期（如果一个球员的处罚先于另一个到期，则先到期球员的球队在剩余时间里将以多打少），这不适用于当前未决处罚。然而，在北美职业冰球联赛中，一支球队必须至少有3名场上球员在场上。因此，10分钟的不当行为（misconduct）处罚由受处罚的球员全额执行，但他的球队可以立即替补一名球员，除非与不当行为同时被判罚小罚或大罚（2+10或5+10）。在这种情况下，球队会指定另一名球员来接受小罚或大罚；2名球员都进入处罚室，但只有指定人员不能被替换，并且在2~5分钟期满后离开处罚室，此时10分钟的不当行为处罚开始。此外，故意对对手造成严重伤害（由裁判决定），或因球杆违规而受到大罚或重复大罚，都会被评估为比赛不当行为（game misconduct）。违规球员将被驱逐出场，并且必须立即离开比赛场地（不待在处罚室）；同时，如果附加小罚或大罚，则被指定的球员必须在处罚室受罚（类似于上述的"2+10"）。在极少数情况下，球员可能会因一系列行为而受到最多19分钟的处罚。与采取报复行为的对方球员打架，可能会受到4分钟双重小罚，在打架后会受到比赛不当行为的处罚。在这种情况下，该球员将被驱逐出场，2名队友必须接受双重小罚和大罚。

图9.10　一名球员正在罚点球，旁边有一名裁判。如果裁判认为球员的犯规阻止了进球机会，被犯规球员将会罚点球（作者 The Pancake of Heaven）

当一名防守球员的违规行为阻止了进攻球员的明显得分机会，通常是当进攻球员形成单刀突破时（breakaway），该进攻球员将获得罚点球（penalty shot）。罚点球时冰球被放于红线中线的中点上，罚球队员在没有其他球员防守的情况下面对守门员射门得分，以弥补之前错失的得分机会。可判罚点球的情况还有：除守门员以外的防守队员在球门区（goal crease）防守冰球；守门员在进攻队员单刀突破时故意移动自己的球门柱以避免进球；后卫在常规比赛还有不到2分钟的时候或加时赛的任何时候，故意把自己的门柱移开；或者球员或教练故意向冰球或控球队员投掷球杆或其他物体，并且扰乱了射门或传球。

裁判也会因为移动冰球的违规行为而选择停止比赛，例如在进攻端用手传球，但没有球员因这些违规行为而受到处罚。唯一的例外是故意摔倒在冰球上或将冰球收到身上、手中拿着冰球以及在防守区内将冰球射出场外（所有这些延误比赛行为都会被罚2分钟）。

在北美职业冰球联赛（NHL）中，对守门员有一种特殊的处罚。现在，守门员被禁止在冰球场靠近本方球门的角打球。如果守门员在此处打球，将导致守门员所在球队被判2分钟小罚。守门员只能在球门线前面和球网后面的区域内（球网两侧各有一条红线作为标志）打球。

另一项规则是两线越位传球（two-line offside pass），该规则从未构成处罚，但直到近期规则更改之前在北美职业冰球联赛（NHL）中一直属于违规行为。在2005—2006 NHL赛季之前，当从一方球队防守区内的传球越过中线时，比赛就会停止，并在违规球队的防守区内进行争球（faceoff）。现在，NHL不再使用中线来判定两线传球犯规，这是国际冰球联合会（IIHF）在1998年通过的一项变化。现在，球员可以将球传给越过蓝线和中场红线的队友。

美国国家冰球联盟（NHL）已经采取措施，通过减少过去经常发生的违规撞击、打架和抱抓的次数，来加快冰球比赛的速度和增强比赛的技巧性。现在对于规则的执行更加严格，导致出现更多的罚球情况，为球员提供了更多的保护和进球机会。美国业余冰球的管理机构实施了许多新规则，以减少球杆击打身体的次数，以及比赛中其他有害的和违规的行为，并对这些违规行为采取"零容忍"（zero tolerance）的态度。

在男子冰球比赛中，防守球员可以用臀部或肩膀撞击另一名正在控球或最后一个接触到冰球的进攻球员，但女子冰球比赛中不行。这种臀部和肩膀的使用被称为身体冲撞（body checking）。并不是所有的身体接触（physical contact）都是合规的——特别是，从背后撞击、击打头部和大多数用球杆用力击打身体的身体接触都是违规的。

当没有控球权的球队犯规时，就会发生延迟判罚（delayed penalty）。在这种情况下，拥有球权的球队可以完成比赛；也就是说，比赛将继续进行，直到进球，或对方球队的球员获得控球权，或者控球球队犯规为止。由于被处罚的球队无法在不停止比赛的情况下控球，因此他们不可能进球。在此情况下，控球的球队可以用额外的进攻球员换下守门员，而不必担心被对手进球得分。然而，控球队可能会错误地将冰球打入自己的球门。如果发出了延迟判罚信号并且控球球队得分，则仍将处罚判给犯规球员，但不执行。2012年，美国全国大学体育协会（NCAA）针对大学级别的冰球比赛更改了这一规则。在大学比赛中，即使控球球队得分，处罚仍然会执行。

图9.11　裁判宣布延迟判罚，这意味着比赛将继续进行，直到进球，或者对方球队重新控球
（作者 brapai）

4.1.3 裁判人员

典型的冰上曲棍球比赛由 2～4 名场上裁判员负责执裁。通常有 2 名边线裁判(linesmen)，主要负责判定越位(offside)和底板球(icing)的违规行为、制止打斗和组织争球，以及 1～2 名主裁判，负责判定进球和所有其他处罚。然而，在某些情况下边线裁判可以向主裁判报告应对违规球员进行的处罚。对这种做法的规定因不同的管理规则而异。场上裁判得到场外裁判的协助，场外裁判分别是进球裁判、计时员和官方记分员。

图 9.12　主裁判即将丢球给两名球员争球
（图片来源：Wikimedia）

图 9.13　4 人制的主裁判，佩戴橙色臂章，以区别于边线裁判
（作者 Bon hein）

最普遍的制度是"三人制",即使用一名主裁判和两名边线裁判。一种不太常用的制度是两名主裁判和一名边线裁判制度。除了一些程序上的变化之外,该制度接近常规的三人制度。从国家冰球联盟(NHL)开始,一些联盟已经实施了"四裁判制度",即增加一名额外的主裁判来协助判罚那些通常难以由一名主裁判单独准确评估的情况。自2001年以来,该系统被用于NHL比赛、IIHF世界锦标赛、奥运会以及北美和欧洲的许多职业和高水平业余联赛。

裁判由所在的联盟选出。业余冰球联盟使用国家管理机构制定的指导方针作为选择裁判人员的基础。在北美,国家冰球管理机构加拿大冰球协会(Hockey Canada)和美国冰球协会(USA Hockey)根据裁判员的经验水平以及他们参加的规则知识和滑冰能力测试来选拔裁判。加拿大冰球协会的裁判级别为Ⅰ至Ⅵ级。美国冰球协会的裁判级别为1至4级。

4.2 冰球场

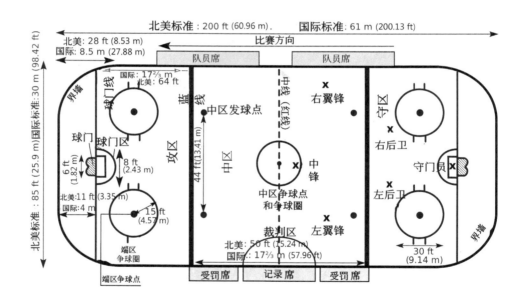

图 9.14 冰球场的详细图解(作者 Ysangkok)

4.2.1 球场规格

冰球场有两种标准尺寸:一种主要用于北美,也被称为国家冰球联盟尺寸;另一种用于欧洲的和国际比赛,也被称为国际冰球联合会或奥运会尺寸。

4.2.1.1 北美冰球场

大多数北美冰场都遵循北美国家冰球联盟(NHL)的规格,面积为 200 ft × 85 ft

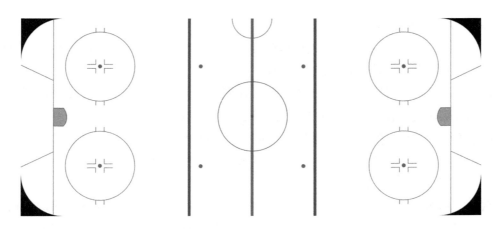

图 9.15　NHL 冰球场(作者 Юкатан)

(60.96 m×25.9 m),边角半径为 28 ft(8.5 m),每条球门线距离底板 11 ft(3.4 m)。北美国家冰球联盟的蓝线距底板 75 ft(22.9 m),间距 50 ft(15.2 m)。

4.2.1.2　国际冰球场

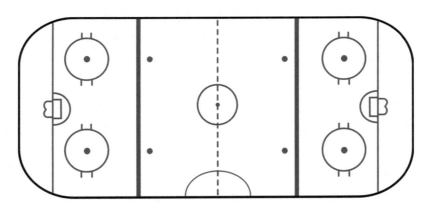

图 9.16　传统的冰球场地布局(作者 Jecowa)

世界其他地区的冰球场都遵循国际冰球联合会(IIHF)的规格,即 60.0 m×30.0 m(196.9 ft×98.4 ft),角半径为 8.5 m(27.9 ft)。两条球门线距离底板 4.0 m(13.1 ft),蓝线距离底板 22.86 m(75.0 ft)。

4.2.2　标记

4.2.2.1　标线

中线是一条粗线,将冰球场横向分成两半,通常作为判断死球的依据。在北美国家冰球联盟(NHL)中必须"包含设计独特的、统一规则的间隔标记,便于将其与 2 条蓝线区分开来"。在使用这种规则的联赛中,它也可以用来判断两线传球违规。

2 条粗蓝线把溜冰场分成 3 个部分,称为区。这两条线是用来判断球员是否越位的依据。如果一名进攻球员在冰球越过对方蓝线前就进入攻区,他就会被判越位。

在冰球场的两端,有一条红色的细球门线横跨整个冰面。它被用来判断进球和死球。

4.2.2.2 争球点和争球圈

冰球场有9个争球点，所有的争球都在这些争球点进行。每队防守区各设2个争球点，中立区两端各设2个争球点，冰球场中央设1个争球点。

在冰球场中心有开球圈，端区有争球点。在端区争球点附近的冰面上画着码标线。圆圈和码标线表示选手在争球或比赛中可以合规站立的位置。

中心争球点和中心争球圈都是蓝色的。圆圈直径30 ft(9 m)，线宽2 in(5.1 cm)，争球点是一个直径12 in(30 cm)的蓝色实心圆。所有其他的争球点和争球圈都是红色的。

4.2.2.3 门柱和网

在冰上的两端各有一个由金属球门框和布网组成的球门，必须将冰球打入球门内才能得分。根据国家冰球联盟和国际冰球联合会的规则，冰球必须整体越过球门线才能算作进球。国家冰球联盟规则和国际冰球联合会规则对于球门尺寸的规定一样：球门的开口宽72 in(180 cm)，高48 in(122 cm)，深40 in(100 cm)。

4.2.2.4 球门区

球门区是球门前的一块特殊区域，作用是让守门员在守门时不受干扰。

根据国际冰球联合会的规定，球门区的规格如下：以球门的中心点为圆心，以180 cm (71 in)为半径，用5 cm(2 in)宽的红线在球门线前画一个半圆；长15 cm(6 in)、宽5 cm(2 in)的"L"型画于半圆内的2个前角；"L"的位置在球门线向前122 cm(48 in)与半圆相交处。这个区域通常是蓝色的，以便识别。

4.2.2.5 裁判区

裁判区是一个半径为10 ft(3.0 m)的半圆形，位于记录席前。根据《美国冰球协会规则》601条(d)款(5)项，当裁判向任何比赛官员报告或咨询时，任何球员进入或停留在裁判区内，都可能被判罚行为不当。《美国冰球案例手册》特别指出，这种处罚是很特殊的，在处罚之前，球员通常会被要求离开裁判区。国家冰球联盟也有类似的规定，也要求对不当行为进行处罚。传统上，只有队长和候补队长才能接近裁判区。

4.2.3 区域

蓝线把冰球场分成3个区域。中间区域被称为中区，靠外的区域被称为端区，但更常用与每个团队攻守状态相关的术语来指代端区。一支球队试图得分的端区称为攻区；球队的球门所在的端区称为守区。

蓝线被认为是冰球所在区域的一部分。因此，如果冰球在中区，蓝线就是中区的一部分，它必须完全越过蓝线才能被认为是在端区。一旦冰球进入了端区，蓝线就成了端区的一部分。冰球必须从另一个方向完全越过蓝线，才能再次被视为进入中区。

4.2.4 界墙

在冰球场，界墙是形成冰球场边界的矮墙，高在40～48 in(100～120 cm)之间。"侧板"是沿着冰球场两条长边的界墙。半场板是球门线和蓝线中间的界墙。位于每个球门后面的冰球场部分被称为"底板"。弯曲的界墙(靠近冰球场的末端)被称为"角板"。

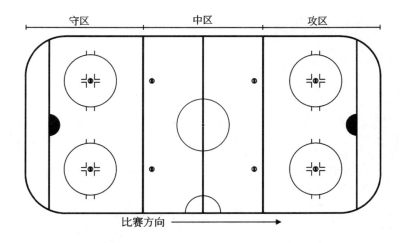

图 9.17　冰球场的区域划分（图片来源：Wikimedia）

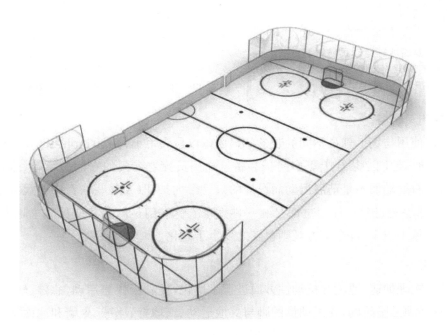

图 9.18　界墙（图片来源：Wikimedia）

4.3　比赛装备

4.3.1　防护装备

由于男子冰球是一项全接触运动，所以身体接触是允许的，受伤也是很常见的。穿戴防护装备是强制性规定，在所有的比赛情况下都必须执行。防护装备包括带有护目镜或全面罩的头盔、垫肩、护肘、护齿、防护手套、厚衬垫短裤（也称为冰球裤）或护腰带、形状不同的男女护裆、护胫、冰鞋以及护颈器（可选择的）。

图 9.19　身着冰球运动员防护装备的模型，如头盔、垫肩、护肘、手套、冰球裤和护胫（作者 Wafulz）

图 9.20　守门员装备（作者 Fabien Perissinotto）

4.3.2　守门员装备

守门员使用与场上球员不同的装备。当冰球以最大每小时 100 mph（160.9 km/h）的速度接近他们时，他们必须穿上更多防护装备。守门员穿着专门的守门员冰鞋（这种冰鞋更多是针对左右运动而不是前后运动而设计的）、一个大护腿（在某些联赛中有尺寸限制）、阻挡手套、接球手套、护胸、守门员面具和一件大球衣。守门员的装备变得越来越大，导致每场比赛进球越来越少，许多官方规则也随之发生了变化。

4.3.3　冰鞋

冰鞋在物理加速、速度和机动性方面进行了优化，更利于快速启动、急停、转弯和变向。此外，冰鞋必须是坚硬的，在运动员的脚与其他运动员、球杆、冰球、界墙和冰面接触时起到保护作用。冰鞋的刚性也提高了滑冰的整体机动性。刀片的长度、厚度（宽度）、曲率和空心半径（横跨刀片宽度）与速滑或花样滑冰的冰鞋刀片有很大的不同。冰球运动员通常根据他们的技术水平、位置和体型来调整这些参数。大多数冰鞋的刀片宽度约为 0.125 in（3.2 mm）厚。

4.3.4　冰球杆

冰球杆由一根长而宽且略弯曲的杆刃与一根杆柄相连构成。球杆的曲线本身对其性能有很大的影响。一个深的曲线可以更容易地挑起冰球，而一个浅的曲线可以更容易地反手击球。球杆的弯曲度也会影响球杆的性能。通常情况下，弹性较小的球杆适合相对强壮的球员，因为相对强壮的球员希望使用具有合适弹性、性能平衡的球杆，这样的球杆容易弯曲,同时能够产生一个强大的"回弹力",使冰球高速飞行。冰球杆与其他运动中的球杆有很大的区别,非常适合击打和控制扁平的冰球。冰球杆独特的形状促进了冰球运动的早期发展。

图 9.21　冰球鞋(作者 Santeri Viinamäki)

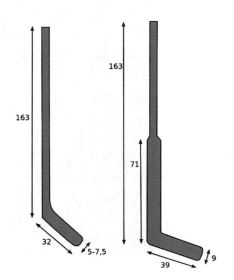

图 9.22　常规曲棍和守门员曲棍,尺寸以厘米为单位(作者 Ohkami)

第五节　基本战术

5.1　防守战术

冰球的防守战术很多,从比较积极的战术到比较保守的战术都有。两个较为典型的防守体系是人盯人防守体系和区域防守体系,很多球队使用两者结合的防守体系。防守技术包括抢断、封堵射门和球杆阻截(防守队员试图用冰球杆抢夺冰球或阻断冰球前进路线)。冰球防守战术的重点是"控制距离"、"卡位"(不让进攻方进入内线)和"守在冰球右侧"等概念。冰球防守战术中另一个流行的概念是打一场"200 ft 比赛"。所谓"200 ft 比赛",指的是在冰球比赛中,一名球员(通常是前锋)能在冰球场的所有 3 个区域内都展现出强大的比赛能力,而冰场的标准长度正好是 200 ft。

一个重要的防守战术是阻截(checking)——试图从对手手中争夺冰球或迫使对手无法参与进攻。用球杆阻截、扫球阻截和戳球阻截都是合规获取冰球控制权的方式。中区拦截的目的是将控球队员隔离在中区,以阻止其进入攻区。身体冲撞是指用肩膀或臀部攻击控制冰球或最后一个接触到冰球的对手(最后一个接触到冰球的人在规则上仍然是"控制"冰球的人,如果他在最后一次触球后超过 2 秒被阻截,通常对手也会被判罚犯规)。在某些联赛中,身体冲撞也被判定为犯规,以减少球员受伤的情况。通常情况下,"checking"一词指

图 9.23　教练在教孩子们如何正确地进行阻截
(图片来源：Wikimedia)

的就是身体冲撞,这是在冰球球迷中普遍使用的说法。

5.2　进攻战术

进攻战术包括通过将冰球从本方区域向对方区域推进,以改善球队在球场上的位置,逐步突破各条界线：首先是越过本方蓝线,然后是本方红线,最终突破对方蓝线。北美职业冰球联赛(NHL)在 2006 赛季制定的规则重新定义了越位规则,使双线传球合规：一名球员可以在本方蓝线后,使冰球越过蓝线和红线,传给处于对方蓝线近端的球员。进攻战术的最终目的是通过射门得分,当一名球员有意将冰球朝对方的球门方向推进时,就被认为要射门了。

如果一支球队在比赛的最后几分钟落后一到两个球,他们通常会选择让守门员上场；也就是说,用一名额外的进攻球员换掉守门员,以期获得足够的进攻优势来进球。然而,这是一种风险极大的行为,因为它有时会导致对方打空门进球,从而扩大领先优势。

一个球队最重要的策略之一就是前场阻截。前场阻截是指在对方防守区域内攻击对方的行为。阻截是抛球追逐策略的重要组成部分(即将冰球射入进攻区,然后追球)。每支球队都会使用自己独特的阵型,但主要阵型是：2-1-2、1-2-2 和 1-4。2-1-2 阵型是最基本的阻截阵型,2 名前锋向前推进,给对方守门员施加压力,第 3 名前锋站在高位,2 名后卫站在蓝线上。1-2-2 阵型比较保守,1 名前锋压迫控球队员,另外 2 名前锋对位对方的边锋,2

图 9.24　2017 年在威瑞森中心举行的 NHL 斯坦利杯季后赛
（作者 Keith Allison）

名后卫守在蓝线上。1-4 阵型是最具防守性的防守阵型，被称为"中区拦截"，其中 1 名前锋将在对方蓝线周围对控球队员施加压力，其他 4 名球员在他们的蓝线旁边大致排成一排，希望对手能被他们其中 1 人阻截。除此之外，另一种策略是左翼锁定，由 2 名前锋对对方的控球队员施压，左翼和 2 名后卫守在蓝线。

在冰球比赛中还有许多其他的小战术。通过沿着攻区的界墙来回运球（cycling），使防守队员疲劳或使他们处于不利的位置来创造得分机会。夹击（pinching）是指进攻方的后卫在对方抢得球权后，阻挡攻区内运球突破的对方翼锋并进行抢断，试图阻止对方进攻并将冰球保持在攻区内。挑传球是指当对方的球杆或身体在传球路线上时使用的传球，这是一种将冰球挑起越过障碍物传给队友的动作。

假动作指的是用身体或球杆做假动作来欺骗防守队员或守门员。许多现代球员，如帕维尔·达特丘克、西德尼·克罗斯比和帕特里克·凯恩，都学会了"晃球"技术，这是一种更花哨的打法，需要更多的控球技巧。

图 9.25　一名队员准备强打（slapshot）
（作者 somegeekintn）

图 9.26　一名守门员下场去替补席,以便让一名额外的进攻球员上场(作者 Eric Kilby)

5.3　打斗

图 9.27　冰球比赛中打架是被官方禁止的,但仍然是北美冰球运动的既定传统
(作者 ArtBrom)

尽管打斗在规则中是被官方禁止的,但在职业水平的比赛中,它并不罕见。打斗的流行既受到了批评,同时也成为这项运动一个颇具吸引力的方面。在北美,职业级别的比赛中,打斗未经官方认可。

执行者和其他队员打斗,可以打击对手的士气,同时激励本队的球员,以及解决与某个对方球员的个人恩怨或进行报复。如果球队中一名技术娴熟的球员受到重击,或者有人受到被视为是肮脏手段的打击,就会爆发一场打斗。业余比赛对打人的处罚更为严厉,在美国全国大学生体育协会联赛或一些青少年联赛中,被罚出场5分钟的球员也会受到至少10分钟的不当行为处罚;在高中和更年轻的比赛,以及一些休闲成人联赛中,他们会受到比赛不当行为处罚和停赛。但观众似乎喜欢观看在冰球比赛中的打斗,打斗时观众都会欢呼雀跃。

冰球术语

冰球:一种坚硬的硫化橡胶圆盘,球员试图使其越过守门员而得分。

冰球场:冰上的比赛场地。

进攻区:对方球门所在的区域。

中区:蓝线之间的区域。

守区:离球队球门最近的区域。

中线:在两个球门中间,横跨冰面的红线。

蓝线:将溜冰场划分为3个区域(攻区、守区和中区)的线。

球门区:冰球球门正前方的涂色区域称为球门区。这是冰球守门员阻止对方进球的地方,该区域内禁止对方球员有干扰守门员的行为。

球门线:位于场地两端的两条边界线。

界墙:围绕冰场的木墙,使冰球保持在球场中。

争球点:场上九个用颜色标出的用以争球的圆,攻区和守区各有两个,中区的四个角落附近各有一个,中场正中一个。

处罚室:让受罚球员待着接受判罚,等待判罚时间结束的地方。

死球:飞出冰球场的冰球,或者球员用手抓住的冰球。

进球:当进攻球员使用球杆击打冰球,使其穿过防守方球门柱之间的红线时,得一分。

空门进球:对方守门员不在场上时的进球。

单刀突破:当一名球员控球向前移动时,在他和对方球门线之间除了守门员之外没有其他防守者。

阻截:用身体接触来阻止对方球员在球场上获得有利位置。

臀部阻截:用臀部有力的一击将对手撞到界墙上或冰面上的身体冲撞。

回守区阻截:在快速滑回本方的守区时阻截对手。

假动作:球员通过对球或自己身体的控制,来欺骗对手移动的动作。

抛球追逐:一种进攻手段,将球直接打过对方蓝线,使球落在本方球员可以去争抢的角落。这样的策略可以快速使本方球员进入攻区。

帽子戏法:是指一名球员在一场比赛中进3个球。

小罚:离场2分钟的判罚。

大罚： 离场5分钟的判罚。

练 习

1. 冰球运动的国际管理机构是什么？
2. 请列举3个重要国际冰球赛事。

第十章

水 球

学习目标

1. 了解水球的发展历史
2. 掌握水球赛事的主要管理机构和重要赛事
3. 熟悉水球比赛规则和专业术语

第一节 概 述

图 10.1 希腊队与匈牙利队的水球比赛(2004 年意大利那不勒斯世界青年锦标赛)(作者 Massimo Finizio)

水球是一项由 2 支队伍在水中进行的集体竞技运动,每队 7 人。比赛包括 4 节,两队通过把球射进对方的球门来得分。比赛结束时进球较多的球队赢得比赛。每队由 6 名场上队员和 1 名守门员组成。除了守门员,球员们同时承担进攻和防守的任务。水球通常在一个全深的泳池里进行,这样运动员就不会碰到池底。

水球比赛中,运动员在泳池游泳、踩水(主要使用打蛋机式蹬腿)、传球和射门。团队合作、战术思维和意识也是水球比赛中非常重要的方面。水球是一项对身体要求很高的运动,经常被认为是最难的运动项目之一。

水球专用装备包括:水球(一个漂浮在水中的彩色的球)、泳帽(有编号和颜色)和2个球门(要么浮在水里,要么系在池边)。

这项运动被认为起源于19世纪中期的苏格兰,当时是一种"水上橄榄球"运动。威廉·威尔逊(William Wilson)被认为在19世纪70年代发明了这项运动。随着伦敦水球联盟(London Water Polo League)的成立,这项运动得到了发展,并在欧洲、美国、巴西、中国、加拿大和澳大利亚的部分地区流行起来。

第二节 主要管理机构

世界游泳联合会(World Aquatics,简称世界泳联),前身为国际游泳联合会(法语:Fédération Internationale de Natation,FINA;英语:International Swimming Federation),是负责管理游泳类水上运动的国际体育组织,获国际奥林匹克委员会认可。它是为国际奥委会和国际社会管理特定运动项目或纪律的几个国际联合会之一。总部设在瑞士洛桑。

国际游泳联合会于1908年成立,并于2023年1月正式更名为世界泳联。世界泳联目前负责监督6项水上运动的赛事:游泳、跳水、高台跳水、艺术游泳、水球和公开水域游泳。世界泳联还负责监管各个项目的"大师赛"(成人)。

在1908年夏季奥运会结束后,国际泳联于1908年7月19日在伦敦的曼彻斯特酒店成立。国际泳联由8个国家的泳联组成:比利时、丹麦、芬兰、法国、德国、英国、匈牙利和瑞典。

第三节 重要赛事

3.1 夏季奥运会水球比赛

自1900年第二届奥运会以来,水球一直是夏季奥运会的比赛项目。2000年夏季奥运会引入了女子水球比赛。匈牙利是男子比赛中最成功的国家,而美国是女子比赛成立以来唯一一支多次夺冠的球队。意大利是第一个也是唯一一个赢得男子和女子水球奥运冠军的国家。

3.2 世界游泳锦标赛水球比赛

世界游泳锦标赛水球比赛(Water Polo at the World Aquatics Championships)是每两

第十章 水 球

图 10.2 2004 年夏季奥运会水球比赛（作者 Vchristos）

年举行一次的国际水球锦标赛，是国际泳联世界游泳锦标赛的一部分。在 2023 年日本福冈世界游泳锦标赛中，匈牙利男子水球队和荷兰女子水球队获得冠军。

3.3 国际泳联男子水球世界杯

国际泳联男子水球世界杯（FINA Men's Water Polo World Cup）是一项国际水球锦标赛，由国际泳联组织，共有 8 支男子国家队参加。国际泳联男子水球世界杯设立于 1979 年，最初在奇数年举行，自 2002 年以来，每 4 年举行一次，在奥运会之间的偶数年举行。

3.4 国际泳联世界水球联赛

国际泳联世界水球联赛（FINA Water Polo World League）是一项由国际泳联组织的国际水球联赛，每年举行一次，通常从冬季到次年 6 月。联赛的特点是从各大洲的男子和女子锦标赛中脱颖而出的顶级球队参加冠军锦标赛（"超级决赛"），联赛冠军球队将加冕。2000 年奥运会使水球运动在世界范围内日益普及，特别是在欧洲、北美和澳大利亚，于是国际泳联在 2002 年设立了男子水球联赛。2004 年，因为观众对女子比赛的兴趣日益增长，于是设立了女子联赛。2022 年 10 月，国际泳联宣布，从 2023 年起，这项赛事将被国际泳联水球世界杯和国际泳联女子水球世界杯所取代。

3.5 欧洲水球锦标赛

欧洲水球锦标赛（European Water Polo Championship）是一项针对欧洲各国国家水球队的体育赛事，目前每两年举行一次，由欧洲游泳联盟（LEN）组织，男子和女子比赛都有。

第一届欧洲水球锦标赛于1926年在匈牙利布达佩斯举行,当时只有男子比赛。女子比赛在1985年(挪威奥斯陆)第一次举行。直到1997年,水球锦标赛一直是欧洲游泳锦标赛(European Aquatics Championships)的一部分,从1999年开始,这项赛事被分离出来,成了一项独立的赛事。

3.6 欧洲游泳联盟冠军联赛

欧洲游泳联盟冠军联赛(LEN Champions League)是欧洲顶级的职业水球俱乐部比赛,参赛球队来自18个不同的国家。

这项比赛由欧洲游泳联盟(LEN)组织,始于1963年的欧洲杯。1996年,由于名称和赛制发生了变化,赛事被重新命名为欧洲冠军联赛,并在1996—1997赛季的欧洲冠军联赛中首次设立了四强赛制。2003—2011年期间,赛事被命名为欧洲游泳联盟欧洲联赛(LEN Euro League)(更名只是为了重塑品牌),2011年至今,赛事名称为欧洲游泳联盟冠军联赛(LEN Champions League)。

欧洲游泳联盟冠军联赛是欧洲大陆最受欢迎的水球联赛,共有24家不同的俱乐部获得过冠军,其中10家不止一次获得过冠军。在这项赛事中最成功的俱乐部是普罗雷科(Pro Recco),到2023年已经赢得了11个冠军。

第四节 比 赛 规 则

4.1 球员人数

成年人比赛每队由7名队员组成(6名场上队员和1名守门员),比赛在泳池的比赛区域进行。2014年,国际泳联(FINA)将U20(及更年轻)比赛的参赛人数减少到6人(5名场上运动员和1名守门员)。如果1名球员离场犯规(严重犯规),那么该队将少1名球员比赛,直到该球员被允许重新进入(通常是20秒后)。如果一名球员有特别暴力的行为,如殴打另一名球员,那么裁判可能会判罚野蛮犯规,在这种情况下,除了犯规球员要被驱逐出场(即他们必须离开球场区域,不能再回来)之外,该队需要在少1名球员的情况下比赛4分钟。此外,根据管理机构的规定,罪魁祸首可能会被禁赛一定场次的比赛。

球员可以在进球后、暂停期间、半场之间和受伤后被换上或换下。在比赛过程中,球员从泳池的角落(称为再入区)或球门前进入和退出比赛。当比赛停止时,球员可以从任何地方进入或退出比赛。

如果在比赛中任何时候,一方的队员人数超过了允许的人数,将会判给对方一个罚球。如果一支球队开场时的场上球员少于6人,第6名球员违规加入比赛,主裁判可能会给教练出示黄牌,认为他允许这种情况发生,并判罚严重犯规,判给对方球队在6 m处罚球。

沙滩水球是水球的一种变体,包括守门员在内有4名队员(含1名守门员),场地较小,还有一些其他不同的规则。

4.2 泳帽

比赛双方球队必须佩戴颜色对比鲜明的泳帽，要求如下：

- 双方场上队员佩戴的泳帽与双方守门员泳帽的颜色对比鲜明；
- 两队必须佩戴与对方队帽颜色形成鲜明对比的泳帽；
- 必须佩戴与球的颜色形成鲜明对比的泳帽。

在实际比赛中，一队通常戴深色的泳帽，另一队戴白色的泳帽（在国际泳联的比赛中，通常主队戴白色的泳帽，客队戴黑色的泳帽）。各队可选择佩戴不同颜色的泳帽（例如各队的传统颜色）。例如，澳大利亚女子水球队佩戴绿色的帽子。

图 10.3　场上队员的泳帽
（图片来源：Wikimedia）

按照美国全国州立高中协会联盟（National Federation of State High School Associations，NFHS）、美国大学水球协会（Collegiate Water Polo Association，CWPA）和全美大学生体育协会（NCAA）规则，主队戴黑色的泳帽，客队戴白色的泳帽。

水球帽用于保护球员的头部和耳朵，帽子上的数字（1～13）使球员（尤其是裁判）从远处就能被辨认出来。2 名守门员都戴红色或红色条纹帽。第一守门员通常被标记为"1"，替补守门员被标记为"13"（根据国际泳联规则）或"1A"（根据全美大学生体育协会和美国全国州立高中协会联盟规则）。

4.3 比赛时间

比赛分为 4 节；时长取决于比赛的水平。国际水球比赛没有加时赛，也没有平局，如果出现平局需要决出胜负，比赛将进行点球大战。大学水平的比赛，比赛分为 2 节，每节 3 分钟；如果打平，之后将进行 3 分钟的"金球制"加时赛，直到一方进球。对于低级别赛事，不同组织的比赛，其加时赛规则也有所不同。每节比赛（包括加时赛/点球大战）之后有 2 分钟的休息时间，但中场休息时间为 5 分钟。

表 10.1　不同级别比赛每节的时间长度

比赛级别	球队级别	每节时长/分	管理机构
奥运会	国家队	8	国际泳联
国际泳联世界水球联赛	国家队		国际泳联
欧洲联赛	俱乐部		欧洲泳联
职业俱乐部比赛	俱乐部	9	国际泳联

(续表)

比赛级别	球队级别	每节时长/分	管理机构
美国大学	大学代表队	8	美国大学水球协会
美国大学	俱乐部	7	美国大学水球协会
美国高中	高中代表队	7	全美州立高中协会联盟
美国高中	高中代表队二队	6	全美州立高中协会联盟
美国高中	高一/高二队	5～6	全美州立高中协会联盟
美国水球协会	14岁及以下年龄队	5～7	美国水球协会

4.4 比赛和进攻时限钟

当比赛暂停时（在犯规和罚球间隔，以及在进球和重新开始的间隔），比赛计时器停止。因此，平均每节的实际时间约为12分钟。除非对方犯规，否则一支球队在没有射门的情况下控球时间不得超过30秒。30秒后，控球权交给对手，计时重新开始。在进球、裁判球或罚球后，进攻时限钟也会重置30秒。

如果一支球队在规定的时间内射门，并重新控制球权（例如球从门柱反弹后），则进攻时限钟重置为20秒。在严重犯规（驱逐出场）、角球或4 m罚球击中门柱反弹后进攻球队又获得控球权，也会重置20秒。

进攻时限钟的出现引出了水球运动的一个关键概念：不需要冒着犯规的风险抢球。球最终会回到你的手中，例如：在进球后；射门尝试失败后；或者在进攻时间结束后。所以，没有必要试图以一种过于激进的方式去抢夺对手手中的球；因为这可能会造成严重犯规，对手会再获得额外20秒进攻时间。严重犯规的后果是球队失去了一名球员，对手获得了更多的进攻时间。所以防守的艺术就是"压制"（即占领有利位置，激怒对手，拦截一个质量不高的传球等）对手（不能出现严重犯规），减慢比赛速度，并等待获得球权。

4.5 球场尺寸

水球场地的尺寸不是固定的，可以在20 m×10 m和30 m×20 m之间浮动（国际泳联批准的比赛要求男子场地为30 m×20 m，女子场地为25 m×20 m），因此可以使用短池作为场地。作为比赛场地的泳池最低水深要求至少为1.8 m（6 ft），但由于许多泳池的一端较浅，往往达不到这个要求。球门宽3 m，高90 cm。

水球场地中间有一条白色的中线。在2005年之前，场上有一条7 m线和一条4 m线（距球门线的距离）。自2005—2006赛季以来，这两条线合并为一条5 m线；自2019—2020赛季以来，增加了一条6 m线，6 m线用黄线标示，它是国际泳联于2019年引入的，关系到普通犯规或严重犯规后的罚球方式。5 m线是罚球的地方，用红线标示。2 m线用红线标示，进攻方的队员不能在2 m线以内的区域接球。这些规定自2020年夏季奥运会（推迟到2021年举行）以来一直在使用。

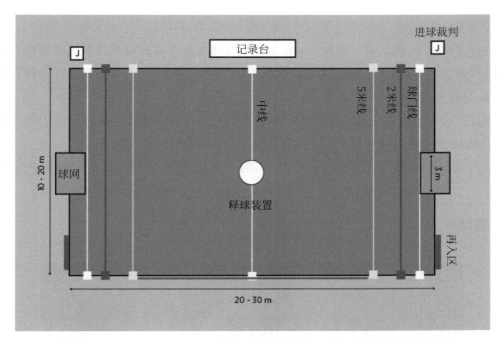

图 10.4　水球场地的布局：2 m 和 5 m 的标记（红色和黄色）、中间线（白色标记）、
两端的球门以及水池的长度和宽度（作者 Jkwchui）

水球一般是黄色的，大小和重量在少年、女子和男子的比赛中规格不同。

在比赛中，如果球飞出比赛区域（或击中泳池边缘然后落回水中），在球出比赛场地前没有最后触球的球队将获得一次罚球（任意球）。

此外，裁判不能在比赛休息时捡起在泳池边的球，并把它交给进攻队，这可能会给进攻队带来优势。

4.6　开球

在全深泳池中，主队从左侧（从记分台面向泳池对面以确定左右）开始比赛。两队在中场休息时交换场地。在有一端是较浅的泳池中，通过掷硬币的方式决定哪一队从哪一边开始。两队在每节结束后交换场地。在每一节开始和每次得分后，各队在自己的球门线上排成一排。最常见的阵型是球门两边各有 3 名球员，而守门员则留在球门内。如果球被抛到场地中心，冲刺争球的球员通常会从球门出发，而守门员在比赛开始时要么在球门里，要么在球门的一边。

图 10.5　开球（作者 Wpktsfs.）

裁判员一声哨响，将球扔到水中，两队快速游到场地的中点争夺球权（称为"争球"）。根据不同的比赛规则，争球会在裁判的一边或在场地的中心进行。在国际比赛中，球通常放在场地中央，由一个浮环支撑。第一个抢到球的球队成为进攻方，直到进球或防守方得到球权为止。

在特殊情况下,两队都可能在触球前犯规。这通常发生在球员利用侧边来帮助自己获得速度优势的情况(即通过拉动侧边来游得更快)。在这种情况下,非犯规队在中线获得一次罚球(任意球)。

争球只在每节比赛开始时及得分后进行。因此,争球在一场比赛中会出现2次、4次或6次,这取决于比赛是采用上下半场、4局还是4局后有加时赛等不同情况。

裁判应在比赛开始前检查球员的指甲(防止刮伤别人)。通常不允许佩戴护目镜和首饰。

4.7 移动球

图10.6 进攻球员(7)运球向前推进(作者 Ryanjo)

球员可以把球抛给队友,也可以通过把球放在身前游泳来移动球。球员不允许将球推入水中以防止对手触球,也不允许推或抱住对方球员,除非对方球员正在持球。如果1名球员在己方控球时将球推到水下,这被称为"球入水"(ball under),将导致失误(turnover),这意味着犯规的球员必须把球权交给对手。不管球员在水下持球是不是被对手强迫的,他们都会被判犯规。

水球是一项激烈的运动,所以犯规是很常见的,犯规会导致罚任意球。罚任意球时,球员不能直接射门,除非他们在6 m线外。如果在6 m线外被判犯规,罚球球员可以选择射门(一个连贯动作,不允许有假动作)、传球或继续运球。

4.8 得分

如果球完全穿过门柱并在横梁下方,就算进球得分。如果球从球门柱上弹回场地,并且球权又被进攻方获得,则射门时间将重置(为20秒),比赛继续进行。如果射门偏出了球门,碰到了绳子,或者落在了地板上(场地外),则防守方发球门球,计时将重置30秒。重新开球和重新计时必须立即开始(时间限制未在规则中规定)。如果守门员是在球出底线前最后一个接触到球的人,或者防守队员故意使球出了底线,那么进攻方就会在2米线上"掷角球"。角球也必须在没有延迟的情况下完成(同样,规则中没有规定时间限制),球员可以运球、射门或传球。如果在射门限制钟到达0或比赛计时器到达00.0之前完成射门,只要球不在球员手中,得分有效。

当守门员阻截了射门,防守方控制住球时,将会把球长传给没有回来防守而是留在进攻端的队友,这被称为"采樱桃"或"海鸥"战术。因为水球不像足球那样有越位规则,所以这种情况时有发生,防守方球员可以"徘徊"在对方的球门附近。

水球比赛也没有足球比赛的"乌龙球"概念,但这种情况确实会发生(极少),这样的进球会被判给最后触球的进攻球员。

4.9　得分后重启比赛

进球后,两队可以在本方半场的任何地方排成一排。在实际比赛中,两队通常是在场地的中心附近各排成一排。当裁判发出开始的信号,未进球的一方将球向后传给队友,比赛重新开始。

4.10　暂停

每队可以(根据所使用的规则)使用不同次数的1分钟暂停(美国/国际泳联规则)或2分钟暂停(美国大学体育协会/全美州立高中协会联盟规则);如果比赛进入加时赛或点球大战,还有一次暂停机会。在比赛中,只有控球的一方可以要求暂停。暂停不会带入加时赛或点球大战。在比赛中没有控球而要求暂停的球队会被处罚。国际泳联水球规则允许每队在一场比赛中暂停2次,可以在同一局叫2次暂停。

暂停时间45秒时(计分员在记分表上提示后),主裁判吹3声短哨,挥手让进攻队员向前推进到对方半场。在60秒时,球被抛给位于中线的守门员(通常),当另一次(单一)长哨吹响时,守门员可以开始发球。

4.11　换人

替补队员可以在比赛间歇、进球后、暂停期间从任何地方进入场地,也可以替换受伤的队员;但在判罚之后不能换人。如果在比赛中进行换人,在替补球员进入场地之前,换下的球员应该在再入区等待,他们都不能举起边绳进出比赛场地。

4.12　行为控制

水球裁判在处理替补席犯规时使用红牌和黄牌。根据违规的严重程度,裁判可能会发出口头警告。

黄牌可以在比赛的任何时候发出,也可以通过"行走黄牌"发出,即裁判在不停止比赛的情况下出示黄牌。在发出"行走黄牌"后,在下一次比赛暂停时,主裁判可以将球拿出场地,通知记录台和搭档裁判已经做出的判罚和出示的黄牌。

图 10.7　一张黄牌和一张红牌(图片来源:Wikimedia)

红牌可以出示给任何球队人员(领队、助理教练、球队经理、球员和球队的其他官员)或其支持者。红牌发出后,被判罚的队员必须离开赛场,并且不能再(以任何方式)参与比赛。红牌将导致违规队员至少停赛一场,并向相应的管理机构提交报告。获得第二张黄牌的球员也会得到一张红牌。

4.13　犯规

4.13.1　普通犯规

图 10.8　从 2 m 线罚角球(图片来源:Wikimedia)

当一名球员阻碍或以其他方式阻止对手的自由移动(虽然对手没有持球,但球在他们的控球范围内或附近)时,就会发生普通犯规。最常见的是当防守球员为了把球击走,伸手越过对手的肩膀,同时在这个过程中阻碍对手。当进攻队员推开防守队员,为传球或射门提供空间时,也可能会被判犯规。

裁判员用一声短哨示意犯规,并将一只手指向进攻队的方向(与犯规位置大致站在一条直线上),进攻队保持控球权。进攻队员必须在没有任何延迟的情况下(规则中没有规定的时间)将球传给另一个进攻队员。如果犯规发生在 6 m 线外,进攻队员可以尝试直接射门,但必须立即以一个连续动作射门(即不能有假动作)。如果进攻球员先假射,然后再真射门，这会导致失去球权。

防守队（通常是犯规的一方）必须后退（规则中没有规定距离，但通常是1.5～2 m）以允许罚球；换句话说，他们不能只是站在原地来阻挡进攻球员。在罚球时，如果防守队员处于合理距离之外，可以举起他的手臂进行阻拦。掷球（以及所有在犯规后的掷球）必须立即进行，这个过程的最长时间通常是3秒左右（规则中也没有明确说明）。

如果同一名后卫多次普通犯规，裁判将会把该球员禁赛30秒。为了避免被罚出场，防守中锋的队员可以犯规2次，然后让边路防守队员与他互换位置，这样防守队员就可以继续对中锋犯规，而不会造成离场犯规。该规则的修改是为了允许重复犯规而不被罚出场，但裁判仍然会根据具体情况进行裁定。

还有相当多的其他违规行为会导致普通犯规，包括站在浅端，延迟掷球（任意球、球门球或角球），不按规定的罚球，用双手触球（如果不是守门员），假装被犯规，浪费时间，以及位于球门2 m以内的区域。

4.13.2 严重犯规

图10.9　防守队员(2)将持球进攻队员压入水下
（图片来源：Wikimedia）

严重犯规（离场犯规和点球犯规）是当防守队员"抓住（特别是用双手）、向后拉拽（水球中的一个关键短语）进攻队员，或将其压入水下"。严重犯规还包括游到对方球员的腿上或背上，阻止对方球员游泳，或以其他方式阻止进攻方球员保持优势。

裁判员发出两声短哨，然后是一声长哨，以示严重犯规，并指示球员必须离开赛场，进入禁区20秒。裁判首先指向犯规的球员并吹响哨子，然后指向处罚区并再次吹响哨子。运动员必须在不影响正常比赛的情况下，在合理的时间内移动到他们的再入区（否则将受到处罚)。被罚出场 3 次的球员必须在剩余的比赛中退场。

还有其他几种可能导致离场犯规的违规行为:
- 坐在台阶上或泳池边。
- 向对手的脸上泼水。
- 干扰任意球、球门球或角球;包括防守队员没有松开球,把球扔出去或移动到其他地方,或者试图在球离开掷球队员的手之前击球。
- 在 6 m 内用双手封堵传球或射门。如果裁判认为这一动作阻止了一个进球,则会判罚点球。
- 在交换球权后,防守队员在进攻方半场的任何地方犯规,这是为了防止在进攻队员(或球)通过中线之前犯规。
- 踢或击打对手(或表现出意图)。如果发生在 6 m 线内,则罚球一次。裁判可以根据意图和后果决定如何惩罚踢人或打人一方,或者判罚不当行为或野蛮犯规。
- 被判离场的球员干扰比赛,或不立即离场。该球员会被再判罚一次离场犯规(个人)并判给对方一次罚球机会。
- 被判离场的球员以不正当方式重新参赛(或替补参赛)。例如,在裁判(或记分台)没有发出信号的情况下,不从再入区进入赛场,或影响球门的摆放(如抬起绳子)。他们将(再次)被判离场犯规(但只有一次个人犯规被记录),并判给对方球队一次罚球(如果该球员所在球队没有控球)。
- 防守方守门员在对方罚球时,在被裁判要求一次后,仍未能站到正确的位置。

球员恶意踢或击打对手或裁判员的行为,被称为暴力犯规。击打行为必须与球员有接触,并且必须带有伤害的意图,才会被判暴力犯规。否则球员将会被判罚不当行为犯规,将被判罚离场,在 20 秒后或交换球权时才能被替换上场。被指控有暴力行为的球员将被红牌罚下,犯规球队将被迫在接下来的 4 分钟时间里,在比对手少一名队员的情况下比赛。除了离场犯规外,如果在实际比赛中发生犯规,对方球队也会获得罚球机会。在此之前,被指控有暴力行为的队伍将被要求在剩下的比赛中减少一名队员。所有的暴力犯规都必须由裁判员上报,相关管理机构可能会实施进一步的处罚,其中可能包括增加停赛场次。

不当行为犯规是一种不符合体育道德的行为,其包括不可接受的语言、暴力或持续犯规、在被判罚离场犯规后继续参加比赛或表现出不尊重。被判不当行为犯规的球员将会被出示红牌,在 20 秒后被替补队员换下。球员可以造成两种类型的不当犯规,包括有身体接触和无身体接触的不当犯规。如果冲突不涉及(或试图涉及)身体接触,裁判也可以对犯规进行不当行为判罚。

4.14 5 m 球

如果防守队员在 6 m 范围内严重犯规(major foul),阻止了一个可能的进球,进攻队将获得罚球(penalty throw)或点球(penalty shot)。通常是当进攻球员在射门时从后面或侧

图 10.10　罚点球(5 m 球)(作者 Иван Ћурчић)

面受到阻碍。根据 2019 年国际泳联规则的变化,裁判在判罚时不再有任何自由裁量权(如,考虑一个射门是否会进球)。

进攻队员位于对方球门前 5 m 线上。其他球员不得在他的前方或在他的 2 m 范围内。防守守门员必须位于门柱之间。裁判用哨声和放下手臂发出信号,罚球的球员必须立即以连贯的动作将球掷向球门(即不能做假动作)。球出手前,罚球队员的身体在任何时候都不能越过 5 m 线。如果罚球队员的身体越过罚球线并射门,将导致进攻队失去球权。如果射门没进,球仍场内,则比赛继续进行。罚点球通常都能进球,有 63.7% 的进球是由罚点球打进的。

还有很多其他违规行为可能会导致点球:被罚离场的球员(excluded player)在离场时干扰比赛、被罚离场的球员在没有裁判(或记录台)信号的情况下进入赛场、球员或替补球员违规离开或进入赛场(例如,在比赛期间抬起绳子)、野蛮犯规、教练或队长在没有球权时请求暂停,以及在把球交给对手时,教练拖延时间。

4.15　加时赛

4.15.1　国际泳联规则

如果两队在正式比赛结束时比分打平,将采用罚点球方式决定胜负。每队的教练选出 5 名球员和 1 名守门员参加罚点球。如果 1 名球员因被处罚(即 3 次个人犯规或红牌)而无法参加比赛,则不能入选。队员们轮流在泳池两端的 5 m 线上射门,直到 5 人全部射门完毕。如果比分仍然打平,同样的球员再次轮流射门,直到一方失球,另一方得分。

4.15.2　美国全国大学生体育协会规则

与国际泳联要求进行点球大战的规则不同,NCAA 的规则要求球队进行 2 次 3 分钟的加时赛,如果仍然打平,则再进行 3 分钟一节的突然死亡赛,可进行多轮比赛,直到一方进球并赢得比赛。

4.16 水球装备

4.16.1 水球

图 10.11　水球：旧款(左)和新款(右)(作者 Antiflu)

水球是用防水材料制成的,可以浮在水面上。表面有纹理,便于球员更好地控制球。男子、女子和青少年比赛的球的大小是不同的。

4.16.2 球门

水球比赛双方各有一个球门。球门可以安装在泳池边,也可以用漂浮物固定在泳池里。

4.16.3 护齿

在大多数比赛中,护齿不是强制性的规定,但推荐使用。

4.16.4 水球服

图 10.12　男泳衣(左)和女泳衣(右)(作者 Hy Crutchett)

男子水球运动员要么穿三角泳裤,要么穿长及大腿的泳裤。女选手必须穿连体泳衣。比赛时,由于球员之间拉拽泳衣犯规很常见,所以球员们经常穿着紧身的水球服,为了增加额外的安全性,他们可能会同时穿几套水球服。许多泳装品牌也出售专门的水球服,这种水球服的特点是加固缝线和使用更坚固的面料。女式水球服一般都是连体泳衣,没有开背,但背部有拉链,这样就不会有容易被抓住的带子。

4.17 球员位置

每队同时有 7 名队员上场,包括 6 名场上球员和 1 名守门员(goalkeeper)。与大多数常见的集体运动不同,这里很少有阵地战(positional play);场上球员通常会根据情况需要在整个比赛中填补多个位置。这些位置通常由 1 名中锋(center forward)、1 名中后卫(center back)、2 名边前锋(wing player)和两名边后卫(driver)组成。能胜任进攻或防守各个位置的球员被称为全能型球员(utility player)。全能型球员往往是替补球员,但不是绝对的。某些体型更适合某些特定的位置,例如左手球员非常适合在球场的右侧,使球队能够在两侧发起进攻。

4.17.1 进攻位置

进攻位置包括一名中锋(位于 2 m 线或附近,大致对着球门中心的位置)、两个边前锋,(分别位于两个球门柱外侧的 2 m 线或附近)、两名边后卫(位于 5 m 线或附近,分别大致在两个球门柱处)和一个距离球门最远的控球后卫(通常位于 5 m 线后,大致对着球门中心的位置)。边锋、边后卫和控卫通常被称为外线球员(perimeter player);中锋(hole-set)负责指挥进攻。美国 NCAA 男子水球一级联赛中的这些位置有一个特有的编号系统。对方守门员右侧的进攻左边锋为 1 号;从 1 号开始逆时针方向依次为 2 号左边后卫(flat)、3 号控球后卫、4 号右边后卫和 5 号右边锋,中锋为 6 号。此外,可以根据球员的惯用手来安排位置,以改善射门或传球角度(例如,右边锋通常是左手队员)。

中锋位于对方守门员的前面,个人得分最高(特别是在低水平比赛中,边后卫没有足够的力量从外线进行有效射门或像篮球比赛的控球后卫和足球比赛的中场球员一样突破传球给队友)。中锋的位置最接近球门,可以近距离进行大力射门。

4.17.2 防守位置

防守位置通常与进攻位置相同,只是从进攻转为防守。例如,中锋在进攻时指挥进攻,在防守时被称为中后卫,防守对方球队的中锋。防守可以是人盯人防守(man-to-man defense),也可以是区域防守(zone defense),例如 2—4 防守(球门线上有 4 名防守队员)。在"M drop"防守战术中可以将 2 种防守战术相结合,在这种防守中,中后卫把对方中锋控制到一个区域,以便更好地防守中锋。在这种防守阵型中,2 名防守边锋的后卫分别位于两侧边线附近,当防守方夺回球权时,他们的反击通道就会比较通畅,有利于进行快速反击。

4.17.3 守门员

守门员的主要职责是阻挡对方射门、指挥防守以及告知队友防守的威胁和缺口。守门员通常是通过将球传给进攻队员来发动进攻。守门员通过传球助攻队友突破进球的情况并不罕见。

图 10.13　门将封堵射门(作者 Juan Fernández)

守门员享有高于其他球员的多项特权,但仅限于本方球门前 5 m 线范围内:
- 可以握紧拳头击球;
- 可以用两只手触球。

一般来说,一个会导致场上球员被罚出场(ejection)的犯规行为,对于守门员来说,可能会判罚 5 m 球。此外,如果守门员将球推入水下,该行为不会像场上球员那样被判罚失误(turnover),而是会被判罚点球(penalty shot)。

第五节　基本战术

5.1　进攻战术

5.1.1　阵型

最基本的阵型被称为"3-3"阵型,在对手球门前排列 2 条进攻线。另一种阵型,更多地由职业球队使用,被称为"弧形"阵型、"伞形"阵型或"蘑菇形"阵型,外线球员围绕球门排列成弧形,中锋突前形成一把伞或蘑菇的形状。另一种进攻阵型被称为 4—2 阵型或双中锋阵型,门前有 2 名中锋球员。双中锋最常用于以多打少的局面(man-up situations),或者当防守方只有一个熟练的中后卫(hole D)时,或者通过中锋吸引防守队员,然后把球传给外线球员射门。

5.1.2　推进球

当进攻方控球时,比赛策略是将球向对方球门推进并射门得分。球员可以通过将球掷给队友或将球放在自己面前来推进球（dribbling）。如果进攻球员用手臂推开防守球员来腾出传球或射门的空间，裁判将判罚失误，防守方将获得球权。如果进攻方无球进入 2 m 线内或在球之前进入 2 m 线内，将被判越位，并将球权交给防守方。如果进攻球员位于水池的另一侧或球位于水池另一侧，越位常常被裁判忽视。

5.1.3 传球

进攻的关键是准确地将球传给位于球门正前方的中锋。任何场上球员都可以向该中锋进行"湿传"（wet pass）。湿传是指传到中锋能够很容易够到的水面的传球。也可以使用干传（dry pass），中锋直接将球接在手中，然后进行射门。这种传球要困难得多，因为如果传球没有被正确接住，裁判很可能会判进攻犯规，从而导致失去球权。中锋试图（在湿传后）控球、射门或造成防守队员犯规。如果防守他的中后卫在他控球前试图阻碍他移动，则会被判轻微犯规。裁判员用一声短哨示意犯规，并将一只手指向犯规地点，另一只手指向罚球队的进攻方向。然后，该中锋在"合理的时间"（通常约为 3 秒；国际泳联对此问题没有规定）内，通过向队友传球来重新开始比赛。在间接任意球（free throw）罚出之前，防守队不能干扰该中锋，但是在裁判判罚犯规后，该中锋不能直接射门，必须先传球给至少一名队友之后才能进行射门。如果该中锋直接射门，则该进球无效且防守方获得球权，除非射门是在 5 m 线外进行的。一旦该中锋获得间接任意球，其他进攻球员就会奋力摆脱（drive）防守球员，快速游向对方球门。处于边后卫位置的其他球员将尝试为边后卫（driver）设置掩护（setting a screen/pick）。如果后卫摆脱了防守队员，就会示意中锋传球给他，并尝试射门。

5.1.4 多打少 (6 对 5)

图 10.14　典型的 4—2 多打少阵型（作者 Prisonblues）

如果防守球员干扰罚球、抱人或压沉未控球的进攻球员或向对手脸上泼水,则防守球员将被罚出场 20 秒,称为"驱逐出场"(kick out/ ejection)。进攻方通常将 4 名球员安排在 2 m 线上,将 2 名球员安排在 5 m 线上(4—2 阵型),在球员之间不断传球,直到空位球员接球进行射门。其他阵型包括 3—3 阵型(2 排,每排 3 名进攻球员)或弧线阵型(进攻球员在球门前形成弧线,一名进攻球员位于球门正前方的 2 m 线)。当防守球队少 1 人时,5 名防守球员在 20 秒内竭尽全力向进攻球员施压、封堵射门并阻止进球。其他防守队员只能用一只手挡球来帮助守门员。如果进攻方得分,或者防守方在 20 秒结束前夺回球权,被驱逐出场的防守球员就可以立即返回赛场。

5.2 防守战术

图 10.15 水球防守:防守球员只能抱、阻挡或拉正在触球或持球的对手(作者 LauraHale)

在防守时,球员们努力夺回球权并防止对手进球。防守方试图从进攻方手中把球打掉或抢断球,或者通过犯规以阻止进攻方球员射门。防守队员试图站在进攻队员和球门之间,这个位置被称为内水(inside water),以阻止进攻队员射门得分。

5.2.1 守门员的防守战术

即使有后卫的大力支持,如果守门员位于球门中间,阻止进攻也会非常困难。最好的防守位置是位于连接 2 个球门柱的半圆线上,根据持球者的位置,守门员位于距离球门大约一米的半圆线上,以减少进攻球员的射门角度。当对手到 7 m 标记附近时,守门员停止用手踩水,并开始用打蛋器式踩水技术(eggbeater technique)抬起上半身,准备封堵射门。最后,守门员试图挡住球,这对于守门员可以防守的范围来说通常很困难,但可以防止进攻队员抢到反弹球(offensive rebound)并进行二次射门。与其他防守球员的一样,如果守门员在进攻队员得分的位置上对射门球员进行侵人犯规,将会判罚点球(penalty shot)。如果发生严重犯规(major foul),守门员也会被驱逐出场20秒。此外,规则规定,在5 m范围内守门员可以用拳头击球。

5.2.2 有利原则

如果进攻球员(例如中锋)在球门前控球,防守球员会试图抢断球或阻止中锋射门或传球。如果防守球员无法达到这些目的,就可能会故意犯规。然后该中锋将获得一个间接任意球,但必须将球传给另一名进攻球员,而不能直接射门。防守方外线球员也可能故意制造一个普通犯规,然后向球门移动,远离被犯规的进攻球员,被犯规的进攻球员必须罚间接任意球。这种技术称为回抢(sloughing),让防守方有机会包夹(double-team)对方的中锋,并有可能抢断对方的传中球,如果裁判认为这会给犯规球队带来优势,则他可以不宣布犯规。这称为有利原则(Advantage Rule)。

水球术语

场上队员: 守门员以外的队员。

边后卫: 3—3进攻中的外线球员,位于中后卫或中锋的两侧,他们试图突破防守队员游向球门、接球并射门得分。

外线球员: 除了中锋以外的5个进攻位置,即翼锋、边后卫和中后卫。外线球员在一次进攻中多次交换位置。

节: 比赛分为4节;每节时间取决于比赛水平。

2 m线: 是指在球门前2 m处横跨泳池两边的线,在泳池边缘用红色标记标出。从2 m标志到球门线的比赛区域边缘用一条红线标记。

再入区: 在赛场两端靠近每队替补席,用红线标出的区域,球员可以在换人或被罚离场时在此处进出赛场。

死球时间: 指在犯规后鸣哨停止计时和球返回比赛后重新计时之间的时间。

传球路线: 持球队员与队友之间的传球路线。

裁判球: 类似于篮球中的跳球;裁判将球抛在两队队员之间进行争球。

有利规则: 如果裁判认为吹犯规暂停比赛将有利于犯规的球队,裁判可以不吹犯规。

任意球: 当裁判判给球队球权后,将球投进赛场,重新开始比赛的方法。除非另有规定,否则必须从犯规发生的地点(或在该点后面的任何地方)罚球。罚球可以由任何球员进行,他们可以传球或运球。除非犯规发生在5 m区外,否则他们不能直接射门。

打蛋机式蹬腿: 一种水中踢腿动作,用于在踩水时保持稳定性和支撑力,类似于交替的蛙泳踢腿。

运球: 游泳的同时将球控制在头前面的技术。

干传: 也称"不落水传球",球传出后,接球者不等球落水就将球接住。

湿传: 也称"落水传球",球员故意把球传到水上,球落在接球队友和防守队员够不着的地方,接球的队友可以向球快速游去,从水里拿起球进行射门或传球。

反手传球：水球传球技术之一,指利用反手将球侧向或背向传出。

湿射：当球接触水面时进行的一种射门动作,通常是快速的、利用手腕发力的射门动作。

吊射：一种高弧度的射门,目的是使球从守门员的手和横梁之间进门。

掷角球：守门员将球挡出底线,或者防守队员故意使球越过底线时判罚给对手的罚球。

射兔子：瞄准守门员头部或靠近头部的位置的劲射得分。

采樱桃：一种战术,当防守方其他队员都在防守时,一名队员待在进攻端,等待本方获得球权后的长传,如果战术成功,常常会获得轻松的进球。

球入水：一种技术犯规,当一名球员在被对手擒抱或拦截时,持球没入水中的行为。

罚球：进攻队员在裁判吹哨后,在5 m线上的任意球。判罚发生在5 m线内阻止进球的犯规。

紧逼：一种最常用的人盯人防守策略。

反攻：一种进攻策略,在交换球权后迅速传球,从而使进攻方获得优势。

双中锋进攻：一种进攻策略,2名进攻者在对方球门前2 m线上,每个门柱前各有一名进攻队员。

坠后：防守队员游回场地中心,以阻止进攻队员的传球和射门,且一名防守队员压迫持球队员,试图造成持球队员匆忙传球。

一般犯规(或轻微犯规)：裁判员发出一声短促的哨声,表示一般犯规,并一只手指向犯规位置,另一只手指向获得球权的一方,比赛立即继续进行。

离场犯规(严重犯规)：是当防守队员"抓住(特别是用两只手)、下沉或向后拉"进攻队员时发生的。包括游到对方球员的腿上或背上,阻止对方球员游泳,或以其他方式阻止进攻方球员保持优势。裁判员用两声短哨示意严重犯规,并指示球员必须在不影响比赛的情况下离场,前往处罚区待20秒。

3-3阵式：一种基本的进攻阵式,由2条线组成,每条线有3名球员：中后卫和两名边后卫沿5 m线排列,中锋与两位边锋沿2 m线排列。

4-2阵式：进攻方4名队员沿2米线上排列,2名队员沿5米线排列,该阵式通常用于多对少的比赛。

练　习

1. 水球运动的国际管理机构是什么？
2. 请列举3个重要国际水球赛事。

参考文献 | References

[1] 2002 FIFA World Cup TV Coverage [EB/OL]. (2008-01-06). https://en.wikipedia.org/wiki/Association_football.

[2] BBC SPORT. Champions League final tops Super Bowl for TV market [EB/OL]. (2010-01-31). https://wikimili.com/en/List_of_most-watched_television_broadcasts.

[3] IFAB. Laws of the game (Law 8: the start and restart of play) [EB/OL]. (2007-09-24). https://www.theifab.com/laws/latest/the-start-and-restart-of-play/#introduction.

[4] England Premiership (2005/2006) [EB/OL]. (2007-06-05). https://spfl.co.uk/league/premiership/archive/293.

[5] IFAB. Video assistant referees (VARs) experiment: protocol (summary) [EB/OL]. (2017-04-26). https://docslib.org/doc/11531458/video-assistant-referees-vars-experiment-protocol-summary.

[6] Laws of the Game 2013/2014 (PDF) [EB/OL]. https://dt5602vnjxv0c.cloudfront.net/portals/9504/docs/fifa%20laws%20of%20the%20games.summary.pdf

[7] SUMMERS C. Will we ever go completely metric? [EB/OL]. (2004-09-02) [2007-10-07]. https://en.wikipedia.org/wiki/Association_football.

[8] IFAB. Laws of the game (Law 1.3 — The field of play) [EB/OL]. (2007-10-11). https://www.theifab.com/laws/latest/the-field-of-play/#field-surface.

[9] Laws of the game (Law 7.3 — The duration of the match) [EB/OL]. (2007-10-19). https://www.theifab.com/laws/latest/the-duration-of-the-match/#periods-of-play.

[10] For example in the FACup prior to the semi-finals [EB/OL]. https://www.givemesport.com/football-fa-cup-semi-final-wembley-stadium-history/.

[11] SHIRTY5. Football League administration penalty raised to 12 points [EB/OL]. [2018-05-17]. https://forum.charltonlife.com/discussion/67966/football-league-administration-penalty-raised-to-12-points.

[12] HONG F, MANGAN J A. Sport in Asian society: past and present [M]. London: Routledge, 2002.

[13] UNITED STATES POLO ASSOCIATION. Rules of the game: sports of polo [EB/OL].

[2017-11-08]. https://www.uspolo.org/sport/rules.

[14] Aspen World Snow Polo Official Website [EB/OL]. (2012-01-25). http://www.aspenvalleypoloclub.com/snowpolo.

[15] Left-handed polo layers [EB/OL]. [2018-01-28]. https://stickandbat.com/can-you-play-polo-if-youre-left-handed/.

[16] LAFFAYE H A. The polo encyclopedia[M]. Jefferson, NC: McFarland Publishing.

[17] World Polo News. Outdoor polo ball [EB/OL]. [2015-02-10]. https://www.worldpolonews.com/2015/outdoor-polo-ball/.

[18] IBAF. IBAF introduces new format of International Tournaments[EB/OL]. (2014-10-04). https://www.wbsc.org/en/news/ibaf-congress-approves-new-format-of-international-tournaments.

[19] WBSC. Premier12 2019 official program. [EB/OL]. [2019-02-11]. https://www.wbsc.org/en/events/2019-premier12/info

[20] LITTLE LEAGUE. Rules, regulations, and policies: Little League [EB/OL]. [2018-03-19]. https://www.littleleague.org/playing-rules/rules-regulations-policies/.

[21] Nationals Finalize 25-Man Roster. Washington Nationals/Major League Baseball [EB/OL]. (2011-07-04). https://www.mlb.com/news/nationals-finalize-25-man-roster-for-nlds/c-97433254.

[22] ZOSS (2004) Official Rules/9.00—The Umpire (PDF) [EB/OL]. (2009-01-18). https://hmong.in.th/wiki/Baseball_game.

[23] Official Rules/1.00—Objectives of the Game (Rules 1.12—1.15) (PDF)[EB/OL]. (2009-01-02). https://www.baseball-almanac.com/rule1.shtml.

[24] GUTTMANN A, THOMPSON L. Japanese sport: a history[M/OL]. Honolulu: University of Hawai'i Press, 2001. (2001-06-01). https://www.jstor.org/stable/j.ctt6wqsmj.

[25] National Sports of Canada Act[EB/OL]. [2022-06-10]. https://www.laws-lois.justice.gc.ca/eng/acts/N-16.7/.

[26] IIHF. The world governing body[EB/OL]. (2018-07-04). https://www.iihf.com/search/getresult?filterValue=the%20world%20govering%20body.

[27] Including former incarnations of them, such as Czechoslovakia or the Soviet Union[EB/OL]. (2021-09-15). https://www.dailyhistory.org/Why_did_the_Soviet_Union_invade_Czechoslovakia_in_1968.

[28] JAMES H M. National Hockey League [EB/OL]. (2012-12-19). https://www.thecanadianencyclopedia.ca/en/article/national-hockey-league.

［29］ ROARKE S P. Stanley Cup has incredible history［EB/OL］.（2017-03-12）. https://www.nhl.com/news/stanley-cup-has-incredible-125-years-of-history-287633638.

［30］ IIHF. IIHF Official Rule Book 2002-2006（PDF）［EB/OL］.（2006-03-09）. https://blob.iihf.com/iihf-media/iihfmvc/media/downloads/rule%20book/iihf_official_rule_book_2018_ih_191114.pdf.

［31］ National Hockey League official rules 2006—2007［M］. Chicago：Triumph Books.